AF564430

Consumer Behaviour and Promotion Management

Consumer Behaviour and Promotion Management

Anshuman Sharma

Consumer Behaviour and Promotion Management

ISBN 978-93-5111-344-7

Published in 2014 in India by

RANDOM PUBLICATIONS

4376-A/4B, Gali Murari Lal, Ansari Road
New Delhi-110 002
Phone : +91-11-43580356, +91-11-23289044
e-mail: randomexports@gmail.com, sales@randompublications.com, info@randompublications.com

Type Setting by : Keystoneprintads, Delhi-110051
Printed at Thomson Press (India) Ltd -110 020

Preface

Consumer behaviour is the study of individuals, groups, or organizations and the processes they use to select, secure, and dispose of products, services, experiences, or ideas to satisfy needs and the impacts that these processes have on the consumer and society. It blends elements from psychology, sociology, social anthropology and economics. It attempts to understand the decision-making processes of buyers, both individually and in groups. It studies characteristics of individual consumers such as demographics and behavioural variables in an attempt to understand people's wants. It also tries to assess influences on the consumer from groups such as family, friends, reference groups, and society in general.

Some customer inquiries are complaints, which generally must be handled in accordance with strict company policies. In some cases, representatives may try to fix problems or suggest solutions. They may have the authority to reverse erroneous fees or send replacement products. Other representatives act as gatekeepers who make sure that complaints are valid before accepting customer returns.

Promotions can be categorized based on the intended coverage of a single promotional message. For instance, a single television advertisement for a major sporting event, such as the Super Bowl, World Cup or Olympics, could be seen by millions of viewers at the same time. Such mass promotion, intended to reach as many people as possible, has been a mainstay of marketers' promotional efforts for a long time.

This book is written with the purpose of blending both concepts and applications from the field of consumer behavior and marketing research.

I thank all members of my team who have helped in the preparation of the book. My special thanks go to "Random Publications" who have published the book.

—Anshuman Sharma

Contents

1

Consumer Behaviour

INTRODUCTION

In a sense, everything an organisation does hinges on the assumptions it makes about people–both the people that are employed and the people served by the organisation. In marketing we tend to think only of the profit-making private sector, but whether they want to admit it or not, governmental organisations and non-profit organisations also engage in marketing exercises. The goal of marketing is determining wants and satisfying them, and this essentially is what government services are about as well. So, the importance of knowing how people will behave is tantamount to knowing the 'secret to organisational success'.

So let us begin with the simplest description of consumer behaviour. Consumer behaviour is simply the individual purchasing and/or consuming decision of an individual–and/or household–whoever buys goods and services for personal consumption. That purchase can be the consumption of a good or service in the marketplace or can even include the purchase of a stock and other investment decisions as well. This good or service can be either publicly supplied or privately produced by the organisation.

Consumer behaviour can be modelled from a number of perspectives. As pointed out by Kotler and Armstrong, consumer purchases are influenced by forces such as:

- *Cultural*: The set of basic values, perceptions, wants and behaviours learned by an individual from being a member of society
- *Social*: The influences of social factors such as the consumer's relation to small groups, family and social roles
- *Individual*: The characteristics of the individual such as the consumer's age, economic situation and occupation
- *Psychological*: The motivation, perception and beliefs and attitudes of the consumer.

Clearly there is some overlap between these four categories, as a person's attitudes may be dependent on the age or economic situation that the person is in; or the other way around; a person's attitudes and motivation may affect personal factors such as occupation and economic situation. But to the extent that the overlap is not perfect, such a broad-based perspective on consumer behaviour will tend to provide a more accurate portrayal of why consumers make the purchase decisions they do.

It is not our intention in this brief introduction to explain each of the factors affecting consumer behaviour in great detail, as the Kotler and Armstrong text does a very good job of this already. Rather as suggested start by presenting a relatively stylised economic interpretation of consumer behaviour and then we'll see what implications this has for the marketing decisions of an organisation. As suggested then contrast this economic version with the social and psychological approaches.

AGE AND CONSUMER BEHAVIOUR OVER THE LIFE-CYCLE

The life-cycle view of consumer behaviour is closely linked to economics, although like any theory about individual behaviour, it has to make some assumptions about human psychology. In this respect, the life-cycle model of consumer behaviour is quite ubiquitous and appears in economics, marketing and gerontology. Each discipline has a slightly different interpretation of the life-cycle model. We review what the life-cycle model has to say regarding consumption and activity patterns as we age.

The first formal use of the life-cycle model in economics stemmed from a puzzle regarding income and consumption. In macroeconomic data sets, consumption and income seemed to rise at a fixed or constant rate. That is, for every £1 increase in national income a fixed portion would be directed into consumption.

The problem for economists occurred when they examined data at the microeconomic level. Individual and household consumption appeared more or less constant and did not vary with income in the same way. One of the answers to this puzzle was provided by Modigliani and Brumberg with their life-cycle theory. Empirically, the life-cycle theory predicts that the consumption and saving behaviour of an individual has less to do with current income and more to do with age, material status and other socioeconomic conditions during various stages of the individual's life.

From the savings side, the life-cycle hypothesis posits that saving is negative for the young, positive for middle-aged households and negative for the retired, so that wealth should be hump-shaped. The idea motivating this model is that people have distinct financial needs at different periods of their life, typically borrowing when young, paying back the loans and then saving for retirement when middle-aged and reducing savings during retirement.

Shares are vehicles for the savings of those preparing for their retirement. It seems plausible therefore that a large middle-aged cohort seeking to save for retirement will push up the prices of financial services and these securities, and that the prices will be depressed in periods when the middle-aged cohort is small. Another strand of the life-cycle literature examines consumer behaviour from the perspective of the opportunity costs of time and time-use decisions.

Specifically, this research stream addresses the well-documented fact that expenditure and labour supply are also hump-shaped over the life-cycle. This means that consumer expenditure rises, peaks and then declines as we age. This hump is present even when economists control for changing family composition. As noted by economists, household consumption is the output of combining market activities and expenditure with time spent in home production.

To the extent that the relative price of time increases with age, individuals will substitute money spent on market goods for time by undertaking less home production and by searching less intensively for cheaper goods and services. It is shown that the large differences in prices paid across households for identical consumption of goods in the same metropolitan area at any given point in time, corresponds directly with the household's opportunity cost of time.

For example, the authors–using a bar or UPC code data that uniquely identifies a good–find that middle-aged households pay 16 per cent higher prices for the same goods and services than 24-year-olds, and eight per cent higher prices than 66-yearolds.

The data suggests that a doubling of shopping frequency lowers the purchase price of a good by 15 per cent. From this, the authors impute an opportunity cost of time for shoppers. Not surprisingly, the cost of time peaks in middle-age, and is roughly 35 per cent higher than that of retirees.

This model has particular relevance for time-use over the life-cycle. In particular, older consumers shop more frequently and also spend more time on each trip. Time spent in home production is therefore driven by two age-related forces: home production needs, such as children, and the opportunity cost of time. The authors find that both forces explain the pattern in the data: home production needs drive the peak found in home production in the late 1930s, while declining opportunity costs of time explain the increase in home production starting in the late 1950s.

A final strand in the literature looks at the stages in the life-cycle and links these to the generic needs of the consumer. A generic need is an inherent need of physical or social life.

These needs are generic in the sense that they tell us when an individual is likely to move from public transportation to the purchase of a car or from the rental to the purchase of a house. The model, of course, cannot predict the colour or the make of the car chosen, but despite this limitation, the life-cycle needs of an individual are useful in predicting which sectors may witness demographic-induced growth and what sectors may face demographic-related challenges.

STAGES IN THE CONSUMER'S LIFE-CYCLE

The household is typically segmented into four stages. The average age for first marriage in the United Kingdom is 29 for females and 31 for males. This varies depending on level of education but we can use this as our benchmark.

- Stage one therefore includes households in their twenties, usually without children. Whether married or not, young groups are more likely to rent than to own, spend more money than other groups on cinema tickets, take-away food, beer and clothes.
- Stage two, which includes households in their thirties and forties, typically involves children and brings with it changes in lifestyle and consumption. Household needs increase and commensurate with this, spending increases on baby clothes, furniture and televisions, and television viewing on children's programming increases. Noisy restaurants and fast food are chosen instead of quiet, expensive dinners. This is a time of high debt; households are borrowing for their car, home and other family purchases.
- In stage three, the household is now middle-aged and here the typical portrait begins to diverge. There are middle-aged married couples with children in their late teens or early twenties experiencing high costs of higher education and car insurance. Middle-aged singles without children may have many of the same needs as married households, but tend to live in apartments or smaller homes. Some middle-aged stage-three households may also be sandwiched between support for children as well as ageing parents. This group typically demands household cleaning services or other types of time-saving services. Stage-three households with no children have higher travel expenditures, enjoy luxury items and may take up gambling, golf and spa treatments.
- In stage four, older married and single households are typically in the 65 and older group. If in good health, the consumption patterns of young retirees are quite distinct from older retirees. Young retirees are frequent travellers and patrons of culture. As people are living longer and healthier, the age range of the actively-retired keeps getting pushed upwards. In the later years, regardless of health status, estate-planning, rearranging insurance, health care, assisted living and retirement homes become important. As frequently noted by gerontologists, this is a good reason to separate stage four into at least two distinct groups.

CONCEPT OF CONSUMER BEHAVIOUR

The study of consumers helps firms and organizations improve their marketing strategies by understanding issues such as how:

- The psychology of how consumers think, feel, reason, and select between different alternatives;

- The psychology of how the consumer is influenced by his or her environment;
- The behaviour of consumers while shopping or making other marketing decisions;
- Limitations in consumer knowledge or information processing abilities influence decisions and marketing outcome;
- How consumer motivation and decision strategies differ between products that differ in their level of importance or interest that they entail for the consumer; and
- How marketers can adapt and improve their marketing campaigns and marketing strategies to more effectively reach the consumer.

One "official" definition of consumer behaviour is "The study of individuals, groups, or organizations and the processes they use to select, secure, use, and dispose of products, services, experiences, or ideas to satisfy needs and the impacts that these processes have on the consumer and society." Although it is not necessary to memorize this definition.

It brings up some useful points:

- Behaviour occurs either for the individual, or in the context of a group or an organization.
- Consumer behaviour involves the use and disposal of products as well as the study of how they are purchased. Product use is often of great interest to the marketer, because this may influence how a product is best positioned or how we can encourage increased consumption. Since many environmental problems result from product disposal this is also an area of interest.
- Consumer behaviour involves services and ideas well as tangible products.
- The impact of consumer behaviour on society is also of relevance. For example, aggressive marketing of high fat foods, or aggressive marketing of easy credit, may have serious repercussions for the national health and economy.

There are four main applications of consumer behaviour:

1. The most obvious is for *marketing strategy—i.e.*, for making better marketing campaigns. For example, by understanding that consumers are more receptive to food advertising when they are hungry, we learn to schedule snack advertisements late in the afternoon. By understanding that new products are usually initially adopted by a few consumers and only spread later, and then only gradually, to the rest of the population, we learn that,
   - Companies that introduce new products must be well financed so that they can stay afloat until their products become a commercial success and
   - It is important to please initial customers, since they will in turn influence many subsequent customers' brand choices.

2. A second application is *public policy*. In the 1980s, Accutane, a near miracle cure for acne, was introduced. Unfortunately, Accutane resulted in severe birth defects if taken by pregnant women. Although physicians were instructed to warn their female patients of this, a number still became pregnant while taking the drug. To get consumers' attention, the Federal Drug Administration took the step of requiring that very graphic pictures of deformed babies be shown on the medicine containers.
3. *Social marketing* involves getting ideas across to consumers rather than selling something. Marty Fishbein went on sabbatical to work for the Centres for Disease Control trying to reduce the incidence of transmission of diseases through illegal drug use. The best solution, obviously, would be if we could get illegal drug users to stop. This, however, was deemed to be infeasible. It was also determined that the practice of sharing needles was too ingrained in the drug culture to be stopped. As a result, using knowledge of consumer attitudes, Dr. Fishbein created a campaign that encouraged the cleaning of needles in bleach before sharing them, a goal that was believed to be more realistic.
4. As a final benefit, studying consumer behaviour should make us better consumers. Common sense suggests, for example, that if you buy a 64 liquid ounce bottle of laundry detergent, you should pay less per ounce than if you bought two 32 ounce bottles. In practice, however, you often pay a size *premium* by buying the larger quantity. In other words, in this case, knowing this fact will sensitize you to the need to check the unit cost labels to determine if you are *really* getting a bargain.

There are several units in the market that can be analysed. Our main thrust in this course is the *consumer*. However, as suggested, also need to analyse our own firm's strengths and weaknesses and those of *competing firms*. Suppose, for example, that we make a product aimed at older consumers, a growing segment. A competing firm that targets babies, a shrinking market, is likely to consider repositioning towards our market. To assess a competing firm's potential threat, we need to examine its assets against pressures it faces from the market. Finally, we need to assess conditions. For example, although we may have developed a product that offers great appeal for consumers, a recession may cut demand dramatically.

THE CUSTOMER SATISFACTION SURVEY

One problem is that the survey takers are largely self-selected. Managers rarely select a random sample of their customers, nor do they do their best to make sure every survey they issue is returned. Instead, they hand out the cards to everyone and accept whatever comes back. Under those conditions, it's impossible to know what those responses represent. We used to do this type of survey at one of the AV dealers I worked for. There were six or seven questions, each answered by checking a box on a five-point scale, where 1 meant very unsatisfied and 5 meant very satisfied. Our sales manager had the cards delivered to a secretary, who would record the results, average them, and report to him monthly.

He used the averages as the basis for a competition between departments. In March, sales might get 4.15 for overall satisfaction, service 3.92, and rental 4.35. In April, sales and service each might improve .2 or so while rental dropped to 3.99. People took these numbers very seriously, but since we didn't control the sample we were measuring the differences had no real meaning. There's an even bigger, conceptual problem as well. It turns out you can't take a meaningful average of this kind of scale. Say you do a survey like this and 15 people return the cards. Five give your company a 1 for miserable service. Five give you a 3 for meets expectations and the remainder a 5 for exceptional service. What do you get for an average?

That's right, a 3, and that meets expectations hides the fact that 1/3 of your customers are so unhappy they'll never talk to you again. Wouldn't it be nice to know the true proportions, so you can try to find out what you're doing so right with some people and so wrong with others? The right way to use a satisfaction survey

If you truly want to learn from this kind of survey, start with these steps:

- Forget about averages. Instead, report how many fall within certain ranges. With our example, it might be best to report 66 percent were satisfied or very satisfied, 33 percent very unsatisfied.
- Leave lots of space for hand-written comments, and make sure those comments are part of any report.
  Susan Lewis says that she limited her survey to five questions, with room for comments on each, plus room for overall comments. "I started out with checkboxes because that makes the card easily approachable. Someone can look at it, mark 5 boxes, and move on. I really wanted the comments, but if I had put the comment line without the boxes, most people would look at it and say, 'Forget it, this takes too much energy.'"
- Ask people to sign the cards and ask for a phone number. Then set up a system where unhappy customers get help and you have confirmation that they do.
  "Most of our customers," Lewis says, "love us and said wonderful things. But every once in a while they'd say something where I'd go 'Ooh.' I would call them at that point and say, I apologize, and what can I do for you?"
- Consider calling the ones who are exceptionally happy as well, then reward staff members who served them.
- Be very careful how you send and collect your surveys. I was good friends with many of the sales people at the AV dealer I worked for, as well as some of the drivers and service technicians. After we

had been doing the survey cards for several months, I realised that many of my friends were throwing away certain surveys. If they knew a customer was unhappy and thought they might be blamed, they just didn't hand out the cards.

It was also possible, given the system we used, that some of our people filled out the cards themselves. Security is an issue any time you reward or punish people based on customer satisfaction.

- Consider an email survey or an online survey with an email invitation to participate. Email is faster and easier to administer, and it's possible to make it quite secure.

The unfortunate truth is a lot of these surveys are meaningless and are essentially ignored, even by the companies that issue them. You know that's true if you've ever voiced a complaint, then written down your name and phone number, hoping someone would call. Lewis, on the other hand, says, "They're a kick to get back.

We'd get them in the mail and it would give us a high." Most AV integrators can expect to get a lot more positive comments than negative. On the other hand, nearly everyone can uncover flaws in their systems and perhaps find out if certain employees treat customers poorly. You'll also find specific unhappy customers and have a chance to satisfy them before they go elsewhere.

In short, be prepared to learn. It's fun to hear when you're doing well, and it's a good thing to uncover problems. They are the reason you're not growing as fast as you want to. Fix them and your company will really take off. This talk grew out of a research project being conducted by INTERCOM President, Nancy Hushion, with whom I had an extensive conversation on the topic.

In presenting the talk I draw on my extensive experience with the Canada Aviation Museum and my related experience with the Canada Science and Technology Museum and the Canada Agriculture Museum during the last 12 years. I propose to give you a sense of our experience and my views on lessons learned under the general headings of: the context for marketing work at our institution; examples of marketing work we have undertaken; and some comments on results and changes in our corporate culture.

SIMPLE VIEW OF CONSUMER BEHAVIOUR

Remember that marketers are presumably interested in two things: why consumer choices differ across consuming agents; and changes in the consumption behaviour of the same consumer over time.

The reason why these consumption patterns may differ depends on two things: preferences and/or constraints. Based on these two reasons, economists typically argue that models where constraints differ are the more interesting cases since these are more likely to be measurable by a researcher and subject to observable change. What happens to tastes and preferences is often hard to determine and therefore not theoretically of interest to mainstream economists, since it is very hard to test these theories with the large-scale empirical data that economists normally have access to.

- *Model* 1: Consumer behaviour is some function of tastes and constraints. In this model both are variable.
- *Model* 2: Consumer behaviour is some function of tastes and constraints. In this model only constraints are variable.

Economists think that they can explain most consumer behaviour in terms of Model 2 and more precisely looking at constraints in terms of prices and income. They even translate non-economic constraints into costs. This has important implications for marketing. Two famous economists, Gary Becker and George Stigler, have even argued that 'tastes neither change capriciously nor differ importantly between people'. This is a pretty radical statement, but is it accurate?

STABILITY OF TASTES AND THE ECONOMIC EXPLANATION OF CUSTOM AND TRADITION

In many cases we observe stable behaviour that we attribute to cultural factors. For example, for as long as anyone can remember, consumption of wine has been higher in France than in Germany, where beer is consumed more than wine. What explains this and other national differences?

The 'common sense' answer would be that there is a custom of beer consumption in Germany and a custom of wine consumption in France. But to prove this assertion, we need to show that prices and incomes have not remained stable. In other words, only when we observe stable behaviour in the face of prolonged or severe changes in the environment can we then say that custom or tradition are important factors in determining choices.

The economic answer to stable patterns of consumer behaviour relies on the cost of decision-making. The making of a decision is costly, because in order to make a decision one requires information, and the information must be analysed.

Therefore, the price of a good or service has to incorporate the cost of search as well as the market price. When a temporary change takes place in the environment, perhaps in price or in income, it generally may not pay to disinvest in the knowledge or skills that one has acquired. As a result, behaviour will appear stable in the face of temporary changes and will reinforce the popular perception that culture is the causal factor.

So returning to our example of wine and beer consumption in France and Germany, is it tradition or some other constraint that is at work? And more importantly, what use can this debate have to marketing departments? It could be argued that in France people have more information about the quality of wine than beer, and consequently they will not switch to beer without:

- A huge increase in information

- A large drop in the market price of beer to counteract the information search costs.

Now what about 'permanent or long-lasting changes' in the environment, for example the shift to a market economy in the former Soviet Union? Typically, one observes a heterogeneous response.

The younger generation usually responds to these changes to a greater extent than older persons. Why? The popular press account is that young persons are more readily seduced away from old customs by the glitter of the Western-style consumer environment. In the economic interpretation, it has nothing to do with fickle or immutable taste differences between old and young; rather it has to do with the cost to older persons of disinvesting in the knowledge of how to do things under the old environment. The older one is, the fewer years one has to collect the returns from investments in certain patterns of behaviour.

Young persons on the other hand are not so encumbered, not because they are more flexible or adaptable to changes in the environment; they simply have a greater incentive to invest in new knowledge and new skills.

A more trivial application of this theory is the discounts given to senior citizens for the cinema. If preferences really differed, then there would be no need to lower the price of cinema tickets if you were over 65 years of age. What you would do is produce films that catered to that group, or you would engage in publicity campaigns aimed at changing their attitudes. Instead, the price cuts apply to all films but are targeted to a consumer group less likely to step out of the house.

INFORMATION SEARCH OF CONSUMERS

Use of Personal Sources Consumers obtain information about products and services from personal sources (e.g., friends or experts) and from no personal sources (e.g., mass or selective media). When purchasing goods, consumers make generous use of both personal and non personal sources because both effectively - convey information about search qualities. Then purchasing services, on the other hand, consumers seek and rely to a greater extent on personal sources for several reasons.

First, mass and selective media can convey information bout search qualities but can communicate little about experience qualities. By asking friends or experts about services, however, the consumers can obtain information vicariously about experience qualities.

Second, non personal sources of information may not be available because (d) many service providers are local, independent merchants with neither the experience nor the funds for advertising;' (b) "co-operative" advertising, or advertising funded jointly by the retailer and the manufacturer, is used in frequently with services because most local providers are both producer and retailer of the service and (c) professional associations banned advertising for so many years that both professionals and consumers tend to resist its use even though it is now permitted. Third, because consumers can discover few attributes before purchase of a service, they may feel greater risk in selecting a little-known alternative.

Personal influence becomes pivotal as product complexity increases and when objective standards by which to evaluate a product decrease (i.e., when experience qualities are high). Most managers in service industries recognize the strong influence of word of mouth in services. Next, consumers may find post purchase information seeking more essential with services than with goods because services possess experience qualities that cannot be adequately assessed before purchase. One model of audience response to communication describes the situation that occurs -frequently when

Consumers select services:

- The consumer selects from among virtually indistinguishable alternatives.
- Through experience the consumer develops an attitude toward the service.
- After the development of an attitude, the consumer learns more about the service by paying attention to messages supporting his or her choice.

In contrast to the conventional view of audience response to communication, where consumers seek information and evaluate products before purchase, with services most evaluation follows purchase. Perceived Risk While some degree of perceived risk probably accompanies all purchase transactions, more risk would appear to be involved in the purchase of 'services than in the purchase of goods 'because services are intangible;, non standardized, and usually sold without guarantees or warranties.

First, the intangible nature of services and their high level of experience qualities imply that services generally must be selected on the basis of less pre-purchase information than is the case for products. Second, because services are non standardized, there will always be uncertainty about the outcome and consequences each time a service is purchased. Third, service purchases may involve more perceived risk than product purchases because, with few exceptions, services are not accompanied by warranties or guarantees. The dissatisfied service purchaser can rarely "return" a service; he or she has already consumed it by the time he or she realises his or her dissatisfaction.

Finally, many services (e.g., medical diagnosis, pestcontrol) are so technical or specialized that consumers possess neither the knowledge nor the experience to evaluate whether they are satisfied, even after they have consumed the service. The increase in perceived risk involved in purchasing services suggests the use of strategies to reduce risk. Where appropriate, guarantees of satisfaction may be offered. To the extent possible, service providers should emphasize employee training and other procedures to standardize their offerings, so that consumers learn to expect a given level of quality and satisfaction.

EVALUATION OF SERVICE ALTERNATIVES

Evoked Set. The evoked set of "alternatives-that group of products a consumer considers acceptable options in given product category-is likely to be smaller with services than with goods. One reason involves differences in retailing between goods and services.

To purchase goods, consumer generally shop in retail stores that display competing products in close proximity, clearly demonetizing the possible alternatives. To purchase services, on the other hand, the consumer visits an stablishment (e.g., a bank, a dry cleaner, or a hair salon) that almost always offers only a single "brand" for sale. A second reason for the smaller evoked set is that consumers are un-likely to find more than one or two businesses providing the same services in a given geographic area whereas they may find number Us retail stores carrying the identical manufacturer's product.

A third reason for a smaller evoked set is the difficulty of obtaining adequate' pre purchase information about services. Faced with the task of collecting and 'evaluating experience qualities, consumers may simply select the first acceptable alternative rather than searching many alternatives. In consumer behaviour terms, the consumer's evoked set of alternatives is smaller with services than with goods. The Internet has the potential to widen the set of alternatives.

For nonprofessional services, consumers' decisions often entail the choice between performing the services for themselves or hiring someone to perform them. Working people may choose between cleaning their own homes or hiring housekeepers, between altering their families' cloth's or taking them to a tailor, even between staying home to take care of their children-or engaging a day care centre to provide child care.

Consumers may consider themselves as sources of supply for many services, inducing lawn care, tax preparation, and preparing meals. This means that the customer's- evoked frequently includes selfprovision of the service. Nonprofessional service providers, must recognize that they often replace or compete with the consumer, which may imply more exacting standards from the consumer and may require more individualized, personal attention from the service provider.

Consumers know what they expect from providers of housecleaning or lawn care or day care because they know what they are accustomed to providing for themselves. The alert service marketer will be certain to research consumers' expectations and demands in such situations. So far, not every consumer is convinced that the cyber mall will replace the local mall. World Research found that consumers who do not buy online have these reasons for continuing to buy the traditional way: fear of hackers (21 per cent), lack of products (16 per cent), inability to see the products (15 per cent), need to reveal personal information (13 per cent) poorly designed site (8 per cent) companies' reputations (6 per cent) and fear of money or merchandise getting lost (6 per cent) Emotion and Mood Emotion and mood are feeling states that influence people's (and therefore customers') perceptions and evaluations of their experiences. Moods are distinguished from emotions in that moods refer t6 transient feeling states that occur at specific times and in specific situations, whereas emotions are more intense, stable, and pervasive.

Because services are experiences, moods and emotions, are critical factors that shape the perceived effectiveness of service encounters. If a service customer is in a "bad mood" when he enters a service establishment, service provision will likely be interpreted more negatively than if he were in a buoyant, positive mood. Similarly, if a service provider is irritable or sullen her interaction with customers will likely be colored by that mood.

Furthermore, when another customer in a service establishment is cranky or fast rated, whether from problems with the service or from existing emotions unrelated to the service, his or her mood affects the provision of service for all customers who sense the negative mood. In sum, any service characterized by human interaction is strongly dependent on the moods and emotions of the service provider, the service customer, and other customers receiving the service at the same time.

In what specific ways can mood affect the behaviour of service customers? First, positive moods can make customers more obliging and willing to participate in behaviours that help service encounters succeed. 12 A customer in a good emotional state is probably more willing to follow an exercise regimen prescribed by a physical therapist, bus his own dishes at a fast-food restaurant, and overlook delays in service. A customer in a negative mood may be less likely to engage in behaviours essential to the effectiveness of the service but that seem difficult or overwhelming: abstaining from chocolates when on a diet programme with Weight Watchers, taking frequent aerobic classes from a health club, or completing homework assigned in a class.

A second way that moods and emotions influence service customers' is to bias the way they judge service encounters arid providers. Mood and emotions enhance and amplify experiences, making them either more positive or more negative than they might seem in the absence of the moods and emotions. 13 After losing a big account, a sales-woman catching an airline flight will be more incensed with delays and crowding than she might be on a day when business went well. Conversely, the positive mood of a services customer at a dance or restaurant...will heighten the experience, leading to positive evaluations of the, service establishment. The direction of the bias in evaluation is consistent with the polarity (that is, positive or negative) of the mood 'or emotion.

Finally, moods and emotions affect the way information about service-is absorbed anti retrieved. AS memories about a service are encoded by a consumer, the feelings associated with the encounter become an inseparable part of the memory.

If travellers fall in love during a vacation in the Bahamas, they may hold favourable assessments of the destination due more to their emotional state than to the destination itself. Conversely, if a customer first realises his level of fitness is poor when 'on a guest pass in a health club, the negative feelings may be encoded and retrieved every time he thinks of the health club or, for that matter, any health club. Service marketers need to be aware of the moods and emotions of customers and of service employees and should attempt to influence those moods and emotions in positive ways. They need to cultivate positive moods and emotions such as joy,' delight, and contentment and discourage negative emotions such as distress, frustration, anger, and disgust.

SERVICE PROVISION AS DRAMA. RESEARCHERS AND MANAGERS

Service businesses have compared service provision with drama, observing that both aim to create and Maintain a desirable impression before an audience, and both recognize that the way to accomplish this is by carefully managing the actors and the physical setting of their behaviour. In fact, the service marketer must play many drama-related roles (including director, choreographer, and writer) to be sure the performances of the actors are pleasing to the audience. The Walt Disney Company explicitly considers its service provision a "performance," even using show-business terms such as "cast member," "onstage," and "show" to - describe the operations at Disneyland and Walt Disney World.

The skill of the service "actors" in performing their routines, the way they appear, and their commitment to the "show" we all pivotal to service delivery. While service actors are present in most service performances, their importance increases when the degree of direct personal contact increases (such as in a hospital, resort, or restaurant), when the services involve repeat contact, and when the contact personnel as actors have discretion in determining the nature of the service and how it is delivered (as in education, medical services, and legal services). The physical setting of the service can be likened to the staging of a theatrical production including scenery, props, and other physical cues' to create desired impressions.

Among a setting's features that may influence that character of a service are the colors or brightness of the service's surroundings; the volume and pitch of sounds in the setting; the smells, movement, freshness, and temperature of the air; the use of space; the style arid comfort of the furnishings; and the setting's design and cleanliness The setting increases in importance when the nature of a service is distinguished by its environment, as is the case with Steak and Ale and Ponderosa Steak-houses or a "downtown" law firm. In essence, the delivery of service can 'be conceived as drama, where service personnel are the "actors," service customers are the "audience," physical evidence of the service is the "setting," and the process of service assembly is the "performance.

The drama metaphor offers a useful way to conceive of service performances. Among the aspects of a service that can be considered in this way are selection of personnel (auditioning the actors), 'training of personnel (rehearsing), clearly defining the role (scripting the performance), creation of the service environment (setting the stage), and deciding which aspects of the service should be performed in the presence of the customer (onstage) and which should be performed in the back" roomJback-stagey.

CONSUMER BUYING BEHAVIOUR

Possibly the most challenging concept in marketing deals with understanding why buyers do what they do (or don't do). But such knowledge is critical for marketers since having a strong understanding of buyer behaviour will help shed light on what is important to the customer and also suggest the important influences on customer decision-making. Using this information, marketers can create marketing programs that they believe will be of interest to customers.

As you might guess, factors affecting how customers make decisions are extremely complex. Buyer behaviour is deeply rooted in psychology with dashes of sociology thrown in just to make things more interesting. Since every person in the world is different, it is impossible to have simple rules that explain how buying decisions are made.

But those who have spent many years analyzing customer activity have presented us with useful "guidelines" in how someone decides whether or not to make a purchase. In fact, pick up any textbook that examines customer behaviour and each seems to approach it from a different angle. The perspective we take is to touch on just the basic concepts that appear to be commonly accepted as influencing customer behaviour.

TYPES OF CONSUMER PURCHASE DECISIONS

Consumers are faced with purchase decisions nearly every day. But not all decisions are treated the same. Some decisions are more complex than others and thus require more effort by the consumer. Other decisions are fairly routine and require little effort.

In general, consumers face four types of purchase decisions:

- *Minor New Purchase*: These purchases represent something new to a consumer but in the customer's mind is not a very important purchase in terms of need, money or other reason (e.g., status within a group).
- *Minor Re-Purchase*: These are the most routine of all purchases and often the consumer returns to purchase the same product without giving much thought to other product options (i.e., consumer is brand loyalty).
- *Major New Purchase*: These purchases are the most difficult of all purchases because the product being purchased is important to the consumer but the consumer has little or no previous experience

making these decisions. The consumer's lack of confidence in making this type of decision often (but not always) requires the consumer to engage in an extensive decision-making process..

- *Major Re-Purchase*: These purchase decisions are also important to the consumer but the consumer feels confident in making these decisions since they have previous experience purchasing the product.

For marketers it is important to understand how consumers treat the purchase decisions they face. If a company is targeting customers who feel a purchase decision is difficult (i.e., Major New Purchase), their marketing strategy may vary greatly from a company targeting customers who view the purchase decision as routine. In fact, the same company may face both situations at the same time; for some the product is new, while other customers see the purchase as routine. The implication of buying behaviour for marketers is that different buying situations require different marketing efforts.

WHY CONSUMERS BUY

Customers make purchases in order to satisfy needs. Some of these needs are basic and must be filled by everyone on the planet (e.g., food, shelter) while others are not required for basic survival and vary depending on the person. It probably makes more sense to classify needs that are not a necessity as wants or desires. In fact, in many countries where the standard of living is very high, a large portion of the population's income is spent on wants and desires rather than on basic needs. In this tutorial when we mention the consumer we are referring to the actual buyer, the person spending the money.

But is should also be pointed out that the one who does the buying is not necessarily the user of what is bought and that others may be involved in the buying decision in addition to the actual buyer. While the purchasing process in the consumer market is not as complex as the business market, having multiple people involved in a purchase decision is not unusual. For example, in planning for a family vacation the mother may make the hotel reservations but others in the family may have input on the hotel choice. Similarly, a father may purchase snacks at the grocery store but his young child may be the one who selected it from the store shelf.

So understanding consumer purchase behaviour involves not only understanding how decisions are made but also understanding the dynamics that influence purchases.

WHAT INFLUENCES PURCHASING

As we discussed the decision-making process for consumers is anything but straight forward. There are many factors that can affect this process as a person works through the purchase decision. The number of potential influences on consumer behaviour is limitless. However, marketers are well served to understand the KEY influences. By doing so they may be in a position to tailor their marketing efforts to take advantage of these influences in a way that will satisfy the consumer and the marketer (remember this is a key part of the definition of marketing).

For the purposes of this tutorial we will break these influences down into three main categories: Internal, External and Marketing. However, those interested in learning more about customer buying activity may want to consult one or more consumer behaviour books where they will find additional methods for explaining consumer buying behaviour. For the most part the influences are not mutually exclusive.

Instead, they are all interconnected and, as we will see, work together to form who we are and how we behave. For each of the influences that are discussed we will provide a basic description and also suggest its implication to marketers. Bear in mind we only provide a few marketing implications for each influence; clearly there are many more.

INTERNAL INFLUENCES

We start our examination of the influences on consumer purchase decisions by first looking inside ourselves to see which are the most important internal factors that affect how we make choices.

Perceptual Filter

Perception is how we see ourselves and the world we live in. However, what ends up being stored inside us doesn't always get there in a direct manner. Often our mental makeup results from information that has been consciously or subconsciously filtered as we experience it, a process we refer to as a perceptual filter.

To us this is our reality, though it does not mean it is an accurate reflection on what is real. Thus, perception is the way we filter stimuli (e.g., someone talking to us, reading a newspaper story) and then make sense out of it.

Perception has several steps:

- *Exposure*: Sensing a stimuli (e.g. seeing an ad)
- *Attention*: An effort to recognize the nature of a stimuli (e.g. recognizing it is an ad)
- *Awareness*: Assigning meaning to a stimuli (e.g., humorous ad for particular product)
- *Retention*: Adding the meaning to one's internal makeup (i.e., product has fun ads)

How these steps are eventually carried out depends on a person's approach to learning. By learning we mean how someone changes what they know, which in turn may affect how they act. There are many theories of learning, a discussion of which is beyond the scope of this tutorial, however, suffice to say that people are likely to learn in different ways.

For instance, one person may be able to focus very strongly on a certain advertisement and be able to retain the information after being exposed only one time while another person may need to be exposed to the same advertisement many times before he/she even recognizes what it is.

Consumers are also more likely to retain information if a person has a strong interest in the stimuli. If a person is in need of new car they are more likely to pay attention to a new advertisement for a car while someone who does not need a car may need to see the advertisement many times before they recognize the brand of automobile.

Marketing Implications

Marketers spend large sums of money in an attempt to get customers to have a positive impression of their products. But clearly the existence of a perceptual filter suggests that getting to this stage is not easy.

Exposing consumers to a product can be very challenging considering the amount of competing product messages (ads) that are also trying to accomplish the same objective (i.e., advertising clutter). So marketers must be creative and use various means to deliver their message. Once the message reaches consumer it must be interesting enough to capture their attention (e.g., talk about the product's benefits). But attending to the message is not enough. For marketers the most critical step is the one that occurs with awareness.

Here marketers must continually monitor and respond if their message becomes distorted in ways that will negatively shape its meaning. This can often happen due in part to competitive activity (e.g., comparison advertisements). Finally, getting the consumer to give positive meaning to the message they have retained requires the marketer make sure that consumers accurately interpret the facts about the product.

Knowledge

Knowledge is the sum of all information known by a person. It is the facts of the world as he/she knows it and the depth of knowledge is a function of the breadth of worldly experiences and the strength of an individual's long-term memory. Obviously what exists as knowledge to an individual depends on how an individual's perceptual filter makes sense of the information it is exposed to.

Marketing Implications

Marketers may conduct research that will gauge consumers' level of knowledge regarding their product. As we will see below, it is likely that other factors influencing consumer behaviour are in large part shaped by what is known about a product. Thus, developing methods (e.g., incentives) to encourage consumers to accept more information (or correct information) may affect other influencing factors.

Attitude

In simple terms attitude refers to what a person feels or believes about something. Additionally, attitude may be reflected in how an individual acts based on his or her beliefs. Once formed, attitudes can be very difficult to change. Thus, if a consumer has a negative attitude toward a particular issue it will take considerable effort to change what they believe to be true.

Marketing Implications

Marketers facing consumers who have a negative attitude toward their product must work to identify the key issues shaping a consumer's attitude then adjust marketing decisions (e.g., advertising) in an effort to change the attitude.

For companies competing against strong rivals to whom loyal consumers exhibit a positive attitude, an important strategy is to work to see why consumers feel positive toward the competitor and then try to meet or beat the competitor on these issues. Alternatively, a company can try to locate customers who feel negatively toward the competitor and then increase awareness among this group.

Personality

An individual's personality relates to perceived personal characteristics that are consistently exhibited, especially when one acts in the presence of others. In most, but not all, cases the behaviours one projects in a situation is similar to the behaviours a person exhibits in another situation.

In this way personality is the sum of sensory experiences others get from experiencing a person (i.e., how one talks, reacts). While one's personality is often interpreted by those we interact with, the person has their own vision of their personality, called Self Concept, which may or may not be the same has how others view us.

Marketing Implications

For marketers it is important to know that consumers make purchase decisions to support their self concept. Using research techniques to identify how customers view themselves may give marketers insight into products and promotion options that are not readily apparent. For example, when examining consumers a marketer may initially build marketing strategy around more obvious clues to consumption behaviour, such as consumer's demographic indicators (e.g., age, occupation, income). However, in-depth research may yield information that shows consumers are purchasing products to fulfil self-concept objectives that have little to do with the demographic category they fall into (e.g., senior citizen may be making purchases that make them feel younger). Appealing to the consumer's self concept needs could expand the market to which the product is targeted.

Lifestyle

This influencing factor relates to the way we live through the activities we engage in and interests we express. In simple terms it is what we value out of life. Lifestyle is often determined by how we spend our time and money.

Marketing Implications

Products and services are purchased to support consumers' lifestyles. Marketers have worked hard researching how consumers in their target markets live their lives since this information is key to developing products, suggesting promotional strategies and even determining how best to distribute products. The fact that lifestyle is so directly tied to marketing activity will be further examined as we discuss developing target market strategies.

Roles

Roles represent the position we feel we hold or others feel we should hold when dealing in a group environment. These positions carry certain responsibilities yet it is important to understand that some of these responsibilities may, in fact, be perceived and not spelled out or even accepted by others. In support of their roles, consumers will make product choices that may vary depending on which role they are assuming. As illustration, a person who is responsible for selecting snack food for an office party his boss will attend may choose higher quality products than he would choose when selecting snacks for his family.

Marketing Implications

Advertisers often show how the benefits of their products aid consumers as they perform certain roles. Typically the underlying message of this promotional approach is to suggest that using the advertiser's product will help raise one's status in the eyes of others while using a competitor's product may have a negative effect on status.

Motivation

Motivation relates to our desire to achieve a certain outcome. Many internal factors we have already discussed can affect a customer's desire to achieve a certain outcome but there are others. For instance, when it comes to making purchase decisions customers' motivation could be affected by such issues as financial position (e.g., *Can I afford the purchase?*), time constraints (e.g., *Do I need to make the purchase quickly?*), overall value (e.g., *Am I getting my money's worth?*), and perceived risk (e.g., *What happens if I make a bad decision?*).

Marketing Implications

Motivation is also closely tied to the concept of Involvement, which relates to how much effort the consumer will exert in making a decision. Highly motivated consumers will want to get mentally and physically involved in the purchase process. Not all products have a high percentage of highly involved customers (e.g., milk) but marketers who market products and services that may lead to high level of consumer involvement should prepare options that will be attractive to this group. For instance, marketers should make it easy for consumers to learn about their product (e.g., information on website, free video preview) and, for some products, allow customers to experience the product (e.g., free trial) before committing to the purchase.

CONSUMER INVOLVEMENT MANAGEMENT

Consumer involvement is about the motivation to attain a goal: the consumer tries to find a way to satisfy himself or herself and a person's perceived relevance of the object is based on their inherent needs, values, and interests. The word 'object' refers to a product, a brand, an advertisement, or a purchase situation.

In addition, Traylor defined involvement as a consumer's understanding or recognition of a specific product. It is that a consumer is stimulated by personal recognition and/or interest in the product under a specific environment. This also indicated that different people have different motivations and goals for distinctive products.

CONSUMER INVOLVEMENT AND DECISION QUALITY

From the previous review, consumer involvement is about personal motivation in the product under a specific environment and it may create awareness of and preference for information that would be expected to increase the amount of time that consumers spend on seeking information. Therefore, high involvement consumers infer that they will search for more information about certain products under certain situations.

With an increasing involvement level, a consumer would search for higher level product information and high level information helps consumers to compare products more in depth in order to increase the decision quality. Consequently, high involvement is assumed to improve the decision quality because of sufficient information, whereas low involvement will lead to a reduction in the decision quality because of a lack of significant information.

The hypothesis between consumer involvement and decision quality can be drawn as follows:

- Consumer involvement has a positive relationship with decision quality.

CONSUMER KNOWLEDGE AND DECISION QUALITY

The relationship between consumer knowledge and decision-making quality is an interesting issue. During purchase processing, consumers' knowledge of the product would not only affect their search behaviour, but may also affect their information treatment and decision-making processing, and would furthermore, affect their purchase intention. Prior experience is also expected to contribute to the consumer's knowledge of the marketplace, of the product, and of decision-making skills.

More precisely, consumer Knowledge is likely to contribute to consumers' decision-making abilities, because it may improve the efficiency with which consumers handle information that would likely decrease the time consumers must devote to gathering a given amount of information. Due to an expert having more knowledge than a novice in a particular product category, the assumption is that experts will make more satisfied and efficient decisions than would novices. However, there are two negative opinions about this relationship, prior experience and complexity of the situation. Firstly, prior purchasing experience is negatively associated with the overall amount of searching undertaken.

An expert consumer is expected to have more experience than a novice. This infers that experts will search for less information than novices, which may lead to low decision quality. Secondly, Alba and Hutchinson pointed out that consumer knowledge should be regarded as a multidimensional construct. This means that different types of product-related experience lead to different dimensions of knowledge, and these different dimensions of knowledge have different effects on product evaluations and choice behaviour.

Therefore, this may indicate that different experts in the same situation may have different decision results because of personal experience or behaviour. The first opposite view can be explained by the ability of differentiating relevant information. As Wu and Lin cited, experts have better ability to differentiate between relevant and irrelevant than novices. Therefore, even experts search for less information than novices, and still can make a good decision. For a second opposite view the experiencebased knowledge is less directly linked to behaviour than objective and subjective knowledge.

Therefore, the assumption about experts and novice is retained, and the hypothesis between consumer knowledge and decision quality is drawn as follows.

- Consumer knowledge has a positive relationship with decision quality.

CONSUMER EDUCATION AND DECISION QUALITY

Consumer education focuses on providing consumers with skills to utilise information and helps to obtain and keep satisfied customers. These two characteristics implied that consumer education could increase consumers' ability to differentiate between relevant and irrelevant information and the possibility to satisfy consumers. Both of these are important factors to achieve a higher decision quality. Moreover, Brennan and Ritter cited that consumer education is necessary to become an effective consumer, which is a main characteristic of a good decision maker.

Therefore, the assumption of consumer education and decision quality is drawn as follows:

- Consumer education has a positive relationship with decision quality.

THE MODERATING EFFECT OF CONSUMER INVOLVEMENT ON DECISION QUALITY

Consumer involvement plays an important role in consumer behaviour. Consumers will seek more information and knowledge because of their inherent needs, values, and interests. Information seekers no longer need to receive information passively.

In contract, they can actively decide what information they want to read, and how long and in what order to read it. With considering consumer education as information or skills, consumer involvement has a significant influence to receive consumer education. In other words, consumers search a lot of information to increase their knowledge when they have interest or involvement in certain circumstance. Therefore, consumer education not only influences decision quality but also needs to consider different degrees of consumer involvement.

Combining all reasons, the hypothesis is as follows:

- Consumer involvement has a moderating effect on decision quality such that the influence of consumer education on decision quality will be greater for highly involved consumer

THE MODERATING EFFECT OF CONSUMER KNOWLEDGE ON DECISION QUALITY

Consumer education has long been seen as a means for creating values or skills for customers and could help to bring about significant changes in the cognitive processes, behaviour, and satisfaction levels of consumers. These values may increase when consumers are knowledgeable possibly regarding them as an expert. In other words, the effect of consumer education for novices on decision quality will be less than that for experts, because novices are a lack of knowledge and skills to improve consumer abilities of evaluating product quality.

Furthermore, as Wu and Lin cited, novices, being unable to differentiate between relevant and irrelevant information, do not benefit from a high degree of control. Burton's research, the ability of existing customers is a practical issue associated with implementing consumer education. Therefore, highly complicated consumer education seems to be not suitable for novices to make a quality decision, because non-expert consumers may not prefer to receive so much information. Besides, the method of delivery also influences the implementation of consumer education and the Internet, which can provide plenty of information in seconds, is chosen as an environment to demonstrate the framework.

CATEGORIES OF CONSUMER INVOLVEMENT

Involvement can be divided into advertising involvement, product involvement, and purchasing involvement. The level of involvement may be influenced by one or more personal factors, object or stimulus factors, and situational factors. As a result, the degree of involvement can be thought of as a continuum, ranging from lack of interest in marketing stimulus at one end to high involvement at the other.

These are opposite to the research in the economics of information literature, which suggests that consumers will continue to seek information as long as the perceived benefits exceed the marginal costs of search activities. The antecedent of this statement is that consumers have to be interested in this marketing stimulus.

IMPACTS OF CONSUMER INVOLVEMENT

On an increasing involvement level, a consumer will search for higher level information when he or she performs product selection and high involvement purchase decisions are likely to involve a more extensive external information search than low involvement purchase decisions. In other words, consumers will search for more information at the high involvement level, especially for external information. In contrast, low involvement consumers will search for little information, and mainly depend on internal information.

CONSUMER KNOWLEDGE MANAGEMENT

Consumer knowledge has a long history in consumer research in both marketing theory and practice. Brucks stated that consumer knowledge is based on memories of consumers and gathering information from consumers. Similarly, Lin and Chen declared that consumer knowledge depends on a consumer's awareness or understanding about the product, or a consumer's confidence in it. Consumer knowledge plays an important role in the consumer behaviour fields, such as consumers' attitudes, consumers' cognition etc.

MODERATING EFFECT OF CONSUMER KNOWLEDGE

The result of this assumption shows that there is no association with decision quality. This may be a result of level of consumer knowledge, quality of consumer education, and perspective of consumer education. First of all, most pervious definitions consider consumer education as a skill to utilize information or neutral information. For experts, most of consumer education is what they already know or are familiar with. Therefore, the utility of consumer education is not useful for them to increase the decision quality. Next, quality of consumer education is not consistent in cosmetics industry. Consumer education is more effective in financial service than in other industries, because most of financial companies try to develop high quality of consumer education to help their clients.

The quality of Consumer education applied in cosmetics industry, however, has a huge different between companies. For instance, some cosmetics brands provide academic research report to show the benefit of certain ingredient whereas other brands only show the make-up tips for consumers. Both of these may not be a good consumer education for high knowledgeable consumers. Firstly, most consumers may not interest in how cosmetics are made, and secondly, make-up tips are useless for them because they already know how to do their make-up well. Therefore, high knowledgeable consumers are hard to receive benefit from consumer education in cosmetics industry.

In other words, there may not have any interactive effects on decision quality. Moreover, most consumer education provided by cosmetics companies is something related to their own products. As a result, high knowledgeable consumers may regard this kind consumer education as company's advertisement rather than general knowledge. For this reason, the utility of consumer education on decision quality would be diminished. The interaction between CK and CE seems to influence greater for low knowledgeable consumers rather than for high knowledgeable consumers.

However, this is hard to test due to a lack of consistency of consumer education, and this is one of limitation in this study. For example, If a company provides a good consumer education for low knowledgeable consumers, then the impact will be for low knowledgeable consumers. In other words, if a company provides a good consumer education for high knowledgeable consumers, then the influence will be for high knowledgeable consumers. Unfortunately, in this study respondents were asked to image a brand by themselves, rather than tested in one brand. Therefore, it is hard to measure the utility of consumer education and hard to define which group is appropriate. As a result, this may regard as a limitation in this study.

CATEGORIES OF CONSUMER KNOWLEDGE

Brucks illustrated three categories of consumer knowledge: subjective knowledge objective knowledge, and experience-based knowledge. These are broadly-used categories of consumer knowledge. Subjective knowledge is what consumers think they know, whereas objective knowledge is an actual knowledge construct as measured by some sort of test. Moreover, experience-based knowledge is the accumulation of purchasing or usage experience with the product.

However, the experience-based measures of knowledge are less directly linked to behaviour than the former types. As a consequence, objective knowledge and subjective knowledge have more essential influence on consumer knowledge. For objective knowledge, it is hard for measures to be entirely objective, because these have to depend on some form of communication with the consumers about their knowledge. As Park *et al.* state, objective knowledge and subjective knowledge are related. Similarly, Alba and Hutchinson also indicated that consumer knowledge should include two parts, expertise and familiarity with product.

Familiarity is defined as the numbers of product-related experiences that have been accumulated by the consumer, which included advertising exposures, information search, interactions with salesperson, decision-making, purchasing, and product usage. Expertise is defined as the ability to perform productrelated tasks successfully, which included cognitive structure and cognitive processes. The relationship between familiarity and expertise is that increased product familiarity results in increasing consumer expertise. Therefore, these will be re-enforced by each other.

From previous researches, consumer knowledge will be different from individuals, and objective knowledge and subjective knowledge have differential influence on consumers' search activities and information processing. High objective knowledge allows consumers to encode information about new alternatives more efficiently, while high subjective knowledge leads to a greater reliance on one's own evaluation skills. On the other hand, consumers high in subjective knowledge should have less well developed category structures stored in memory than consumers high in objective knowledge who tend to keep themselves updated about market conditions.

DIFFERENCE BETWEEN EXPERTS AND NOVICES

Expert consumers prefer to search and update information in certain product categories, and develop a good knowledge in this category. In contrast, novice consumers rarely search for relevant information, and make decisions by their own knowledge. Furthermore, experts are people who gain their expert knowledge through experience or training, and differ from novices in many dimensions of information processing, such as memorisation ability, information selection, problem solving, etc. Lin and Chen reviewed the literature and reports in consumer knowledge, and concluded three measurements of product knowledge. The first measurement is how much consumers know about the product. Secondly, the measurement is the amount, type and organisation of what consumers have remembered in their memory. Finally, the amount of purchasing and usage experience the consumers have. Consequently, experts tend to memorise the technical attributes of a product, whereas novices tend to focus on the benefit of a product.

CONSUMER BUYING BEHAVIOUR

Consumer Buying Behaviour the decision processes and acts of final household consumers associated with evaluating, buying, consuming, and discarding products for personal consumption. Consider the purchase an automobile. You generally will not consider different options until some event triggers a need, such as a problem needing potentially expensive repair. Once this need has put you "on the market", you begin to ask your friends for recommendations regarding dealerships and car models. After visiting several dealerships, you test drive several models and finally decide on a particular model. After picking up your new car, you have doubts on the way home, wondering if you can afford the monthly payments, but then begin to wonder if instead you should have purchased a more expensive but potentially more reliable model.

Over the next five years, the car has several unexpected breakdowns that lead you to want to purchase a different brand, but you have been very happy with the services of the local dealership and decide to again purchase your next car there.

In this particular case, the following generic model of consumer decision making appears to hold:

- Need recognition
- Information search
- Evaluation of alternatives
- Purchase decision
- Postpurchase behaviour

Now consider the purchase of a quart of orange juice. This product when you do your grocery shopping once per week. You have a favourite brand of orange juice and usually do your grocery shopping at the same store. When you buy orange juice, you always go to the same place in the store to pick it up, and never notice what other brands are on the shelf or what are the prices of other brands.

How is it that the generic model works differently in this second scenario? Why does it work differently? Why would we generally need the ministrations of a sales person in the sale of a car, but we generally do not need the help of a salesperson in the purchase of orange juice?

How can the marketer of orange juice get a consumer like you to exert more effort into information search or to consider alternative products? How is it that the marketer of your brand got you to ignore alternative competing brands?

What is the involvement of salespeople in *sales promotions* that might be associated with products such as orange juice? Consumer behaviour researchers are not so interested in studying the validity of the above generic model, but are more interested in various factors that influence how such a model might work.

GROUP INFLUENCES ON CONSUMER BEHAVIOUR

Culture

Culture the set of basic values, beliefs, norms, and associated behaviours that are learned by a member of society, Note that culture is something that is *learned* and that it has a relatively long lasting effect on the behaviours of an individual. As an example of cultural influences, consider how the salesperson in an appliance store in the U.S. must react to different couples who are considering the purchase of a refrigerator. In some subcultures, the husband will play a dominant role in the purchase decision; in others, the wife will play a more dominant role.

Social Class

Social Class a group of individuals with similar social rank, based on such factors as *occupation, education,* and *wealth*

Reference Groups

Reference groups, often temporary, that affect a person's values, attitude, or behaviours:

- E.g., your behaviours around colleagues at work or friends at school are probably different from your behaviours around your parents, no matter your age or stage in the family life cycle. If you were a used car salesperson, how might you respond differently to a nineteen year old prospect accompanied by her boyfriend from one accompanied by two girlfriends?
- Opinion leadera person within a reference group who exerts influence on others because of special skills, knowledge, personality, etc.
  - You might ask the webmaster at work for an opinion about a particular software application. Software manufacturers often give away free beta copies of software to potential opinion leaders with the hope that they will in turn influence many others to purchase the product.

Family

Family a group of people related by blood, marriage, or other socially approved relationship

INTERNAL INFLUENCES ON CONSUMER BEHAVIOUR

Personality

Personality a person's distinguishing psychological characteristics that lead to relatively consistent and lasting responses to stimuli in the environment

We are each unique as individuals, and we each respond differently as consumers. For example, some people are "optimizers" who will keep shopping until they are certain that they have found the best price for a particular item, while other people are "satisficers" who will stop shopping when they believe that they have found something that is "good enough." If you are a salesperson in a retail shoe store, how might you work differently with these two personalities?

Lifestyle and Psychographics

- Lifestyle is a pattern of living expressed through a person's activities, interests, and opinions
- Psychographics is a technique for measuring personality and lifestyles to developing lifestyle classifications

Motivation: Multiple Motives

Consumers usually have multiple motives for particular behaviours. These can be a combination of:

- Manifest known to the person and freely admitted
- Latent unknown to the person or the person is very reluctant to admit

Note: different motives can lead to the same behaviour; observing behaviour is not sufficient to determine motives.

Involvement

Involvement has to do with an individual's:

- *Intensity of interest* in a product and the
- *Importance* of the product for that person

The purchase of a car is much more risky than the purchase of a quart of orange juice, and therefore presents a higher involvement situation. This modifies the way that the generic model works.

As involvement increases, consumers have greater motivation to comprehend and elaborate on information salient to the purchase. A life insurance agent, for example, would typically be more interested in contacting a young couple who just had a baby than an eighteen year old college student - even though the new parents might be struggling to make ends meet while the student is living more comfortably. Although the annual investment into a policy is much lower if started at a younger age, most young college students are not open to thinking about long term estate planning. A young couple with a new child, however, is much more open to thinking about issues associated with planning for the child's future education, saving to buy a house, or even saving to take an extended vacation upon retirement.

TYPES OF CONSUMER PROBLEM-SOLVING PROCESSES

Routenized

- Used when buying frequently purchased, low cost items
- Used when little search/decision effort is needed
- E.g., buying a quart of orange juice once per week

Limited Problem Solving

- Used when products are occasionally purchased
- Used when information is needed about an unfamiliar product in a familiar product category

Extended Problem Solving

- Used when product is unfamiliar, expensive, or infrequently purchased
- E.g., buying a new car once every five years

POST-PURCHASE CONSUMER BEHAVIOUR

Satisfaction

After the sale, the buyer will likely feel either satisfied or dissatisfied. If the buyer believes that s/he received more in the exchange than what was paid, s/he might feel satisfied. If s/he believes that s/he received less in the exchange than what was paid, then s/he might feel dissatisfied. Dissatisfied buyers are not likely to return as customers and are not likely to send friends, relatives, and acquaintences. They are also more likely to be unhappy or even abusive when the product requires post-sale servicing, as when an automobile needs warranty maintenance.

The idea can be modelled as Homans' basic exchange equation:

Profit = Rewards–Costs

Unfortunately, even a buyer who "got a good deal" with respect to price and other terms of the sale might feel dissatisfied under the perception that the salesperson made out even better.

This idea is called equity theory, where we are concerned with:

Outcomes of A Inputs of A

vs.

Outcomes of B Inputs of B

Consider value is listed at $16,000. You are probably delighted with the purchase until you accidentally meet the prior owner who had received a trade-in of $10,000 on the car just a few days before. That the dealer appears to have received substantially greater benefit than you could lead to extreme dissatisfaction, even though you received good value for the money spent.

An issue related to this is attribution theory. Attribution theory, people tend to assign cause to the behaviour of others. Mary's life insurance agent advises her to purchase a whole life policy, while her accountant advises her, "buy term insurance and invest the difference.". The reason, explains the accountant, "is that insurance agents receive substantially higher commission payments on sales of whole life policies."

If Mary believes that the insurance agent is recommending a product merely because he receives a higher commission, she will likely be displeased with the relationship and will not take his recommendation. If the agent is able to show Mary that the recommended product is the best solution for her situation, then she will likely attribute his recommendation to having her best interests in mind and will not be concerned about how it is that he is compensated for his services.

Cognitive Dissonance

Cognitive dissonance has to do with the doubt that a person has about the wisdom of a recent purchase. It is very common for people to experience some anxiety after the purchase of a product that is very expensive or that will require a long term commitment. Jane and Fred, for example, signed a one year lease on an apartment, committing themselves to payments of $1500 per month. A week later, they are wondering if they should have instead leased a smaller $900 apartment in a more rough part of town; they are not sure if they really can afford this much of a monthly obligation. Dick and Sally, on the other hand, ultimately rented the $900 apartment, and now are wondering if the savings in rent will be offset by noisy and sometimes unsafe conditions in this neighbourhood.

Perhaps neither couple would be experiencing this anxiety if their landlords had given them just the smallest of assurances that they had made a good decision. After a close on products that are expensive or that require a long term commitment, the salesperson should provide the prospect with some reasons to be happy with the decision. Allow the car buyer to reinforce her own positive feelings by calling her a week after the purchase to ask how things are going. Call the new life insurance policy holder after two months to see if there are any questions; a lack of questions can only help the buyer to convince himself that he did the right thing.

2

Consumer Research Methods

INTRODUCTION

Market research is often needed to ensure that we produce what customers really want and not what we *think* they want.

RESEARCH SEQUENCE

In general, if more than one type of research is to be used, the more flexible and less precise method—such as focus groups and/or individual interviews—should generally be used before the less flexible but more precise methods are used. Focus groups and interviews are flexible and allow the researcher to follow up on interesting issues raised by participants who can be probed. However, because the sample sizes are small and because participants in a focus group are influenced by each other, few data points are collected. If we run five focus groups with eight people each, for example, we would have a total of forty responses. Even if we assume that these are independent, a sample size of forty would give very imprecise results.

We might conclude, for example, that somewhere between 5% and 40% of the target market would be interested in the product we have to offer. This is usually no more precise than what we already reasonably new. Questionnaires, in contrast, are highly inflexible. It is not possible to ask follow-up questions. Therefore, we can use our insights from focus groups and interviews to develop questionnaires that contain specific questions that can be asked to a larger number of people. There will still be some sampling error, but with a sample size of 1,000+ responses, we may be able to narrow the 95% confidence interval for the percentage of the target market that is seriously interested in our product to, say, 17-21%, a range that is much more meaningful.

CAUTIONS

Some cautions should be heeded in marketing research. First, in general, research should only be commissioned when it is worth the cost. Thus, research should normally be useful in making specific decisions. Secondly, marketing research can be, and often is, abused. Managers frequently have their own "agendas". Often, a way to get your way is to demonstrate through "objective" research that your opinions make economic sense.

One example of misleading research, which was reported nationwide in the media, involved the case of "The Pentagon Declares War on Rush Limbaugh." The Pentagon, within a year of the election of Democrat Bill Clinton, reported that only 4.2% of soldiers listening to the Armed Forces Network wanted to hear Rush Limbaugh. However, although this finding was reported without question in the media, it was later found that the conclusion was based on the question "What single thing can we do to improve programming?" If you did not write in something like "Carry Rush Limbaugh," you were counted as *not* wanting to hear him.

PRIMARY VS. SECONDARY RESEARCH METHODS

There are two main approaches to marketing. *Secondary* research involves using information that others have already put together. For example, if you are thinking about starting a business making clothes for tall people, you don't need to question people about how tall they are to find out how many tall people exist—that information has already been published by the U.S. Government. *Primary* research, in contrast, is research that you design and conduct yourself. For example, you may need to find out whether consumers would prefer that your soft drinks be sweater or tarter.

Research will often help us *reduce risks* associated with a new product, but it *cannot take the risk away entirely*. It is also important to ascertain whether the research has been complete. For example, Coca Cola did a great deal of research prior to releasing the New Coke, and consumers seemed to prefer the taste. However, consumers were *not* prepared to have this drink replace traditional Coke.

Surveys are useful for getting a great deal of specific information. Surveys can contain open-ended questions or closed-ended, where the respondent is asked to select answers from a brief list. Open ended questions have the advantage that the respondent is not limited to the options listed, and that the respondent is not being influenced by seeing a list of responses. However, open-ended questions are often skipped by respondents, and coding them can be quite a challenge. In general, for surveys to yield meaningful responses, sample sizes of over 100 are usually required because precision is essential. For example, if a market share of twenty per cent would result in a loss while thirty per cent would be profitable, a confidence interval of 20-35% is too wide to be useful.

Surveys come in several different forms. Mail surveys are relatively inexpensive, but response rates are typically quite low—typically from 5-20%. Phone-surveys get somewhat higher response rates, but not many questions can be asked because many answer options have to be repeated and few people are willing to stay on the phone for more than five minutes. Mall intercepts are a convenient way to reach consumers, but respondents may be reluctant to discuss anything sensitive face-to-face with an interviewer. Surveys, as any kind of research, are vulnerable to bias. The wording of a question can influence the outcome a great deal.

For example, more people answered no to the question "Should speeches against democracy be allowed?" than answered yes to "Should speeches against democracy be forbidden?" For face-to-face interviews, interviewer bias is a danger, too. Interviewer bias occurs when the interviewer influences the way the respondent answers.

For example, unconsciously an interviewer that works for the firm manufacturing the product in question may smile a little when something good is being said about the product and frown a little when something negative is being said. The respondent may catch on and say something more positive than his or her real opinion. Finally, a response bias may occur—if only part of the sample responds to a survey, the respondents' answers may not be representative of the population.

Focus groups are useful when the marketer wants to launch a new product or modify an existing one. A focus group usually involves having some 8-12 people come together in a room to discuss their consumption preferences and experiences. The group is usually led by a moderator, who will start out talking broadly about topics *related broadly* to the product without mentioning the product itself.

For example, a focus group aimed at sugar-free cookies might first address consumers' snacking preferences, only gradually moving towards the specific product of sugar-free cookies. By not mentioning the product up front, we avoid biasing the participants into thinking only in terms of the specific product brought out. Thus, instead of having consumers think primarily in terms of what might be good or bad about the product, we can ask them to discuss more broadly the ultimate benefits they really seek. For example, instead of having consumers merely discuss what they think about some sugar-free cookies that we are considering releasing to the market, we can have consumers speak about their motivations for using snacks and what general kinds of benefits they seek.

Such a discussion might reveal a concern about healthfulness and a desire for wholesome foods. Probing on the meaning of wholesomeness, consumers might indicate a desire to avoid artificial ingredients. This would be an important concern in the marketing of sugar-free cookies, but might not have come up if consumers were asked to comment directly on the product where the use of artificial ingredients is, by virtue of the nature of the product, necessary.

Focus groups are well suited for some purposes, but *poorly suited for others*. In general, focus groups *are very good for getting breadth—i.e.*, finding out what kinds of *issues* are important for consumers in a given product category. Here, it is helpful that focus groups are completely "open-ended:" The consumer mentions his or her preferences and opinions, and the focus group moderator can ask the consumer to elaborate. In a questionnaire, if one did not think to ask about something, chances are that few consumers would take the time to write out an elaborate answer.

Focus groups also have some drawbacks, for example:

- They represent *small sample sizes*. Because of the cost of running focus groups, only a few groups can be run. Suppose you run four focus groups with ten members each. This will result in an *n* of 4(10)=40, which is too small to generalize from. Therefore, focus groups *cannot* give us a good idea of:
- What proportion of the population is likely to buy the product.
- What price consumers are willing to pay.
- The groups are inherently *social*. This means that:
- Consumers will often say things that may make them look good even if that is not true.
- Consumers may be reluctant to speak about embarrassing issues.

Personal interviews involve in-depth questioning of an individual about his or her interest in or experiences with a product. The benefit here is that we can get really into depth but this method of research is costly and can be extremely vulnerable to interviewer bias.

To get a person to elaborate, it may help to try a common tool of psychologists and psychiatrists—simply repeating what the person said. He or she will often become uncomfortable with the silence that follows and will then tend to elaborate. This approach has the benefit that it minimizes the interference with the respondent's own ideas and thoughts. He or she is not influenced by a new question but will, instead, go more in depth on what he or she was saying.

Personal interviews are highly susceptible to inadvertent "signaling" to the respondent. Although an interviewer is looking to get at the truth, he or she may have a significant interest in a positive consumer response. Unconsciously, then, he or she may inadvertently smile a little when something positive is said and frown a little when something negative is said.

Consciously, this will often not be noticeable, and the respondent often will not consciously be aware that he or she is being "reinforced" and "punished" for saying positive or negative things, but at an unconscious level, the cumulative effect of several facial expressions are likely to be felt. Although this type of conditioning will not get a completely negative respondent to say all positive things, it may "swing" the balance a bit so that respondents are more likely to say positive thoughts and withhold, or limit the duration of, negative thoughts.

Projective techniques are used when a consumer may feel embarrassed to admit to certain opinions, feelings, or preferences. For example, many older executives may not be comfortable admitting to being intimidated by computers. It has been found that in such cases, people will tend to respond more openly about "someone else." Thus, we may ask them to explain reasons why *a friend* has not yet bought a computer, or to tell a story about a *person in a picture* who is or is not using a product. The main problem with this method is that it is difficult to analyse responses.

Projective techniques are inherently inefficient to use. The elaborate context that has to be put into place takes time and energy away from the main question. There may also be real differences between the respondent and the third party. Saying or thinking about something that "hits too close to home" may also influence the respondent, who may or may not be able to see through the ruse.

Observation of consumers is often a powerful tool. Looking at how consumers select products may yield insights into how they make decisions and what they look for. For example, some American manufacturers were concerned about low sales of their products in Japan. Observing Japanese consumers, it was found that many of these Japanese consumers scrutinized packages looking for a name of a major manufacturer—the product specific-brands that are common in the U.S. were not impressive to the Japanese, who wanted a name of a major firm like Mitsubishi or Proctor and Gamble. Observation may help us determine how much time consumers spend comparing prices, or whether nutritional labels are being consulted.

A question arises as to whether this type of "spying" inappropriately invades the privacy of consumers. Although there may be cause for some concern in that the particular individuals have not consented to be part of this research, it should be noted that there is no particular interest in what the individual customer being watched does.

The question is what consumers—either as an entire group or as segments—do. Consumers benefit, for example, from stores that are designed effectively to promote efficient shopping. If it is found that women are more uncomfortable than men about others standing too close, the areas of the store heavily trafficked by women can be designed accordingly. What is being reported here, then, are averages and tendencies in response. The intent is not to find "juicy" observations specific to one customer.

The video clip with Paco Underhill that we saw in class demonstrated the application of observation research to the retail setting. By understanding the phenomena such as the tendency towards a right turn, the location of merchandise can be observed.

It is also possible to identify problem areas where customers may be overly vulnerable to the "but brush," or overly close encounter with others. This method can be used to identify problems that the customer experiences, such as difficulty finding a product, a mirror, a changing room, or a store employee for help.

Online research methods. The Internet now reaches the great majority of households in the U.S., and thus, online research provides new opportunity and has increased in use.

One potential benefit of online surveys is the use of "conditional branching." In conventional paper and pencil surveys, one question might ask if the respondent has shopped for a new car during the last eight months. If the respondent answers "no," he or she will be asked to skip ahead several questions—*e.g.*, going straight to question 17 instead of proceeding to number 9. If the respondent answered "yes," he or she would be instructed to go to the next question which, along with the next several ones, would address issues related to this shopping experience. Conditional branching allows the computer to skip directly to the appropriate question. If a respondent is asked which brands he or she considered, it is also possible to customise brand comparison questions to those listed.

Suppose, for example, that the respondent considered Ford, Toyota, and Hyundai, it would be possible to ask the subject questions about his or her view of the relative quality of each respective pair—in this case, Ford vs. Toyota, Ford vs. Hyundai, and Toyota vs. Hyundai. There are certain drawbacks to online surveys. Some consumers may be more comfortable with online activities than others—and not all households will have access. Today, however, this type of response bias is probably not significantly greater than that associated with other types of research methods. A more serious problem is that it has consistently been found in online research that it is very difficult—if not impossible—to get respondents to carefully read instructions and other information online—there is a tendency to move quickly. This makes it difficult to perform research that depends on the respondent's reading of a situation or product description.

Online search data and page visit logs provides valuable ground for analysis. It is possible to see how frequently various terms are used by those who use a firm's web site search feature or to see the route taken by most consumers to get to the page with the information they ultimately want. If consumers use a certain term frequently that is not used by the firm in its product descriptions, the need to include this term in online content can be seen in search logs. If consumers take a long, "torturous" route to information frequently accessed, it may be appropriate to redesign the menu structure and/or insert hyperlinks in "intermediate" pages that are found in many users' routes. *Scanner data*. Many consumers are members of supermarket "clubs." In return for signing p for a card and presenting this when making purchases, consumers are often eligible for considerable discounts on selected products.

Researchers use a more elaborate version of this type of programme in some communities. Here, a number of consumers receive small payments and/or other incentives to sign up to be part of a research panel. They then receive a card that they are asked to present any time they go shopping. Nearly all retailers in the area usually cooperate. It is now possible to track what the consumer bought in all stores and to have a historical record.

TRAINING AND RESEARCH

Psychoanalytic training in the United States, in most locations, involves personal analytic treatment for the trainee, conducted confidentially, with no report to the Education Committee of the Analytic Training Institute; approximately 600 hours of class instruction, with a standard curriculum, over a four-year period. Classes are often a few hours per week, or for a full day or two every other weekend during the academic year; this varies with the institute; and supervision once per week, with a senior analyst, on each analytic treatment case the trainee has.

The minimum number of cases varies between institutes, often two to four cases. Male and female cases are required. Supervision must go on for at least a few years on one or more cases. Supervision is done in the supervisor's office, where the trainee presents material from the analytic work that week, examines the unconscious conflicts with the supervisor, and learns, discusses, and is advised about technique.

Many psychoanalytic Training Centers in the United States have been accredited by special committees of the American Psychoanalytic Association or the International Psychoanalytical Association. Because of theoretical differences, other independent institutes arose, usually founded by psychologists, who until 1987 were not permitted access to psychoanalytic training institutes of the American Psychoanalytic Association. Currently there are between seventy-five and one hundred independent institutes in the United States.

As well, other institutes are affiliated to other organizations such as the American Academy of Psychoanalysis and Dynamic Psychiatry, and the National Association for the Advancement of Psychoanalysis. At most psychoanalytic institutes in the United States, qualifications for entry include a terminal degree in a mental health field, such as Ph.D., Psy.D., M.S.W., or M.D.

A few institutes restrict applicants to those already holding an M.D. or Ph.D., and most institutes in Southern California confer a Ph.D. or Psy.D. in psychoanalysis upon graduation, which involves completion of the necessary requirements for the state boards that confer that doctoral degree.The first training institute in America to educate non-medical psychoanalysts was The National Psychological Association for Psychoanalysis., in New York City. It was founded by the world famous analyst Theodor Reik.

Some psychoanalytic training has been set up as a post-doctoral fellowship in university settings, such as at Duke University, Yale University, New York University, Adelphi University, and Columbia University. Other psychoanalytic institutes may not be directly associated with universities, but the faculty at those institutes usually hold contemporaneous faculty positions with psychology Ph.D. programmes and/or with Medical School psychiatry residency programmes.

The International Psychoanalytical Association is the world's primary accrediting and regulatory body for psychoanalysis. Their mission is to assure the continued vigour and development of psychoanalysis for the benefit of psychoanalytic patients. It works in partnership with its 70 constituent organizations in 33 countries to support 11,500 members. In the US, there are 77 psychoanalytical organizations, institutes associations in the United States, which are spread across the states of America.

The American Psychoanalytic Association has 38 affiliated societies, which have ten or more active members who practice in a given geographical area. The aims of the APSaA and other psychoanalytical organizations are: provide ongoing educational opportunities for its members, stimulate the development and research of psychoanalysis, provide training and organize conferences. There are eight affiliated study groups in the USA. A study group is the first level of integration of a psychoanalytical body within the International Psychoanalytic Association, followed by a provisional society and finally a member society.

The Division of Psychoanalysis of the American Psychological Association was established in the early 1980s by several psychologists. Until the establishment of the Division of Psychoanalysis, psychologists who had trained in independent institutes had no national organization. The Division of Psychoanalysis now has approximately 4,000 members and approximately thirty local stages in the United States.

The Division of Psychoanalysis holds two annual meetings/conferences and offers continuing education in theory, research and clinical technique, as do their affiliated local stages. The European Psychoanalytical Federation is the scientific organization that consolidates all European psychoanalytic societies. This organization is affiliated with the IPA. In 2002 there were approximately 3900 individual members in twenty-two countries, speaking eighteen different languages. There are also twenty-five psychoanalytic societies.

The National Membership Committee for Psychoanalysis in Clinical Social Work was also started in the mid-eighties to represent social work psychoanalysts. Founded by Crayton Rowe, MSW it included in its membership Rueben and Gertrude Blanck who were well known ego psychologists. Other notable members are Joyce Edward, Jean Sanville and Diana Siskind. Recently, NMCOP changed its name to the American Association of Psychoanalysis in Clinical Social Work. The organization holds a bi-annual national conferences as well as numerous annual state and area meetings in 16 area stages. These conferences provide sessions on theory, technique and research.

CRITICISM

Early critics of psychoanalysis believed that its [theories were based too little on quantitative and experimental research, and too much on the clinical case study method. Some even accused Freud of fabrication, most famously in the case of Anna O.. An increasing amount of empirical research from academic psychologists and psychiatrists has begun to address this criticism. A survey of scientific research suggested that while personality traits corresponding to Freud's oral, anal, Oedipal, and genital phases can be observed, they do not necessarily manifest as stages in the development of children. These studies also have not confirmed that such traits in adults result from childhood experiences. However, these stages should not be viewed as crucial to modern psychoanalysis. What is crucial to modern psychoanalytic theory and practice is the power of the unconscious and the transference phenomenon.

Numerous studies have shown that its efficacy is related to the quality of the therapist, rather than the psychoanalytic school or technique or training, while a French 2004 report from INSERM says instead, that psychoanalysis therapy is far less effective than other psychotherapies.

The idea of "unconscious" is contested because human behaviour can be observed while human mental activity has to be inferred. However, the unconscious is now a popular topic of study in the fields of experimental and social psychology. The idea of unconscious, and the transference phenomenon, have been widely researched and, it is claimed, validated in the fields of cognitive psychology and social psychology, though a Freudian interpretation of unconscious mental activity is not held by the majority of cognitive psychologists.

Recent developments in neuroscience have resulted in one side arguing that it has provided a biological basis for unconscious emotional processing in line with psychoanalytic theory *i.e.*, neuropsychoanalysis, while the other side argues that such findings make psychoanalytic theory obsolete and irrelevant. Both Freud and psychoanalysis have been criticized in very extreme terms.

Exchanges between critics and defenders of psychoanalysis have often been so heated that they have come to be characterized as the Freud Wars. Karl Popper argued that psychoanalysis is a pseudoscience because its claims are not testable and cannot be refuted; that is, they are not falsifiable. Karl Kraus, an Austrian satirist, was the subject of a book written by noted libertarian author Thomas Szasz. The book Anti-Freud: Karl Kraus's Criticism of Psychoanalysis and Psychiatry, originally published under the name Karl Kraus and the Soul Doctors, portrayed Kraus as a harsh critic of Sigmund Freud and of psychoanalysis in general.

Other commentators, such as Edward Timms, author of Karl Kraus - Apocalyptic Satirist, have argued that Kraus respected Freud, though with reservations about the application of some of his theories, and that his views were far less black-and-white than Szasz suggests. Grünbaum argues that psychoanalytic based theories are falsifiable, but that the causal claims of psychoanalysis are unsupported by the available clinical evidence.

A prominent academic in positive psychology wrote that 'Thirty years ago, the cognitive revolution in psychology overthrew both Freud and the behaviourists, at least in academia.... Thinking... is not just a [result] of emotion or behaviour.... Emotion is always generated by cognition, not the other way around.' Michel Foucault and Gilles Deleuze claimed that the institution of psychoanalysis has become a center of power and that its confessional techniques resemble the Christian tradition.

Jacques Lacan criticized the emphasis of some American and British psychoanalytical traditions on what he has viewed as the suggestion of imaginary "causes" for symptoms, and recommended the return to Freud. Together with Gilles Deleuze, Félix Guattari criticised the Oedipal structure. Luce Irigaray criticised psychoanalysis, employing Jacques Derrida's concept of phallogocentrism to describe the exclusion of the woman from Freudian and Lacanian psychoanalytical theories.

Shlomo Kalo explains that Materialism that flourished in the 19th Century severely harmed religion and rejected whatever called spiritual. The institution of the confession priest in particular was badly damaged. The empty void that this institution left behind was swiftly occupied by the newborn psychoanalysis. In his writings Kalo claims that psychoanalysis basic approach is erroneous. It represents the mainline wrong assumptions that happiness is unreachable and that the natural desire of a human being is to exploit his fellow men for his own pleasure and benefit.

Freud's psychoanalysis was criticized by his wife, Martha. René Laforgue reported Martha Freud saying, "I must admit that if I did not realise how seriously my husband takes his treatments, I should think that psychoanalysis is a form of pornography." To Martha there was something vulgar about psychoanalysis, and she dissociated herself from it. Marie Bonaparte, Martha was upset with her husband's work and his treatment of sexuality.

Gilles Deleuze and Felix Guattari, in their 1972 work Anti-Œdipus, take the cases of Gérard Mendel, Bela Grunberger and Janine Chasseguet-Smirgel, prominent members of the most respected associations to suggest that, traditionally, psychoanalysis enthusiastically embraces a police state:

E. Fuller Torrey, writing in Witchdoctors and Psychiatrists, stated that psychoanalytic theories have no more scientific basis than the theories of traditional native healers, "witchdoctors" or modern "cult" alternatives such as est. Frank Cioffi, author of Freud and the Question of Pseudoscience, cites false claims of a sound scientific verification of the theory and its elements as the strongest basis for classifying the work of Freud and his school as pseudoscience.

Among philosophers, Karl Popper argued that Freud's theory of the unconscious was not falsifiable and therefore not scientific. Popper did not object to the idea that some mental processes could be unconscious but to investigations of the mind that were not falsifiable. In other words, if it were possible to connect every conceivable experimental outcome with Freud's theory of the unconscious mind, then no experiment could refute the theory. Noam Chomsky has also criticized psychoanalysis for lacking a scientific basis.

The philosopher Paul Ricoeur argued that psychoanalysis can be considered a type of textual interpretation or hermeneutics. Like cultural critics and literary scholars, Ricoeur contended, psychoanalysts spend their time interpreting the nuances of language. He classified psychoanalysis as a hermeneutics of suspicion. By this he meant that psychoanalysis searches for deception in language, and thereby destabilizes our usual reliance on clear, obvious meanings.

Jacques Derrida incorporated aspects of psychoanalytic theory into his theory of deconstruction in order to question what he called the 'metaphysics of presence'. Derrida also turns some of these ideas against Freud, to reveal tensions and contradictions in his work. For example, although Freud defines religion and metaphysics as displacements of the identification with the father in the resolution of the Oedipal complex, Derrida insists in The Postcard: From Socrates to Freud and Beyond that the prominence of the father in Freud's own analysis is itself indebted to the prominence given to the father in Western metaphysics and theology since Plato.

Some post-colonialists argue that psychoanalysis imposes a white, European model of human development on those without European heritage, hence they will argue Freud's theories are a form or instrument of intellectual imperialism.

NATURE OF MOTIVATION RESEARCH

In its true sense the task of motivation research is to find out just what makes people behave as they do, regardless of the technique or method used for the purpose. As a matter of fact, the term "motivation research" is equally applicable to all methods and techniques designed to discover reasons why people act or think the way they do, whether in the capacity of ultimate consumers, purchasing agents, store buyers, or in any other capacity. So far, however, the term has been applied principally to consumer motivation studies dealing with consumer buying and patronage motives, and with consumer attitudes.

An attitude may be defined as a tendency to respond favorably or unfavorably toward a person, an institution, a thing, or an idea. An individual's attitude in any given situation is usually a result of a variety of past influences, including his assumptions or beliefs, his social frame of reference, and sensations or feelings that he has experienced. Since an attitude is an effect of what one has experienced, it is also something of a prophet of future action in the sense that a consumer's conscious or unconscious feelings or moods largely determine whether and how he will react to certain selling appeals.

For this reason, marketing researchers attempt to discover consumer attitudes and, whenever possible, to measure the magnitude of such reactions. Manufacturers and marketing institutions are interested not only in the motivations of their customers, but also in the attitudes of those who have not used, or have discontinued to use, their products. Although research in consumer motivation has been popularized to a high degree in recent years, it is not essentially a new concept. Some marketing books devoted considerable attention to consumer motivation, and elaborate classifications of buying motives were presented in the early 1920's. Contemporary developments have included refinements in research methodology and increased appreciation, on the part of marketing executives, of the practical application of motivation knowledge to marketing problems. This may be better understood by giving brief attention to methods of motivation research and to actual illustrations of such research findings.

Motivation Research Methods

Methods used to obtain information about consumer attitudes or buying behaviour may be classified into three groups, namely, observation of consumer action, consumer surveys, and psychological approaches. Most early classifications of buying motives depended largely upon careful observation of consumer reactions to different kinds of stimuli. If an advertisement stressed a selling appeal directed to a particular buying motive, and if this evoked considerable favorable response, then it was concluded that this particular motive was of considerable importance to consumers purchasing the product. In many instances a change in selling appeals provoked such a significant response that the importance of certain motives could be inferred with reasonable certainty. While this is an old method, it continues to be highly relevant in situations where consumer reaction to certain stimuli is quite pronounced.

This may be illustrated by reference to patronage motives under modern conditions. In the 1950's, discount houses grew in importance in many metropolitan markets. When such stores are located outside the main stream of shopping traffic and hence are relatively inaccessible to many consumers, and when they do not offer the usual range of customer services available in regular stores, it does not take an elaborate survey or psychological analysis to determine that price appeal constitutes the principal patronage motive. Consumer surveys have often been utilized when consumer motivations cannot be inferred from direct observation of consumer actions in the market. This approach usually involves selection of a representative sample of the presumed market for a particular product.

Consumers are asked to state why they buy particular products or patronize certain institutions or are asked to rank or evaluate given factors which are related to particular motives. Analysis of such replies may reveal what motives or attitudes are of great importance to many consumers and which are of only incidental or no significance in the situation being investigated. Such surveys have revealed that consumers prefer to shop in downtown stores rather than in outlying shopping centers because of the broader assortments of merchandise available, the greater emphasis upon bargain or clearance sales, and the feasibility of combining shopping with other things that one may want to do.

At the same time they have revealed that many prefer to shop in outlying centers because of lower cost for transportation, better parking facilities, more convenient store hours, ease of taking children on shopping trips, and other reasons. In connection with selective buying motives, such surveys may reveal that most consumers buy one brand of a product rather than another because of a price differential, a reusable package, or some premium that is offered in connection with the product.

Such surveys are a particularly appropriate method for motivation research in kinds of situations where consumers know why they have reacted in a given manner and when they are willing to state their reasons or attitudes. More elaborate psychological approaches have become popular because of recognition that consumer behaviour in some situations is a result of complex personality variables rather than a simple reaction to easily identified stimuli. Often, the consumer has given little systematic thought to buying situations and may not actually be aware of all the considerations that entered into his purchasing decisions.

Moreover, consumers may know why they bought something or what their attitude is regarding a situation but are reluctant or unwilling to state their true motives or opinions when asked straightforward questions. Such circumstances have led to a number of refinements in research techniques, treatment of which is beyond the scope of this text.

In general, they involve the use of probing procedures, depth interviewing, and other projective techniques that have been borrowed from the fields of personality studies and clinical psychology where they have been used for many years.

Motivation Research Findings

Motivation research studies, whether of the general survey or psychological approach type, reveal that consumers often do not think in terms of general classifications of buying motives but rather in terms of quite specific features of a product or a service.

From very concrete consumer reactions, it is necessary to form hypotheses or generalizations about the basic underlying motives. The nature of such findings and the character of their application to questions of marketing strategy are illustrated below.

Product Examples

Several examples are presented to show how motivation research findings have been applied in the marketing of specific goods or services.

- The State Farm Mutual Automobile Insurance Company attained a dominant position in its industry by advertising emphasis upon low cost. To broaden the company's appeal further, extensive motivation research was undertaken to learn more about why people buy automobile insurance and what qualities they look for in an insurance company. Techniques included large-sample consumer surveys supplemented by projective studies conducted by trained psychologists with a much smaller sample. The company learned that an insurance company may be unconsciously resented at the same time it is accepted as a protector of individual welfare; that even though people are generally happy not to have had an accident, they are inclined to resent the fact that they have had to pay for something on which they have had no opportunity to collect; and that policyholders are greatly interested in prompt, courteous and expert service. As a result of these findings, the company's advertising was changed. While low cost was still stressed, more emphasis was placed on providing answers to important questions which people have about automobile insurance, on illustrating the availability of desired services through convincing case histories, and on reflecting the size and stature of the company.

- Encouraged by its success with Wildroot Cream Oil Charlie, a hair conditioner for men, the Wildroot Company decided to produce a shampoo for women and call it Lady Wildroot. A research company was retained to make a study to determine how the proposed product should be marketed and whether the name was good or should be changed. A sample of 250 consumers was selected and interviewed on a nondirective basis. It was learned that the name was a major handicap. Through its advertising for Cream Oil Charlie, the company had established a reputation as a "masculine" company and a concept of a special type of man as the ideal male. This male was forward and aggressive in the minds of women. They tended to resent the implication that by merely having a stock of hair smoothed down with cream oil, this type of man can prevail over them. These findings were validated by a test. Two control groups of women were selected and members of each group were given bottles of the new product-some bottles labeled Lady Wildroot, the others by a quite different name. In the group testing Lady Wildroot, user comments were critical or negative, but in the other group the product was quite acceptable.
- In a study conducted by Social Research, Inc., for the Chicago Tribune, considerable light was shed upon primary and selective motives which are important to people in purchasing automobiles. It was found that the meanings which the automobile embodies are grouped around five central ideas:
  - A mechanical object which satisfies practical needs for transportation;
  - A sizable investment with an important place in family economics, partly in terms of original price but to a greater extent in relation to cost of operation and upkeep;

- An indicator of the individual's social status, his position, his place in the scheme of things, and the role the car plays in social companionship, like family vacations, car pools, dates, etc.;
- A symbol of self-control, signifying personal mastery, through a sense of power, with the thrill of speeding, or many other opportunities for showing personal superiorities; and
- As an avenue of self-expression, or a clearly understood way of conveying in our society the characteristics, feelings, and motives that typify a particular individual.

  As a result of these findings, it was recommended that automobile advertising should appeal to two types of motivations:
- The foregoing basic wishes for ownership of automobiles in general and
- Specific personality attributes of a particular brand which an individual purchaser can identify with his own understanding of himself, his social situation, and his aspirations.

• A prune growers' association, while suffering a continuing decline in sales, decided to find out what consumers thought about prunes. In detailed interviews it was learned that consumers thought prunes were dry and wrinkled-ugly things to behold; that they were believed to be without particular food value or were to be used only as a laxative. As a result of this research, marketing strategy was changed. Most prunes are now distributed in cans or glass jars. They appear on supermarket shelves as fat, juicy "prune plums." They are associated with fruit and with the quality of freshness. Sales have improved, bringing more consumer satisfaction with increasing consumption and with benefits to the producing industry.

CONCEPT OF BRAND IMAGE

An important contribution of motivation research has been the development of the concept of "brand image." Brands, like types of products, are perceived by people as images.

The image results from the total of all the impressions that the consumer receives from many sources: actual experience and hearsay about the brand, its packaging, its name, the company making it, the kind of stores in which it is sold, the types of people the consumer has seen using or buying the brand, what has been said in the advertising for the brand, the tone and format of the advertising, the type of advertising media used.

The total of such impressions results in an image which tends to be similar for the consuming public at large, particularly for well-publicized brands, but different groups of consumers may have different attitudes toward it. For example, users of a given brand may think of it as "first and best on the market" while nonusers regard it as "an oldfashioned brand." Both groups, however, may agree that it is "an old, well-established brand. The preceding example of Lady Wildroot illustrates the power of a brand image when attempting to market a new product under an established name. In another study dealing with brands of gasoline, it was found that motorists tended to think of Gulf, among other things, as a "friendly" gasoline.

Such a notion was supported by name associations reminding people of the out-of-doors, "Gulf of Mexico," etc.; by the "sunny" yellow colour used in the brand emblem; by a "friendly" approach in advertising copy (Go Gulf); and by the nature of an advertising programme, "We the People," which, although off the air at the time of the study, had contributed to the brand image.

CONCEPT OF STORE PERSONALITY

Somewhat similar to the concept of brand image is the idea of store character or store personality. Individual patronage motives, as listed in a preceding section, sometimes are adequate to explain why a consumer will go to one store rather than another. It often happens, however, that many alternative establishments would be similarly ranked in regard to various specific patronage motives. In many metropolitan areas, for example, housewives have at their command a number of supermarkets which carry just about the same assortments and variety of merchandise, sell at comparable prices, render similar services, and are about equally convenient. Each organization is still likely to have a distinct personality based on the totality of all the impressions that consumers have of it.

One store that, over-all, reflects an atmosphere of sophistication and elegance will tend to attract patrons who feel at home in such surroundings while it may not appeal to others who would be more comfortable in a store with a severely functional atmosphere. Some stores have clear-cut personalities because all of the things that the organization does make impressions of a consistent character. Others may have a vague or dull personality in the minds of consumers because advertising reflects one kind of personality, store layout another, and the nature of personal selling effort still a third, with the result that one kind of activity undermines rather than builds upon the impressions made by others.

Some studies have attempted to determine the personality attributes of people as well as the personality attributes of particular brands of products or stores. When the brands or stores actually used by people are matched with their own personalities, the findings are usually that people tend to select those brands or stores they conceive as being consistent with their own personalities, even though they are unable to describe their own personality attributes which are revealed by psychological testing.

DYNAMICS OF MOTIVATION

The foregoing examples demonstrate that consumers have attitudes toward products and services which are directly influenced by the shortrun policies and plans of marketing executives in a particular company and by the action of persons employed in individual business establishments. While consumer attitudes toward the general question of branded merchandise are well grounded and relatively stable, attitudes toward a particular brand of a prepared food product may change radically and within a very short period of time merely as a result of a barely perceptible change in flavoring, the adoption of a new shape or type of container, or the modification of some other product characteristic.

Likes and dislikes about a particular make of car may be drastically altered with the introduction of a new model with different style and engineering characteristics. Consumer attitudes toward a specific retail store may be considerably different before and after thorough modernization programs have been carried out in competing stores in the same shopping district. Such attitudes may also undergo rapid change if a lax personnel policy results in discourtesy on the part of salespeople, if a stricter customer return and adjustment policy is adopted, if the store begins to feature a price rather than a quality appeal, or for numerous other reasons.

Motivations of individuals are also influenced by a host of other considerations. To a large extent, personal motivations reflect values in society. As cultural values change, motivations are modified. In our country there has been a decline in Puritanism, or the feeling that it is wrong to get too much pleasure out of life. This has enabled many advertisers to make forceful and direct appeals to the motive of comfort which would not have been as appropriate in former generations.

Individuals also tend to follow behaviour patterns of socioeconomic classes to which they belong or to which they aspire.Everyone feels that there are certain things which "are all right for people like us," but which would not be appropriate for people in altogether different socioeconomic classifications. As one moves from one class to another, perhaps as a result of a successful business career, the family takes on a whole new set of motivating characteristics.

Each person is also influenced by close associates, friends or neighbours, who may be regarded as taste setters because they are intellectual, economically successful, travel a lot, or are social leaders.Because of the multitudinous product and source of supply choices open to consumers and the possibility of unexpected change in consumer attitudes, it is difficult to formulate generalizations about motivations which can be continuously applied in connection with the marketing of any specific product. The consumer's reaction at any given time is a function of a complex set of factors involving

- The make-up of the individual and
- The environmental situation as it exists at the time of the reaction.

Many illuminating facts have come to light through motivations studies; but for the most part, to be of value from the standpoint of marketing management, they must be acted upon promptly after they become known. The mere application of the results in a large-scale marketing programme changes the environmental situation in which the consumer is expected to respond.Nevertheless, motivation research has made significant contributions to our understanding of consumer behaviour.

It has provided much insight into the nature of motives that influence behaviour, the complexity of multiple motives in given situations, the importance of understanding motivation as a basis for predicting behaviour, and the dynamics of motivation as affected by cultural change, social class status, and one's close associates.

THE MARKETING RESEARCH PROCESS

There are basically four steps in the marketing research process that franchisors must follow:

- Define the problem and research objectives.
- Develop a research plan for collecting information.
- Implement the research plan by collecting and analyzing the data.
- Interpret and report the findings.

When defining the problem and research objectives, it is important that the franchisors doing the research work closely with the decision makers to determine what research is needed and how it will be used.

If this step is skipped, the results generally will not address the major problem. In a franchise setting, the research people must work closely with those people in the franchise who handle recruitment of potential franchisees. They must also work with the franchisees themselves to understand the needs of the market.

Marketing research is designed to reduce uncertainty and provide knowledge for the franchisor. Thus, marketing research will help determine what is going right and what went wrong. Research can help the franchisor understand consumers' buying motivations and determine the strengths and weaknesses of the products or services.

When developing a research plan, there are three objectives of market research to remember:

- *Exploratory*: To gather primary information that will better define problems and suggest improvements.
- *Descriptive*: To describe the market potential for a product or the demographics and attitudes of consumers who buy the products.
- *Causal*: To understand the cause and effect relationships in market practices.

The three major functional roles in marketing research are descriptive, diagnostic, and predictive. The descriptive role focuses on gathering and presenting statements of fact. For example, what has been the sales trend for the franchise outlet during the last five years? What are the consumers' attitudes toward the product or service? The second role of research goes beyond description and is diagnostic. A researcher attempts to explain the data. What was the impact on sales when we introduced the new product? Have sales increased as a result of the new product line introduced? The final function of research would be predictive. Will this individual operate a franchise in a manner consistent with franchise philosophy? Can we predict how a new advertising campaign will affect sales? If we replace the manager, will we improve on employee morale and performance?

The third stage of a marketing research project is implementing the research plan by collecting and analyzing the data. The franchisor must determine the best instrument to use to collect data for the project. Interviews, focus groups, and surveys can all be used to collect data, but the costs, ease, and depth of information vary from one method to another. For example, when conducting research about a franchisee's goals, more in-depth information will probably be required than can be provided by a simple questionnaire.

The fourth step in marketing research is interpreting and reporting the findings where conclusions are drawn to the franchisors. The purpose of this research is not to overwhelm management but provide information which will be useful for making decisions.

The Franchise Dilemma

The franchise dilemma is that franchisors have two distinct and different target markets, including:

- The prospective franchisee and
- The end consumer.

Unlike most major retail or service outlets, the franchisor does not sell directly to an end consumer but through a franchising organization. The franchises are generally owned and operated by franchisees who actually run, manage, or supervise the outlet stores. It is, therefore, important for the franchisor to first develop a success profile for prospective franchisees.

Using Research to Create a Franchisee Profile

The successful franchisee profile is best developed by devising a preference research model. Such an approach involves research using both personal interviews and a general survey instrument. The personal interview is generally completed with existing successful franchisees. The purpose of the interview is to measure franchisees' attitudes toward their managing experience, as well as general demographic information. The franchisees selected for the study are generally among the top quartile or top third in sales or other success criteria as determined by the franchisors.

In addition to the personal interview, a general survey is made of all franchisees concerning what they believe would be a success profile for franchisees. This general survey is often developed by first using focus groups.

The focus group generally includes 6-10 people gathered together for a few hours with a trained interviewer to talk about franchisees, managers, and successful management techniques.

These individuals may be the franchisor's franchisees, but they may also include other managers and owners of different types of businesses, as long as they have some understanding of management and ownership responsibilities. The trained interviewer generally begins with broad questions before moving to specific issues. The interviewer encourages open discussion, hoping that the interactions between the participants bring out actual experiences and recommen-dations for successful franchisees. These discussions are generally taped for future playback and study.

Once a focus group has determined critical factors that lead to successful franchisees, a survey of franchisees can begin. The purpose of the survey is to obtain primary data concerning attitudes toward the franchisor and the franchise system, and goals of the franchisee, as well as demographics. It is with this information that the franchisor can begin to understand where problems with relationships with their franchisees are occurring.

Using Market Research To Create A Customer Profile

One of the most typical functions of a marketing research programme is to understand the habits and attitudes of customers. This information, when provided to franchisees by the franchisor, can build stronger channel relationships. The customer profile is often conducted through exit interviews as well as a general survey.

The exit interview generally is conducted as customers leave a store. At this time, their attitudes about the product or service are measured.

In addition, perception indicators can indicate how individuals felt about the quality of the product or service being sold compared to competitors'offerings. Also, demographic information will provide valuable information about the customer segment currently visiting the franchisee's outlet. With the customer profile for each outlet, franchisors may be able to tailor their franchise programme to better meet the unique needs of each franchisee, hence reducing conflict within the relationship.

Additionally, marketing research may be conducted with focus groups which will allow for greater insights into the end consumer. Focus groups may indicate the strengths or weaknesses of a particular company, product, or service. The focus groups may easily be divided up into heavy users, moderate users, light users, or non-users of a particular franchise outlet.

Marketing research can play an integral part in proper decision making in a franchising organization. More and more franchisors are recognizing the benefits of implementing a marketing research programme. Along with the commonly recognized benefits of marketing research, franchisors should also recognize that marketing research can be an effective tool in building strong relationships with its franchisees. First, marketing research can help franchisors select franchisees whose goals are consistent with system-wide growth. Second, franchisors can conduct customer research and share the findings with franchisees.

Marketing research provides information which franchisors can use to properly determine the profile for both the successful franchisee and the target customer. When both the franchisee and customer profiles have been developed, the franchisor will be better able to select franchisees who can manage the franchising outlet and serve the customer. Marketing research becomes one tool to reducing unnecessary conflict within franchise channels.

The increasing efforts by marketers to target diverse groups of consumers call for a closer examination of the ethical implications of market segmentation and differentiated marketing. Previous research suggests that marketers and consumers often differ in their perceptions of marketing ethics. Based on contingency theory, this research proposes an integrated framework-which includes the nature of the product, consumer characteristics, and market selection-to analyse the ethical complexities of the marketing exchange. Interactions among these factors lead to various contingencies with different ethical implications for marketing managers and public policy makers. Marketers should assess consumer interests and the ethics of marketing programmes before their implementation

In the last several decades, targeting distinctive consumer segments with differentiated marketing has been a popular strategy among many marketers. The distinctive nature of various consumer groups such as children, the elderly, women, and ethnic minorities has made them attractive market segments. However, market segmentation and targeted marketing have, from time to time, met with tremendous difficulties. Targeting potentially harmful products at vulnerable and disadvantaged consumers such as children, the elderly, and inner-city residents has received negative publicity and been subjected to damaging litigation. The increasing willingness of some large corporations to exploit vulnerable consumers indicates unfair treatment of these consumers and a lack of justice in the marketplace.

On the other hand, cases of discrimination and redlining still occur in certain product and market areas, such as the discrimination directed at minority consumers by insurance and mortgage companies. Disenchanted consumers are increasingly rallying consumer interest groups to put pressure on firms that they consider to be predatory or discriminatory in their marketing practices. Companies such as R. J. Reynolds, Prudential Insurance, and Texaco Oil Company have suffered from tarnished images, consumer boycotts, and court penalties of hundreds of millions of dollars.

Although the modern marketing concept emphasizes its mission to satisfy consumer needs and wants, that promise, in reality, is sometimes lost or misplaced, resulting in outcomes that are not in the best interests of either the customers or society. A lack of understanding of the ethical issues associated with market segmentation and selection has contributed to these problems, which have tremendous social and economic costs. While targeting harmful products at vulnerable consumers has received harsh criticism, restricting the marketing of certain products and labeling some consumers as vulnerable are considered equally troublesome, suggesting that the ethical implications of marketing practices are complicated. Although researchers have examined the ethics of market segmentation and selection, effort is lacking in synthesizing various issues to provide a holistic understanding of the ethical implications of the marketing exchange.

Based on contingency theory, we integrate previous research and propose a three-dimensional framework--which includes the nature of the product, consumer characteristics, and market selection--to analyse the ethics of market segmentation and related marketing strategies. Interactions among these variables lead to various scenarios with different ethical implications for marketing management and public policy making. Particular attention is given to areas in which marketers and consumers differ in their perceptions of ethical propriety with respect to the nature of the product and market selection. To avoid ethical conflicts in marketing, we suggest that companies consider consumers'interest and assess the ethical implications of their marketing plans before implementation.

In the marketing field, market segmentation and the differentiation of the marketing mix have become so prevalent that they are almost synonymous with competitive strategies. While targeted marketing has largely been beneficial to both consumers and marketers, cases of consumer discontent from time to time raise questions about the ethical implications of market segmentation and targeted marketing, most notably the targeting of harmful products at vulnerable consumers, such as targeting alcohol and cigarettes at inner-city consumers and churning insurance policies to the elderly. Meanwhile, the opposite of targeting--the exclusion of certain consumers from a company's offerings--is just as controversial.

These problems are not unique to marketers of consumer goods. Business service providers and public and nonprofit organizations are not immune to such challenges. Organizations, including educational institutions and government agencies, that cater to certain segments of society have also become the targets of public scrutiny and face the prominent possibility of consumer discontent and legal actions. While consumers and marketers continue to struggle with these complicated issues and seek viable solutions, researchers have studied the ethics of market segmentation and market selection. Recent studies have focused on the ethical implications of targeted marketing of harmful products at vulnerable consumers.

Targeted Marketing

Targeted marketing, as a popular marketing strategy, refers to the concentrated marketing of a product to a segment of consumers due to the attractiveness of the group, in terms of such factors as its size and growth rate. Theoretically speaking, there is nothing inherently wrong with targeted marketing.

When marketers promote a product beneficial to a group of consumers, targeted marketing is largely ethical and welcome by consumers. For instance, some restaurants and hotels have special promotion programmes aimed at children, and indirectly at their parents, with inexpensive toys and special vacation packages. In recent years, however, many cases of targeting potentially harmful products at vulnerable consumers have raised ethical concerns in terms of justice and fairness, such as targeting sweepstakes at the elderly and handguns at women. Even indirect and subtle targeting of potentially harmful products at vulnerable consumers has received criticism, such as targeting children with R-rated movies and using animal characters to promote cigarettes and alcohol.

Product Harm

Many products in the marketplace, such as wholesome food and medicine, are beneficial or at least beneficial to the target group. However, products that are intended to be beneficial have from time to time been found harmful to some consumers, resulting in "market failures". For instance, unless a pharmaceutical company tests a new product on everyone (instead of limited clinical trials), it is difficult to determine whether the product will cause any harm. The key issue here is the marketer's knowledge of the product's potential harm, even to a small group of people.

If a company discovers that a small percentage of people may suffer negative reactions from its products and it immediately takes corrective measures, the company may be deemed as acting ethically, believing that it should take responsibility for the incident as part of its business liability. If the company had prior knowledge of the side effect and it took no remedial measures upon such discovery, it would be considered as intentionally harming the consumers. Having prior knowledge of the harmfulness of a product and withholding that information have been used as evidence against companies, such as in the Dow Corning case of silicone breast implants and the legal battle against tobacco companies.

However, the evaluation of a product's harmfulness is not always clear-cut. Even the marketing of seemingly beneficial and harmless products can sometimes take an unexpected turn, because such products can be harmful to consumers who have known characteristics. Some products, even though not inherently harmful, can be potentially harmful to consumers due to abuse or misuse. For instance, targeting alcoholic beverages at poor inner-city consumers is particularly problematic, as this segment already suffers from a greater number of alcohol-related health and social problems than the general population. Thus, ethical evaluations of many products depend on their interaction with consumer characteristics and marketing practices.

Vulnerable Consumers

Recently, consumer vulnerability has drawn much attention in studies of marketing ethics. In numerous legal cases, the court system in the U.S. has defined vulnerable consumers as a group of people who, due to various idiosyncrasies, are sensitive and susceptible to the potential negative effects associated with using a particular product. For instance, a small group of people, due to their body biology, may suffer side effects from using certain medications. Moreover, children do not have the same level of knowledge, experience, or maturity as adults to process commercial information.

Many elderly people, due to their physical and/or mental conditions, also face challenges as consumers. In addition, some consumers may be prone to addiction or compulsion while others may be disadvantaged due to their social and economic conditions. Such examples of targeting vulnerable consumers include the targeting of high interest loans of credit cards to consumers with poor credit histories and less financial sophistication. Thus, product harmfulness is heightened for consumers at a risk or disadvantage, and poses ethical concerns.

Discrimination

While much recent research has examined the ethics of targeting harmful products to vulnerable consumers, some researchers continue to investigate the opposite case: the exclusion of certain consumers in marketing. Discrimination in marketing refers to the practice of denying access to products to a group of consumers due to their racial or ethnic background, age, gender, or other characteristics.

Discrimination may also have to do with discrepancies in product quality and variety, and the terms of exchange such as pricing and payment method. Since the 1960s, many studies have investigated pricing discrimination against the poor and minority consumers. Despite the tremendous progress in the last few decades, discrimination and redlining have persisted in areas such as housing, mortgage lending, and financial services. Here, the important gauge points are the equivalence or proportionality in marketing intensity and the disparate treatment of consumers.

Existing studies have made significant progress in conceptualizing the ethics of market segmentation and differentiated marketing. In several important respects, their findings have elevated our understanding of the ethical implications of the marketing exchange. First, these studies emphasize that the concern with the ethical consequences of marketing practices in the United States is well grounded in the fundamental beliefs in social and moral equity, fairness, and justice for all people.

Second, researchers have emphasized the ethical risks inherent in market segmentation and differentiated marketing. Dunfee, Smith and Ross suggest that due to the boundary-expanding nature of marketing, ethical concerns may arise in certain situations when marketers cross such boundaries. For instance, marketing products to youth that are intended for mature consumers, such as alcoholic beverages, leads to different ethical evaluations. According to Star, the social discontent and ethical concerns associated with marketing stem from the functional limitations of the marketing concept. Contemporary marketing practices often rely on market segmentation, which divides consumers into submarkets based on characteristics such as age, gender, race, and nationality.

To provide unique values to consumers and to avoid head-on competition, each market segment may require a unique marketing mix. Thus, segmentation and subsequent marketing practices often imply differential albeit unequal treatment of various consumer groups, and raise ethical concerns. Third, extant studies have found that ethical concerns or dilemmas often arise when a marketer's perception is in conflict with that of consumers or the public. In fact, the customer interface represents the area of marketing in which conflicts in the perception of the ethical propriety of marketing practices frequently occur. Thus, marketers must study the perception of the public when formulating marketing strategies in order to avoid potential misunderstandings.

QUANTITATIVE RESEARCH VS QUALITATIVE RESEARCH

In general, research methods can be classified into two types, namely qualitative and quantitative research. The data gathering process of qualitative research is unstructured and more flexible comparing to quantitative research. Qualitative research involves small samples of respondents who are carefully selected in relation to the research topic, and the data produced by qualitative research is non-quantifiable insights into behaviour, attitudes feelings and motivations of consumers.

On the other hand, quantitative research is undertaken using a structured approach and requires larger number of respondents to provide a quantifiable answer for particular behaviours, motivations and attitudes. Both the quantitative research and qualitative research have their own advantages and disadvantages.

Gephart, there are three research traditions: positivism, interpretive research, and critical postmodernism. The key assumption of the positivism are that the reality is external and objective, and that the knowledge is only of significance if it is based on observations of this external reality. Regarding the advantages of this paradigm and quantitative methods, they can provide a highly structured methodology and a quantifiable observation that are statistically analysed. However, the main disadvantage of positivism paradigm and quantitative methods are inflexible and artificial.

There is a lack of understanding the rationale behind consumer's action or behaviour. Furthermore, the analysis only shows a recent phenomenon, and therefore, it is hard to infer what should be made in the future. Interpretive research aims to described subjective meanings and in-depth understanding of people's actions. Hence, interpretivism tends to qualitative viewpoint. Therefore, the researcher has to be inside the subject, and analyses the issue in-depth. Obviously, the main benefit of this paradigm is to understand people's meanings or rationale behind their behaviour.

However, the disadvantages of this paradigm are time consuming and the difficulty of analyzing data. Beside, due to no standard procedure to be followed, interpretivism is considered to have low credibility. In other words, researcher's bias have a great influence on the results. Critical postmodernism combines critical theory and postmodern thought to uncover hidden interests and contradictions.

Moreover, this paradigm describes dominant and subordinated meanings, displays the power implications of meanings, and encourages critical reflexivity to make people aware of the constraints on their own meanings and actions. These can be the benefits of this paradigm. Nevertheless, there are similar disadvantages with interpretive research. Time consuming, difficulty of analysing data, and researcher's influence are also valid in this paradigm. Quantitative method may be the most appropriate approach to apply here because of several reasons. First of all, quantitative research is easier to assess data from large sample size.

In order to realise relationships among the factors, a great amount of respondents is required. Secondly, as Bell and Eisingerich's researches showed, the research in consumer education and relatives could be credible demonstration by quantitative researches. Finally, quantitative approach is chosen because of the short time available for this research. However, the ideal method may be a mixed approach included qualitative and quantitative approaches. Quantitative research could provide relationships among variables, whereas qualitative research could explore the reasons for these relationships. This means that a mixed approach could eliminate disadvantages of each approach. Nevertheless, because of time constraints, a mixed method approach was not applied in this research.

SAMPLE

The main purpose of choosing samples is to infer the results to whole population. However, because of a lack of database of the whole cosmetics users and the cost constraints, the non-probability sampling Techniques would be used in this research. Moreover, a convenience sample was chosen to conduct respondents via Internet. This method is easy, fast, and least expensive.

However, the limitation of this method is that there is no indication of how the information gathered from the sample can be inferred to the whole population. There are two reasons to define the sample in this research.

Firstly, the purpose of this research is to find the utility of consumer education provide by cosmetics company on their website, and secondly, the main users of cosmetics are female. As a consequence, the target sample for this study is female who search cosmetics information via Internet. To consider the convenience and efficiency, the sample is chosen from UK female residents via Internet.

In August 2008, a total of 169 respondents participated in this research, and 128 effective questionnaires were collected. There are nearly 40 questionnaires incorrectly completed because not every respondent has an experience in searching information about cosmetics products and purchasing them online. As Nie and Erbring suggested, only 52% of the consumers use the Internet for product information and 24% for buying. As a consequence, 128 effective questionnaires of 169 respondents are acceptable.

MEASURES

There are five constructs under consideration in this research, consumer education, consumer involvement, consumer knowledge, decision quality, and consumer loyalty. Each of constructs was assessed through Likert scale survey questions derived from the published literature.

Measures of Consumer Involvement

Consumer involvement is about the motivation to attain a goal. The involvement can separate into advertising involvement, product involvement, and purchasing involvement. Involving in different objects would lead to different results. For instance, involvement with purchase leads consumer to search for more information and spend more time searching for the right selection. The measures of involvement can be classified into personal, physical, and situational motivation. He further indentified five items to measure involvement degree. Similarly, Lin and Chen also used six items to conduct involvement degree.

These items are all related to four preferences: search for product information, alternative evaluation, perception of brand difference, and brand preference. The level of consumer involvement can be defined.

All preferences have positive relationship with consumer involvement, and therefore, higher involvement means higher search for product information, higher alternative evaluation, higher perception of brand difference, and higher brand preference. To sum up, there are five items to measure the consumer involvement in this research.

Consumer Involvement Variables:

- I would be interested in reading information about how the cosmetics are made
- I would be interested in reading consumer reports and articles about cosmetics
- I have compared brands of cosmetics in terms of the product features
- I think there are a great deal of differences among different brands of cosmetics
- I have a most preferred brand of cosmetics

Measures of Consumer Knowledge

Form previous discussion, consumer knowledge is defined as a consumer's understanding level of a particular product. Consumer knowledge has two main components: familiarity and expertise, whereas Brucks divided into three categories: objective knowledge, subjective knowledge, and experience-based knowledge.

These have widely used by researchers to conduct the attitudes about consumer knowledge. For instance, Flynn and Goldsmith used five items to measure consumer subjective knowledge, while Bell and Eisingerich used three items to measure consumer expertise. Nevertheless, all of the measures help to build consumer knowledge in different perspectives. By adapting all items used in previous researches, five delicate items is used to conduct the consumer knowledge in this research.

Consumer Knowledge Variable:

- I know a lot about cosmetics
- I know how to use cosmetics to best effect
- Among my circle of friends, I am one of the experts on cosmetics
- Compared with most other people, I know how to do my make-up well
- I have used a lot of cosmetics product in the past year

Measures of Consumer Education

Consumer education is about attitudes, skills, knowledge and ability to assess an effective consumer and to utilize information. Furthermore, consumer education is not information for a specific product, but neutral knowledge about using certain product category. The measures of consumer education include the increase of consumer knowledge about certain consumer education topics, the ability to compare within certain markets, the efficiency of consumer. By extending and modifying the 4 items by previous research, the measures of consumer education consist of six items.

Consumer Education Variables:

- The website keep me very well informed about what is going on using cosmetics
- The website explain utility of cosmetics in a meaningful way
- The website show recommendations in a meaningful way
- The website always offers me as much information as I need
- The website explain the pros and cons of the different cosmetic product
- The website help me to compare different products

Measures of Decision Quality

Decision quality is about consumer's ability to choose a high-quality product. The consumer needs to have a better understanding of relationship between the attribute functions of the product and his or her goals for purchasing it in order to choose the appropriate alternative. The information control and expertise matrix can be used to realise the decision quality under different situations, and the ability to differentiate relevant and irrelevant is also essential to make a quality decision. On the other hand, Lin and Chen used information intention and purchase intention to present the decision quality, and developed six items to measure these two intentions. Besides when evaluating possible alternatives, comparisons matrix help consumer to select an appropriate choice among alternatives. In addition, a good decision means that consumer will be more satisfied with his or her choice.

Dooley and Fryxell used six items to test the decision quality for hospital strategies. The items asked participates' perceptions of the quality of the information, whether the decision fit the objectives, and whether the decision contributed to the overall effectiveness. These items almost included all the consideration of decision process, and therefore the items used in this study will base on Dooley and Fryxell's measures. Besides, the differentiation of relevant and irrelevant information and satisfaction of purchases are also important figures to measure the decision quality. There are five items conducted in this research.

Decision Quality Variables:

- I was able to differentiate between relevant and irrelevant information about cosmetics product
- The decision I made was based on the best available information
- The decision I made was made based on valid assumptions
- The decision I made always helped myself achieve my objectives/ get what I needed
- I was satisfied with cosmetics product that I bought

Measures of Consumer Loyalty

Consumer loyalty is defined as customers' intentions to stay with a organization or brand, and can be seen as a repeat purchasing behaviour of the same brand. Bell and Eisingerich both used four items to measure the consumer loyalty in the financial industry.

By adapting form previous researches, there are three items to measure consumer loyalty in cosmetic industry. Besides, switching cost is also an important factor that is highly relevant with consumer loyalty. Hence, there are two items to measure this factor, and the relationship is that if consumers perceive a high switching cost, they will stay in the same brand with high possibility.

Consumer Loyalty Variables:

- I will purchase more products form [Brand Name] in the future
- The likelihood of me trying [other Brand Name] products is very good
- I try to use [Brand Name] products for most of my cosmetics

- Switching Cost:
  - By continuing with [Brand Name] I receive particular privileges I would not receive elsewhere
  - A lot of energy, time and effort have gone into building and maintaining the relationships with
  - [Brand Name] for you

QUESTIONNAIRE DESIGN

The questionnaire design in this chapter includes six parts, which are consumer involvement, consumer knowledge, consumer education, decision quality, consumer loyalty, and a respondent's basic information. The questions were asked respectively. Before answering the questions about consumer education, and decision quality and consumer loyalty, participates were required to recall a past purchase on a cosmetics website or to choose a website and imagine that they are going to buy a product off the website.

The purpose of this action is to measure the utility of consumer education, and find out the relationship among decision quality and consumer loyalty in a consistent way for individuals. However, this recall and imagination process presented a limitation in this research. All participants chose a cosmetics brand based on previous experience or self-preference. Therefore, there is a lack of consistency among individuals. This may influence the credibility of this research. A way to solve the limitation is to find one cosmetics brand and only use consumers of this brand. Nevertheless, because the data is unavailable and time is limited, the imaginative method will be used in this study.

CONTROL VARIABLES

Age, gender, and Internet experience are controlled in this research. Females comprise the main population of purchasing cosmetics. Obviously, gender has significant influences on consumer behaviour in the cosmetic industry. Besides, in comparison with men, women appeared to have a lower threshold for elaborating on message cues and thus made greater use of such cues in judging products. Furthermore, older consumers, due to their greater accumulation of wealth over time, may demonstrate differences in loyalty due to the accumulation of switching costs and a degree of inertia. Internet experience has been shown to have an influence on the information assessment.

Therefore, the high frequency of surfing on the Internet would infer a high probability of increasing information quality. In other words, Internet experience might be associated with consumer involvement and decision quality. Gender was indicated as male and female. Age was divided into six groups, which were adopted from Key Note: 15-24, 25-34, 35-44, 45-54, 55-64, 65+. Moreover, Internet experience was measure by asking how often respondents have surfed the Internet per week. However, this study will place less emphasis on these factors. Hence, these factors have already been conducted in previous researches.

3

Consumer Decision-Making

INTRODUCTION

How do consumers make decisions? This question is at the core of much of marketing examination over the past 60 or 70 years. As marketers manipulate the various principles of marketing, so do the consumers they seek to reach—choosing which products and services to buy, and which not to buy, choosing which brands to use, and which brands to ignore. The focus of this document is to examine the major decision- making models, strategies, and theories that underlie the decision processes used by consumers and to provide some clarity for marketing executives attempting to find the right mix of variables for their products and services.

THREE DECISION-MAKING MODELS

Early economists, led by Nicholas Bernoulli, John von Neumann, and Oskar Morgenstern, puzzled over this question. Beginning about 300 years ago, Bernoulli developed the first formal explanation of consumer decision-making. It was later extended by von Neumann and Morgenstern and called the Utility Theory. This theory proposed that consumers make decisions based on the expected outcomes of their decisions. In this model consumers were viewed as rational actors who were able to estimate the probabilistic outcomes of uncertain decisions and select the outcome which maximized their well-being.

However, as one might expect, consumers are typically not completely rational, nor consistent, nor even aware of the various elements that enter into their decision-making. In addition, though consumers are good at estimating relative frequencies of events, they typically have difficulty translating these frequencies into probabilities. This Utility model, even though it had been viewed as the dominant decision-making paradigm, had serious shortcomings that could not be explained by the model. Nobel Laureate Herbert Simon proposed an alternative, simpler model in the mid-1950s. This model was called Satisficing, in which consumers got approximately where they wanted to go and then stopped the decision-making process.

An example of this would be in the search for a new apartment. Under the Utility Theory, consumers would evaluate every apartment in a market form a linear equation based on all the pertinent variables, and then select the apartment that had the highest overall Utility Score. With Satisficing, however, consumers might just evaluate apartments within a certain distance to their desired location, stopping when they found one that was "good enough." This theory, though robust enough to encompass many of the shortcomings of Utility Theory, still left significant room for improvement in the area of prediction.

After all, if a marketing executive couldn't predict consumer behaviour, then what use would a decision-making paradigm be? Simon and others have extended this area in the investigation of the field of bounded rationality. Following Simon, additional efforts were made to develop better understandings of consumer decision-making, extending beyond the mathematical optimization of Utility Theory and the somewhat unsatisfying Satisficing Theory. In the late 1970s, two leading psychologists, Daniel Kahneman and Amos Tversky, developed the Prospect Theory, which expanded upon both the Utility Theory and Satisficing Theory to develop a new theory that encompassed the best aspects of each, while solving many of the problems that each presented.

Two major elements that were added by Kahneman and Tversky were the concepts of value and endowment, in which an item is more precious if one owns it than if someone else owns it. Value provided a reference point and evaluated both gains and losses from that reference point. Additionally, gains and losses had a marginally decreasing increase from the reference point. For example, there was a much greater value for the first incremental gain from the reference point than for subsequent gains.

SEVEN DECISION-MAKING STRATEGIES

What this all led to was the development and exploration of a series of useful consumer decision-making strategies that could be exploited by marketers. For each product, marketers needed to understand the specific decision-making strategy utilized by each consumer segment acquiring that product. If this were done, marketers could position their product in such a manner that the decision-making strategy would lead consumers to select their product. The first two strategies are called compensatory strategies.

In these strategies, consumers allow a higher value of one attribute to compensate for a lesser value of another attribute. For example, if a consumer is looking at automobiles, a high value in gas mileage might compensate for a lower value in seating space. The attributes might have equal weight or have different weights for the attributes. An example of the latter might be to place twice as much importance on gas mileage than seating space. The next three strategies are called noncompensatory strategies. In these strategies, each attribute of a specific product is evaluated without respect to the other attributes, and even though a product may have a very high value on one attribute, if it fails another attribute, it is eliminated from consideration. From Simon, the first of these is Satisficing, in which the first product evaluated to meet cutoff values for all attributes is chosen, even if it is not the best. The second of these strategies, Elimination by Aspects, sets a cutoff value for the most important attribute, and allows all competing products that meet that cutoff value to go to the next attribute and its cutoff value.

The third strategy, Lexigraphic, evaluates the most important attribute, and if a product is clearly superior to others, stops the decision process and selects that product; otherwise, it continues to the next most important attribute. The next two strategies are called partially compensatory strategies, in that strategies are evaluated against each other in serial fashion and higher values for attributes are considered. The first of these strategies is called Majority of Conforming Dimensions, in which the first two competing products are evaluated across all attributes, and the one that has higher values across more dimensions, or attributes, is retained. This winner is then evaluated against the next competitor, and the one that has higher values across more dimensions is again retained.

The second partially compensatory strategy is called Frequency of Good and Bad Features, in which all products are simultaneously compared to the cutoff values for each of their relevant attributes, and the product that has the most "good" features that exceed the cutoff values is the winner. There are other expansions upon these seven basic consumer decision-making strategies, but they are generally captured. However, two major areas of marketing theory also help to provide additional explanatory power to these strategies.

TWO MARKETING THEORIES

The first marketing theory is called Consideration. In this theory, consumers form a subset of brands from which the decision-making strategies are applied. For example, if asked to enumerate all the restaurants that one could recall, the list might be quite extensive for most consumers. However, when a consumer first addresses the question of where to dine that evening, a short list of restaurants that are actively considered is utilized for the decision-making process. Multistage decision-making models were summarized by Allan Shocker, in which the increasing complexity of a decision produces more steps in the decision process.

In essence, more cognitive effort would be expended in evaluating members of the consideration set and reducing that number to an eventual choice. The second marketing theory is called Involvement, in which the amount of cognitive effort applied to the decision- making process is directly related to the level of importance that the consumer places on acquisition of the specific product. For example, there is rarely a significant amount of decision-making applied to the selection of a pack of chewing gum at the grocery store checkout counter, but there is a much greater amount of decision-making effort applied to the purchase of a new cell phone. This degree of involvement is not necessarily a function of the price, but is more related to the perceived impact on the quality of life of the consumer. The quality of life can come directly from the benefits supplied by the product, or can come indirectly from the social accolades or sanctions provided by members of the peer group.

ATTITUDE AND CONSUMER DECISION-MAKING

In everyday life, consumers receive a variety of marketing communications about what they should buy and they should not. They come to know about different claims and standings of the brands. On the basis of inputs received from various sources, consumers develop their assessment of the brands, better known as the brand-image. The brand image helps consumers in believing which brand is more likely to have a particular benefit or a feature. It should be noted here that since these brand beliefs are based on consumer perception, they may sometimes be at variance with reality.

Thus, a potential car buyer may believe that the brand A of car has style but it may not be actually true about the brand A. In a similar vein, a potential lipstick buyer may believe that the brand B of the lipstick has the attribute of social prestige. In reality, it may not be so. Thus, consumer attitude are based on the perception, true or otherwise. But they provide a very important clue as to whether the consumers will take a particular course of action or not.

Thus, a person after having been bombarded by a string of newspapers ads on various TV brands available in India, may suddenly observe: "Oh, the TV ads! I can't stand them any more!" Similarly, a typical housewife may have this to say to her husband, after having viewed the sunday morning transmission: "You know something, the TV ads are so fascinating that they have taught a lot to our children in making brand choices for grocery". These two statements express a summary evaluation of a marketing stimulus *i.e.*, promotional methods, and indicate how these will act in case of consumers who were asked to respond. Thus, the first consumer will probable zap the TV commercials or skip them. The second housewife may regulate the viewing hours of the television for the children.

THE CONSTITUENTS OF CONSUMER ATTITUDE

In the subsequent block 3, as suggested deal with the major variables that a buyer would face during information search for the purpose of evaluating and reaching a choice. The key variable that would guide the customer in the process, is the consumer attitude. Since an attitude provides a series of cues to marketers with reference to evaluation procedure, an understanding of consumer attitude can help marketers predict future purchases; and gauge the strength or otherwise of their its present sales. Even they redesign their marketing mix efforts. Attitude, as a concept, however, is far from simple. An attitude consists of three constituents. These are affective; cognitive and conative. Affective part of the attitude refers to the feelings that a consumer has. The cognitive part refers to the information and knowledge basis of these consumers. The third and final part of the attitude–the conative, refers to tae intention of the customer. A schematic conception of attitudes is attempted in Figure.

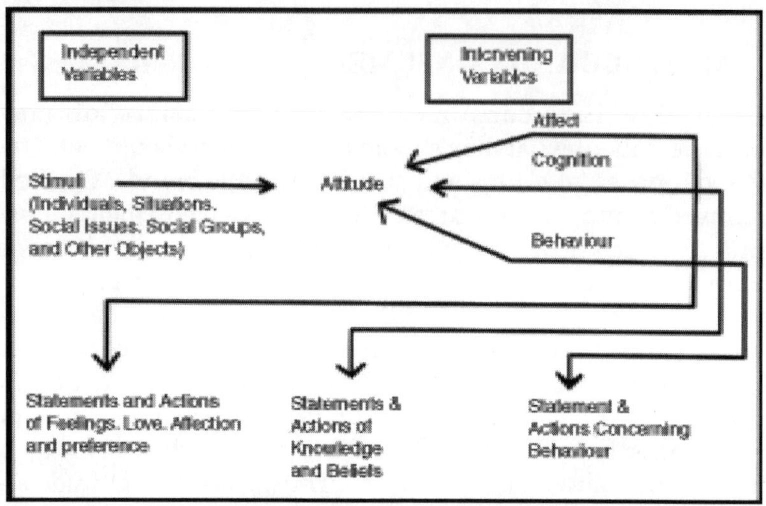

Fig. Schematic Conception of Attitudes.

The Figure can be amplified by an hypothetical example of the attitude formation in respect of an individual as well as a institutional buyer. For instance, assume that a research study reveals that Indian females have a favourable attitude towards ONIDA Television. Similarly, assume that TATA Steel too has indicated its favourable attitude towards HCL Fax machines.

In operational terms, these findings summarize the knowledge of these buyers as to what ONIDA TV and HCL Fax machine may possess. Secondly, they indicate how the female buyers and the TATA Steel feel about these brands. Thirdly, they indicate the likely action if these buyers are asked to go for these respective products, *i.e.*, ONIDA Television and HCL Fax machine. To sum up, attitude indicates knowledge, feelings and intended action for the given stimulus.

THE FUNCTIONS OF CONSUMER ATTITUDE

Notwithstanding the importance of consumer attitude, two serious criticisms have been levelled against it. The foremost criticism is that it makes a rather naive assumption that attitudes influence the specific and overt behaviour of consumer. The real facts don't support it so clearly. Yet, the functions of attitude are too important to be left un-described. Consumer attitudes in their most rudimentary form, renders the following function as explained in figure.

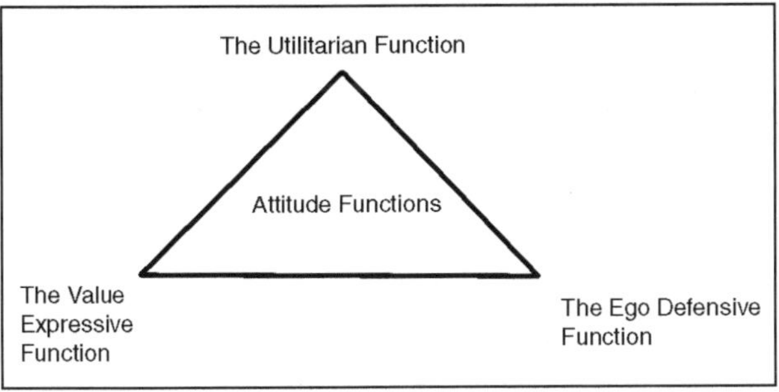

Fig. Functions of Attitude

THE UTILITARIAN FUNCTION

Consumer attitudes fulfil a utilitarian function as they guide consumers in achieving their desired needs. Thus, if the TV buyers consider technology and after-sales service support as the two most important criteria in TV selection, the buyers will be most attracted by the messages of those brand alternatives that claim to possess the two attributes. Such attitudes towards these brands will help the consumer achieve what he wants. Also, it will assist them in avoiding failure and disappointment in brand evaluation.

THE EGO DEFENSIVE FUNCTION

This function protects consumers against internal and external anxieties and environment. Herein, the marketing stimuli and more particularly, products become an instrument of the protection process. Many consumer psychologists have led marketers to believe that a positiveconsumer attitude towards expensive jeweler wrist watches and other visible prestige products serve as mechanism of Defence for these consumers.

It should be cautioned here, however, that expensive items alone do not constitute a mechanism of Defence for consumers. The low priced products like mouthwash deodorants too can serve the same protection function from anxiety etc.

THE VALUE-EXPRESSIVE FUNCTION

Often consumer attitudes are an expression of their values and self-concept. Value expressive attitudes maintain self-identity among consumers and lead them to expression and determination. The projection is often strong, evident and extreme because consumers openly express opinions that reflect their strong beliefs and self-concept.

The application of this function is all too evident in consumer selection and evaluation of products, their price, promotional items and the distributive outlets. Thus, a consumer, in order to express his simple and Gandhian values in life, will always select and wear handloom and Khadi, support products of the small scale industries and may have a negative attitude against conspicuous consumption and their public endorsement by the commercial houses. Normally, there is a tendency on the part of consumers to flaunt this kind of attitude.

UTILITY FUNCTION

After having ascertained that the consideration-set of alternative brands, possesses all the desired attributes, consumers will identify how their satisfaction will vary in response to changing levels of performance in those attributes, Thus, the potential car buyer will decide how much will it mean to him in utility terms if brand 'x' of car possesses 4/10 level of performance in fuel-efficiency, instead of, say, 6/10 level of performance. The same could be argued in the case of the female lipstick buyer. The advantage of utility function is that by combining the performance levels of salient attributes, consumers can make up what is called an 'ideal' brand.

CONSUMER ATTITUDE: THE MODELS

Model-making in attitudes have been attempted in a variety of ways. Most prominent among them are the multi-attribute attitude models.

MULTI-ATTRIBUTE ATTITUDE MODELS

Multi-attribute attitude models explain how consumers may combine their beliefs about product attributes to form their attitudes about various brand alternatives. These models assume that the brand which receives the best attitude, will be chosen. They further assume that consumers will go through the standard Hierarchy of Effects sequence.

A careful scrutiny of all multi-attribute attitude models establishes two general categories of these models. Category I comprises the models that emphasize the Attitude- Towards—Objects. Hence, they are termed as ATO models. Category II consists of those models that focus on predicting the behavioural intentions of consumers to perform certain action. This action could be purchase or non-purchase. For brevity sake, it is termed as BI Model. Figure illustrates the point.

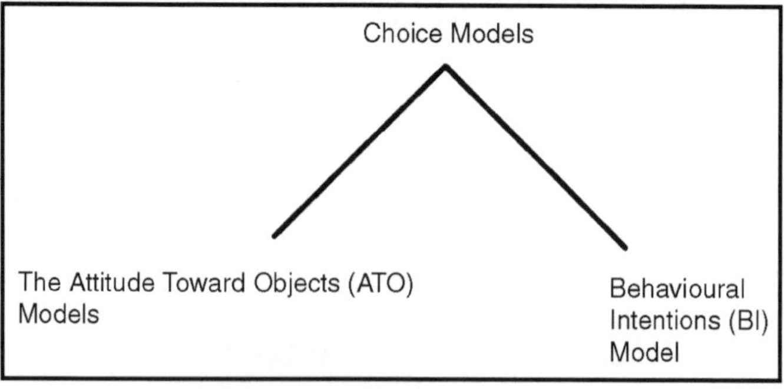

Fig. Multi-attributes of choice Models

Criticisms

The ATO models, however, suffer from a major weakness. They fail to consider that quite often, consumer attitude does not fully equate with behaviour. Thus, a potential car buyer in spite of having the most positive attitude towards 'Maruti', may never engage in the behaviour of buying it. This happens because of the adverse opinion of other important people or due to temptation of investing the funds more profitably elsewhere. Situational influences may prevent him from engaging the act of buying. The Behaviour Intentions model attempts to rectify this weakness in alternative evaluation.

The Behaviour Intentions Model

The BI model is in effect, an extension of Fishbein's ATO model. The model does not attempt to predict behaviour *per se* but intentions to behave algebraically, the model is as follows:

B = BI = W_1 (A_B) + W_2 (SN): where

B = behaviour; BI = Behaviour Intention

A_B = attitude towards performing the behaviour

SN = the subjective norm

W_1 and W_2, are empirically determined weights, through regression analysis.

A_B and SN are obtained directly from consumers via questionnaires. Thus, A_B is obtained from the following equation:

Where,

$$A_B = \sum_{i=1}^{n} b_i e_i,$$

A_B = attitude towards the behaviour

b_i = the person's belief taht performing the behaviour will result in consequence

e_i = the person's evluation of consequence

n = the number of beliefs

The equation has one major difference over the earlier Fishbein's ATO Model. It is that the BI Model assesses the person's belief that performing a particular behaviour will result in a particular consequence. They are termed as Subjective Norms (SN).

The equation for obtaining the subjective norms is as follows:

$$SN = \sum_{j=1}^{n} NB_j \ MC_j$$

where,

SN = subjective norm;

NB_j = the normative belief that a reference group of persons j thinks that the consumer should or should not perform the behaviour;

MC = the motivation to comply with the influence of the referent j and

n = number of relevant reference groups of individuals.

Various research studies have found the BI model to be superior to the standard multi-attribute choice models, though eye-brows have been raised concerning the calculation of the subjective norms (SN). In practice, this exercise is never so simple.

PROCESS OF DECISION-MAKING

The most basic and important requirement for the marketer is to understand how consumers make choices. Ajzen and Fishbein have attempted to explain human choice behaviour in their theory of reasoned action which states that: "Generally speaking-human beings are usually quite rational and make systematic use of information available to them. People consider the implications of their actions before they decide to engage or not to engage in a given behaviour."

Thus, making a decision is a rational and conscious process in which the consumer evaluates each of the available alternatives to select the best amongst them. Each decision you make involves an elaborate mental thought process, a degree of active reasoning, though on the surface it may not always seem to be so.

This may be because over a period of time you have taken certain decisions so many times that they now seem to be made almost automatically but that is not true at all. Even your daily decision of buying a loaf of bread involves the element of active reasoning as buying a new sofa set for your drawing room. However, in the former case, the extent and intensity of active reasoning may be much less as compared to the latter case.

In the case of bread, the only decision variables may be which brand, quantity and retail outlet. But in case of buying a sofa set the decision variables are far more in number.

These may be:

- Ready-made or made to order
- From a furniture shop or to be built at home
- Type of material for frame: Wood, Steel, Aluminium
- Type of material for cushion: cloth, rexine, leather
- Design: with or without arm-rests, height, depth of seat, seating capacity, loose or fixed cushion.

Thus, depending on the type of decision being made, the degree and strength of active reasoning will vary.

There are three factors which influence the degree of active reasoning that is undertaken by the consumer in his process of decision-making. These are:

- *Involvement*: When a product is perceived to be of great personal importance to the customer, such as personal clothing, or its purchase involves a great deal of money or risk such as jewellery, car, house, company shares, the level of involvement in making the decision is likely to be very high. The consumer is likely to spend a great deal of time before arriving at the final decision. In contrast, when buying items which do not reflect much on the consumer's personality or their purchase involves small amounts of money.or the risk associated with them is not high, the degree of involvement of the consumer is likely to be low. Products such as shoes, polish, toilet soap, toothpaste, biscuits etc. would fall in this category.

- *Differentiation*: When the consumer perceives that the various alternatives which are available are very different from one another in terms of their features and benefits offered, he is likely to spend more time in gathering information about and evaluating these different features. On the other hand, in case of products which are not very different from one another either in terms of their features or benefits offered, the consumer is bound to perceive them as being almost the same and buy the first available product/brand which satisfies his minimum expectation. He will not like to spend much time in evaluating the various alternatives. The various brands of washing powder available in the market today are an excellent example of low level of differentiation with the consumer perceiving the different brands to be offering almost identical benefits. All the brands, such as Nirma, Vimal, Vijay, etc. look similar with identical packing and carry almost the same price tag.
- Till a few years ago, the two wheel scooter market in,India was highly undifferentiated with Vespa and Lambretta offering almost identical scooter to the consumers in terms of basic features. But today the same market is highly differentiated. The consumers have a wide range of brands to choose from such as Kinetic-Honda, Lohia, Bajaj etc. each offering a variety of shapes, horse power and many other innovative features to choose from. A potential consumer of scooter would have to spend considerable time in evaluating each brand before he is in a position to make his decision.
- Time Pressure: When you are under pressure to make a decision quickly, you cannot afford to spend a long time finding out about the various products or brands. You would probably buy whatever is readily available. While traveling in your car to a hill station your car tyre bursts and you need to buy a new one. At that time you would buy the brand that is available at whatever price without giving it too much thought. But under a different situation, when you need to buy new tyres, you would certainly like to find the features of nylon and radial tyres and evaluate various brands *e.g.* Modi, MRF, Dunlop and Apollo etc. on their individual advantages and disadvantages.

DECISION-MAKING AND CONSUMER CHOICE

One model of consumer decision making involves several steps. The first one is problem recognition-you realise that something is not as it should be. Perhaps, for example, your car is getting more difficult to start and is not accelerating well. The second step is information search-what are some alternative ways of solving the problem? You might buy a new car, buy a used car, take your car in for repair, ride the bus, ride a taxi, or ride a skateboard to work. The third step involves evaluation of alternatives. A skateboard is inexpensive, but may be ill-suited for long distances and for rainy days. Finally, we have the purchase stage, and sometimes a post-purchase stage. In reality, people may go back and forth between the stages. For example, a person may resume alternative identification during while evaluating already known alternatives.

Consumer involvement will tend to vary dramatically depending on the type of product. In general, consumer involvement will be higher for products that are very expensive or are highly significant in the consumer's life in some other way.

It is important to consider the consumer's motivation for buying products. To achieve this goal, we can use the Means-End chain, wherein we consider a logical progression of consequences of product use that eventually lead to desired end benefit. Thus, for example, a consumer may see that a car has a large engine, leading to fast acceleration, leading to a feeling of performance, leading to a feeling of power, which ultimately improves the consumer's self-esteem. A handgun may aim bullets with precision, which enables the user to kill an intruder, which means that the intruder will not be able to harm the consumer's family, which achieves the desired end-state of security. In advertising, it is important to portray the desired end-states. Focusing on the large motor will do less good than portraying a successful person driving the car.

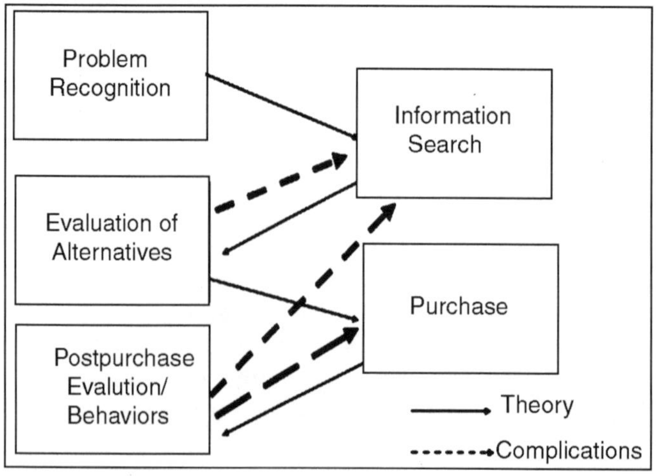

INFORMATION SEARCH AND DECISION-MAKING

Consumers engage in both internal and external information search. Internal search involves the consumer identifying alternatives from his or her memory. For certain low involvement products, it is very important that marketing prigrammes achieve"top of mind" awareness. For example, few people will search the Yellow Pages for fast food restaurants; thus, the consumer must be able to retrieve one's restaurant from memory before it will be considered.

For high involvement products, consumers are more likely to use an external search. Before buying a car, for example, the consumer may ask friends' opinions, read reviews in Consumer Reports, consult several web sites, and visit several dealerships. Thus, firms that make products that are selected predominantly through external search must invest in having information available to the consumer in need-e.g., through brochures, web sites, or news coverage.

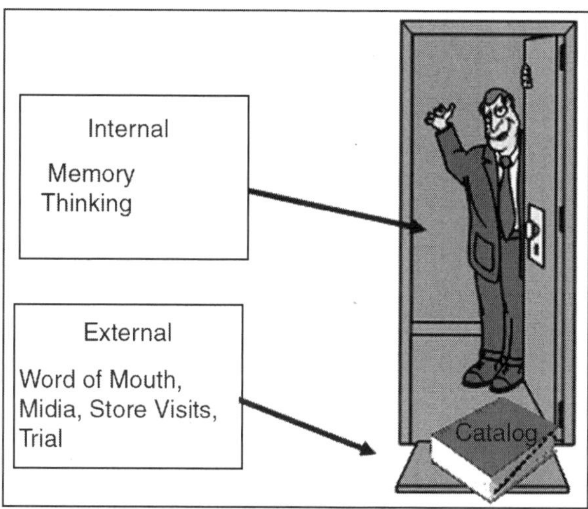

A compensatory decision involves the consumer"trading off" good and bad attributes of a product. For example, a car may have a low price and good gas mileage but slow acceleration. If the price is sufficiently inexpensive and gas efficient, the consumer may then select it over a car with better acceleration that costs more and uses more gas.

Occasionally, a decision will involve a non-compensatory strategy. For example, a parent may reject all soft drinks that contain artificial sweeteners. Here, other good features such as taste and low calories cannot overcome this one"non-negotiable" attribute.

The amount of effort a consumer puts into searching depends on a number of factors such as the market, product characteristics, consumer characteristics, and situational characteristics.

Two interesting issues in decisions are:

- *Variety seeking* where consumers seek to try new brands not because these brands are expected to be "better" in any way, but rather because the consumer wants a "change of pace," and
- *"Impulse" purchases*—unplanned buys. This represents a somewhat "fuzzy" group. For example, a shopper may plan to buy vegetables but only decide in the store to actually buy broccoli and corn. Alternatively, a person may buy an item which is currently on sale, or one that he or she remembers that is needed only once inside the store.

A number of factors involve consumer choices. In some cases, consumers will be more *motivated*. For example, one may be more careful choosing a gift for an in-law than when buying the same thing for one self. Some consumers are also more motivated to *comparison shop* for the best prices, while others are more *convenience* oriented. *Personality* impacts decisions. Some like variety more than others, and some are more receptive to stimulation and excitement in trying new stores. *Perception* influences decisions.

Some people, for example, can taste the difference between generic and name brand foods while many cannot. *Selective* perception occurs when a person is paying attention only to information of interest. For example, when looking for a new car, the consumer may pay more attention to car ads than when this is not in the horizon. Some consumers are put off by perceived *risk*.

Thus, many marketers offer a money back guarantee. Consumers will tend to change their behaviour through *learning*—e.g., they will avoid restaurants they have found to be crowded and will settle on brands that best meet their tastes. Consumers differ in the *values* they hold. As suggested, consider the issue of lifestyle under segmentation.

TYPES OF PURCHASE DECISION BEHAVIOUR

Consumer buying behaviour varies with the type of buying decision. Earlier, we stated that while a decision for buying bread was almost made automatically, the decision for buying a sofa set was more deliberate and time consuming. Similarly, there is a great deal of difference in buying a tube of toothpaste, clothes for yourself and a refrigerator for your home.

We shall now distinguish three types of buying behaviour:

- *Routinised response behaviour*: This occurs when the consumer already has some experience of buying and using the product. He is familiar with the various brands available and the attributes of each and has a well established criteria for selecting his own brand. Consumers do not give much thought or time when buying such products and already have a preferred brand. The degree of involvement in buying such products is low. Frequently purchased and low cost products such as razor blades, coffee powder, toothpaste, soap, soft drinks, etc. fall in this category. Marketers dealing in products involving routinised response behaviour must ensure the satisfaction of existing customers by maintaining consistent quality, service and value. Also, they must attempt to attract new customers by introducing novel features, using point-of-purchase promotional material and special displays.

- *Limited Problem Solving*: In this type of buying behaviour, the consumer is familiar with the product and the various brands available, but has no established brand preference. The consumer would like to gather additional information about the brands to arrive at his brand decision. For instance a housewife buys refined vegetable oil for her cooking. She is familiar with the concept of vegetable oil and also knows that Postman, Dalda and Ruby are some of the prominent brands available. But to establish her choice of brand, she would like to check with her friends and regular shopkeeper about the attributes of each. Limited problem solving also takes place when a consumer encounters an unfamiliar brand in a known product category. The housewife who buys refined vegetable oil, on her next visit to the market, sees a new brand of oil, Saffola. Apart from being a new brand, this brand of oil also claims the unique attribute of being low in cholesterol. To arrive at a decision, whether or not to buy this brand, the housewife needs to gather information about the new brand which will allow her to compare it with the known brands. The marketer's task in a situation where he is introducing a new brand in a well known product category is to design a communication strategy that gives complete information on all the attributes of the brand, thus increasing the consumer's confidence and facilitating his or her purchase decision.
- *Extensive Problem Solving*: Extensive problem solving occurs when the consumer is encountering a new product category. He needs information on both the product category as well as the various brands available in it. This kind of decision is by far the most complex. For instance, you are thinking of buying a Flat colour television to replace your existing black and white TV set. You do not have much idea about how to judge the quality of a, colour TV set. You have heard about the various brands, such as Videocon, BPL, Samsung, LG, Sony, Thomson etc. but you do not know what t heir respective quality ranking is in colour TV. Each brand makes claims of foreign technology, latest features such as flat square tube and channel display. Further, t here is a range of models to choose from within each brand, models with remote control. different cabinet colour finish, vertical monitor styling etc. To arrive at a decision, you have to gather information at three levels and also

establish a criteria for evaluating this information. The three levels of information gathering and evaluation are at generic product level, brand level and model level within each brand. The marketing strategy for such buying behaviour must be such that it facilitates the consumer's information gathering and learning process about the product category and his own brand. The marketer must be able to provide his consumer with a very specific and unique set of positive attributes regarding his own brand, so that the purchase decision is made in his favour. The concept of EPS is most applicable to new products. The product may be new at the generic product concept level or it may be an established product concept but new for a particular consumer. In case of a new product concept such as ready to cook instant snack, the entire consumer universe is unfamiliar with the product. The marketer has to spend large amounts of money in educating the consumers about his product. The consumers in turn need a great deal of information before they can take a decision; and the decision process takes a long time. On the other hand, you may have the situation where the product concept is well understood by a majority of the consumers, but it is being bought or used by a particular consumer for the first time. To take a very simple example, a tribal who is exposed to the concept of toothpaste for the first time in his life will seek a lot of information and take a long time to decide. For him, buying a toothpaste is a EPS behaviour, whereas for most of us it simply requires a routinised response behaviour.

4

Consumer Behaviour in Services Management

SERVICE SECTOR GROWTH

From 1978 to 2004, the service sectors of China and India achieved high annual growth averaging 10.8 per cent in China and 7.0 per cent in India. The difference in these growth rates matches the difference in the rates of GDP growth in the two countries. During the same period, an average annual growth rate of 9.7 per cent was recorded for the Chinese economy compared to 5.4 per cent for India. At the disaggregate level, the structures of the service sector in China and India are very similar.

In both countries, the service sector is still dominated by the traditional or old services, followed by business services (finance, insurance and real estate) and transport and communications. However, the new service sectors are catching up rapidly.

From 1999 to 2003, communication services showed the strongest growth in both countries (with an average annual rate of 16.8 per cent in China and 23.9 per cent in India), followed by education (8.6 per cent) and research (11.9 per cent) in India, and real estate (8.8 per cent) and research (8.9 per cent) in China. Though growing rapidly in recent years, research-related services are still relatively small in both countries.

OUTPUT AND EMPLOYMENT SHARES

The development of the service sectors can also be examined by analysing the sectoral shares of output and employment over the national totals in the two countries. Output shares of the service sector in China and India have grown steadily since 1978. The role of services in the Indian economy is clearly more significant than that in the Chinese economy. Accordingly, since 1990, India's service sector has grown faster (annual growth rate of 7.5 per cent) than the manufacturing sector (6.0 per cent) while the opposite is true in China where the manufacturing sector grew at 12.1 per cent and the service sector, at only 8.4 per cent.

In contrast, the employment share of India's service sector has grown very slowly according to available statistics covering the period from 1983 to 1999, though the absolute figure was much higher than that in China in the 1980s. The employment share of China's service sector has, however, been growing steadily since 1978, in particular since the early 1990s. As a result, China's service sector has absorbed relatively much more labour than India's since the mid-1990s.

In terms of creating new jobs, services have played a vital role in both economies. For example, during the decade of 1995 to 2004, more than 62 per cent of the new jobs created in China were in the service sector while India's services provided about 54 per cent of new jobs in the country from 1994 to 1999. As both countries must relocate a large pool of rural surplus labour, further employment growth in the service sector will be indispensable.

FUNCTION OF CUSTOMER SERVICE

Customer Service Representaives provide a valuable link between customers and the companies who produce the products they buy and the services they use. They are responsible for responding to customer inquiries and making sure that any problems they are experiencing are resolved. Although most customer service representatives do their work by telephone in call centres, some interact with customers by e-mail, fax, post, or face-to-face.

Many customer service inquiries involve simple questions or requests. For instance, a customer may want to know the status of an order or wish to change his or her address in the company's file. However, some questions may be somewhat more difficult, and may require additional research or help from an expert. In some cases, a representative's main function may be to determine who in the organization is best suited to answer a customer's questions.

Some customer inquiries are complaints, which generally must be handled in accordance with strict company policies. In some cases, representatives may try to fix problems or suggest solutions. They may have the authority to reverse erroneous fees or send replacement products. Other representatives act as gatekeepers who make sure that complaints are valid before accepting customer returns.

Although selling products and services is not the primary function of a customer service representative, some customer services representatives may provide information that helps customers to make purchasing decisions. For instance, a representative may point out a product or service that would fulfill a customer's needs.

Customer service representatives use computers, telephones, and other technology extensively in their work. When the customer has an account with the company, a representative will usually open his or her file in the company's computer system. Representatives use this information to solve problems and may be able to make specific changes as necessary. They also have access to responses for the most commonly asked questions and specific guidelines for dealing with requests or complaints. In the event that the representative does not know the answer or is unable to solve a specific problem, a supervisor or other experienced worker may provide assistance.

Many customer service workers are located in call centres, where they spend the entire day speaking on the telephone. Companies usually keep statistics on their workers to make sure they are working efficiently. This helps them to keep up with their call volume and ensures that customers do not have to wait on hold for extended periods of time. Supervisors may listen in on or tape calls to ensure customers are getting quality service.

Almost every industry employs customer service representatives, and their duties may vary greatly depending on the nature of the organization. For instance, representatives who work in banks may have similar duties to tellers, whereas those in insurance companies may be required to handle paperwork, such as changes to policies or renewals. Those who work for utility and communication companies may assist customers with service problems, such as outages. Representatives who work in retail stores often handle returns and help customers to find items in their stores.

Work environment. Although customer service representatives work in a variety of settings, most work in areas that are clean and well lit. Those who work in call centres generally have their own workstations or cubicle spaces equipped with telephones, headsets, and computers. Because many call centres are open extended hours or are staffed around the clock, these positions may require workers to take on early morning, evening, or late night shifts.

Weekend or holiday work is also common. Because peak times may not last for a full shift, many workers are part-time or work a split shift. As a result, the occupation is well suited to flexible work schedules. Many companies hire additional employees at certain times of year when higher call volumes are expected.

Call centres may be crowded and noisy, and work may be repetitious and stressful, with little time between calls. Also, long periods spent sitting, typing, or looking at a computer screen may cause eye and muscle strain, backaches, headaches, and repetitive motion injuries. A growing number of employers are hiring telecommuters, who provide customer service from their own homes. Although this remains somewhat rare, it can be a major advantage for workers who need to remain in their homes during the day.

Customer service representatives working in retail stores may have customers approach them in person or contact them by telephone. They may be required to work later in the evenings or on weekends, as stores are generally open during those times. Evenings and weekends tend to be peak hours for customer traffic. Customer service representatives may have to deal with difficult or irate customers, which can be challenging. However, the ability to resolve customers'problems has the potential to be very rewarding.

CHARACTERISTICS OF CONSUMER SERVICE

Existing studies suggest that consumer capability is the most salient factor in ethical evaluations of marketing practices. Clearly, consumer capability/ vulnerability is multifaceted. Consumers need mental, physical, and economic abilities to effectively execute a marketing exchange. At times, however, some consumers may lack one or another type of ability to the extent that they can not make informed decisions about a product or benefit from it. Lack of such capabilities may lead to some degree of vulnerability.

In general, a consumer's ability falls on a continuum that runs from being sophisticated to being vulnerable. Here, we group consumers into three categories: sophisticated, at-risk, and vulnerable. Many consumers may be sophisticated due to maturity, education, prior experience, or professional background.

Some consumers are considered at-risk when they are prone to addiction or compulsion even though they may possess basic skills and capabilities. These consumers also include those who are socio-economically disadvantaged. For instance, some consumers may be at greater risk if they already suffer from a disproportionate occurrence of harmful behaviour patterns, including those who may not be able to control their own behaviour, such as alcoholics, smokers, or other drug addicts. Moreover, some consumers may be vulnerable due to personal characteristics such as age, education, and physical and mental health.

Market Selection

With respect to any consumer group, a marketer basically has the following options: to target the group with a unique marketing mix, to market to the group via integrated mass marketing, or to exclude the group from marketing programmes. While integrated mass marketing remains a popular strategy for many products, targeted marketing is considered more effective for companies to gain competitive advantages.

When a product has universal benefits, market selection involves decisions about the inclusion of one group of consumers or the exclusion of another, and may be perceived as unequal or unfair. When a company's marketing programmes exclude certain consumers inadvertently or by design, consumers may have limited choice or incur higher switching costs of going elsewhere.

According to the contingency approach, each of the dimensions discussed above is important in ethical evaluations of marketing activities. However, none of the dimensions alone can determine the ethicality of a marketing situation. The degree of negative or positive ethical evaluation depends on the interaction among the three dimensions. To inform marketing practice and provide ethical guidelines, a normative framework of marketing ethics should enable decision-makers to make better moral judgments that are applicable to specific and often complex situations. Thus, analyzing the specific contingencies of a given marketing activity would be more helpful for assessing the ethical evaluations of marketing than would offering a limited set of general prescriptions.

Contingencies and Ethical Implications

They have different ethical implications due to differences in perceptions between marketers and the public based on the universal principles of equality, fairness, and justice. Each block provides a unique interaction of the three factors. The white block indicates positive or non-negative ethical evaluation. Black indicates negative ethical evaluation that marketers should avoid. These two areas often represent situations of universal agreement about ethical practice.

The gray block suggests caution due to potential ethical concerns and represents the area in which there are different ethical perceptions and hence disagreement on the ethicality of marketing practices. Based on contingency theory, we describe the following seven common marketing practices and discuss their ethical implications.

Scenario 1. Mainstream Marketing

First, companies may market beneficial products to sophisticated and at-risk consumers through targeted marketing or mass marketing, as in the blocks from A1B1C1 to A2B1C2. In these cases, companies will receive positive evaluations from consumers and should proceed. Ringold suggests that marketing transactions with equal participants (i.e., capable and informed consumers) are typically regarded as fair and ethically sound.

While many consumers are sophisticated and will not be considered at-risk or vulnerable under normal circumstances, this is not to say that unethical practices would not occur in these situations. Unethical practices may affect capable consumers (who do have bounded rationality and are sometimes vulnerable to unscrupulous marketing) as evidenced by numerous fraudulent investment schemes. As well, in the case of silicone breast implants, many sophisticated consumers fell victim to unethical practices.

Scenario 2. Positive Targeting and Social Marketing

Second, targeting and integrated marketing to vulnerable consumers is positive as long as the products are beneficial, and may be meaningful in some product categories (blocks A1B1C3 and A2B1C3). Children, due to their body size and stage of mental development, are often targeted with beneficial products and features such as specially formulated medications, safety caps for medication containers, and educational toys. Targeting beneficial products at vulnerable consumers mostly receives positive ethical evaluation. Based on the concept of social responsibility, many businesses provide beneficial products to vulnerable and disadvantaged consumers, such as charitable donations to those who are weak and poor. Social marketing programmes also target beneficial products at these consumers, such as free vaccinations for the children of poor families, and low interest rate mortgages for households with limited income. Marketers should receive positive evaluations from the public for these goodwill practices that contribute to consumer well being.

Scenario 3. Marketing Potentially Harmful Products

Third, the gray areas are the most challenging for marketing organizations and merit caution (blocks A1B2C1 and A2B2C2 are coded gray). Targeting products that are harmful due to abuse/misuse at any consumers is generally a questionable practice. The marketing of such products to consumers who are already at risk and disadvantaged is even more problematic.

For instance, targeted marketing of malt liquor of higher alcohol content to inner-city minorities by some companies led to severe criticism and consumer boycotts due to the disproportionate consumption of such products and more frequent alcohol-related health problems among these groups. Therefore, when marketing products that are potentially harmful due to abuse or misuse, it is important that marketers examine the characteristics of their target markets and use extreme caution to avoid marketing such products to consumers at risk or a disadvantage.

Scenario 4. Predatory Marketing

Fourth, marketing of harmful products to any consumer group is unethical, as indicated by blocks from A1B3C1 to A1B3C3, which are coded black. Targeted marketing is appropriately met with intense public scrutiny and even consumer boycotts when products are detrimental to consumer well being and lead to health and social problems. For this reason, the marketing of cigarettes has been curtailed in the U.S. and many other countries.

Negative ethical evaluations are even stronger when harmful or potentially harmful products are targeted at vulnerable consumers, because companies are considered to be preying on the weaknesses of such consumers (A1B2C3 and A2B2C3).

Because cigarettes and other nicotine products are detrimental to consumer health, it is even more problematic when they are targeted towards the vulnerable (e.g., young children). The U.S. Food and Drug Administration recently ordered several companies to stop making lollypops that contained nicotine due to their potential to harm children.

Scenario 5. Discrimination and Redlining

Fifth, the exclusion of certain consumer groups, particularly vulnerable and disadvantaged consumers, from access to beneficial products is unethical because such actions limit consumer choices. It is also illegal to exclude any consumer groups from marketing programmes specified under U.S. laws such as the Fair Lending Act and the Fair Housing Act.

However, segmentation and targeted marketing often mean the inclusion of some groups and exclusion of others, which results in inadvertent redlining. For instance, when marketers launch new products or expand into new geographical markets, they often select business locations based on criteria such as demographic statistics, the cost of doing business, and crime rates. Naturally, companies choose areas where consumers are affluent and the cost of doing business and crime rates are low, thus bypassing poor communities.

Hence, the conflict between consumer interest and corporate objectives poses an ethical dilemma. A number of banks, insurance underwriters, and mortgage companies, such as American Family Insurance and Chevy Chase Bank, faced lawsuits by minority consumers for alleged discrimination and redlining under the Fair Lending Act and the Fair Housing Act.

Although the companies admitted no wrongdoing in the consent decrees, it is the effect, not the intent, of these marketing practices that causes cries of "redlining" from those experiencing the lack of equity and fairness. In such cases, marketers need to ensure that their market selection and marketing activities are based solely on valid business criteria and consumer characteristics that are not directly related to factors such as age, gender, or ethnicity.

Scenario 6. Demarketing

However, not all exclusive marketing practices are unethical. Some exclusion is not only positive but also necessary to protect consumers (blocks A3B3C1 to A3B2C3). Many social marketing programmes are designed to dissuade consumers from adopting harmful of potentially harmful products, such as alcoholic beverages, cigarettes, and other addictive drugs. In addition to efforts by government agencies and civic organizations, many corporations also sponsor and participate in these programmes.

To encourage responsible consumption of alcohol products and to prevent drunk driving, Anheuser Busch Company, for instance, sponsored a consumer education programme that included advertising, designated drivers, and free taxi rides. These demarketing efforts play a critical role in educating and protecting consumers and minimizing the potential harm to them.

Scenario 7. Reverse Discrimination

Finally, targeting beneficial products at vulnerable and disadvantaged consumers is not entirely without controversies, especially when other groups are not included in these programmes. While marketers may face discontent from disadvantaged consumers—who are the traditional targets of discrimination—lawsuits also come from the non-target segments. For instance, long distance telephone carriers and airlines have designed special promotions for certain nationality groups who make more calls or travel more often to certain destinations. These and other affinity programmes give the target consumers special rates or discounted fare. Members of other ethnic groups, who are automatically disqualified, may cry discrimination for exactly the same reasons as traditional victims of discrimination.

Although most reverse discrimination cases have to do with employment-related issues, some are directly related to social marketing programmes that are designed to assist the disadvantaged. In a number of cases, white entrepreneurs have charged the U.S. Small Business Administration with reverse discrimination, in that these non-members of protected groups have been discriminated against precisely due to their ethnic background. Thus, marketers need to pay attention to the perceptions and responses of non-target groups, who may derive different meanings from such marketing efforts. Any targeted marketing programme should be fair and sensitive to non-target consumer segments.

CUSTOMER EXPECTATION OF SERVICE MANAGEMENT

As the consumer market segment of the Internet economy continues to grow, the role of customer service in the emerging logistics supply chain systems will continue to change. Therefore, the need to improve logistics customer service (LCS) to consumers is greater than ever before. Finding meaningful ways to meet consumer service expectations requires LCS programmes that strategically blend website service activities (e.g., online ordering procedures) with offline logistics supply chain activities (e.g., order delivery).

This balance may be a key strategy in satisfying and maintaining loyalty relationships with online consumers. Yet very little is understood about the nature of website-enabled LCS and the impact on online customer loyalty, although the level of e-logistics service expectations is often thought to be higher than that demanded by customers in brick-and-mortar environments.

The purpose of this study is to examine:

- The factors that determine the level of perceived LCS quality in the Internet-enabled logistics supply chain, and
- The impact of LCS quality on customer loyalty towards online retailers'websites.

Internet-enabled logistics supply chain refers to the total logistics system of transportation, warehousing, inventory, order processing, information flow, and website-enabled order processing procedures that drive the level of perceived quality of LCS in this system. Perceived LCS quality is defined as the level of expectation-minus performance gap and customer intended loyalty is defined as the tendency of online consumers to repurchase from the same website, as reflected in repurchase intentions or intention to recommend a website to peers. Following conventional practice, LCS was defined as the total output of the logistics system, but with emphasis on cognitive impact:

perceived service speed and consistency of service speed, perceived availability of merchandise on the retailer's website and in the supply chain, and perceived responsiveness of the retailer.

This study contributes to the literature on two levels. At the conceptual level, the study provides an empirical validation of the logistics customer service-customer loyalty linkage in the online environment. While this linkage has been widely established in traditional business-to-business markets, it remains to be established in the online environment where the impersonal and self-service nature of customer service may raise doubts about the validity of the LCS-customer linkage.

At the managerial level, the study suggests ways to create a consumer-oriented online logistics customer service strategy by identifying the relevant web-based and traditional supply chain logistics activities that are important in creating and maintaining loyalty relationships with online consumers. As with all service activities, not all website features are likely to be relevant to consumer perception of online LCS quality. Moreover, different website features are likely to play different roles in consumer perception of LCS quality. Thus, this study provides insight into which website features should be emphasized in the different phases of the Internet-enabled logistics supply chain.

The following discussion presents an overview of the influence of website design strategy on LCS quality assessment among online consumers. Using the consumer disconfirmation theory as a theoretical foundation, a conceptual framework is proposed including the hypotheses isolating influences of key website design features on LCS quality, followed by the field study that was conducted to specifically examine the service encounter evaluation of 373 online transactions. Finally, analysis and findings are discussed followed by a discussion of the managerial implications and suggestions for future research.

VALUES AND ATTITUDES DIFFER ACROSS CULTURES

Values and attitudes help to determine what members of a culture think is right, important, and/or desirable. Because behaviours, including consumer behaviours, flow from values and attitudes, services marketers who want their services adopted across, cultures must understand these differences While American brands often have an "exotic" appeal to other cultures, U.S. firms should not count on this as a long-term strategy.

In the late 1990s, Wal-Mart found that the cachet of U.S. brands was falling in Mexico. The Mexican news media alerted consumers to shoddy foreign goods and some Wal- Mart customers turned to a spirit of nationalism. The retailer responded with an "Hecho en Mexico" programme similar to the "Made in the U.S.A." programme that was successful in the United States. In some situations it is more than a case of nationalism: Brand attitudes are negatively influenced by specific prejudices toward "dominating" cultures. The Korean ban on Japanese movies and the French phobia about Euro Disney are good examples of the latter.

STRATEGIES MANAGEMENT IN CUSTOMER SERVICE

The customer service study revealed that no specific tactic, technology, or mission statement is the key to effective customer service delivery. In fact, what is clear is that effective customer service delivery is organization specific, since services are designed around the targeted customers' desires and the frontline employees delivering the services.

The components of the process for producing effective customer service delivery include appropriately identifying and targeting the ideal customer, establishing a customer-focused vision that is consistent with the prioritized desires of the target customers, establishing the operational procedures and internal infrastructure that support customer service, continuously measuring customer and employee satisfaction, embracing change, and striving persistently to improve.

The customer service literature clearly demonstrates that both profit-seeking and public agencies that implement effective customer service strategies realise financial benefits, either through increased profits or through reduced costs associated with long-term, informed customers; customer referrals; employee retention; improved information exchange; and streamlined service delivery.

Child support enforcement, in this case, is like any other business. In order to implement effective customer service strategies and reap the benefits of good customer service, the Office of Child Support Enforcement (OCSE) agencies will need to implement the process of developing effective customer service.

In an effort to become "more results-oriented and responsive to customers," the Office of Child Support Enforcement (OCSE) contracted with Circle Solutions, Inc. to undertake a study of public and private sector practices and outcomes in customer service. The study included a review of customer service literature, a review of the annual reports and Web sites of 40 companies mentioned in the literature, telephone interviews with companies sited as leaders in customer service in the literature, and site visits to three agencies—two private and one child support agency.

Throughout the study, an advisory group of four State child support enforcement directors provided input and feedback. As a final product of the study, this report summarizes the literature on effective approaches to customer service delivery, highlights four promising practice case studies, conjectures about the transferability of these concepts to child support, and offers future research recommendations. Child support enforcement agencies can refer to this report as a guide for improving customer service, as a resource to learn the costs and benefits of effective customer service delivery, and to inspire future inquiries into effective customer service delivery. In the 1990s, IBM conducted global research on the question, "What will keep CEOs and senior management awake at night as we begin the twenty-first century?" The study found that, regardless of the industry or geographic location, the most common response was a desire to generate a more customer-oriented culture or business vision.

Customer service is not merely customer relations or how nice frontline workers are to customers. Rather, satisfying or even delighting customers is the goal of excellent customer service. Because customers for different types of services have different needs, customer service strategies will differ and must be tailored to the target customer.

It improves trust and information exchange: In the public sector, including child support offices, good customer service generates satisfied or delighted customers. Satisfied customers lead to increased compliance, improved information exchange, improved relationships, increased trust, and, potentially, decreased workloads or costs.

For instance, police departments across the Nation have embraced the concept of community policing. Through community policing, police departments incorporate a customer focus as well as an attitude of partnership with customers, to increase satisfaction and trust and even reduce fear of crime in the community. Customers actually participate in addressing crime and disorder problems, thus reducing the workload on patrol officers.

It saves money and increases profit: In the private sector, good customer service leads to satisfied or delighted customers, which generates customer loyalty, which produces increased revenues and reduced costs. For example, during the early 1990s, IBM transformed itself into a customer-driven organization. From 1994–1999, customer satisfaction increased by 5.5 per cent, revenue increased from $63 billion to over $80 billion, cost and expense savings equaled $7 billion, and stock prices improved over 1,000 per cent.

Upon becoming CEO of Greater Southeast Hospital, a private, nonprofit community hospital, Tom Chapman refocused customer service strategy to save the faltering hospital. Instead of trying to attract more clientele outside the community or turning away the uninsured in the community it served, under Chapman's leadership, Greater Southeast sought to provide better customer service—improving the quality of life and creating community-specific services. The emphasis shifted to treating people when it was cheapest—not in the emergency room but rather when their problems were minor—and to instituting preventative care.

He opened a clinic in the high school to address minor health issues and provide health education resources to teach students about prevention. Additionally, Mr. Chapman improved coordination with the local health clinic and obtained the specific technology from which patients served by the hospital would benefit. Before his arrival, Greater Southeast spent only

$20,000–$30,000 a year on a blood pressure programme, although a single stroke victim could cost $30,000 to treat. The public and private sector customer service literature concurs on the process for delivering great customer service, even if outcomes differ. The current literature supports an outside-in strategy of customer service, rather than the traditional inside-out model for providing services. In the private sector, profit and growth are the *outcomes,* not goals.

Profit and growth are generated by customer loyalty. Loyalty is generated by customer satisfaction. Customer satisfaction is the *goal* that companies should seek and focus on, because high customer satisfaction, as a matter of course, produces customer loyalty and subsequently profit and growth. At this point, the public and private sectors converge—customer satisfaction is the *goal.*

Customer satisfaction is achieved by providing valued services and products, where value is the positive difference between customers' actual experiences and their service delivery expectations. Productive employees also create value.

Employee productivity stems from employee loyalty, and loyalty is a product of employee satisfaction. Satisfaction is generated by high-quality support services (people, information, and technology) and by being empowered to provide value and resolve customer complaints. This customer service culture must be supported by leadership that emphasizes the importance of each customer and employee. These leaders must be creative and energetic (not lofty or conservative), participatory and caring (not removed or elitist), that is, one who can be a coach, teacher, or listener (not just a supervisor or manager).

Such a leader demonstrates company values (rather than simply institutionalizing policies) and motivates by mission (rather than by fear). Some components of this model are cyclical. A 1991 study of property and casualty insurance companies found that employees who felt that they were meeting customer needs had twice the job satisfaction level of employees who did not believe they were meeting customer needs. In that study, when a frontline service worker left the company, customer satisfaction levels dropped from 75 to 55 per cent.

In the customer service literature, five guiding principles are adopted by public as well as private agencies delivering excellent customer service:

- Embrace change and persistently strive to improve (be a learning organization).
- Continually ask the target customers what they want and then give it to them.
- Empower, support, and reward frontline personnel.
- Harness the power of information.
- Establish an enabling infrastructure.
- Identify the Target Customer.

  - Begin by identifying the target customers and by considering the point of purchase, point of service delivery or receipt, and point of consumption.
  - Cluster or segment target customers based on their common behaviours, knowing that targeting the wrong customers can have adverse effects on the organization.
  - Determine the priorities of various clusters of customers, knowing that the capabilities of the organization are crucial in addressing these priorities.
  - When possible, focus on customers with high current or future value. (Perhaps in child support this is a custodial parent with many children in the system.) This does not mean that other customers will not receive service, but it may mean that they will receive a different level of service. Consider the frequent flier programmes that airlines and hotels offer to their customers with high current and future value. This does not mean that other passengers will not receive services, but services may not be at the same level.
  - Discourage non-target customers, those who are not likely to be satisfied by the services, and those to whom it is expensive to provide services, which is a necessary part of a customer focus. A simple example is offered as an illustration. A fire department could discourage residents from contacting the department to remove cats from trees by charging a $20 fee for performing the service and by advertising their busy emergency call load. The equipment and time investment of sending a ladder truck and several firefighters may reduce the effectiveness of the department at responding to an emergency and may not be the most prompt means of accomplishing the task for the customer.
- Determine What Customers Want..
  - Determine what target customers want (not just what they need right now) by asking them in person or as part of a mail or telephone survey or by using other mechanisms (e.g., electronic tracking and researching marketing trends) to determine what they want. Be aware that advertising, word of mouth, and public relations influence customers'expectations. Meeting customers'basic needs or expectations does not always bring high levels of satisfaction. Exceeding expectations produces high satisfaction-therefore, determine customers'ideal desires.
  - Determine how the target customers prioritize their "wants."Generally, customers want convenience, quality products and services, variety or selection, low prices, and protection or security. However, each organization must identify what is most important to its customers.

- Weigh how important the customer-identified"wants"are to the organization. Are the services something that the organization does, is capable of doing, or wants to pursue?
- Determine how well the organization can meet the customers'"wants"in comparison with competitors. The success of other companies at meeting and exceeding customer expectations changes a customer's frame of reference and increases a customer's expectations.
- Determine which"wants,"if performance delivery were to be improved, would most impact the organization's bottom line (profit, cost, loyalty, trust, or compliance).

• Establish an Organizational Culture Supportive of Customer Service.
  - Utilizing the information gathered, establish the company's customer-focused vision. The vision statement should be simple and may also identify what the company does not want to be. Some examples of simple vision statements include"Absolutely, Positively Overnight"by Federal Express and L.L. Bean's promise "Guaranteed. Period."
  - Live up to what is promised by concurrently developing and applying externally and internally oriented strategic service concepts that reflect the vision. If the organization does not implement both internally and externally oriented service strategies consistent with the vision, the organization will have good intentions but poor customer service (Thompson).
  - Continually reflect on the vision and goals and the way services are delivered to customers. Be creative about the mechanisms used to create and deliver new services. Be willing to change existing practices to integrate improvements.

• Implement an Externally Oriented Strategic Service Concept. The externally oriented strategic service concept establishes how the organization's service is designed, marketed, and delivered to target customers.
  - Take into account the costs of providing services and ways to minimize those costs while implementing quality control. The service concept must be developed with the frontline worker at its centre. Determine the necessary financial, human, and technological resources necessary, as well as how the organizational structure and flow can enable the frontline worker to delight the customer and deliver the promised vision.
  - Use advertising/educational strategies to set appropriate customer expectations.
  - When planning, realise that control of information can take the place of assets. For instance, the Rural/Metro Fire Department in Scottsdale (AZ) has reduced the size of its crew and trucks

because of technology that allows crews to view microfiche floor plans on the way to a fire. The added knowledge of the building layout allows fewer fire fighters to accomplish the same task that requires more firefighters when they do not have this advance knowledge.

- Provide a feedback loop for incorporating customer comments and complaints into the planning processes. Customer complaints are an invaluable resource and source of information without which organizations cannot be successful. Complaints brought to the organization are one of the most efficient and least expensive ways to obtain information about customer expectations of products and services. Complaints are a more direct means of obtaining information than conducting research studies of customer expectations, conducting transaction studies, or reviewing customer expectations in parallel industries. Another means of soliciting customer feedback that has been implemented by a number of service leaders is to interview lost customers-those who have switched service providers. (Perhaps in child support these customers were custodial parents who had been making timely payments but who stopped doing so.) Still other options are holding customer meetings, hosting social events, and attending seminars or conferences where customers are present.

  Ensure that the complaint resolution strategy supports the customer-focused vision. Most research shows, "...if customers believe their complaints are welcomed and responded to, they will more likely repurchase." British Airways found that 67 per cent of its complaining passengers fly again if their complaints are handled well. British Airways even implemented a creative and convenient way to allow customers to complain by installing video booths at Heathrow Airport so that customers could immediately go into a booth and state a complaint, even during non-business hours. The videotapes are reviewed and addressed during business hours.
- One final element of an externally oriented service strategy is to regularly measure customer satisfaction or delight in the products and services.

• Implement an Internally Oriented Strategic Service Concept.

The internally oriented strategic service concept establishes how the organization's internal processes will support the customer-focused vision. The premise behind the internally oriented strategic service concept is "...capable workers who are well trained and fairly compensated provide better service, need less supervision, and are much more likely to stay on the job. As a result, their customers are likely to be more satisfied...". A study by

Sears in 1989 found that "employee turnover and customer satisfaction are directly correlated." Stores with high customer service ratings had a 54 per cent sales force turnover versus 83 per cent in stores with low customer service ratings. This is supported by examples throughout the literature. Taco Bell found that the 20 per cent of stores with the lowest employee turnover rates have 55 per cent higher profits (an outcome of customer satisfaction) than the 20 per cent of stores with the highest turnover rates.

A number of other studies provide convincing evidence as to why companies should avoid employee turnover. Merck and Co. found in 1990 that turnover costs were 1.5 times an employee's annual salary. Clearly this varies based on a number of cost factors (e.g., workers compensation claims, hiring process costs, training costs, and lost business), but it is commonly noted that employee turnover is an expensive problem. Abt Associates studied an automobile dealer's sales and determined that it cost $36,000 to replace a salesperson with 5–8 years of experience with a salesperson with less than 1 year of experience.

The economic costs of excessive employee turnover in one trucking company were analysed, and it was determined that the company could increase profits by 50 per cent by cutting driver turnover in half.

- Ensure that leaders of the learning organization exhibit the company values. Leaders must foster the creation and testing of new ideas and be unabashedly willing to change existing practices to integrate improvements.
- Identify employee groups important to implementing the externally oriented service concept. Frontline workers are of central importance.
  - Identify the characteristics and needs of the employee group(s) and how well those needs are met. This may include resources needed to successfully perform the job or needs can refer to compensation, work environmental factors, or personal needs. Understanding employee needs helps an organization to develop successful processes as well as employee retention policies. Learn how targeted employees perceive the proposed customer services. An organization cannot change without the participation of its employees.
- Focus on recruiting employees who support the customer service vision. The costs of employing people who do not support the customer service vision are considerable. Forum Corporation research in the service industry showed, "...only 14% [per cent] of customers who stop patronizing service businesses do so because they are dissatisfied with what they bought. More than two-thirds defect because they find service people indifferent or unhelpful." Oftentimes, the right employees are those that fit in with the corporate culture's customer service vision, not necessarily those

with the most experience in the industry. Additionally, develop career paths that allow successful customer-oriented employees to remain on the frontline.

- Focus on training and employee development throughout employment. A study by Ryder Truck from 1988 through 1989 found that increased training meant lower employee turnover.
- Empower frontline employees to do what it takes to satisfy the customer. Management must support employee empowerment by clearly defining the parametres of the empowerment, while remaining flexible within the parametres. This will encourage creativity. Rules should be simple and few—Continental Airlines actually had an employee handbook burning party to signify the change from a procedural environment to one of empowered customer service. Also, in support of internal customers, the Department of Defence reduced its 230 pages of travel regulations to 17 pages.
- Ensure that management supports employee decisions and judgment calls, even if this means that the cost of satisfying customers initially increases. In positions of high customer contact, quality control is not met by increased supervision, but by the use of incentives to emphasize quality, making service providers highly visible to customers, and by building a peer group to instill a sense of pride and teamwork.
- In addition to skills and empowerment, equip frontline personnel with the technology, information, and internal resources to do what it takes to satisfy the customer. The literature is replete with examples of how incorporating the latest information technology can improve employee productivity. For example, Charles Schwab developed IWIN, a system that allows an agent to identify and view electronically Charles Schwab literature to respond to customer questions received by telephone. Before this system was implemented, agents who were unfamiliar with the literature in question could not provide immediate and succinct answers to customer questions.
- Ensure that divisions and individuals within the organization communicate. Frontline employees and other employees need information and a support network. A customer should never have to tell one employee what another employee already knows.
- Develop cross-functional teams for operations and improvement tasks. First ask those who are doing the work for suggestions to improve productivity. The Social Security Administration nearly doubled its telephone-answering capacity by implementing automated features, utilizing additional technology to change the

way employers' reports of wages are recorded, and cross training its employees to work outside their normal areas of responsibility during peak periods.

- Link all employees' compensation to (and offer rewards for) good customer service performance. Rewards can be money, status, praise, acknowledgement, or perks such as trips or special events. While Charles Schwab does provide monetary incentives based on the amount of money a broker team brings into the company, if the customer service survey for the quarter does not show strong customer service by the team, the reward is reduced or even eliminated for the quarter. This policy in a profit-seeking environment leaves no doubt that customer satisfaction is the primary goal.
- Finally, measure employee satisfaction regularly. Leaders in the service industry have employed such methods as toll-free numbers, periodic roundtable meetings, and surveys to collect employee satisfaction information.

DETERMINE WHAT CUSTOMERS SERVICE

Want and Give It to Them

A number of child support agencies, including those in Texas and California, have implemented customer surveys. Customer surveys can and should be used to determine what child support customers most want from child support services and to seek input on improving services, collect baseline information by which to measure results of improvements to the system, and to reinforce a customer focus.

The Urban Institute prepared a sample customer survey for OCSE from which questions could be gleaned, and child support agencies also may use one another as a resource for samples.

Implement an Externally Oriented Strategic Service Culture

Establishing an externally oriented strategic service culture in child support follows the same process as similar procedures in the private sector. In this culture, management places an emphasis on minimizing costs, increasing quality control measures, educating customers, establishing a customer complaint mechanism and resolution strategy, and measuring customer satisfaction.

Both First Interstate Bank and Cherner Automotive Group offer creative quality control procedures. At Cherner and FIB, frontline supervisors serve as coaches or mentors and are trained to serve in this capacity. FIB has a policy to"inspect what they expect."In child support services, rather than relying only on statistics or monthly reports about the quality of services at field offices, central office management could regularly visit child support field offices. The visit would include discussions with field office managers regarding operations, observations of customer interactions with staff, auditing and reviewing measures identified as important to customer service, addressing patterns of complaints, brainstorming on improvement opportunities, and rewarding excellent customer service practices.

A creative customer education tool used by FIB is the I-Beetle. Employees of FIB drive a Volkswagen Beetle painted with an advertisement for FIB's Web site. This takes the message to the customers-during traffic jams, on trips to the supermarket, while shopping at the mall, etc. Opportunistic marketing may be something worth considering in child support. Messages about responsible parenting or a new child support Web site or call centre telephone number could be distributed where child support customers are already going-whether at the supermarket, on downtown streets, at shopping malls, at job placement centres, or at the town ball field.

California Child Support Services has automated its complaint tracking and established an Interagency Agreement with the Department of Social Services, State Hearing Office, to conduct State hearings when appropriate.

Implement an Internally Oriented Strategic Service Culture: Implementing an internally oriented strategic service culture in child support means hiring the right people; continually training employees in customer service; seeking input from employees; empowering, rewarding, and supporting frontline personnel; utilizing technology to reduce the workload on CSOs and other frontline personnel and to provide easy access to information; creating an enabling environment where discretion is clearly defined and frontline judgment calls are supported by management; utilizing cross-functional teams; and measuring employee satisfaction.

This may mean hiring staff with an aptitude and attitude for customer service, even if child support skills must subsequently be learned. Such a culture may also be actualized through software that categorizes and automatically queues cases for attention by CSOs, based on the status of the case. This means instituting incentives for providing great customer service, whether perks, recognition, or merit raises. It also means that divisions or departments within child support services must communicate and cooperate with one another. It includes proactively attempting to deter burnout of CSOs and call takers by encouraging staff to take appropriate breaks and eat lunch away from work, use vacation time, and modify the work that a person does.

What Recommendations or Lessons Learned Do the Model Agencies Interviewed Offer to OCSE?

- Understand that good customer service takes time, patience, persistence, consistency in message at all levels, accountability, courtesy, respect, and emphasis on team players.
- Make sure upper management and executives at the top are sold on a customer service culture.

- Put a human face on customers—treat them with a personal touch, rather than as a collective.
- Make it easy for customers to do business with the service.
- Listen to customers to learn what they need and want.
- Address the immediate needs of the customer.
- Hire the right people by hiring on attitude and training on the skill.
- Mentor new employees.
- Manage by staying close to the frontline.
- Train the frontline on how to address customer problems.
- "Inspect" what you "expect."
- Don't focus energies on the bad apples—put energies and resources into those employees that want to work in customer service.
- Ensure that management/executives listen to their employees' complaints (without interruption) and have trust in their employees.
- Ask open-ended questions.
- Have uniform expectations of the customers.
- Establish uniform processes, policies, and procedures to collect payments. Customers must be able to expect the same expertise, collection efforts, production, recovery, and professional delivery regardless of which branch or individual is working.
- Develop working relationships with other partners (e.g., courts, credit card companies, vendors, or other banks) that play a role in debt collection.
- When working with a customer complaint, try to understand the customer as well as those available to help address the problem.
- Frontline employees should mentally separate themselves from problems in an effort to address the issue so that the outcome is positive for all involved.
- Maintain an orderly work atmosphere.

The results of this study provide a glimpse of how child support agencies may be able to strategically plan and implement a customer-focused culture and the benefits that child support agencies should expect from successfully implementing excellent customer service. The study also suggests several possible areas for future study:

- OCSE may consider selecting one or several elements of the process for further study. For example, what specific performance measures may be appropriately implemented for child support officers when the agency has a customer focus? Circle Solutions, Inc. (Circle) has recently received a contract from the Department of Justice to conduct a school resource officer performance measures study and pilot programme with four police agencies that are implementing community policing in schools. Under this programme, customers and stakeholders in school safety are participating in the development of the performance measures. A similar pilot programme could be adapted and utilized for child support agencies.

- OCSE may consider studying the effectiveness of specific customer service strategies in child support enforcement in pilot states that implement the customer service process outlined in this study.
- OCSE may wish to highlight many more promising customer service practices in child support across the Nation. Case examples or a compilation of examples within the structure of the customer service process could offer States a point from which to brainstorm.
- OCSE may wish to create a toolkit for developing a customer-focused culture. Circle Solutions recently completed a"Collaboration Toolkit"for the Department of Justice. The Toolkit is a nuts-and-bolts guide for law enforcement and their partners to develop, fix, and sustain productive law enforcement-community partnerships to support the advancement of community policing. The Toolkit offers worksheets and exercises for working through pitfalls and organizing these efforts, and it refers the reader to resources to learn more. A similar toolkit presentation of the customer service process may be useful for State child support agencies.
- OCSE may also wish to explore in more detail some creative strategies of serving customers related to co-location of child support with other offices or businesses, payment choices, call management, training strategies, etc.

Certainly, this study lends itself to a great deal of further exploration. The study revealed that no specific tactic, technology, or mission statement is the key to effective customer service delivery. In fact, what is clear is that effective customer service delivery is organization specific, since services are designed around the targeted customers' desires and the frontline employees delivering them. The components of the process for producing effective customer service delivery include appropriately identifying and targeting the ideal customer, establishing a customer-focused vision that is consistent with the prioritized desires of the target customers, establishing operational procedures and internal infrastructure that support customer service, continuously measuring customer and employee satisfaction, embracing change, and striving persistently to improve.

The customer service literature clearly demonstrates that both profit-seeking and public agencies that implement effective customer service strategies realise financial benefits, either through increased profits or through reduced costs associated with long-term, informed customers, customer referrals, employee retention, improved information exchange, and streamlined service delivery. In this case, child support enforcement is like any other business. In order to implement effective customer service strategies and reap the benefits of good customer service, child support agencies will need to implement the process of developing effective customer service.

SERVICESCAPE TYPES, SERVICESCAPE EFFECTS ON BEHAVIOUR

Servicescape is a concept that was developed by Booms and Bitner to emphasize the impact of the physical environment in which a service process takes place. If you were to try to describe the differences a customer encountered when entering a branch of say like McDonald's compared with a small family restaurant, the concept of servicescapes may prove useful. Booms and Bitner defined a servicescape as "the environment in which the service is assembled and in which the seller and customer interact, combined with tangible commodities that facilitate performance or communication of the service".

Servicescape may be likened to 'landscape'. It includes facilities exterior (landscape, exterior design, signage, parking, surrounding environment) and facilities interior (interior design and decor, equipment, signage, layout, air quality, temperature and ambiance). Servicescape along with other tangibles like business cards, stationary, billing statements, reports, employee dress, uniforms, brochures, web pages and virtual servicescape forms the 'Physical Evidence' in marketing of services. Servicescape is not defined as above. The definition above is the definition for physical evidence. Physical evidence consist of servicescape combined with the tangible elements, so servicescape is a part of physical evidence.

5

Customer Management Systems

INTRODUCTION

Companies need a method for viewing all customer and marketing-related information in an integrated way. Often marketing organizations maintain multiple databases for each business and marketing activity with data that is not easily integrated for strategic or operational purposes. A new generation of software that is Internet based gathers information from customer service, Web sites, direct mail operations, telemarketing, field sales, customer service, distributors, retailers and suppliers for the purpose of managing marketing, sales and customer service activities.

The major applications families are commonly referred to as sales force automation (SFA) and customer relationship management (CRM) systems. Some CRM systems are fully integrated with SFA applications and some are standalone. The worldwide market for such systems is projected to grow five times faster than the overall software market, from $5 billion in 1999 to more than $22 billion in 2003.

SALES FORCE AUTOMATION

The fastest growing elements of the MkIS. SFA applications are often integrated with the CRM system. SFA involves the application of information technology to the sales function or, more appropriately, to the activities leading to a sale. These activities include acquiring sales leads, managing the sales opportunity, closing the sale and managing the customer relationship.

The historic role of personal selling has been to move the product—to generate transactions. As selling has become increasingly more professional, sales people emphasize building relationships with customers that will generate loyalty-based repeat transactions over time. Relationship building often necessitates that the sales person has consultative and advisory skills in addition to product knowledge and sales abilities. Team-based selling places emphasis on role specialization, collaboration and coordination. Customers have become more sophisticated as well. Requirements for customised solutions, rapid response times and the need for concurrent and post-sale service have greatly increased the need for information technology in the sales process. The goals of SFA are to increase the effectiveness of the sales organization, improve its efficiency and to create superior value for the customer.

Sales effectiveness focuses on getting the sale by improving lead generation, qualifying prospects, coordinating sales efforts, and tracking commitments. Effectiveness is a function of improving the sales process. *Sales efficiency* is evaluated by measuring the return on sales efforts. SFA can improve sales efficiency by reducing sales cycle time, by managing workflow, and tracking the current status of critical activities related to the sale. Proposal generation, opportunity management, fulfillment, and follow up are facilitated by SFA. *Superior customer value* is achieved when the customer expectations are exceeded. It is a primary determinant of customer satisfaction. SFA enables better understanding of customer expectations and management of the customer account.

CUSTOMER RELATIONSHIP MANAGEMENT

The Internet has facilitated a fundamental shift in market power from sellers to buyers. Customers, newly endowed with the power of market information, have much different expectations than before. Customers can easily move their business to another vendor with the click of a mouse. They have access to the same cost data as their suppliers and they demand 24x7 customer service. Customers now have almost unlimited ability for interactions with organizations through the Web in addition to the traditional phone and mail methods. Company web sites facilitate information search, shopping and customer support. E-mail communication can target specific offers on a one-to-one basis. Understanding and meeting demanding expectations has placed a renewed emphasis on managing customer relationships.

The primary goal of CRM systems is to increase the return on marketing expenditures by enabling the understanding of the complete history of a firm's interactions with its customers. CRM applications can deliver targeted solutions that promote customer loyalty as measured by increased response to promotions, purchase frequencies and volume, and minimizes the time between orders. CRM systems are able to target marketing communications to likely buyers, facilitate sales efforts and deliver customer service. CRM systems increase revenue, lower costs and optimize customer lifetime value.

Design Principles

The CRM field is rapidly evolving into an integrated discipline that manages all of a company's touches with the customer.

Accordingly, several design principles have evolved as the foundation for CRM development:

- The CRM system should offer the customer multiple channels for communication such as the telephone, e-mail, fax, on-line or some combination. Each channel should lead to an interaction that satisfies customer expectations. Customers must be able to choose the method that best meets their needs on each occasion.

- Each CRM interaction should deliver value to the customer. The CRM system must be able to determine what value is required and deliver it quickly whether it is a product or service transaction or a customer service request.
- The CRM system integrates the customer throughout the firm's value chain. Customers should be able to reach into all necessary functions of the organization not just to the sales organization, or customer service, but to manufacturing and even the CEO. Better integration of the customer into the process can lead to higher levels of trust, loyalty and repeat purchases. The cost of acquiring a new customer often far exceeds that of retaining existing ones.
- Knowledge is captured during each CRM interaction. The CRM system should capture knowledge about the customer and the customer's relationship with the company over time. Sales and customer support histories should be analysed for indications of how well the vendor is doing in meeting customers' needs and how valuable the customer is to the marketer.

Functions

CRM applications provide the customer-related information that is necessary to drive a firm's ebusiness activities. Better customer information enables more effective demand forecasting, product launches and marketing campaigns. CRM functions are sometimes referred to as the company's "front office."

CRM functionality includes:

- E-commerce support
- Sales force automation
- Telesales and call centre automation
- Direct mail and catalog sales
- Email and e-newsletter response
- Web sales and personalization
- Analysis of Web generated data
- Traditional customer support and service
- On-line support and customer service
- Mobile support through laptops, handheld devices.
- Training

Modern CRM systems are fully integrated with the "back office" elements of the enterprise resource planning (ERP) system such as accounting, manufacturing, project management, and human resources. This integration enables the sharing of customer information that can impact the operations of the enterprise and vice versa. Common customer definitions, price lists, employee definitions, service requests, call histories, order histories, contracts, service level agreements are accessible by all who need them. Correspondingly, marketing can access information on items such as new product development, product costs, order status, delivery dates and backorders.

CUSTOMERS WORKING MANAGEMENT

FMC stresses the importance of creating a holistic customer service culture by beginning with upper-level management and actualizing this goal among all staff including frontline personnel. The framework for the customer service culture at FMC includes learning what the customers want; implementing steps to provide for those wants for which a business case can be made; equipping frontline employees with training, information, empowerment, and motivation; and monitoring success through customer and employee feedback mechanisms.

When the U.S. call centres were being developed, the director researched other call centres to find a model for their design. In favour of economies of scale (related to technology, resources, and personnel), FMC implemented call centre access on a national scale at four sites. Even with this consolidated design, FMC is committed to providing personalized service.

Call centre management utilizes customer telephone and mail survey results as well as focus group findings to guide implementation. Once analysed, this information is provided to the areas within the call centre for which it applies. (For example, customer feedback about loan rates goes to employees responsible for making policy decisions about rates. Customer input about experiences and interactions with personnel are provided to staff in training and human resources.)

Call centre managers are expected to coach and mentor call takers, based on performance during quality control checks. FMC management utilizes formal feedback initiatives to ensure that communication between the frontline and management remains open. One of these programmes is the Voice of the Customer Committee. On this committee, frontline workers meet with management during a monthly meeting at which staff relay what customers want, based on their interactions with customers that month and over time. Another mechanism, the Ideas Programme, offers an opportunity for frontline personnel to submit a proposal to management on how to improve customer service. Employees are rewarded for submitting proposals, and when ideas are implemented, a gift card is provided.

Frontline employees, especially through the Voice of the Customer Committee, have made important contributions to improving customer service at FMC. For example, frontline staff identified necessary changes in the voice menu wording, suggested options that should be added and some to omit from the phone tree menu, and identified customers' information needs. Frontline personnel are encouraged not only to report to management any processes that are not working, but to offer potential solutions.

The key to hiring someone on the front line, according to FMC management, is to hire staff with a passion for customer service. Training for FMC staff includes training on teams, as well as learning how to give and receive feedback, how to be a good team member, and how to improve telephone communication skills.

One important motivator for employees is the policy within the company that includes customer satisfaction as a determining factor in employee compensation. Quarterly, customer telephone survey results are tabulated, and employees receive bonuses that are tied directly to their scores. Also, prizes are offered for customer letters or phone calls of praise. Lunches are offered to teams who perform well in customer service.

In an effort to make the payment process as convenient as possible for customers, FMC piloted a phone pay system through Western Union. Currently, this programme produces 350,000 transactions each month. Other pay options include direct electronic payments from a bank account or payroll deduction and Internet-based payment processing. Twenty-two per cent of FMC payments are processed electronically. At the time of this report, they are also considering whether to permit credit card payments.

During a month when the customer simply cannot pay, FMC works with customers who struggle to make full and timely payments. For example, a customer may be permitted to skip a payment and add that payment to the end of the loan. Another option is reducing the amount of the monthly payment and extending the length of the loan. Accountability is enforced through late payment charges and reports made to the credit bureau.

Customer service is key to the day-to-day operation of Cherner Automotive Group (Cherner). This sentiment is echoed from the frontline employee to the upper-level executive. The Cherner philosophy of customer service delivery is customer satisfaction through continued friendly communication and interaction, coupled with accessibility and responsiveness. Cherner's approach is very individualized, and they believe that customer service is relative to the customer being served. In no case did a Cherner employee claim to be in the business of selling vehicles; rather, employees view themselves as"in the people business."Building customer relationships is underscored. Cherner employees realise that exemplary customer service brings in new customers, as well as repeat customers. This is accomplished by reputation or referral.

Cherner operates two dealerships, both of which are located in the Northern Virginia technology corridor. Cherner has a wide customer base that includes retired persons, business professionals, members of Congress, and community residents. Many Cherner customers are repeat customers or referrals.

Cherner is a family-owned and -operated business. The corporate culture embraces change; strives to learn what customers want and gives it to them; and seeks both customer and employee loyalty. Cherner considers customers'first impressions to be important and strives to create a warm and inviting environment. Cherner employees attempt to make customers feel welcome and to provide individualized attention.

The only"formal"policies for making this occur include the"10-foot rule,"whereby employees who are in the area should acknowledge customers within this range and ask to be of assistance, and a policy that all customers who enter the dealership are acknowledged within 30 seconds. Cherner employees understand the value of smiling and being pleasant to all customers.

According to Cherner staff at all levels of the company, customers deserve responsiveness. The ability to individualize service is, in their opinion, what sets them apart in customer service delivery. There are no written guidelines, but employees have a degree of autonomy in making decisions.

For example, the service advisor has the latitude to refund money or to adjust a charge ticket. The core ideology is that each employee is encouraged to do whatever it takes within reason-based on the situation-to serve a customer immediately. Employees are discouraged from having a"this is my job or that is not my job"attitude. Rather, all employees work for the same company and every employee is responsible for serving customers and making them happy.

Integral to Cherner's customer service delivery is the need to understand customer expectations. Cherner listens to their customers and provides convenient forums for customer feedback. The most widely used method is their customer satisfaction survey. Each customer who purchases an automobile receives a questionnaire from Ford Motor Company. The results are shared with the dealer. Also, Cherner hires an outside company to phone a sample of their service customers to collect data on customer satisfaction. These findings are presented in the monthly report"Viewpoint."The service area also has a customer feedback/suggestion box, posted beside the cash register.

Staff at all levels of the organization articulated their customer service orientation as:

- Being pleasant and smiling at customers.
- Being a good listener (and being empathetic to customers'situations).
- Doing the job right the first time.
- Being accountable.
- Building trusting relationships with customers.
- Treating people fairly.
- Making customers fully happy.
- Being willing to apologize.

Cherner's owners and managers set the tone for the company. Managers are expected to"lead by example."The general manager adheres to a policy of"Management by Walking Around."In other words, he and other managers try to stay connected with employees throughout the organization by working side-by-side with them. Senior-level executives have an open-door policy and solicit employee input during staff meetings. Calls are not screened, so customers also can contact managers directly.

Managers attempt to empower employees by providing a supportive environment in which employees are encouraged to make decisions. Managers are expected to coach frontline staff. During interviews, frontline personnel indicated that if a frontline employee were experiencing difficulties, managers would speak with that individual and coach him/her. However, frontline staff felt that improvement would be expected and that the employee would be held accountable for improving, or the employee would be terminated. As an employee's experience increases, so does the amount of discretion allotted to the employee.

Cherner frontline personnel perceive that they are supported by management in that whatever they feel they cannot handle can be turned over to management, with frontline staff confident that the situation will be addressed. Management also listens and responds to the needs of the employees.

This is handled in different ways. For example, when employees in service determine that they need some training or equipment to do the job better, they can write the request on a white board designed for this purpose, and a member of management will address the request (and keep the notation on the board until the request is resolved). The white board is also an information-sharing tool for frontline employees. Employee meetings are an another forum for raising and addressing issues.

Most of the dealership's employees have longevity with the company. During each discussion with Cherner employees, regardless of organizational level, the interviewee acknowledged that to deliver great customer service, a company must hire and retain the right people. Managers added that "the right person" is one who can get along with others, possesses good judgment, can work on a team, is motivated, and possesses the desire to grow and learn. Cherner wants to hire sales personnel who are motivated not by money, but rather by the desire to help people.

Cherner offers multifaceted, ongoing training for employees. In order to continually provide effective customer service, employees are trained both in-house and by the manufacturers. Ford Star Satellite training, Ford's training facility in Centreville (VA) and printed training materials from KIA and ISUZU are designed to keep employees current on various features and aspects of the products being sold and serviced. Other training offered is designed to enhance selling techniques and customer service and to update technicians on vehicle and repair technology. In the past, employees received gender sensitivity training that was offered to improve customer service for female customers.

Among the most creative training strategies is Cherner's frontline mentoring system, whereby a senior salesperson mentors a new salesperson for 90 days. The senior salesperson is responsible for teaching sales basics, orienting the new employee to Cherner culture and attitude, describing Cherner products, and detailing processes. One frontline employee stated that this type of mentoring is a key component to great customer service that is transferable to other organizations.

At all levels of the organization, employees reported being very self-motivated—driven by personal pride and the desire to do a great job. This may be a result of Cherner's hiring policies as well as employees' positive perceptions of their work environment.

Most of those that were interviewed commented that separate and distinct from the actual family ownership of the dealership, the working environment feels like a family environment. Employees know and talk with one another, even across departments; employees support one another; employee picnics and gatherings allow families to get to know each other; and employees simply "get along." This family environment proves to be a strong motivator for Cherner employees at all levels.

Another motivator that was mentioned comes directly from individual customers. Employees reported receiving Christmas cards, gifts, notes, and personal appreciation and friendship from satisfied customers. Cherner, as well as the vehicle manufacturers, offers incentives to foster and sustain employee motivation. Cherner sponsors contests, and the winners are given free tickets to sporting events or dinner coupons, monetary awards, and other "per's" (e.g., use of a vehicle, recognition, etc.) Rewards are also offered based on customer survey scores, reported by Ford. At times, there are luncheons or dinners.

Rather than a point-in-time formalized evaluation process, employees are continuously recognized for good service. Similarly, management addresses negative behaviour as it is observed or identified via customer surveys or complaints and seeks to correct this behaviour through mentoring and coaching.

Technology is a resource primarily used for training and in the service area. Service employees are linked to each of the manufacturer's databases and have access to sophisticated on-line reference manuals. They are connected to nationwide databases that have background information on the history of the car, as well as customer history. This allows for a more detailed, efficient, and expedient service call and better customer service.

Ford Star is a satellite training initiative that allows employees to remain at the dealership while receiving training. Employees can even take the required tests and receive their scores via the Internet. This lends convenience for employees being trained.

The attitude of customer responsiveness holds true for complaints. Employees echoed the same sentiment: "If you receive it, handle it. If you can't handle it, find someone who can until the problem is solved." Employees explained that complaints are an information resource for them, and that they utilize the information to improve services. Cherner boasts a low turnover rate, estimated at approximately 10 per cent. In fact, an average employee will remain with Cherner for 10 years. The General Manager has been with Cherner for 29 years. This low turnover is attributed to the family-oriented atmosphere, competitive wages, and knowledge that the jobs at Cherner are secure (as Cherner does not have a history of layoffs).

One challenge to this positive environment has been a recent decision to respond to customer and manufacturer desires to operate on Saturdays. As such, employees who used to be off each weekend now find themselves working on some Saturdays. In an effort to reduce employee burnout or turnover that such a change may produce, Cherner offers special incentives to these employees. For example, an employee who works on Saturday may choose to take the following Monday off (service advisors can take Friday) or to be paid for an extra day of work at overtime rates. Management also provides lunch for employees who work on Saturday.

Cherner focuses on outcomes rather than the process. Cherner offers its vehicle repair customers a shuttle back to work, within a reasonable distance, or to the transit station. However, Cherner recognizes that because of local traffic conditions, offering this service during evening rush hour is counterproductive.

Therefore, customers are reimbursed for cab fare back to Cherner when traveling from the transit station to Cherner to pick up a vehicle during evening rush hour. While Cherner could have told customers that the shuttle does not run during rush hour and that transportation would have to be arranged on their own or during non-rush hours, Cherner went the extra mile with customers and found a mutually beneficial way of providing this service.

Cherner aims to exceed customer expectations. When customers have their vehicles at Cherner to be serviced, they are provided with complementary car washes. Cherner proclaims that the benefits of customer service delivery are happier customers, high employee morale, employee and customer loyalty, free advertising (word of mouth), and sales generation. "If you do it right the first time, you won't have to do it again." This is the premise from which they operate.

Satisfaction the first time results in not having to spend more labour hours rectifying a situation. This, in turn, makes daily business operations more fluid and service more efficient. Satisfaction the first time also enhances the dealership's community reputation as that of a professional, people-oriented business. This business stance generates a larger customer base. High employee morale is also a benefit of good customer service. Employees take pride in their work.

The costs to Cherner for delivering great customer service include employee incentive costs, salaries, and bonuses; training costs; car wash expenses; shuttle service expenses; and write-off costs for services performed but not charged to the customer. As part of its external customer service strategy, the Child Support Division in Texas has developed a programme called *Compact with Texans,* which outlines the vision, guiding principles, and goals of the division and explains how external customers can continue to provide feedback on child support.

The guiding principles are:

- Always do what is best for the child, by putting children first.
- Treat everyone with dignity, respect, honesty, and courtesy.
- Walk in the customer's shoes—have empathy.
- Be a leader in doing the right thing, not just in doing things right.
- Participate and contribute in finding solutions—work as a team.
- Maintain objectivity and be nonjudgmental.
- Respect customer' privacy.
- Bear in mind that the customers' perceptions of reality are their reality.

These principles are designed as the framework for action at the agency and individual levels when serving both internal and external customers. Everyone in the division is provided with a copy of these principles to hang on their office walls, and these principles are also posted in conference rooms and hallways throughout the office.

To advance these principles, the customer service action plan addresses:

- Improving access to services and staff by implementing regional call centres; expanding and publicizing the Office of the Attorney General (OAG) Child Support Web site—including online application for services; publicizing the complaint process on posters and the Internet; considering a plan to increase office hours; and putting computers in six office lobbies, on which customers may access some case information as well as conduct job searches.
- Ensuring comprehensive, accurate, and easily accessible information that is easy to understand by recording information about billing and interest, credit bureau reporting, and license suspension laws on a toll-free line; providing telephone access to information about mail-out dates; providing call takers with screen pops; providing parents with an information packet and video (and also including it on the Web site) about customer expectations, services, procedures, and timeframes when they first enter the system; providing presentations in public forums or for selected groups regarding child support; comprehensively training new employees; and providing staff with information online.
- Ensuring prompt action on new case information and responses to customer requests and inquiries by instituting several policies, including: the service delivery process must begin within 20 days of receiving an application for services; telephone messages must be addressed within 2 business days, and action must be taken

within 2 business days of information receipt; actions taken on a case or information received must immediately be documented; responses must be made to written inquiries within 10 days; follow-up efforts to telephone inquiries must be undertaken within 15 business days; automated wage withholdings must be acted upon within 2 business days of receiving information about a new employer; either customers are seen when they walk in or appointments must be scheduled to occur within 10 days of the customer's request. Additionally, prompt action is actualized by improving the automated computer system and allowing parents to make address changes on an automated toll free line.

- Improving accuracy and quality by revising forms, standardized letters, and publications as necessary to ensure that they are clear and current and that they use plain language; training all central office staff in writing techniques; training managers in leadership development; creating a compliment-tracking system; establishing an employee recognition programme (including revising performance plans and defining merit raise criteria); providing automated management reports; conducting a workload study; sharing best practices; and creating a customer service advisory team.
- Treating customers professionally, courteously, and respectfully by pilot testing privacy measures in waiting rooms, providing customer service and other professional training to all staff, creating individual staff training plans, attaching information about court procedures to court notices (including expected wait time), and instituting a regular customer feedback process.

The Child Support Division of the Texas OAG works with mothers, fathers, and legal guardians of children to locate absent parents; establish paternity; establish, enforce, and adjust child and medical support orders; and collect and distribute the money associated with these orders. They have over 1 million active cases.

In 1997, the Texas legislature mandated the Sunset Advisory Commission to review the OAG Child Support Division to determine whether the OAG should continue to administer the State's child support programme. Legislators were receiving too many complaints about the Division from constituents.

The Sunset Commission conducted its review in 1998 and recommended that the OAG continue to administer the programme for a 2-year probationary period. The Commission made a number of recommendations for improving the programme. The highest priority was improving customer service and, in particular, accessibility.

Too often, customers needing information about their cases could not get through to staff for information. Of the 1.5 million calls a month that child support received, only 14 per cent of those who wished to speak with staff could do so. Thousands of calls each day were abandoned. A customer service survey revealed that 48 per cent of customers were dissatisfied. Shortly after the Commission issued its report, a new Attorney General took office. He hired a new Deputy Assistant Attorney General for child support, and they both made customer service a top priority, with answering the phones as the number one objective.

A full-time staff person was hired to develop the customer service strategy and action plan. The process included focus groups with internal and external customers, a customer satisfaction survey, and an employee satisfaction survey, as well as and soliciting input from various special interest groups. Customers said that they were most concerned with obtaining timely and accurate information, preserving their personal dignity, and being respected. Employees wanted empowerment and discretion.

To make the plan "stick," the administration realised that they needed to communicate, improve staff development, measure performance, and increase employee accountability and recognition. Quarterly, the regions report on their progress through action plans.

In the quarter from March through May 2001, regional progress reports revealed that regions:

- Maintained telephone answer rates at approximately 95 per cent.
- Implemented external customer surveys and suggestion boxes.
- Sought employee input through surveys, suggestion boxes, and staff meetings.
- Rewarded employees with merit increases, promotions, donated food, gift certificates, tickets, and special events, as well as via a recognition board or e-mail commendations.
- Implemented flex and optional work schedules.
- Focused on improving relationships with other agencies/individuals within the system, especially court personnel (one region instituted court greeters).
- Instituted a job pool to reduce hiring delays.
- Implemented quality control procedures such as "mystery callers."
- Maintained on-the-job training efforts.
- Improved office appearance.

Overall, after the first year of implementation, a general customer satisfaction survey revealed a statewide increase in customer satisfaction to 63 per cent (up from 52 per cent in 1999). Furthermore, in Spring 2001, a survey of custodial parents who had recently had an establishment performed reported an 82 per cent satisfaction rate. Intuitively, management claims that staff stress levels are down and that morale and job satisfaction are on the rise.

Efforts to improve customer service are continuing through the undertaking of the "e-degree" project (in which employees use educational leave and agency computers to take up to 3 hours of online college-level courses per semester) and the WorkSMART model office-reengineering project. The WorkSMART project is in the planning stages. WorkSMART embodies an ideal for service in which customers gain empowerment over their cases through increased access to online information online.

Customers will be able to electronically enter their case into the child support system via a streamlined application process, use a graphical roadmap to know the status of their case, and review frequently asked questions and answers while experiencing shorter processing times. Much of the detailed development of these action plans has been pushed down to the regional level (e.g., training strategies, measurement strategies, reward systems, and customer input mechanisms).

Texas is working on maintaining consistency in these procedures while allowing each region some discretion. This strategy was designed to increase buy-in and ownership at the regional level. As a result of this autonomy, different offices may vary in their customer service strategies and levels of success. While executive management has found this autonomic setup effective, the downside is that its varied measurement strategies do not lend themselves to easy statewide assessment.

At the beginning of the customer service implementation, the Director closed the central call centre and created regional call centres. At the regional level, managers focus on getting the phones answered and supporting employees—through training and cross-training, by clearly outlining expectations, through consistent management, by serving as role models, by rewarding good work and good customer service, and by encouraging open communication.

A regional call centre manager stressed the importance of his own attitude (attitude filters from the top down, according to this manager) as a means of setting the tone of the office and keeping employees productive and willing to provide the best services possible. In support of this belief, every day he walks around the office and greets each employee, offers assistance, provides answers to questions, and maintains an open-door policy.

He emphasizes results and delivering a consistent message. As long as the center's goals are being met, he offers flexibility (e.g., in scheduling lunch breaks and requests for time off). He has instituted strategies to cope with the unit when it is not fully staffed, by flexing lunch schedules and by having management serve as backup.

He tries to handle most problems by talking with all of the staff instead of isolating an individual. However, individual accountability does play an important part in the management strategy. This particular call centre succeeds both in meeting its telephone answering goals (staff and managers answer 96 per cent of all incoming calls) and in maintaining low employee turnover (approximately 22 per cent in the region, but of those who have left, every person still works within the Texas Child Support Division via transfer or promotion).

Call centre management has trained employees that their role is to accurately handle as many incoming phone calls as possible. The purpose is to free up time child support officers (CSOs) to be able to process cases. Brief interviews with frontline call centre staff suggested that call centre employees and managers share a rapport and can rely on one another for help or answers to questions.

Two people said that the best part of their job is the feeling of helping someone. Another person took pride in thoroughly addressing all of the callers' issues so as to deflect calls for CSOs. One call taker even assigns "ticklers" on his calendar so that he knows to check the system to make certain that appropriate action has been taken on a call he has received.

Call takers reported some challenges, including balancing the target talk time (about 4 minutes) with providing thorough information to the caller, dealing with callers who are not truthful, and handling concerns that caseworkers may not be able to perform requested follow-up. However, the call centre statistics show that 95 per cent of calls are answered, the average wait time since inception of the regional call centres is approximately 30 seconds, and that call takers spend an average of 3 minutes of talk time per call.

Management places the same emphasis on hiring call centre staff as they do in hiring CSOs. Call centre staff are paid at the CSO level. Some call centre staff were hired from field offices, as well as from county child support offices, and others were hired with customer service backgrounds but with no child support experience. Management for the six call centres includes personnel from the central office, some of whom had worked in field offices and others from general hiring pools.

All child support staff receive 2 days of basic training in customer service, even those personnel serving internal customers only. New staff also receive this training. During this training, instructors stress that the Division's guiding principles apply to both internal and external customer service. Managers receive advanced customer service training on how to support staff to deliver great customer service. Training is offered regionally, and therefore staff from all levels train together. In addition to customer service training, staff are trained in how to deal with hostile customers. The next initiative is to design and implement a follow-up course in customer service.

Motivation is addressed on a number of levels:

- Staff participated in the internal focus groups that led to the Compact with Texans. This participation generated introspection, and executive personnel believe that this introspection may be a positive motivation.
- Additionally, some regions cross train and cross work. For example, personnel in Dallas train on both call centre and field office tasks and then, depending on the workload, staff can assist in either location. This additional knowledge helps the employees in one location understand the impact of their actions on their coworkers.

- The call centre manager sets high expectations of staff and strives to provide employees with the training, information, and resources needed to meet them.
- The customer service culture has clearly been established as a permanent priority. Executive staff stress the importance of adhering to the customer service philosophy and individual accountability, and staff are aware that they can be dismissed for a lack of customer service.
- Performance plans include customer service measures and clearly outline performance expectations and standards.
- Staff are rewarded with merit increases, promotions, food, gift certificates, tickets, and special events, as well as via a recognition board or e-mail commendations. (Worth noting: during one office recognition celebration, staff from another field office came to offer phone support so that everyone could attend the event.)

According to Texas Child Support Division executives, one of the keys to the improvement of customer service in Texas child support is technology. In particular, six regional call centres were established and were equipped with technology and systems to improve efficiency, information availability, and information exchange. The call centres handle approximately 25 per cent of all customer service contacts.

First, a model- the Erlang C Formula-was used to understand the relationship between the amount of incoming calls, time taken to handle those calls, wait time for callers, and number of call centre staff. With this formula, executive personnel determined the number of staff needed given call volume, target maximum wait times, and handling times for calls. Initially, the number of required staff calculated by this method was higher than that of actual staff available for the effort. As a result, Texas had to address another factor in the formula-handle time.

Efficiencies in call handling have been gained through a number of innovations:

- Calls are automatically disseminated to call takers based on availability of their lines. Once a call taker hangs up, the call taker has a pre-set amount of time to perform call wrap up activities, and then the line automatically becomes part of the call queue once again. (Previously, call takers had to proactively re-set their "ready" buttons.) The system includes a way to put a line on "break" as necessary.
- Screen pops were designed to utilize the incoming phone number to pull up a case, rather than requiring the call taker to obtain a case or social security number upon answering the call. This feature saves an average of 15 seconds per call.
- A Graphical User Interface ("GUI") screen was developed to contain the core information used on typical calls to child support. This feature was created so that call takers spend less time flipping from

screen to screen. This feature also can save an average of 76 seconds per call. Additionally, data entry options on GUI save additional data entry time-about 92 seconds per call.

The database of cases (TXCSES) includes a diary function that permits staff members, whether in a call centre or field office, to make a notation on the case so that anyone who opens the case will be current on action taken or contact made on the case. It also allows staff to e-mail one another directly. Another useful feature allows call centre staff to mark the correspondence or case so that the call taker receives a reminder notice to perform follow-up.

Still other call centre technology allows call centre staff to be acutely aware of the number of calls coming in and the length of wait time. First, a digital light board posted in the office provides this real-time information. Additionally, a computer tracking system provides aggregate statistics on the calls and is located in the break room.

Intellicenter software is used by call centre managers to provide quality control by periodically screening calls and coaching staff, as appropriate. At the call centre, everyone agreed that technology has made their jobs easier.

Another technological improvement for customer service has been the interactive Web site. On the site, customers can provide information, obtain payment information, and make complaints. Customers are using the site for all of these things.

The Web site was designed to reduce the number of phone calls, while increasing information access for customers. Web site use has been increasing since inception. In August 2001, there were 196,403 transactions from individuals who had entered their pin number and were actually accessing case information. On average, the site receives 3,967 hits daily. Ten per cent of all customer service contacts are over the Web site. The Web site won an award from Computer World Magazine.

CONSUMER MARKET

The consumer market is composed of individuals who buy a specific good or service. Rarely does one product interest the entire population. This statement applies even to staples, such as sugar, flour, and salt. A small percentage of households do not eat these products, so even if a company did target the entire population, not everyone would be a potential consumer. The same statistical truth applies to cultural products. However, because of the extremely fragmented nature of the cultural sector, some distinctions are in order.

For example, looking at this sector as a whole, it can be said that nearly 100% of the population consumes one type of cultural product or another. Indeed, in its broadest sense, the cultural sector encompasses everything from the performing arts to heritage, compact disks, movies, book and magazine publishing, and radio and television, with each of these disciplines appropriating a more or less important share of global demand.

In Canada, for example, statistics1 show that 37.0% of families attend a performing arts event at least once a year: movies 62.2%, museums and art galleries 32.9%. In the United States the figures for cultural consumption are: classical music 15.6%, opera 4.7%, musicals 24.5%, plays 15.8%, ballet 5.8%, art museums 34.5%, and historical parks 46.9%.2 In Australia3 the figures are: musical theatre 19.3%, classical music 7.7%, festivals 21.9%, concerts 23%, and museums 27.8%. Of course, within each of these sectors, consumers cluster just as to specific poles of interest.

This leads to sharper market segmentation. The consumer makes a discriminating choice among various cultural products to acquire or consume the type of product desired. The distribution of consumers just as to various market segments differs in both time and space. Markets undergo and reflect the influence of opinion leaders, trends, tastes, and societal characteristics.

Markets also vary from country to country just as to different social structures. Over the past 40 years, various surveys focusing on the sociodemographic profile of consumers of cultural products have been carried out in nearly every European country as well as in Canada, the United States, Australia, and Japan.4 It is fascinating to note that, regardless of whether the surveys were conducted in the 1970s, 1980s, or 1990s, they all obtained the same attendance rates and the same sociodemographic profiles.

Differences in the measuring tools used can sometimes make it difficult to compare countries; nonetheless, these studies have consistently and systematically revealed strong polarization of audiences between high art and popular culture across all countries over the past four decades. They show, for example, that cultural products catering to high art attract educated consumers, whereas those catering to popular culture draw on all segments of the population, in accordance with the relative weight of each.

The proportion of university graduates making up Canadian audiences, for example, ranges between 50% and 70% for high art, compared with 10% to 25% for popular culture. By way of comparison, the overall percentage of university graduates in Canada is 25%. Similar results have been found in other countries, most notably in France5 but also in Russia, where university graduates make up 50% of performing arts audiences but only 7% of the general population.

Other sociodemographic variables are also linked to attendance, including average income and type of occupation. It should be pointed out once again that this profile is based on averages. Less-educated individuals with lower income may be great consumers of culture, as is the case for students and those specialized or working in the cultural milieu.

Indeed, it is well known that, as a rule many people active in the arts are highly educated yet so ill paid that they struggle to stay above the poverty line. On the other hand, there are people with both very high salaries and very high educational levels who are not interested in the arts and gladly keep their distance. Four factors are known to influence an individual's penchant for complex cultural products: family values that encourage or discourage high art; the educational milieu and the value it places on high art; the fact of having attended performances or visited museums as a child; and amateur art practice.

A more detailed analysis of the typical cultural consumer's traits reveals other nuances based on the different disciplines. For example, dance audiences are relatively younger and even more female in composition than those of the other performing arts; similarly, more women than men read novels, although a larger proportion of men read daily newspapers. In the film sector, there are two very different segments of avid cinema-goers; one of these segments is dominated by a young clientele, while the other is made up of educated people. The majority of consumers in the film sector belong to one or the other of these two segments.

BUSINESS BUYING BEHAVIOUR

The business market is comprised of organizations that, in some form, are involved in the manufacturer, distribution or support of products or services sold or otherwise provided to other organizations. The amount of purchasing undertaken in the business market easily dwarfs the total spending by consumers. Because the business market is so large it draws the interest of millions of companies worldwide that market exclusively to business customers.

For these marketers understanding how businesses make purchase decisions is critical to their organizations' marketing efforts. In some ways understanding the business market is not as complicated as understanding the consumer market. For example, in certain business markets purchase decisions hinge on the outcome of a bidding process between competitors offering similar products and services.

In these cases the decision to buy is often whittled down to one concern– who has the lowest price. Thus, unlike consumer markets, where building a recognizable brand is very important, for many purchase situations in the business market this is not the case. However, in many other ways business buying is much more complicated. For instance, the demand by businesses for products and services is affected by consumer purchases and because so many organizations may have a part in creating consumer purchases, a small swing in consumer demand can create big changes in business purchasing.

Automobile purchases are a good example. If consumer demand for cars increases many companies connected with the automobile industry will also see demand for their products and services increase. Under these conditions companies will ratchet up their operations to ensure demand is met, which invariably will lead to new purchases by a large number of companies. In fact, it is conceivable that an increase of just one or two per cent for consumer demand can increase business demand for products and services by five or more per cent. Unfortunately, the opposite is true if demand declines. Trying to predict these swings requires businesses to not only understand their immediate customers but also the end user, which as suggested, discuss, may be well down the supply chain from where the business operates.

Principles of Marketing Tutorials discusses the unique characteristics of the business market. As suggested, see that marketers must appeal to business customers in ways that are distinct from how they would approach consumers. While marketers selling to other businesses operate with most of the same marketing tools used by marketers of consumer products, how they employ these tools to reach their marketing objectives may be quite different.

SUPPLY CHAIN MARKET

The supply chain consists of mostly for-profit companies engaged in activities involving product creation and delivery. Essentially the chain represents major steps needed to manufacture a product that will eventually be sold as a final product. Each member of the supply chain purchases products and services enabling them to carry out its business objectives. When making purchase decisions supply chain members may be motivated by such factors as: product cost, return on investment, assurance of consistent supply, reciprocity with supplying firm, and much more. Examples of purchasing occurring in the supply chain include: manufacturing and plant equipment, information technology, office supplies, professional business services, etc.

In the table we arbitrarily identify five main categories of supply chain members primarily based on the stage at which they contribute to the manufacturing process. However, it is conceivable that these categories can be further divided in order to flush out more specific activities.

Supply Chain Member	What They Do	Example
Raw Material Suppliers	These companies are generally considered the first stage in the supply chain and provide basic products through mining, harvesting, fishing, etc., that are key ingredients in the production of higher-order products.	Copper is mined and extracted from copper ore. Copper is then refined to remove impurities.
Processed Materials or Basic Component Manufacturers	Firms at this level use raw materials to produce more advanced materials or products contained within more advanced components.	Copper is purchased by electrical wire manufacturers.
Advanced Component Manufacturers	These companies use basic components to produce products that offer a significant function needed within a larger product.	Electrical wire is purchased by a manufacturer of electrical power supplies.
Product Manufacturers	This market consists of companies that purchase both basic and advanced components and then assemble these components into a final product designated for a user. These products may or may not be sold as stand-alone products. Some may be included within larger products.	Power supplies are purchased by manufacturers of desktop computers.
Support Service Firms	These companies offer services at almost any point in the supply chain and also to the business user market. Some services are directly related to the product while others focus on areas of the business not directly related to production.	Distribution companies, such as truck firms and storage facilities, assist in moving products from one supply chain member to another. However, in most cases they do not take ownership of products that pass through the supply chain.

BUSINESS USER MARKETS

Besides selling final products and services to supply chain companies, several additional user markets also make purchases either for their own consumption or they buy with the intention of redistributing to others.

Market	What They Do	Considerations When Buying	What They Buy
Government	Made up of Federal, State, Local and International governments. They use purchases to assist with the functioning of the government that may include redistributing to others.	Mostly require suppliers to be approved, meet specifications and to bid for purchases.	Defense equipment, heavy equipment for public works projects, office supplies, pharmaceuticals, etc.
Not-For-Profit	Organizations whose tax structure precludes earning profits from operations and whose missions tend to be oriented to assisting others.	Look for purchases that will fit within tight budgetary restrictions and also within the mission of the organization.	Office equipment and supplies, office rental, professional services, etc.
Reseller	Also called distributors, these companies operate in both the consumer and the business markets. Their function involves purchasing large volumes of products from manufacturers and selling these products in smaller quantities. Includes wholesalers, retailers and industrial distributors.	Seek products that are of interest to the reseller's customers. Other issues include how delivery is handled and whether the supplier offers incentives to help the reseller promote the product.	Consumer and industrial products to be redistributed to other businesses and co

In these purchase situations the buyer generally does not radically change the product from its form when it was purchased from a Product Manufacturer. While technically these markets are also part of the supply chain, members of the business user market do not, in most cases, engage or directly assist in production activities.

BUSINESS VS CONSUMER MARKETS

For marketers, the selling environment of business markets present uniquely different circumstances when compared to selling to consumers.

At the beginning of this tutorial we saw two ways in which consumer and business markets differ:

- Business markets are more likely to be price driven than brand driven, and
- Demand in business markets tends to be more volatile than consumer markets.

However, the two markets are dissimilar in other ways requiring marketers to take a different approach when selling to business customers than to consumers.

These differences include:

- How Decisions Are Made
- Existence of Experienced Purchasers
- Time Needed to Make Buying Decision
- Size of Purchases
- Number of Buyers
- Type of Promotional Effort Needed to Reach Buyer

BUYING DIFFERENCES

Buying Centre Decisions

In the consumer market a very large percentage of purchase decisions are made by a single person. As we discussed in the Consumer Buying Behaviour tutorial, there are situations in which multiple people may be involved in a consumer purchase decision, such as a child influencing a parent to choose a certain brand of cereal or a husband and wife deciding together to buy a house, but most of the time purchases are individual decisions. The business market is significantly different. While single person purchasing is not unusual, especially within a small company, a significant percentage of business buying, especially within larger organizations, requires the input of many.

In the marketing literature those associated with the purchase decision are known to be part of a Buying Centre, which consists of individuals within an organization that perform one or more of the following roles:

- *Buyer*: Responsible for dealing with suppliers and placing orders
- *Decider*: Has the power to make the final purchase decision
- *Influencer*: Has the ability to affect what is ordered such as setting order specifications
- *User*: Those who will actually use the product when it is received
- *Initiator*: Any Buying Centre member who is the first to determine that a need exists
- *Gatekeeper*: Anyone who controls access to other Buying Centre members

For marketers confronting a Buying Centre it is important to first identify who plays what role. Once identified the marketer must address the needs of each member, which may differ significantly. For instance, the Decider, who may be the company president wants to make sure the purchase will not negatively affect the company's bottom line while the Buyer wants to be assured the product will be delivered on time. Thus, the way each Buying Centre member is approached and marketed to requires careful planning in order to address the unique needs of each member.

Experienced Purchasers

As noted in the discussion of the Buying Centre, organizations often employ purchasing agents or professional buyers whose job is to negotiate the best deals for their company. Unlike consumers, who often lack information when making purchase decisions, professional buyers are generally as knowledgeable about the product and the industry as the marketer who is selling to them.

Decision Making Time

Depending on the product, business purchase decisions can drag on for an extensive period. Unlike consumer markets where impulse purchasing is rampant, the number of people involved in business purchase decisions results in decisions taking weeks, months or even years.

Size of Purchases

For products that are regularly used and frequently purchased, businesses will often buy a larger volume at one time compared to consumer purchases. Because of this business purchasers often demand price breaks for higher order levels.

Type of Promotions

Companies who primarily target consumers often use mass advertising methods to reach an often widely dispersed market. For business-to-business marketers the size of individual orders, along with a smaller number of buyers, makes person-to-person contact by sales representatives a more effective means of promotion.

TYPES OF BUSINESS PURCHASE DECISIONS

While it would appear business customers face the same four purchase situations faced by consumers, the nature of the business market has led many marketing academics to group business purchase situations into only three categories.

The reason is that the idea of a minor order may not hold as well in the business market, where buyers tend to place larger orders and where suppliers' marketing efforts are directed toward the most profitable buyers.

- *Straight Re-Purchase*: These purchase situations involve routine ordering. In most cases buyers simply reorder the same products or services that were previously purchased. In fact, many larger companies have programmed re-purchases into an automated ordering system that initiates electronic orders when inventory falls a certain pre-determined level. For the supplier benefiting from the re-purchase this situation is ideal since the purchaser is not looking to evaluate other products. For competitors who are not getting the order it may require extensive marketing efforts to persuade the buyer to consider other product or service options.
- *Modified Re-Purchase*: These purchases occur when products or services previously considered a straight re-purchase are for some reason now under a re-evaluation process. There are many reasons why a product is moved to the status of a modified re-purchase. Some of these reasons include: end of purchase contract period, change in who is involved in making the purchase, supplier is removed from an approved suppliers list, mandate from top level of organization to re-evaluate all purchasing, or strong marketing effort by competitors. In this circumstance the incumbent supplier

faces the same challenges they may have faced when they initially convinced the buyer to make the purchase. For competitors the door is now open and they must work hard to make sure their message is heard by those in charge of the purchase decision.

- *New Task Purchase*: As the name suggests, these purchases are ones the buyer has never or rarely made before. In some ways new task purchases can be considered as either minor or major depending on the total cost or overall importance of the purchase. In either case the buyer will spend considerably more time evaluating alternatives. For example, if faced with a major new task purchase, which often involves complex items, such as computer systems, buildings, robotic assembly lines, etc., the purchase cycle from first recognizing the need to placement of the order may be months or even years.

CUSTOMER INTEGRATION MANAGEMENT (CIM)

Customer Interaction Management helps organisations execute effective and efficient interactions with their customers and prospects. These interactions must be consistent and tailored to the customer needs, based on the segment of the customer, the service required and the used channel.

IMPORTANT

Today's competitive environment requires companies to ensure that the customer has a consistent experience across interactions and channels, giving him a clear sense of brand value and differentiation.

Customer Interaction specialists at Deloitte focus on the following offerings:

- *Customer Experience*: We support the organisation in describing and assessing the experience of its customer or prospect across their lifecycle, providing actionable recommendations for enriching the customer experience.
- *Multi-channel interaction management*: We provide advice regarding the ways the organisation can best reach its customers. By implementing right-channelling, we help companies maximize interaction value in a cost-efficient way.
- *Service Organisational design*: Our organisational design methods consider people and processes in order to put in place the right service models, contact flows and escalation rules
- *Service request and SLA management*: We provide methods and tools to improve service request management and implement the appropriate service level agreements.
- *Contact Centre Implementation and Transformation*: Deloitte has a proven track-record in implementing multi-channel interaction centres, including integration with CRM processes and tools.

PREDICTIVE CUSTOMER INTERACTION MANAGEMENT

Introduction

Every business needs to efficiently manage outbound and inbound interactions with customers. These interactions can occur through many channels including the web, call centres branch offices, ATMs, and e-mail. With inbound interactions, customers offer their attention. They visit a web site, make a call, or access an ATM because they want something at that moment – information about a product or help with a problem.

These interactions usually present an opportunity to communicate with a customer who is engaged by choice and ready to share information regarding his or her wants and needs. Outbound interactions are typically used to target products to particular customer segments based on analysis of customer data. The success of these interactions – whether through e-mail, direct mail, or other channels – depends to a great extent on the organization's understanding of the customer's wants and needs at the time of the offer. This document describes an architecture that manages inbound and outbound interactions in a consistent manner to present a unified, real-time view of each customer.

Requirements for Effective Customer Interaction Management

The following list summarizes requirements for such an architecture:

- Provides consistent customer interaction management of outbound and inbound communications.
- Addresses the uniqueness and complexities of various inbound and outbound channels. For example, in an inbound call, the business logic might dictate that the CSR should not make an offer if the call time is greater than a given threshold.
- Allows businesses that are aligned along product lines to use both customer knowledge and data mining to publish product propensities.
- Allows customer data to be distributed across multiple systems.
- Combines rules, policies, inferencing, and analytics – both statistical and probabilistic – to produce complex models of reasoning via events, customer data, time, and analytics.
- Leverages existing investment in data mining tools such as SAS, SPSS, and others.
- Handles the low latency requirements of real-time customer interactions with sophisticated caching techniques.
- Provides flexibility, scalability, and high availability.

Key Aspects of Customer Interaction Management

How a business treats customers and manages customer relationships is a key differentiator and is critical to succeeding in highly competitive and dynamic environments. The solution proposed in this document addresses three important aspects of customer interaction management:

1. Maintaining customer relationships using relationship events over time.
2. Driving up-sell and cross-sell opportunities using both inbound and outbound events.
3. Incorporating a feedback model to calculate the effectiveness of models over macro and micro dimensions.

Architecture

Effective customer interaction management requires an event-driven architecture that is application and database agnostic.

High-level components of such a solution include:

- Channel adapters.
- Customer interaction engine also referred to as a recomm-endation engine
  - Knowledge models maintained by business users.
  - Analytical models maintained by business users or reused from existing investments.
- Virtual data source
  - SOA platform to integrate customer and other information from various data sources. A typical implementation will require integration with customer and product data from operational stores and/or data warehouses

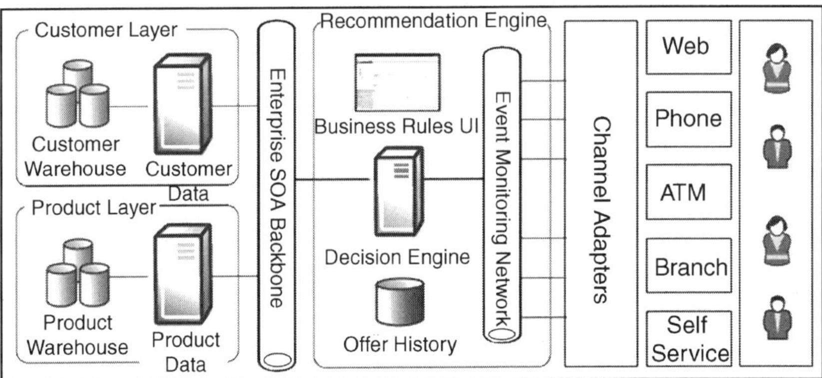

Channel Adapters

In the context of this solution, channel adapters have two key roles:

1. *Sense*: Channel adapters, either intrusively or non-intrusively, publish relevant events to the recommendation engine. The solution contains pre-defined adapters for various technologies used in the channels.

2. *Respond*: Channel adapters provide a mechanism to initiate a dialogue with the customer. The response is inferred and initiated by the recommendation engine to the channel adapters.

Recommendation Engine

The recommendation engine provides the following functions:

- A glossary of terms and vocabulary that form the basis of marketing strategies.
- Integration with channels using events.
- Pattern matching of a set of events with the policies, knowledge, and analytical models to generate a set of responses.
- Generic offers such as "Offer of the Day."
- Maintain history of offers and customer responses.
- A business user interface to create and represent marketing strategies or business "rules" based on the vocabulary of terms and events. TIBCO provides a recommendation engine based on TIBCO BusinessEvents™ software, a market-leading complex event processing application.

Virtual Data Source

The virtual data source integrates all relevant customer and product data. TIBCO BusinessWorks™ is an extensible SOA enablement platform that uses a no-coding approach to developing, deploying, and running integration projects and building serviceoriented architectures. It simplifies some of the more complex implementation issues that are critical for the glue and sequence between connected systems, such as process orchestration and transformation.

Customer Examples

Today's leading retail banks recognize that customers are their most important and strategic asset and are rapidly adopting customer-centric IT strategies to achieve competitive advantage. This part presents a number of practical examples showing how a real-time, event-driven, multi-channel, application-agnostic architecture delivers immediate value to the retail banking business and a unique banking experience to their customers.

Retail banks have traditionally used customer resource management systems to capture the inbound customer data stream and store the information in a central repository. Using a post-processing procedure, data mining tools are then used to analyse the data and apply rules to execute marketing campaigns.

TIBCO's approach to customer interaction management uses CEP software to enable:

- Real-time matching of customer profiles and product lines across all banking channels.

- Real-time, rules-based product recommendations based on statistical, relationship, or experience models per business line.

Example: Multi-Channel Customer Interaction

The following example shows how banks can use real-time information to provide more effective service:

- Mick and his wife have a new baby girl named Nora.
- While using the bank's internet portal, Mick updates his Personal Profile to include the new family member.
- Still using the portal, he checks the bank's mortgage packages and requests several brochures because he is thinking about renovating or buying a new home.
- The next day he and his wife get a present from the bank congratulating them on the new family member and offering a baby savings account especially tailored for them.
- One week later, while visiting the local branch, the local branch officer congratulates Nick on Nora's birth, offers him an informational appointment with the bank's mortgage advisor, and offers to increase the credit limit on the family credit card at no charge and with no paperwork. In the example, complex event processing software allows the bank to:

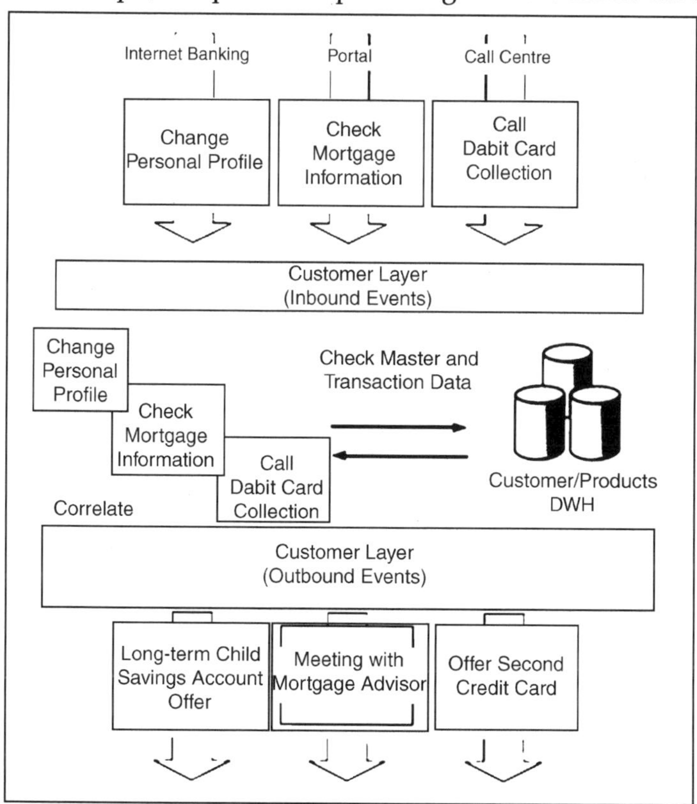

- Capture all events through all channels in real-time.
- Seek out patterns and correlate information with the goal of identifying important events, such as the birth of a child.
- Consult historical information to determine, for instance, the customer's demographic profile and to estimate the bank's share of wallet
- Apply different models, or rules, to assess which marketing campaign, if any, is most suited to the customer.
- Execute appropriate marketing strategies and recommend products in real-time. By tracking customer interactions, capturing other vital, non-traditional customer events that help flesh out the customer profile – birth of a child, starting or ending school, landing a first job, getting married, renting a house, purchasing a new car, moving, changing a job, buying a house – and responding with relevant offers and services, banks have an opportunity to extend the customer relationship and demonstrate that the customer is the bank's most important asset.

CONSUMER PROTECTION

Consumer protection laws are designed to ensure fair competition and the free flow of truthful information in the marketplace. The laws are designed to prevent businesses that engage in fraud or specified unfair practices from gaining an advantage over competitors and may provide additional protection for the weak and those unable to take care of themselves. Consumer Protection laws are a form of government regulation which aim to protect the interests of consumers. For example, a government may require businesses to disclose detailed information about products—particularly in areas where safety or public health is an issue, such as food. Consumer protection is linked to the idea of "consumer rights" and to the formation of consumer organizations which help consumers make better choices in the marketplace.

Consumer is defined as someone who acquires goods or services for direct use or ownership rather than for resale or use in production and manufacturing. Consumer interests can also be protected by promoting competition in the markets which directly and indirectly serve consumers, consistent with economic efficiency, but this topic is treated in Competition law. Consumer protection can also be asserted via non-government organizations and individuals as consumer activism.

CONSUMER LAW

"Consumer protection law" or "consumer law" is considered an area of law that regulates private law relationships between individual consumers and the businesses that sell those goods and services. Consumer protection covers a wide range of topics, including but not necessarily limited to product liability, privacy rights, unfair business practices, fraud, misrepresentation, and other consumer/business interactions. Such laws deal with credit repair, debt repair, product safety, service and sales contracts, bill collector regulation, pricing, utility turnoffs, consolidation, personal loans that may lead to bankruptcy and much more.

Germany

A minister of the federal cabinet is responsible for consumer rights and protection. In the current cabinet of Angela Merkel, this is Ilse Aigner. When issuing public warnings about products and services, the issuing authority has to take into account that this affects the supplier's constitutionally protected economic liberty.

Republic of China

Consumer Protection Law in the Republic of China is the national special law which specifically protects the interests and safety of end-user using the products or services provided by business operators. Consumer Protection Commission of Executive Yuan serves as an ombudsman supervising, coordinating, reporting any unsafe products/services and periodically reviewing the legislation.

United Kingdom

The United Kingdom, as member state of the European Union, is bound by the consumer protection directives of the EU. Domestic laws originated within the ambit of contract and tort but, with the influence of EU law, it is emerging as an independent area of law.

In many circumstances, where domestic law is in question, the matter judicially treated as tort, contract, restitution or even criminal law. Consumer Protection issues are dealt with when complaints are made to the Director-General of Fair Trade.

The Office of Fair Trading will then investigate, impose an injunction or take the matter to litigation. The Office of Fair Trading also acts as the UK's official consumer and competition watchdog, with a remit to make markets work well for consumers, and at a local, municipal level by Trading Standards departments. General consumer advice can be obtained from Consumer Direct or via a local branch of the Citizen's Advice Bureau.

Other Commonwealth Countries

In Australia the corresponding agency is the Australian Competition and Consumer Commission or the individual State Consumer Affairs agencies. The Australian Securities and Investments Commission has responsibility for consumer protection regulation of financial services and products. In New Zealand, the corresponding agency is the Ministry of Consumer Affairs and the New Zealand Commerce Commission.

United States

In the United States a variety of laws at both the federal or state levels regulate consumer affairs. Among them are the federal Fair Debt Collection Practices Act, the Fair Credit Reporting Act, Truth in Lending Act, Fair Credit Billing Act, and the Gramm-Leach-Bliley Act.

Federal consumer protection laws are mainly enforced by the Federal Trade Commission and the U.S. Department of Justice. At the state level, many states have a Department of Consumer Affairs devoted to regulating certain industries and protecting consumers who use goods and services from those industries.

For example, in the U.S. state of California, the California Department of Consumer Affairs regulates about 2.3 million professionals in over 230 different professions, through its forty regulatory entities. In addition, California encourages its consumers to act as private attorneys general through the liberal provisions of its Consumers Legal Remedies Act, Cal. Civil Code § 1750 et seq. California has the strongest consumer protection laws of any US state, partly because of rigorous advocacy and lobbying by groups such as Utility Consumers' Action Network, Consumer Federation of California and Privacy Rights Clearinghouse.

Other states have been the leaders in specific aspects of consumer protection. For example Florida, Delaware and Minnesota have legislated requirements that contracts be written at reasonable readability levels as a large proportion of contracts cannot be understood by most consumers who sign them.

THE CONSUMER PROTECTION ACT, 1986

The Act enshrines all the consumers' rights which are internationally accepted. As per the Act, the consumer protection councils have been established at Central, State and District levels to promote and protect the consumer rights.

They are:

- *Right to Safety*: To be protected against the sale of goods and services which are spurious/hazardous for the life.
- *Right to Information*: To know the quality, quantity, weight and the price of goods/services being paid for, so that one is not cheated by unfair trade practices.
- *Right to Choose*: To be assured, wherever possible, access to a variety of goods and services at competitive prices.
- *Right to be Heard*: To be heard and to be assured that the interest would receive due consideration at appropriate fora.
- *Right to Seek Redressal*: To seek legal redressal against unfair or restrictive trade practices or exploitation.
- *Right to Consumer Education*: To have access to consumer education.

At present there are 35 State Commissions, one in each State/UT and 571 district forum besides the National Commission. The state governments are responsible to set up the district forum and the State Commissions. States have been empowered to establish additional District Forum and also additional members in the State Commission to facilitate constituting benches and also for holding circuit benches. The Central Government is required to set up the National Commission.

It has been empowered to appoint additional members to facilitate creation of more benches and holding of circuit benches. The second bench of the National Commission started functioning from 24 September 2003.

The government is monitoring the disposal of cases by the consumer courts through National Commission. Since its inception and up to March 2004, 32,910 cases were filed out of which 24,974 cases disposed of in the National Commission. Similarly 3,01,485 cases were filed and 1,97,797 cases disposed of in the State Commissions and 18,86,236 cases were filed and 16,46,698 cases disposed of in the district forum.

Overall 18,69,469 cases have been disposed of out of 22,20,631 cases filed with a remarkable disposal rate of 84.2 per cent. The government has declared 24 December as 'National Consumer Day', since the President gave his assent on that day to the enactment of the historic Consumer Protection Act, 1986. Besides this, 15 March is observed as 'World Consumer Rights Day' every year.

CUSTOMER PRODUCT PACKAGING

This relates to the package the final customer receives in exchange for their payment. When the final customer makes a purchase he or she is initially exposed to the Primary Package – the outermost container that is seen and touched by the final customer. This primary package can be further divided into the following:

- *First-Level Package* : This is packaging that holds the actual product (e.g., Tylenol Bottle). In some cases this packaging is minimal since it only serves to protect the product. For instance, certain frozen food products are sold to consumers in a cardboard box with the product itself contained in a plastic bag found inside the box. This plastic bag represents the first-level package. In other cases frozen food products are sold in the plastic bag that contains the product. In these cases the plastic bag is both first-level package and the primary package for convey product information.
- *Second-Level Package:* In some cases the first-level package is surrounded by one or more outer packages (e.g., box holding the Tylenol Bottle). This second-level package may act as the primary package for the product.
- *Package Inserts*: Marketers use a variety of other methods to communicate with customers after they open the product package.

These methods are often inserted within, or sometimes on, the product's package. Insertions include information such as instruction manuals and warranty cards, promotional incentives such as coupons, and items that add value such as recipes and software.

DISTRIBUTION PACKAGING

This packaging is used to transport the customer package through the supply chain. It generally holds multiple customer packages and also offers a higher level of damage protection than that of customer packaging.

Factors to Consider

Packaging decisions are important for several reasons including:

- *Protection:* Packaging is used to protect the product from damage during shipping and handling, and to lessen spoilage if the protect is exposed to air or other elements.
- *Visibility*: Packaging design is used to capture customers' attention as they are shopping or glancing through a catalog or website. This is particularly important for customers who are not familiar with the product and in situations, such as those found in grocery stores, where a product must stand out among thousands of other products. Packaging designs that standout are more likely to be remembered on future shopping trips.
- *Added Value:* Packaging design and structure can add value to a product. For instance, benefits can be obtained from package structures that make the product easier to use while stylistic designs can make the product more attractive to display in the customer's home.
- *Distributor Acceptance:* Packaging decisions must not only be accepted by the final customer, they may also have to be accepted by distributors who sell the product for the supplier. For instance, a retailer may not accept packages unless they conform to requirements they have for storing products on their shelves.
- *Cost:* Packaging can represent a significant portion of a product's selling price. For example, it is estimated that in the cosmetics industry the packaging cost of some products may be as high as 40% of a product's selling price. Smart packaging decisions can help reduce costs and possibly lead to higher profits.
- *Expensive to Create* : Developing new packaging can be extremely expensive. The costs involved in creating new packaging include: graphic and structural design, production, customer testing, possible destruction of leftover old packaging, and possible advertising to inform customer of the new packaging.
- *Long Term Decision:* When companies create a new package it is most often with the intention of having the design on the market for an

extended period of time. In fact, changing a product's packaging too frequently can have negative effects since customers become conditioned to locate the product based on its package and may be confused if the design is altered.

- *Environmental or Legal Issues:* Packaging decisions must also include an assessment of its environmental impact especially for products with packages that are frequently discarded. Packages that are not easily bio-degradable could draw customer and possibly governmental concern. Also, caution must be exercised in order to create packages that do not infringe on intellectual property, such as copyrights, trademarks or patents, held by others.

Labelling

Most packages, whether final customer packaging or distribution packaging, are imprinted with information intended to assist the customer. For consumer products, labelling decisions are extremely important for the following reasons.

- Labels serve to capture the attention of shoppers. The use of catchy words may cause strolling customers to stop and evaluate the product.
- The label is likely to be the first thing a new customer sees and thus offers their first impression of the product.
- The label provides customers with product information to aid their purchase decision or help improve the customer's experience when using the product (e.g., recipes).
- Labels generally include a universal product codes (UPC) and, in some cases, radio frequency identification (RFID) tags, that make it easy for resellers, such as retailers, to checkout customers and manage inventory.
- For companies serving international markets or diverse cultures within a single country, bilingual or multilingual labels may be needed.
- In some countries many products, including food and pharmaceuticals, are required by law to contain certain labels such as listing ingredients, providing nutritional information or including usage warning information.

CATEGORIES OF CONSUMER PRODUCTS

In addition to categorizing by type of offering, most products intended for consumer use can be further categorized by how frequently and where they are purchased.

- *Convenience Products:* These are products that appeal to a very large market segment. They are generally consumed regularly and purchased frequently. Examples include most household items such as food, cleaning products, and personal care products. Because of the high purchase volume, pricing per item tends to be relatively low and consumers often see little value in shopping around since additional effort yields minimal savings. From the marketer's perspective the low price of convenience products means that profit per unit sold is very low. In order to make high profits marketers must sell in large volume. Consequently, marketers attempt to distribute these products in mass through as many retail outlets as possible.

- *Shopping Products:* These are products consumers purchase and consume on a less frequent schedule compared to convenience products. Consumers are willing to spend more time locating these products since they are relatively more expensive than convenience products and because these may possess additional psychological benefits for the purchaser, such as raising their perceived status level within their social group. Examples include many clothing products, personal services, electronic products, and household furnishings. Because consumers are purchasing less frequently and are willing to shop to locate these products, the target market is much smaller than that of convenience goods. Consequently, marketers often are more selective when choosing distribution outlets to sell their products.
- *Specialty Products:* These are products that tend to carry a high price tag relative to convenience and shopping products. Consumption may occur at about the same rate as shopping products but consumers are much more selective. In fact, in many cases consumers know in advance which product they prefer and will not shop to compare products. But they may shop at retailers that provide the best value. Examples include high-end luxury automobiles, expensive champagne, and celebrity hair care experts. The target markets are generally very small and outlets selling the products are very limited to the point of being exclusive.

In addition to the three main categories above, products are classified in at least two additional ways:

- *Emergency Products*: These are products a customer seeks due to sudden events and for which pre-purchase planning is not considered. Often the decision is one of convenience (e.g., whatever works to fix a problem) or personal fulfilment (e.g., perceived to improve purchaser's image).
- *Unsought Products:* These are products whose purchase is unplanned by the consumer but occur as a result of marketer's actions. Such purchase decisions are made when the customer is exposed to promotional activity, such as a salesperson's persuasion or purchase incentives like special discounts offered to certain online shoppers. These promotional activities often lead customers to engage in Impulse Purchasing.

CATEGORIES OF BUSINESS PRODUCTS

The amount spent on business purchasing far exceeds consumer purchasing. Products sold within the b-to-b market fall into one of the following categories:

- *Raw Materials:* These are products obtained through mining, harvesting, fishing, etc., that are key ingredients in the production of higher-order products.
- *Processed Materials:* These are products created through the processing of basic raw materials. In some cases the processing refines original raw materials while in other cases the process combines different raw materials to create something new. For instance, several crops including corn and sugar cane can be processed to create ethanol which has many uses including as a fuel to power car and truck engines.
- *Equipment:* These are products used to help with production or operations activities. Examples range from conveyor belts used on an assembly line to large buildings used to house the headquarters staff of a multi-national company.
- *Basic Components:* These are products used within more advanced components. These are often built with raw material or processed material. Electrical wire is an example.
- *Advanced Components:* These are products that use basic components to produce products that offer a significant function needed within a larger product. Yet by itself an advanced component does not stand alone as a final product. In computers the motherboard would be an example since it contains many basic components but without the inclusion of other products (e.g., memory chips, microprocessor, etc.) would have little value.
- *Product Component*: These are products used in the assembly of a final product though these could also function as stand alone products. Dice included as part of a children's board game would be an example.
- *MRO (Maintenance, Repair and Operating) Products*: These are products used to assist with the operation of the organization but are not directly used in producing goods or services. Office supplies, parts for a truck fleet and natural gas to heat a factory would fall into this category.

Core Benefits

Consider what we have talked about many times in this tutorial; people make buying decisions that satisfy their needs. While many needs are addressed by the consumption of a product or service, some needs are not. For instance, customers may need to be perceived highly by other members of their group or need a product that is easy to use or need a risk-free purchase. In each of these cases, and many more, the core product itself is the benefit the customer receives from using the product.

In some cases these core benefits are offered by the product itself (e.g., floor cleaner) while in other cases the benefit is offered by other aspects of the product (e.g., the can containing the floor cleaner that makes it easier to spread the product). Consequently, at the very heart of all product decisions is determining the key or core benefits a product will provide. From this decision, the rest of the product offering can be developed.

Actual Product

The core benefits are offered through the components that make up the actual product the customer purchases. For instance, when a consumer returns home from shopping at the grocery store and takes a purchased item out of her shopping bag, the actual product is the item she holds in her hand. Within the actual product is the consumable product, which can be viewed as the main good, service or idea the customer is buying.

For instance, while toothpaste may come in a package that makes dispensing it easy, the Consumable Product is the paste that is placed on a toothbrush. But marketers must understand that while the consumable product is, in most cases, the most critical of all product decisions, the actual product includes many separate product decisions including product features, branding, packaging, labelling, and more. Full coverage of several of these important areas is provided later in this tutorial.

CUSTOMER RELATIONSHIP

Customer relationship management (CRM) covers methods and technologies used by companies to manage their relationships with clients. Information stored on existing customers (and potential customers) is analyzed and used to this end. Automated CRM processes are often used to generate automatic personalized marketing based on the customer information stored in the system.

Customer relationship management is a corporate level strategy, focusing on creating and maintaining relationships with customers. Several commercial CRM software packages are available which vary in their approach to CRM. However, CRM is not a technology itself, but rather a holistic approach to an organisation's philosophy, placing the emphasis firmly on the customer.

CRM governs an organization's philosophy at all levels, including policies and processes, front-of-house customer service, employee training, marketing, systems and information management. CRM systems are integrated end-to-end across marketing, sales, and customer service.

A CRM system should:

- Identify factors important to clients.
- Promote a customer-oriented philosophy

- Adopt customer-based measures
- Develop end-to-end processes to serve customers
- Provide successful customer support
- Handle customer complaints
- Track all aspects of sales
- Create a holistic view of customers' sales and services information

There are three fundamental components in CRM:

- Operational - automation of basic business processes (marketing, sales, service)
- Analytical - analysis of customer data and behaviour using business intelligence
- Collaborative - communicating with clients

Operational CRM provides automated support to "front office" business processes (sales, marketing and service). Each interaction with a customer is generally added to a customer's history, and staff can retrieve information on customers from the database as necessary.

According to Gartner Group operational CRM typically involves three general areas:

- *Sales force automation (SFA)*: SFA automates some of a company's critical sales and sales force management tasks, such as forecasting, sales administration, tracking customer preferences and demographics, performance management, lead management, account management, contact management and quote management.
- *Customer service and support (CSS)*: CSS automates certain service requests, complaints, product returns and enquiries.
- *Enterprise marketing automation (EMA)*: EMA provides information about the business environment, including information on competitors, industry trends, and macroenvironmental variables. EMA applications are used to improve marketing efficiency.

Integrated CRM software is often known as a "front office solution", as it deals directly with customers. Many call centers use CRM software to store customer information. When a call is received, the system displays the associated customer information (determined from the number of the caller). During and following the call, the call center agent dealing with the customer can add further information. Some customer services can be fully automated, such as allowing customers to access their bank account details online or via a WAP phone.

Analytical CRM

Analytical CRM analyses data (gathered as part of operational CRM, or from other sources) in an attempt to identify means to enhance a company's relationship with its clients. The results of an analysis can be used to design targeted marketing campaigns, for example:

- Acquisition: Cross-selling, up-selling
- Retention: Retaining existing customers (antonym: customer attrition)
- Information: Providing timely and regular information to customers

Other examples of the applications of analyses include:

- Contact optimization
- Evaluating and improving customer satisfaction
- Optimizing sales coverage
- Fraud detection
- Financial forecasts
- Price optimization
- Product development
- Programme evaluation
- Risk assessment and management
- Strategic Marketing
- Operational marketing

Data collection and analysis is viewed as a continuing and iterative process. Ideally, business decisions are refined over time, based on feedback from earlier analyses and decisions. Most analytical CRM projects use a data warehouse to manage data.

Collaborative CRM

Collaborative CRM focuses on the interaction with customers (personal interaction, letter, fax, phone, Internet, e-mail etc.)

Collaborative CRM includes:

- Providing efficient communication with customers across a variety of communications channels
- Providing online services to reduce customer service costs
- Providing access to customer information while interacting with customers

Driven by authors from the Harvard Business School (Kracklauer/Mills/ Seifert), Collaborative CRM also seems to be the new paradigma to succeed the leading Efficient Consumer Response and Category Management concept in the industry/ trade relationship.

In its broadest sense, CRM covers all interaction and business with customers. A good CRM programme allows a business to acquire customers, provide customer services and retain valued customers.

Customer services can be improved by:

- Providing online access to product information and technical assistance around the clock
- Identifying what customers value and devising appropriate service strategies for each customer
- Providing mechanisms for managing and scheduling follow-up sales calls

- Tracking all contacts with a customer
- Identifying potential problems before they occur
- Providing a user-friendly mechanism for registering customer complaints
- Providing a mechanism for handling problems and complaints
- Providing a mechanism for correcting service deficiencies
- Storing customer interests in order to target customers selectively
- Providing mechanisms for managing and scheduling maintenance, repair, and on-going support
- Scalability: the system should be highly scalable, as the volume of data stored in the system grows over time
- Communication channels: CRM can interface with a variety of different channels (phone, WAP, Internet etc.)
- Workflow - a company's business processes need to be represented by the system with the ability to track the individual stages and transfer information between steps
- Assignment - the ability to assign requests, such as service requests, to a person or group.
- Database - the means of storing customer data and histories (in a data warehouse)
- Customer privacy considerations, such as data encryption and legislation.

Improving Customer Relationships

CRM applications often track customer interests and requirements, as well as their buying habits. This information can be used to target customers selectively. Furthermore, the products a customer has purchased can be tracked throughout the product's life cycle, allowing customers to receive information concerning a product or to target customers with information on alternative products once a product begins to be phased out.

Repeat purchases rely on customer satisfaction, which in turn comes from a deeper understanding of each customer and their individual needs. CRM is an alternative to the "one size fits all" approach. In industrial markets, the technology can be used to coordinate the conflicting and changing purchase criteria of the sector.

The data gathered as part of CRM raises concerns over customer privacy and enables persuasive sales techniques. However, CRM does not necessarily involve gathering new data, but also includes making better use of customer information gathered as a result of routine customer interaction.

The privacy debate generally focuses on the customer information stored in the centralized database itself, and fears over a company's handling of this information. For example, there is virtually no way a consumer can determine if the company shares private (personally identifiable) data with third parties. Furthermore, companies may not always accurately declare to the consumer the types of information collected by CRM systems and the specific purposes for which the information is used. CRM is also important to non-profit organizations, which sometimes use the terms "constituent relationship management", "contact relationship management" or "community relationship management" to describe their information systems for managing donors, volunteers and other supporters. salesforce.com, a popular CRM service that is on demand, offers its products for free to nonprofit organizations

6

Product Management

INTRODUCTION

Product management is an organizational lifecycle function within a company dealing with the planning or forecasting or marketing of a product or products at all stages of the product lifecycle. Product management and product marketing are different yet complementary efforts with the objective of maximizing sales revenues, market share, and profit margins. The role of product management spans many activities from strategic to tactical and varies based on the organizational structure of the company. Product management can be a function separate on its own and a member of marketing or engineering.

While involved with the entire product lifecycle, product management's main focus is on driving new product development. Product Development and Management Association, superior and differentiated new products - ones that deliver unique benefits and superior value to the customer - is the number one driver of success and product profitability.

CHARACTERISTICS

Depending on the company size and history, product management has a variety of functions and roles. Sometimes there is a product manager, and sometimes the role of product manager is held by others. Frequently there is Profit and Loss responsibility as a key metric for evaluating product manager performance. In some companies, the product management function is the hub of many other activities around the product. In others, it is one of many things that need to happen to bring a product to market.

Product management often serves an inter-disciplinary role, bridging gaps within the company between teams of different expertise, most notably between engineering-oriented teams and business-oriented teams. For example product managers often translate business objectives set for a product by Marketing or Sales into engineering requirements. Conversely they may work to explain the capabilities and limitations of the finished product back to Marketing and Sales. Product Managers may also have one or more direct reports such as a Product Executive who can manage operational tasks or a Change Manager who can oversee new initiatives.

Product Planning

- Identifying new product candidates
- Gathering market requirements
- Determine business-case and feasibility
- Scoping and defining new products at high level
- Evangelizing new products within the company
- Building product roadmaps, particularly Technology roadmaps
- Working to a critical path and ensuring all products are produced on schedule
- Ensuring products are within price margins and up to spec
- Product Life Cycle considerations
- Product differentiation
- Detailed Product planning
- 7 functions of marketing

Product Marketing

- Product positioning and outbound messaging
- Promoting the product externally with press, customers, and partners
- Bringing new products to market
- Monitoring the competition
- more detail on Product marketing.

PRODUCT DECISIONS MANAGEMENT

Marketing starts with the product since it is what an organization has to offer its target market. As we've stressed many times in this tutorial, organizations attempt to provide solutions to a target market's problems. These solutions include tangible or intangible (or both) product offerings marketed by an organization. In addition to satisfying the target market's needs, the product is important because it is how organizations generate revenue. It is the "thing" that for-profit companies sell in order to realise profits and satisfy stakeholders and what non-profit organizations use to generate funds needed to sustain itself. Without a well-developed product strategy that includes input from the target market, a marketing organization will not have long-term success.

PRODUCT

In marketing, the term "product" is often used as a catch-all word to identify solutions a marketer provides to its target market. We will follow this approach and permit the term "product" to cover offerings that fall into one of the following categories:

- *Goods*: Something is considered a good if it is a tangible item. That is, it is something that is felt, tasted, heard, smelled or seen. For example, bicycles, cell phones, and donuts are all examples of tangible goods. In some cases there is a fine line between items that affect the senses and whether these are considered tangible or intangible. We often see this with digital goods accessed via the Internet, such as listening to music online or visiting an information website. In these cases there does not appear to be anything that is tangible or real since it is essentially computer code that is proving the solution. However, for our purposes, we distinguish these as goods since these products are built (albeit using computer code), are stored (e.g., on a computer hard drive), and generally offer the same benefits each time (e.g., quality of the download song is always the same).

- *Services:* Something is considered a service if it is an offering a customer obtains through the work or labour of someone else. Services can result in the creation of tangible goods (e.g., a publisher of business magazines hires a freelance writer to write an article) but the main solution being purchased is the service. Unlike goods, services are not stored, they are only available at the time of use (e.g., hair salon) and the consistency of the benefit offered can vary from one purchaser to another (e.g., not exactly the same hair styling each time).
- *Ideas:* Something falls into the category of an idea if the marketer attempts to convince the customer to alter their behaviour or their perception in some way. Marketing ideas is often a solution put forth by non-profit groups or governments in order to get targeted groups to avoid or change certain behaviour. This is seen with public service announcements directed toward such activity as youth smoking, automobile safety, and illegal drug use.

While in some cases a marketer offers solutions that provide both tangible and intangible attributes, for most organizations their primary offering — the thing that is the main focus of the marketing effort — is concentrated in one area. So while a manufacturer may offer intangible services or a service firm provides certain tangible equipment, these are often used as add-ons that augment the organization's main product.

COMPONENTS OF A PRODUCT

On the surface it seems a product is simply a marketing offering, whether tangible or intangible, that someone wants to purchase and consume. In which case one might believe product decisions are focused exclusively on designing and building the consumable elements of goods, services or ideas.

For instance, one might think the key product decision for a manufacturer of floor cleaners is to focus on creating a formula that cleans more effectively. In actuality, while decisions related to the consumable parts of the product are extremely important, the Total Product consists of more than what is consumed.

The total product offering and the decisions facing the marketer can be broken down into three key parts:

- Core Benefits
- Actual Product
- Augmented Product

Augmented Product

Marketers often surround their actual products with goods and services that provide additional value to the customer's purchase. While these factors may not be key reasons leading customers to purchase (i.e., not core benefits), for some the inclusion of these items strengthens the purchase decision while for others failure to include these may cause the customer not to buy.

Items considered part of the augmented product include:

- *Guarantee:* This provides a level of assurance that the product will perform up to expectations and if not the company marketing the product will support the customer's decision to replace, have it repaired or return for a refund.
- *Warranty*: This offers customers a level of protection that often extends past the guarantee period to cover repair or replacement of certain product components.
- *Customer Service*: This consists of additional services that support the customer's needs including offering training and assistance via telephone or online.
- *Complementary Products* : The value of some product purchases can be enhanced with add-on products, such as items that make the main product easier to use (e.g., laptop carrybag), enhance styling (e.g., cellphone face plates) or extend functionality (e.g., portable keyboard for PDAs).
- *Accessibility:* How customers obtain the product can affect its perceived value depending on such considerations as how easy it is to obtain (e.g., stocked at nearby store, delivered directly to office), the speed at which it can be obtained, and the likelihood it will be available when needed.

KEY PRODUCT DECISIONS

The actual product is designed to provide the core benefits sought by the target market. The marketer offers these benefits through a combination of factors that make up the actual product. Below we discuss in detail four key factors that together help shape the actual product.

These factors include:

- Consumable Product Features
- Branding
- Packaging
- Labeling

Consumable Product Features

Features are characteristics of a product that offer benefits to the customer. In most cases, the most important features are those associated with the consumable product since they are the main reason a customer makes a purchase. For this tutorial we separate the benefits of consumable product features into two groups: functional and psychological.

FUNCTIONAL BENEFITS

Are benefits derived from features that are part the consumable product. For instance, a plasma television includes such features and benefits as:

Feature	Functional Benefit
Screen size	Offers greater detail and allows for more distant viewing
Screen resolution	Viewing provides clear, more realistic picture
Surround sound	Immerses all senses in the viewing experience
Remote control	Allows for greater comfort while viewing

These features are called functional because they result in a benefit the user directly associates with the consumable product. For marketers functional benefits are often the result of materials, design and production decisions. How the product is built can lead to benefits such as effectiveness, durability, speed, ease-of-use, and cost savings to name just few.

PSYCHOLOGICAL BENEFITS

Are benefits the customer perceives to receive when using the product though these may be difficult to measure and may vary by customer. These benefits address needs such as status within a group, risk reduction, sense of independence, and happiness. Such benefits are developed through promotional efforts that target customer's internal makeup.

In addition to determining the type of features to include in a product, the marketer faces several other decisions related to features:

- *Quantity & Quality vs. Cost:* For the marketers an important decision focuses on the quantity and quality of features to include in a product. In most cases the more features included or the higher the quality level for a particular feature, the more expensive the product is to produce and market.
- *Is More Better?:* Even if added cost is not a major concern, the marketer must determine if more features help or hurt the target market's perception of the product. A product with too many features could be viewed as too difficult to use. This was often the case when video cassette recorders (VCR) were the principle device for taping television programs and watching rented movies. Many of the higher-level features introduced in the 1990s as the product matured, such as advanced television recording, proved too difficult for the average consumer to master.

- *Who Should Choose the Features*?: Historically marketers determined what features to include in a product. However, technology, and especially the Internet, offer customers the opportunity to choose their own features to custom build a product. For instance, companies offering website hosting services allow website owners to choose from a list of service options that best suits their needs. Also, for traditional products, such as clothing, companies allow customers to stylize their purchases with logos and other personalized options.

PRODUCT PLACEMENT

Product placement, or embedded marketing, is a form of advertisement, where branded goods or services are placed in a context usually devoid of ads, such as movies, the story line of television shows, or news programmes. The product placement is often not disclosed at the time that the good or service is featured. Product placement became common in the 1980s.

In April 2006, Broadcasting & Cable reported,"Two thirds of advertisers employ'branded entertainment' - product placement - with the vast majority of that in commercial TV programming." The story, based on a survey by the Association of National Advertisers, said"Reasons for using in-show plugs varied from'stronger emotional connection' to better dovetailing with relevant content, to targeting a specific group."

Product placement dates back to the nineteenth century in publishing. By the time Jules Verne published the adventure novel Around the World in Eighty Days he was a world-renowned literary giant to the extent transport and shipping companies lobbied to be mentioned in the story as it was published in serial form; however if he was actually paid to do so remains unknown. Product placement is still used in books to some extent, particularly in novels.

Placement in Movies

Although recognizable brand names probably had appeared in movies prior to the 1920s, the weekly trade periodical Harrison's Reports published its first denunciation of that practice with respect to Red Crown gasoline appearing in the comedy film The Garage, directed by and co-starring Fatty Arbuckle.

During the next four decades, Harrison's Reports frequently cited cases of on-screen brand-name products, always condemning the practice as harmful to movie theaters. Publisher P. S. Harrison's editorials strongly reflected his feelings against product placement in films. An editorial in Harrison's Reports criticized the collaboration between the Corona Typewriter company and First National Pictures when a Corona typewriter appeared in the film The Lost World. Harrison's Reports published several incidents about Corona typewriters appearing in films of the mid-1920s.

Among the famous silent films to feature product placement was Wings, the first film to win the Academy Award for Best Picture. It contained a plug for Hershey's chocolate. Another early example in film occurs in Horse Feathers where Thelma Todd's character falls out of a canoe and into a river. She calls for a life saver and Groucho Marx's character tosses her a Life Savers candy.

In the film Love Happy, Harpo Marx's character cavorts on a rooftop among various billboards and at one point escapes from the villains on the old Mobil logo, the "Flying Red Horse". Harrison's Reports severely criticized this scene in its film review and in a front-page editorial of the same issue. The film It's a Wonderful Life, directed by Frank Capra, depicts a young boy with aspirations to be an explorer, displaying a prominent copy of National Geographic. In the film noir Gun Crazy, the climactic crime is the payroll robbery of the Armour meat-packing plant, where a Bulova clock is prominently seen.

In other early media, e.g., radio in the 1930s and 1940s and early television in the 1950s, programmes were often underwritten by companies. "Soap operas" are called such because they were initially underwritten by consumer, packaged-goods companies such as Procter & Gamble or Unilever. When television began to displace radio, DuMont's Cavalcade of Stars television show was, in its era, notable for not relying on a sole sponsor in the tradition of NBC's Texaco Star Theater and similar productions. Sponsorship exists today with programmes being sponsored by major vendors such as Hallmark Cards. The conspicuous display of Studebaker motor vehicles in the television series Mr. Ed, which was sponsored by the Studebaker Corporation from 1961 to 1963, is another example of product placement. Incorporation of products into the actual plot of a film or television show is generally called "brand integration".

An early example of such "brand integration" was by Abercrombie & Fitch when one of its stores provided the notional venue for part of the romantic-comedy film Man's Favourite Sport? starring Rock Hudson and Paula Prentiss. A recent example is HBO's Sex and the City, where the plot revolved around, among other things, Absolut Vodka, a campaign upon which one of the protagonists was working, and a billboard in Times Square, where a bottle prevented an image of the model from being pornographic. Knight Rider, a television series featuring a talking Pontiac Trans Am, is another example of brand integration.

The earliest example of product placement in a computer or video game occurs in Action Biker for Skips crisps, a product by KP Snacks. Video games, such as Crazy Taxi, feature real retail stores as game destinations. However, sometimes the economics are reversed and video-game makers pay for the rights to use real sports teams and players. Today, product placement in online video is also becoming common. Online agencies are specializing in connecting online video producers, which are usually individuals, with brands and advertisers.

Self Promotion

Twentieth Century Fox, a subsidiary of News Corporation, has promoted its parent company's own Sky News channel through including it as a plot device when characters are viewing news broadcasts of breaking events. The newscaster or reporter in the scene will usually state that the audience is viewing Sky News, and reports from other channels are not shown. One notable example is the film Independence Day.

Sports

Product placement has long been prevalent in sports as well, from professional sports to college sports, and even on the local level with high school sports. This can be attributed to sports being prevalent on television, which increases exposure to these products. The Green Monster at Fenway Park in Boston, Massachusetts, was originally built to have such advertisements, but since 1947 has largely been devoid of such advertisements. The Citgo sign overlooking Fenway Park can also be considered a form of product placement, despite the Boston Red Sox having a sponsorship deal with Gulf Oil.

Outside of baseball product placement in sports began to rise in the 1970s, when NASCAR began to allow sponsors to cover the cars they were sponsoring with their logos. This has subsequently followed with the uniforms the drivers themselves wear having sponsor logos. The Arena Football League, NFL Europe, and several association football leagues eventually allowed sponsors of the uniforms. The National Hockey League began allowing sponsors to line along the interior walls of the ice rinks in the early 1980s. This, combined with new rules mandating players to wear helmets, arguably gave the NHL a different look in the 1980s than compared with the 1970s.

NFL

While the now-defunct NFL Europe allowed liberal use of sponsors with the team's uniforms, the main National Football League has long been more stringent. For instance, the league prohibits logos of sponsors painted onto the fields, although Gillette Stadium in Foxborough, Massachusetts, does have a disposable razor painted onto the field in honour of naming-rights sponsor Gillette. In 2008, the league allowed sponsors on the practice jerseys of the uniforms, but not the game-worn uniforms.

The NFL's strict policy contradicts several other policies on the uniforms. In 1991, the league allowed the individual uniform suppliers to display their logo on the products they made in conjunction with the rest of the sports world, and since 2002, Reebok has been the official uniform supplier for the entire league.

In addition, two of the league's flagship teams — the Green Bay Packers and the Pittsburgh Steelers — adopted some form of their identity from corporate sponsors. The Packers adopted the nickname "Packers" because they were sponsored by the Indian Packing Company, and later had "ACME PACKERS" written on their uniforms in the early 1920s after the Acme Packing Company bought Indian Packing.

The Steelers adopted their current logo in 1962 as a product-placement deal with the American Iron and Steel Institute, which owned the rights to the Steelmark logo. The Steelers later were allowed to add "-ers" to the Steelmark logo the following year so that they could own a trademark on the logo.

Categories and Variations

Actual product placement falls into two categories: products or locations that are obtained from manufacturers or owners to reduce the cost of production, and products deliberately placed into productions in exchange for fees.

Sometimes, product usage is negotiated rather than paid for. Some placements provide productions with below-the-line savings, with products such as props, clothes and cars being loaned for the production's use, thereby saving them purchase or rental fees. Barter systems and service deals are also common practices. Producers may also seek out companies for product placements as another savings or revenue stream for the movie, with, for example, products used in exchange for help funding axdvertisements tied-in with a film's release, a show's new season or other event.

A variant of product placement is advertisement placement. In this case an advertisement for the product is seen in the movie or television series. Examples include a Lucky Strike cigarette advertisement on a billboard or a truck with a milk advertisement on its trailer.

Another variant is the widespread use of promotional consideration in which a television game show would award an advertiser's product as a prize or consolation prize in return for a subsidy from the product's manufacturer.

Product-placement companies work to integrate their client company brands with film and television productions. Jay May, president of Feature This!, a branded entertainment company, explains the process: "The studio sends us the script. We break it down. We look for our clients' demographics and then we tell our client this movie is available with this actor, with this director, with this producer, do you want it?"

Measuring Effectiveness

Quantification methods track brand integrations, with both basic quantitative and more demonstrative qualitative systems used to determine the cost and effective media value of a placement. Rating systems measure the type of placement and on-screen exposure is gauged by audience recall rates. Products might be featured but hardly identifiable, clearly identifiable, long or recurrent in exposure, associated with a main character, verbally mentioned and/or they may play a key role in the storyline. Media values are also weighed over time, depending on a specific product's degree of presence in the market.

NEW PRODUCT DEVELOPMENT

In business and engineering, new product development is the term used to describe the complete process of bringing a new product or service to market. There are two parallel paths involved in the NPD process: one involves the idea generation, product design and detail engineering; the other involves market research and marketing analysis.

Companies typically see new product development as the first stage in generating and commercializing new products within the overall strategic process of product life cycle management used to maintain or grow their market share.

PROCESS

- Idea Generation is often called the "fuzzy front end" of the NPD process
  - Ideas for new products can be obtained from basic research using a SWOT analysis, Market and consumer trends, company's R&D depart-ment, competitors, focus groups, employees, salespeople, corporate spies, trade shows, or Ethnographic discovery methods may also be used to get an insight into new product lines or product features.
  - Idea Generation or Brainstorming of new product, service, or store concepts - idea generation techniques can begin when you have done your OPPORTUNITY ANALYSIS to support your ideas in the Idea Screening Phase.
- Idea Screening
  - The object is to eliminate unsound concepts prior to devoting resources to them.
  - The screeners should ask several queWill the customer in the target market benefit from the product?

    b. What is the size and growth forecasts of the market segment/ target market?

    c. What is the current or expected competitive pressure for the product idea?

    d. What are the industry sales and market trends the product idea is based on?

    e. Is it technically feasible to manufacture the product?

    f. Will the product be profitable when manufactured and delivered to the customer at the target price?
- Concept Development and Testing
  - Develop the marketing and engineering details

a. Investigate intellectual property issues and search patent data bases
b. Who is the target market and who is the decision maker in the purchasing process?
c. What product features must the product incorporate?
d. What benefits will the product provide?
e. How will consumers react to the product?
f. How will the product be produced most cost effectively?
g. Prove feasibility through virtual computer aided rendering, and rapid prototyping
h. What will it cost to produce it?

- Testing the Concept by asking a sample of prospective customers what they think of the idea. Usually via Choice Modelling.

- Business Analysis
  - Estimate likely selling price based upon competition and customer feedback
  - Estimate sales volume based upon size of market and such tools as the Fourt-Woodlock equation
  - Estimate profitability and breakeven point
- Beta Testing and Market Testing
  - Produce a physical prototype or mock-up
  - Test the product in typical usage situations
  - Conduct focus group customer interviews or introduce at trade show
  - Make adjustments where necessary
  - Produce an initial run of the product and sell it in a test market area to determine customer acceptance
- Technical Implementation
  - New prigramme initiation
  - Finalize Quality management system
  - Resource estimation
  - Requirement publication
  - Publish technical communications such as data sheets
  - Engineering operations planning
  - Department scheduling
  - Supplier collaboration
  - Logistics plan
  - Resource plan publication
  - Prigramme review and monitoring
  - Contingencies - what-if planning
- Commercialization
  - Launch the product
  - Produce and place advertisements and other promotions

  - Fill the distribution pipeline with product
  - Critical path analysis is most useful at this stage
- New Product Pricing
  - Impact of new product on the entire product portfolio
  - Value Analysis
  - Competition and alternative competitive technologies
  - Differing value segments
  - Product Costs
  - Forecast of unit volumes, revenue, and profit

These steps may be iterated as needed. Some steps may be eliminated. To reduce the time that the NPD process takes, many companies are completing several steps at the same time. Most industry leaders see new product development as a *proactive* process where resources are allocated to identify market changes and seize upon new product opportunities before they occur. Many industry leaders see new product development as an ongoing process in which the entire organization is always looking for opportunities.

Great amounts of uncertainty and change may exist, which makes it difficult or impossible to plan the complete project before starting it. In this case, a more flexible approach may be advisable.

Because the NPD process typically requires both engineering and marketing expertise, cross-functional teams are a common way of organizing projects. The team is responsible for all aspects of the project, from initial idea generation to final commercialization, and they usually report to senior management.

In those industries where products are technically complex, development research is typically expensive, and product life cycles are relatively short, strategic alliances among several organizations helps to spread the costs, provide access to a wider skill set, and speeds the overall process. Also, notice that because engineering and marketing expertise are usually both critical to the process, choosing an appropriate blend of the two is important. Observe that this substance is slanted more toward the marketing side.

People respond to new products in different ways. The adoption of a new technology can be analysed using a variety of diffusion theories such as the Diffusion of innovations theory.

A new product pricing process is important to reduce risk and increase confidence in the pricing and marketing decisions to be made. Bernstein and Macias describe an integrated process that breaks down the complex task of new product pricing into manageable elements.

FUZZY FRONT END

The Fuzzy Front End is the messy "getting started" period of new product development processes. It is in the front end where the organization formulates a concept of the product to be developed and decides whether or not to invest resources in the further development of an idea. It is the phase between first consideration of an opportunity and when it is judged ready to enter the structured development process. It includes all activities from the search for new opportunities through the formation of a germ of an idea to the development of a precise concept. The Fuzzy Front End ends when an organization approves and begins formal development of the concept.

Although the Fuzzy Front End may not be an expensive part of product development, it can consume 50% of development time and it is where major commitments are typically made involving time, money, and the product's nature, thus setting the course for the entire project and final end product. Consequently, this phase should be considered as an essential part of development rather than something that happens "before development," and its cycle time should be included in the total development cycle time.

Koen et al. distinguish five different front-end elements:

1. Opportunity Identification
2. Opportunity Analysis
3. Idea Genesis
4. Idea Selection
5. Concept and Technology Development

The first element is the opportunity identification. In this element, large or incremental business and technological chances are identified in a more or less structured way. Using the guidelines established here, resources will eventually be allocated to new projects.... which then lead to a structured NPPD strategy. The second element is the opportunity analysis. It is done to translate the identified opportunities into implications for the business and technology specific context of the company. Here extensive efforts may be made to align ideas to target customer groups and do market studies and/or technical trials and research..

The third element is the idea genesis, which is described as evolutionary and iterative process progressing from birth to maturation of the opportunity into a tangible idea. The process of the idea genesis can be made internally or come from outside inputs, e.g. a supplier offering a new material/technology, or from a customer with an unusual request. The fourth element is the idea selection. Its purpose is to choose whether to pursue an idea by analyzing its potential business value.

The fifth element is the concept and technology development. During this part of the front-end, the business case is developed based on estimates of the total available market, customer needs, investment requirements, competition analysis and project uncertainty. Some organizations consider this to be the first stage of the NPPD process. The Fuzzy Front End is also described in literature as "Front End of Innovation", "Phase 0", "Stage 0" or "Pre-Project-Activities".

A universally acceptable definition for Fuzzy Front End or a dominant framework has not been developed so far. It is the Fuzzy Front End generally consists of three tasks: strategic planning, concept generation, and, especially, pre-technical evaluation. These activities are often chaotic, unpredictible, and unstructured. In comparison, the subsequent new product development process is typically structured, predictable, and formal. The term *Fuzzy Front End* was first popularized by Smith and Reinertsen, R.G.Cooper describes the early stages of NPPD as a four step process in which ideas are generated

- Subjected to a preliminary technical and market assessment
- And merged to coherent product concepts
- Which are finally judged for their fit with existing product strategies and portfolios
- Cooper and Edgett affirm that vital predevelopment activities include:
  - Preliminary market assessment.
  - Technical assessment.
  - Source-of-supply-assessment:suppliers and partners or alliances.
  - Market research: market size and segmentation analysis,VoC research.
  - Product concept testing
  - Value-to-the customer assessment
  - Product definition
  - Business and financial analysis.

These activities yield vital information to make a Go/No-Go to Development decision.

In the in-depth study by Khurana and Rosenthal front-end activities include:

- Product strategy formulation and communication,
- Opportunity identification and assessment,
- Idea generation,
- Product definition,
- Project planning, and
- Executive reviews.

Economical analysis, benchmarking of competitive products,and modeling and prototyping are also important activities during the front-end activities.

The outcomes of FFE are the:

- Mission statement
- Customer needs
- Details of the selected concept
- Product definition and specifications
- Economic analysis of the product
- The development schedule
- Project staffing and the budget, and a
- Business plan aligned with corporate strategy.

Husig, Kohn and Huskela was proposed a conceptual model of Front-End Process which includes early Phases of Innovation Process.

This model is structured in three phases and three gates:

- *Phase 1*: Environmental screening or opportunity identification stage in which external changes will be analysed and translated into potential business opportunities.
- *Phase 2*: Preliminary definition of an idea or concept.
- *Phase 3*: Detailed product, project or concept definition, and Business planning.

The gates are:

- Opportunity screening;
- Idea evaluation;
- Go/No-Go for development.

The final gate leads to a dedicated new product development project. Many professionals and academics consider that the general features of Fuzzy Front End make difficult to see the FFE as a structured process,but rather as a set of interdependent activities. However, Husig et al.,2005 argue that front-end not need to be fuzzy,but can be handled in a structured manner.

Peter Koen argue that in the FFE for incremental,platform and radical projects,three separate strategies and processes are typically involved. The traditional Stage Gate process was designed for incremental product development,namely for a single product.The FFE for developing a new platform must start out with a strategic vision of where the company wants to develop products and this will lead to a family of products.

Projects for breakthrough products start out with a similar strategic vision,but are associated with technologies which require new discoveries.It is worth mentioning what are incremental,platform and breakthrough products.

Incremental products are considered to be cost reductions, improvements to existing product lines,additions to existing platforms and repositioning of existing products introduced in markets. *Breakthrough products* are new to the company or new to the world and offer a 5-10 times or greater improvement in performance combined with a 30-50% or greater reduction in costs.

Platform products establish a basic architecture for a next generation product or process and are substantially larger in scope and resources than incremental projects.

PRODUCT DECISIONS MANAGEMENT

Marketers think of a product as a bundle of physical, service, and symbolic characteristics expected to yield benefits to the consumer. Products may range from goods to services, although most products will have some degree of both characteristics.

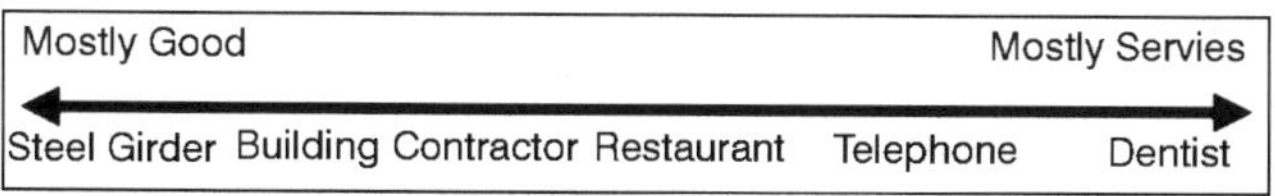

A product item is a specific version of a product that has a unique designation in the seller's list of products. A product line is a series of related product items. A product mix is the company's total assortment of product items.

The product mix may be described by three characteristics:

- Width: the number of product lines
- Depth: the average number of items per line
- *Consistency*: how closely related the product lines are

American Brands, for example, has five major product lines: tobacco products, distilled spirits, office products, home improvement and hardware, and golf and leisure. The tobacco line itself consists of several lines: cigarettes, cigars, pipe tobacco, and roll-your-own supplies. The home improvement and hardware line includes Master Lock and Moen products. A particular style of kitchen faucet would be a product item within the Moen line.

There are several ways to classify products. A popular way is to think of four categories based on the amount of effort a consumer might be expected to expend on obtaining the product: convenience, shopping, specialty, and unsought. In general, a person will expend little effort to obtain a convenience product, so marketers will focus on maximizing product availability via distribution and will try to build brand identity and competitive prices. Shopping products are items people do not buy as frequently, expending a moderate amount of effort to obtain the item and/or compare different alternatives. Distribution can be more selective, and marketers will attempt to build brand differentiation through promotion and the type of outlet carrying the merchandise. If consumers do not believe there really are brand differences, then price will be very important.

Specialty products are not bought very often and will usually be more expensive items. Consumers will expend maximum effort to obtain what they want. Marketers want to build an image of exclusiveness through promotion and distribution; only exclusive outlets will carry the merchandise. Unsought goods are generally those that consumers will expend no effort to obtain and are bought only after extensive promotion by the marketer. Life insurance might be an example of an unsought good. There are thousands of "new" products introduced every year. It has been estimated that only about 10 per cent of these are new in the sense that they did not exist before. More than half of "new" products are really product modifications or product improvement.

Consumers tend to perceive "newness" based on the amount of behaviour change necessary to use the product:

- Discontinuous innovation: pioneering products so new that no previous product performed an equivalent function; necessitate new consumption or usage patterns
- Dynamically continuous innovation: changes and improvements that do not strikingly change buying and usage patterns; these occupy the middle range on the continuum of newness

- Continuous innovations: ongoing, commonplace changes, such as minor product alterations or imitative products

Although definitions of success and failure vary, there is no doubt that the majority of new products are not successes.

Common reasons for failure include:

- Inadequate product superiority or uniqueness, as when a "me too" product does not offer a relative advantage
- Inadequate or inferior planning, such as failing to do proper marketing research to understand consumers' needs or failure to develop realistic estimates of demand
- Poor execution, which may occur when management believes the product is so good it will succeed without resources to support it
- Technical problems, as when a product fails because of design or production problems
- Poor timing, as when a company enters a market too early or too late in the product life cycle or when the marketing environment changes

The typical process for developing new products looks like this:

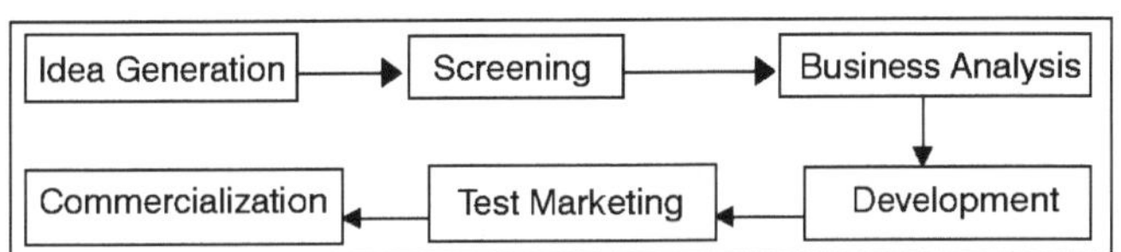

Step 1: *Idea Generation*: Perfom a continuous, systematic search for new ideas. Sources of ideas include scientists, consumers, salespeople, top management, and competitors.

Step 2: *Screening*: Delete from further consideration those ideas that are not consistent with company objectives and resources or with the market needs that the company tries to serve. Common tools include screening checklists and concept testing.

Step 3: *Business Analysis*: Do financial and marketing analyses to see whether the product idea appears to be profitable and what type of marketing efforts it will require.

Step 4: *(Product) Development*: See if the idea can actually be realised. Is it technically and commercially feasible? This stage often involves a host of other decisions, such as package design, brand name selection, trademark registration, etc.

Step 5: *Test Marketing*: Put the product on the market in limited areas to gauge market reaction. The amount of test marketing needed varies by product. Generally little or no test marketing is done when development costs are low, management is very confident, the innovation is a minor product modification or is an imitative product, and/or the product is a high-ticket item.

Step 6: *Commercialization*: Introduce and market the new product. Decisions include when, where, to whom, and how. Once a product is launched, it enters a product life cycle. The PLC describes how a typical new product category follows a set of four stages, the important thing being the marketing implications that accompany each stage.

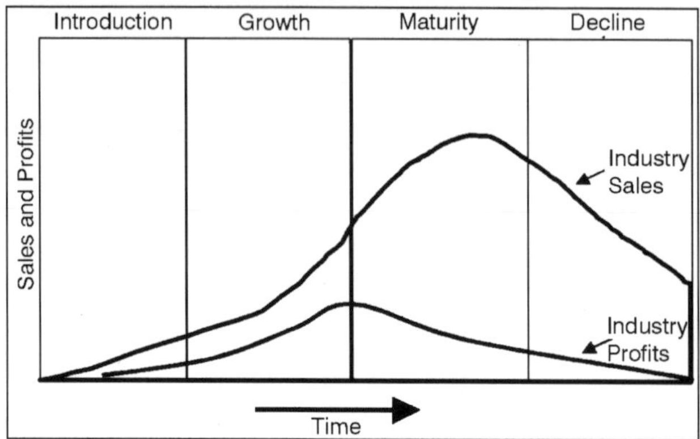

In the introduction stage, the firm faces little if any direct competition for its new product. The objective is to gain awareness and acceptance in the market both by consumers and by middlemen who might carry the product. Price is typically set high, both to take advantage of the fact that the earliest buyers of a new product are often willing to pay premium prices for something new and to begin to regain some of the investment expenses incurred in developing the product.

Sometimes, especially if competition might be expected early, a low price is used to discourage competition from entering. Promotion is designed to inform and educate the market about the new product. Distribution is limited to those few middlemen who might be willing to accept a new product. In the growth stage, competitors enter the market with their own versions of the product, and competition often is based on real product differences.

The strategic focus now becomes building market share and establishing product differentiation. Price tends to remain high but will fall toward the end of the stage as it becomes more of a competitive tool. Distribution will expand considerably, and the tone of promotion shifts to being more persuasive, stressing product differences.

The maturity stage is marked by stable sales and high total industry profits. Many competitors dominate the market, although many more marginal ones that entered during the growth stage have left. The objective now is maintaining the market built in the growth stage. Although firms will have full product lines with many variations, real product differences are fewer. Price tends to fall, being used more competitively. Distribution will be at its maximum. Promotion is of a "reminder" nature.

In the decline stage, sales are falling, as are profits. Firms begin to exit the industry, and the objective now becomes one of trying to pull as much profit as possible from the product in its waning days. The product lines are pruned, with only the few best versions remaining. Both promotion and distribution are reduced as much as possible to help pare back costs. Because the maturity stage is the most profitable, firms will derive strategies for prolonging it as much as possible through either product or market modifications.

Product modifications may include the following:

- *Quality improvements*: Quality is defined by *consumers* and measures how well a product does what it is supposed to do. Marketers need to
  - Provide the desired level of quality,
  - Work constantly to improve quality, and
  - Accurately communicate quality to market.
- *Design improvements*: Styling, aesthetics, and/or function of a product is altered to offer more convenience, safety, efficiency, or versatility.
- *Style improvements*: The aesthetic appeal of the product is increased, especially with an eye toward creating a unique look.

The Product Life Cycle results from a diffusion process that is the the sequence of acceptance of new products by the members of a community or social system.

Five groups are visible in the diffusion process, based on the speed with which they adopt an innovation:

- Innovators initially purchase a new product. They are motivated by novelty and tend to be younger, more affluent, better educated, and confident about their decision-making ability.
- Early Adopters are similar to innovators. They are motivated more by improvement than novelty and are generally considered the most important group because of their opinion leadership qualities—others will follow them.
- Early Majority members are aware of and willing to accept change. They tend to be average in age, affluence, and education.
- Late Majority members are less aware of and less willing to accept change. They may be of an older average age and a little below average in affluence and education; they tend to be conservative and traditional.
- Laggards are the last group to adopt a product. They are generally the oldest, most conservative group.

Part of the "product decision area" involves branding, packaging, and labeling. Both consumers and marketers rely on branding. Think how much easier it is to buy products based on your familiarity with the brand—it certainly makes the search and evaluation stages much simpler than when buying a brand you aren't familiar with. For consumers, benefits include quality assurance, a reduced search/selection time, a known quantity, and prestige. For marketers, benefits include differentiation of their product from competitors', improved brand identity, and more effective marketing communications.

There are several terms to be familiar with:

- *Brand*: A name, term, sign, symbol, design, or combination thereof used to identify and differentiate a company's products from competitors'
- *Brand name*: The element of the brand that can be vocalized
- *Brand mark*: The element of the brand that cannot be vocalized
- *Trademark*: A brand or part of a brand that is registered with the U.S. Patent and Trademark office. This provides the owner of the brand with legal protection for excluding competitors from use of the same or very similar name or logo.
- *Service mark*: the "trademark" for services

Marketers must choose from several brand strategies. One choice involves the sponsor of the brand. A national brand is owned by a manufacturer who then bears the cost of marketing the brand. A distributor or private brand is owned by a retailer or wholesaler, although the product generally is made by a well-known manufacturer. The retailer or wholesaler is responsible for any marketing of the brand. A generic brand has no visible brand name—ownership cannot be determined, and usually no marketing outside of distribution is done.

Another decision is "family vs. individual" branding. In a family, one name is used for a set of products, such as the Craftsman name on a variety of tools. A variation on this is licensing, where the owner of a trademark permits others to use it on various products. In multibranding, each product has its own name, such as with Procter and Gamble's Tide, Cheer, and Ivory Snow laundry detergents.

In a combination strategy, combined family and individual brands are used, such as with Kellogg's Frosted Flakes and Kellogg's Corn Flakes. As with other marketing decisions, there is no one best way; each strategy carries certain advantages and drawbacks.

Ideally, marketers try to build "brand equity," which reflects the value a brand has beyond its basic functional value. Brand equity has a financial dimension to it that results from having a large enough part of the market desiring that brand above others.

Typically, brand equity results from a long-term strategy that leads a market to that point in a series of stages:

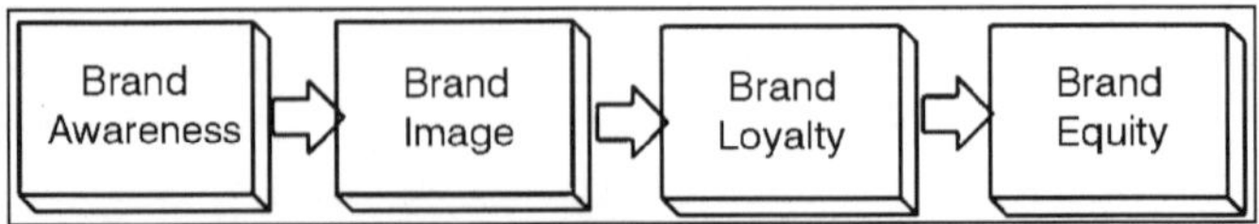

First, the market must realise that the brand exists in the marketplace. Next, the marketer builds strong, positive associations with the brand. From that comes preference, where the ideal is for the consumer to buy that brand exclusively. From long-term use comes consumer identification with the brand. The importance of packaging and labeling differs by product. Packaging may serve various functions. For many consumer products, especially those typically bought in self-serve environments, promotion is a critical element in helping the consumer identify the product and in increasing the product's visibility in a retail setting.

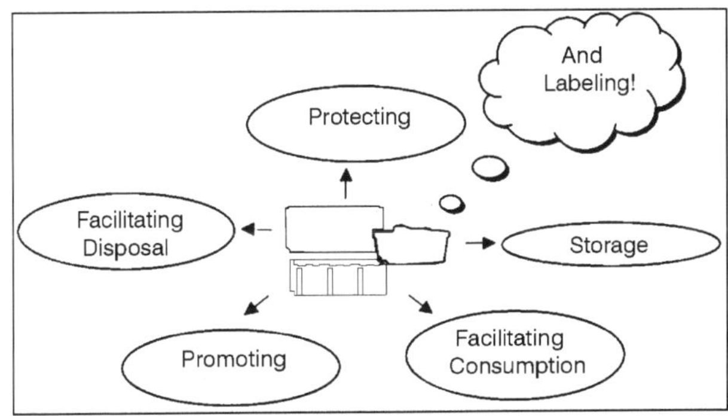

Services differ from goods in several distinct ways.

The diagram shows these key differences:

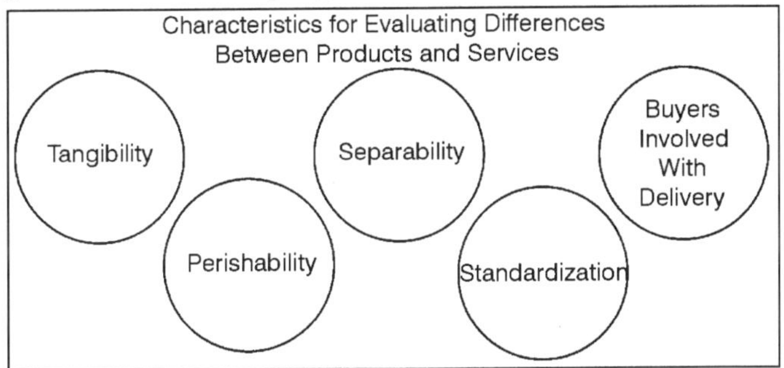

Goods are tangible; services are intangible. Although some goods have very short lifespans, they can be stored for at least a while before consumption; if services are not used when available, they are unrecoverable. Goods can be separated from their makers, but services cannot be separated from the provider.

Goods may be made just as to a standard procedure that makes consistency of output; service delivery is difficult to standardize, so delivery is always, to some degree, inconsistent. Finally, goods may be bought from someone other than the actual producer; with services, the buyer is directly involved with the process: the dental hygienist cannot clean your teeth without you being there.

Because of these differences, the marketing mix elements must be modified for services:

- *Product*: Can be classified like goods. Same marketing mix ideas would then apply. Things like packaging and labeling are of minimal or no importance.

- *Pricing*: Harder to determine because cost of "production" is often more difficult to determine. Price negotiation may be more prevalent for services.
- *Place*: Channels are usually short. Storage, transportation, and inventory are of minimal or no concern.
- *Promotion*: Can be "tangibilized" by linking service to a specific benefit. Creation of a favourable image is critical. Desire for "personal relationship" with provider increases importance of personal selling.

The intangibility of services makes it very difficult for consumers to judge the quality of the service.

Hence, consumers rely on a variety of indicators to suggest quality:

- *Reliability*: Is the service likely to be delivered as expected?
- *Tangibles*: What are the physical characteristics of the place of delivery?
- *Responsiveness*: How willing is the provider to deliver the service?
- *Empathy*: How willing is the provider to take time to determine the exact nature of the service desired?
- *Assurance*: How confident does the consumer feel that the service will be provided as expected?

MANAGING PRODUCT MOVEMENT ANALYSIS

In addition to enlisting the assistance of retailers and wholesalers to make products available to customers, marketers also face additional concerns when trying to meet their distribution objectives. In this section we examine the tasks that must be carried out in order to physically move products to customers. In some cases the marketer will take on the responsibility of carrying out some functions, while other tasks may be assigned to distribution service providers. Whether handled by the marketer or contracted to others, these functions are crucial to having a cost-effective and efficient distribution system.

We explore the movement of product by first examining how physical distribution decisions often involve analyzing the trade-off between the service level the marketer offers to customers versus the costs associated with providing these services. Next we provide an in-depth examination of three major tasks that the marketer or distribution service providers may need to carryout in order to ship products to customers.

These tasks include:

- Ordering and Inventory Management
- Product Storage
- Transportation

It is worth noting that while most physical distribution is concerned with moving tangible products, some of the issues covered here are also applicable to intangible products, such as services and to digital products.

TRADE-OFF ANALYSIS: SERVICE-LEVEL VS. COST

The distribution activities we discuss in this part of the Principles of Marketing tutorial are important elements in the marketer's overall customer service package. Marketers strive to deliver an optimal level of service to their customers. However, "optimal" does not always translate into providing the "best" service options to customers. The service-level marketers' offer for their distribution activities, like the service-level offered by other company-related activities that impact customers (e.g., customer help desk), is determined using trade-off analysis.

With service-level trade-off analysis, the marketer compares the number and quality of distribution features (e.g., speed of delivery, ease of placing orders, order tracking, etc.) they would like to offer versus the cost of providing the features. For instance, when it comes to transportation options (e.g., truck, railroad, air, etc.), trade-off analysis may show that choosing the fastest method for delivery may not make economic sense since options for fast delivery often are very expensive compared to slower methods. While the customer may appreciate having their order arrive quickly, the marketer may find fast delivery to be an expensive proposition that significantly reduces their profit margin.

Since most distribution activities are non-revenue producing (i.e., are used to support the selling of a product but do not actually create a sale) and, thus, represent a cost to the marketer, it should be understood that the marketer's distribution system choice may not be the overall best available in terms of getting the product into customer's hand as fast as possible. Rather, the marketer's choice for what is optimal will be determined by analyzing distribution features and costs and evaluating how these fit within the marketer's overall objectives (e.g., financial objectives, product positioning, etc.).

ORDERING AND INVENTORY MANAGEMENT

Having products available when customers want to make purchases may seem like a relatively straightforward process. All a seller needs to do is make sure there is product (i.e., inventory) in their possession and ready for the customer to purchase. Unfortunately, being prepared for customer purchasing is not always easy.

Having the right product available when the customer is ready to buy requires a highly coordinated effort involving order entry and processing systems, forecasting techniques, customer knowledge, strong channel relationships and efficiency at physically handling products.

Order Entry and Processing System

The marketer must have a system allowing customers to easily place orders. This system can be as simple as a consumer walking to the counter of small food stand to purchase a few vegetables or as complicated as automated computer systems where an electronic order is triggered from a retailer to a manufacturer each time a consumer purchases a product at the retailer's store. In either case, the order processing system must be able to meet the purchasing needs of the customer. In some cases, an efficient ordering system can be turned into a competitive advantage. Firms such as Amazon.com, turned their order handing system into a product feature with the patented "1-click" ordering option that streamlines online ordering by reducing the number of clicks needed to make purchases.

Forecasting

Inventory management is often an exercise in predicting how customers will respond in the future. By predicting purchase behaviour the marketer can respond by making sure the right amount of product is available. For most large-scale resellers effective inventory forecasting requires the use of sophisticated statistical tools that look at many variables, such as past purchase history, amount of promotional effort that triggers an increase in customer ordering, and other market criteria to determine how much of the product will be needed to meet customer demand.

Customer Knowledge

Inventory management can be fine-tuned to respond to customer's needs. As a marketer learns more about a customer they begin to observe trends in how and when purchases are made. Combining customer knowledge with forecasting techniques allows the marketer to better estimate product demand and inventory requirements.

The key to understanding customers is to have in place a customer relationship management (CRM) system that tracks all customer activity and allows for data mining activities that analyse customer information in order to identify patterns in customer activity.

Channel Relationships

While the marketer who uses channel members to sell consumer products has access to information for their immediate customers (e.g., resellers) they often do not have access to sales and customer behaviour information controlled by the party selling to the final consumer (e.g., retailer). Knowing the demand patterns at the final consumer level can give marketers good insight into how the reseller may order.

Developing strong relationships with the holder of consumer information can result in the reseller sharing this information with the marketer. In fact, some retailers allow marketers direct access to real-time, store-level inventory information so the marketer can monitor how products are selling in stores and be in a position to respond quickly if inventory needs change.

Physical Product Handling

An often overlooked area of inventory management involves the actions and skills needed to prepare a product to move from one point to another. Some products require special attention be given to ensure the product is not damaged during shipment. Such efforts must be carefully balanced against increased costs that arise (e.g., stronger packaging) in order to provide greater protection to products. Because of this, many marketers will accept the fact that some small level of damage to occur during the distribution process.

PRODUCT STORAGE

The second important element in physical distribution concerns storing products for future delivery. Marketers of tangible products, and even digital products, may have storage concerns. Storage facilities, such as warehouses, play an important role in the distribution process for a number of reasons including:

- *Hold Wide Assortment:* Many resellers allow their customers to purchase small quantities of many different products. Yet to obtain the best prices from suppliers, resellers must purchase in large quantities. The need, thus, exists for storage facilities that not only hold a large volume of product, but also can hold a wide-variety of resellers' inventory. Additionally, these facilities must be organized in a way that permits resellers to easily fill orders for their customers.
- *Meet Unanticipated Demand:* Holding products in storage offers a safeguard in cases of unexpected increases in demand for products.
- *Needed for Large Shipping Quantities:* As we noted in our discussion of transportation, manufacturers generally prefer to ship in large product quantities in order to more effectively spread transportation costs. This often means manufacturers must create storage areas in which the manufactured goods can build up in the quantities needed for such shipments to occur.
- *Offer Faster Response:* Additional storage facilities, strategically located in different geographical areas, allows a marketing organization to respond quickly to customers' needs. The ability to respond with quick delivery can be a major value-added feature since it reduces the buyer's need to maintain large inventory at their own locations.
- *Security and Backup:* For digital products, additional storage facilities are not only needed to offer customers faster access to products (e.g., online content and software) but are also needed to protect against technical glitches and security threats.

Types of Warehouses

The warehouse is the most common type of storage though other forms do exist (e.g., storage tanks, computer server farms). Some warehouses are massive structures that simultaneously support the unloading of numerous in-bound trucks and railroad cars containing suppliers' products while at the same time loading multiple trucks for shipment to customers.

Below we discuss five types of warehouses:

- *Private Warehouse:* This type of warehouse is owned and operated by channel suppliers and resellers and used in their own distribution activity. For instance, a major retail chain may have several regional warehouses supplying their stores or a wholesaler will operate a warehouse at which it receives and distributes products.
- *Public Warehouse:* The public warehouse is essentially space that can be leased to solve short-term distribution needs. Retailers that operate their own private warehouses may occasionally seek additional storage space if their facilities have reached capacity or if they are making a special, large purchase of products. For example, retailers may order extra merchandise to prepare for in-store sales or order a large volume of a product that is offered at a low promotional price by a supplier.
- *Automated Warehouse:* With advances in computer and robotics technology many warehouses now have automated capabilities. The level of automation ranges from a small conveyor belt transporting products in a small area all the way up to a fully automated facility where only a few people are needed to handle storage activity for thousands of pounds/kilograms of product. In fact, many warehouses use machines to handle nearly all physical distribution activities such as moving product-filled pallets (i.e., platforms that hold large amounts of product) around buildings that may be several stories tall and the length of two or more football fields.
- *Climate-Controlled Warehouse:* Warehouses handle storage of many types of products including those that need special handling conditions such as freezers for storing frozen products, humidity-controlled environments for delicate products, such as produce or flowers, and dirt-free facilities for handling highly sensitive computer products.
- *Distribution Centre:* There are some warehouses where product storage is considered a very temporary activity. These warehouses serve as points in the distribution system at which products are received from many suppliers and quickly shipped out to many customers. In some cases, such as with distribution centers handling perishable food (e.g., produce), most of the product enters in the early morning and is distributed by the end of the day.

TRANSPORTATION FEATURES AND MODES

A key objective of product distribution is to get products into customers' hands in a timely manner. While delivery of digital products can be handled in a fairly smooth way by allowing customers to access their purchase over the Internet (e.g., download software, gain access to subscription material), tangible products require a more careful analysis of delivery options in order to provide an optimal level of customer service. But as we noted earlier, "optimal" does not always translate into fastest.

In terms of delivering products to customers, there are six distinct modes of transportation: air, digital, pipeline, rail, truck, and water. However, not all modes are an option for all marketers. Each mode offers advantages and disadvantages on key transportation features that include:

- *Product Options:* This feature is concerned with the number of different products that can realistically be shipped using a certain mode. Some modes, such as pipeline, are very limited in the type of products that can be shipped while others, such as truck, can handle a wide-range of products.
- *Speed of Delivery:* This refers to how quickly it takes products to move from the shipper's location to the buyer's location.
- *Accessibility:* This transportation feature refers to whether the use of a mode can allow final delivery to occur at the buyer's desired location or whether the mode requires delivery to be off-loaded onto other modes before arriving at the buyer's destination. For example, most deliveries made via air must be loaded onto other transportation modes, often trucks, before they can be delivered to the final customer.
- *Cost:* The cost of shipment is evaluated in terms of the cost per item to cover some distance (e.g., mile, kilometre). Often for large shipments of tangible products cost is measured in terms of tons-per-mile or metric-tons-per-kilometre.
- *Capacity:* Refers to the amount of product that can be shipped at one time within one transportation unit. The higher the capacity the more likely transportation cost can be spread over more individual products leading to lower transportation cost per-item shipped.
- *Intermodal Capable:* Intermodal shipping occurs when two or more modes can be combined in order to gain advantages offered by each mode. For instance, in an intermodal method called piggybacking truck trailers are loaded onto railroad cars without the need to unload the trailer. When the railroad car has reached a certain destination the truck trailers are off-loaded onto trucks for delivery to the customer's location.

MANAGING PRODUCTS MARKETERS

Marketers are confronted with many issues when building the product component of their marketing strategy. While product decisions represent just one aspect of marketer's overall activities, these decisions are often the most important because they lead directly to the reasons (i.e., benefits offered, solutions to problems) for why the customer decides to choose the organization's goods, services or ideas.

The coverage of product decisions by exploring additional product issues facing the marketer. In particular, we examine four important areas. First, we categorize the roles played by those involved in product management and show how the scope of a manager's responsibilities changes as these roles take on greater importance.

Second, we return to a discussion of branding by focusing on overall branding strategies that may be adopted by the marketing organization. Third, we spend a large part of this tutorial covering the importance of new product development including an analysis of the steps firms may follow to bring new products to market. Finally, we will see that once new products have been established in the market numerous factors force the marketer to continually adjust their product decisions.

PRODUCT MANAGEMENT RESPONSIBILITIES

While this tutorial touches on basic concepts and strategies applicable to a large percentage of marketing situations, the reader should understand that no two marketing situations are the same. Yet while some concepts and strategies important to one marketer may not hold the same weight with another, in general, the basic principles of marketing (e.g., satisfying target markets, support decisions using research, etc.) hold no matter the type of industry, type of company or type of product being sold. What is often different between two marketing situations is the level of complication and challenge that arises as a marketer's scope of responsibility increases.

For our purposes a marketer's level of responsibility is measured in terms of:

- The number and variety of tasks that must be performed (i.e., what has to be done)
- The value these tasks represent to the organization (i.e., how important marketing is perceived within the company)
- The overall financial stake the marketing position holds (i.e., total sales volume and profit generation).

As responsibilities change so to do the marketer's tasks. For instance, with regard to product decisions, as a marketer's responsibilities become greater her or his day-to-day job shifts from being involved in specific product issues (e.g., finding a graphics design company to create a new label) to decisions concerning many products and focusing on setting the future marketing direction of the company (e.g., developing marketing plans for numerous products).

We can see this in greater detail by examining the responsibilities associated with four different marketing management levels:

- *Product Item Level:* At this level responsibilities are associated with marketing a single product or brand. By "single" we are limiting the marketer's responsibility to one item. For instance, a startup software development company may initially market just one product. In some organizations the person in charge has the title Product Manager, though in smaller companies this person may simply be the Marketing Manager.

- *Brand Product Line Level:* At this level responsibilities are associated with managing two or more similar product items. By "similar" we are referring to products carrying the same brand name that fit within the same product category and offer similar solutions to customers' needs. Procter & Gamble, one of the largest consumer products companies in the world, markets Tide laundry detergent in several different packaging sizes (e.g., 50oz., 100oz., 200oz.), in different forms (e.g., powder, liquid) and with different added features (e.g., softener, bleach). Tide's product line consists of over 100 different versions of the product. Differences in the product offerings indicate these are targeted to different segments within the larger market (e.g., those preferring liquid vs. those preferring powder), however, it may also represent a choice for the same target market who may seek variety. A product line is often measured by its depth, relative to competitors, with deep product lines offering extensive product items. Brand product lines are often managed by a Brand or Product Line Manager.
- *Category Product Line Level*: At this level responsibilities are associated with managing two or more brand product lines within the same product category. In this situation the marketer may manage products that offer similar basic benefits (e.g., clean clothes) but target their offerings to slightly different needs (e.g., product for tough to clean clothing vs. product to clean delicate clothing). Multiple brand product lines allow the marketer to cover the needs of more segments and, consequently, increase their chance to generate sales. Often in larger companies category product lines are the responsibility of the Product Category or Divisional Marketing Manager who may have Brand Product Managers reporting to him/her.
- *Product Mix Level:* At this level responsibilities include two or more category product lines that are directed to different product categories. In some cases the category product lines may yield similar general solutions (e.g., cleaning) but are aimed at entirely different target markets (e.g., cleaning dishes vs. cleaning automobiles). In large companies, the product lines are very diverse and offer different solutions.

  For example, BIC sells writing instruments, shaving products, and lighters. This diversification strategy cushions against an "all-eggs-in-one-basket" risk that may come if a company directs all resources to one product category. A product mix can be classified based on its width (how many different category product lines) and its depth (how many different brand product lines within a category product line). Generally responsibility for this level belongs to a company's Vice President for Marketing.

PRODUCT LIFECYCLE MANAGEMENT

Product lifecycle management, sometimes "product life cycle management", represents an all-encompassing vision for managing all data relating to the design, production, support and ultimate disposal of manufactured goods.

PLM concepts were first introduced where safety and control have been extremely important, notably the aerospace, medical device, military and nuclear industries. These industries originated the discipline of configuration management, which evolved into electronic data management systems, which then further evolved to product data management.

Over the last ten years, manufacturers of instrumentation, industrial machinery, consumer electronics, packaged goods and other complex engineered products have discovered the benefits of PLM solutions and are adopting efficient PLM software in increasing numbers.

PLM SOLUTIONS

PLM can be thought of as both:

- A repository for all information that affects a product, and
- *A communication process between product stakeholders*: Principally marketing, engineering, manufacturing and field service.

The PLM system is the first place where all product information from marketing and design comes together, and where it leaves in a form suitable for production and support.

A few analysts use "PLM" as an umbrella term that includes engineering CAD. But product information creation tools include word processors; spreadsheet and graphics prigrammes; requirements analysis and market assessment tools; field trouble reports; and even emails or other correspondence. In our view, a PLM tool focuses exclusively on managing data that covers the breadth of a product's lifecycle, without regard to how that data is developed.

The essential elements of PLM:

- Manages design and process documents
- Constructs and controls bill of material records
- Offers an electronic file repository
- Includes built-in and custom part and document metadata
- Identifies materials content for environmental compliance
- Permits item-focused task assignments
- Enables workflow and process management for approving changes
- Controls multi-user secured access, including "electronic signature"
- Exports data for downstream ERP systems

LIMITATIONS

The PLC model is of some degree of usefulness to marketing managers, in that it is based on factual assumptions. Nevertheless, it is difficult for marketing management to gauge accurately where a product is on its PLC graph.

A rise in sales per se is not necessarily evidence of growth. A fall in sales per se does not typify decline. Furthermore, some products do not experienced a decline. Coca Cola and Pepsi are examples of two products that have existed for many decades, but are still popular products all over the world. Both modes of cola have been in maturity for some years.

Another factor is that differing products would possess different PLC "shapes". A fad product would hold a steep sloped growth stage, a short maturity stage, and a steep sloped decline stage. A product such as Coca Cola and Pepsi would experience growth, but also a constant level of sales over a number of decades. It can probably be said that a given product may hold a unique PLC shape, and the typical PLC model can only be used as a rough guide for marketing management. This is why its called the product life cycle.

PRODUCT LIFE CYCLE

A product's life cycle can be divided into several stages characterized by the revenue generated by the product. If a curve is drawn showing product revenue over time, it may take one of many different shapes, an example of which is shown below:

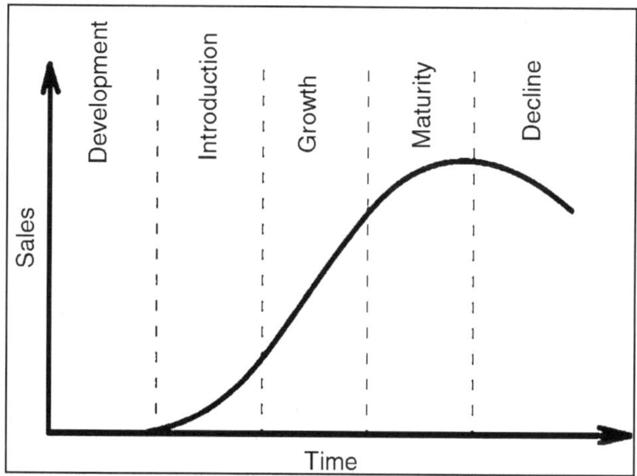

Fig. Product Life Cycle Curve

The life cycle concept may apply to a brand or to a category of product. Its duration may be as short as a few months for a fad item or a century or more for product categories such as the gasoline-powered automobile. Product development is the incubation stage of the product life cycle. There are no sales and the firm prepares to introduce the product. As the product progresses through its life cycle, changes in the marketing mix usually are required in order to adjust to the evolving challenges and opportunities.

INTRODUCTION STAGE

When the product is introduced, sales will be low until customers become aware of the product and its benefits. Some firms may announce their product before it is introduced, but such announcements also alert competitors and remove the element of surprise. Advertising costs typically are high during this stage in order to rapidly increase customer awareness of the product and to target the early adopters.

During the introductory stage the firm is likely to incur additional costs associated with the initial distribution of the product. These higher costs coupled with a low sales volume usually make the introduction stage a period of negative profits. During the introduction stage, the primary goal is to establish a market and build primary demand for the product class.

The following are some of the marketing mix implications of the introduction stage:

- *Product*: One or few products, relatively undiffer-entiated
- *Price*: Generally high, assuming a skim pricing strategy for a high profit margin as the early adopters buy the product and the firm seeks to recoup development costs quickly. In some cases a penetration pricing strategy is used and introductory prices are set low to gain market share rapidly.
- *Distribution*: Distribution is selective and scattered as the firm commences implementation of the distribution plan.
- *Promotion*: Promotion is aimed at building brand awareness. Samples or trial incentives may be directed toward early adopters. The introductory promotion also is intended to convince potential resellers to carry the product.

GROWTH STAGE

The growth stage is a period of rapid revenue growth. Sales increase as more customers become aware of the product and its benefits and additional market segments are targeted. Once the product has been proven a success and customers begin asking for it, sales will increase further as more retailers become interested in carrying it.

The marketing team may expand the distribution at this point. When competitors enter the market, often during the later part of the growth stage, there may be price competition and/or increased promotional costs in order to convince consumers that the firm's product is better than that of the competition. During the growth stage, the goal is to gain consumer preference and increase sales.

The marketing mix may be modified as follows:

- *Product*: New product features and packaging options; improvement of product quality.
- *Price*: Maintained at a high level if demand is high, or reduced to capture additional customers.
- *Distribution*: Distribution becomes more intensive. Trade discounts are minimal if resellers show a strong interest in the product.
- *Promotion*: Increased advertising to build brand preference.

MATURITY STAGE

The maturity stage is the most profitable. While sales continue to increase into this stage, they do so at a slower pace. Because brand awareness is strong, advertising expenditures will be reduced. Competition may result in decreased market share and/or prices. The competing products may be very similar at this point, increasing the difficulty of differentiating the product.

The firm places effort into encouraging competitors' customers to switch, increasing usage per customer, and converting non-users into customers. Sales promotions may be offered to encourage retailers to give the product more shelf space over competing products. During the maturity stage, the primary goal is to maintain market share and extend the product life cycle.

Marketing mix decisions may include:

- *Product*: Modifications are made and features are added in order to differentiate the product from competing products that may have been introduced.
- *Price*: Possible price reductions in response to competition while avoiding a price war.
- *Distribution*: New distribution channels and incentives to resellers in order to avoid losing shelf space.
- *Promotion*: Emphasis on differentiation and building of brand loyalty. Incentives to get competitors' customers to switch.

DECLINE STAGE

Eventually sales begin to decline as the market becomes saturated, the product becomes technologically obsolete, or customer tastes change. If the product has developed brand loyalty, the profitability may be maintained longer. Unit costs may increase with the declining production volumes and eventually no more profit can be made.

During the decline phase, the firm generally has three options:

- Maintain the product in hopes that competitors will exit. Reduce costs and find new uses for the product.
- Harvest it, reducing marketing support and coasting along until no more profit can be made.
- Discontinue the product when no more profit can be made or there is a successor product.

The marketing mix may be modified as follows:

- *Product*: The number of products in the product line may be reduced. Rejuvenate surviving products to make them look new again.
- *Price*: Prices may be lowered to liquidate inventory of discontinued products. Prices may be maintained for continued products serving a niche market.
- *Distribution*: Distribution becomes more selective. Channels that no longer are profitable are phased out.
- *Promotion*: Expenditures are lower and aimed at reinforcing the brand image for continued products.

LIMITATIONS

The term "life cycle" implies a well-defined life cycle as observed in living organisms, but products do not have such a predictable life and the specific life cycle curves followed by different products vary substantially. Consequently, the life cycle concept is not well-suited for the forecasting of product sales. Furthermore, critics have argued that the product life cycle may become self-fulfilling. For example, if sales peak and then decline, managers may conclude that the product is in the decline phase and therefore cut the advertising budget, thus precipitating a further decline.

Nonetheless, the product life cycle concept helps marketing managers to plan alternate marketing strategies to address the challenges that their products are likely to face. It also is useful for monitoring sales results over time and comparing them to those of products having a similar life cycle.

BRANDING STRATEGY

Branding is an important decision designed to enhance the identity of the product through the use of unique brand names, symbols and other distinctive measures. With competition growing more intense in almost all industries, establishing a strong brand allows an organization's products to stand out and avoid potential pitfalls, such as price wars, that have befallen many products. Therefore, a clear understanding of branding strategy is essential in order to build solid products and product lines. In particular, marketers should be aware of various branding approaches that can be pursued.

By branding approach we are referring to different product identification strategies that can be deployed to establish a product within the market. As we will see, the purpose of these approaches is to build a brand that will exist for the long term. Making smart decisions up front is crucial since a company may have to live with the decision for a long time.

Branding approaches include the following:

- *Individual Product Branding*: Under this branding approach new products are assigned new names with no obvious connection to existing brands offered by the company. Under individual product branding the marketing organization must work hard to establish the brand in the market since it cannot ride the coattails of previously introduced brands. The chief advantage of this approach is it allows brands to stand on their own thus lessening threats that may occur to other brands marketed by the company. For instance, if another company brand receives negative publicity this news is less likely to rub off on the company's other brands that carry their own unique names. Brands can create financial gains through the concept known as brand equity. Under an individual branding approach, each brand builds its own separate equity which allows the company, if they choose, to sell off individual brands without impacting other brands owned by the company. The most famous marketing organization to follow this strategy is Procter and Gamble, which has historically introduced new brands without any link to other brands or even to the company name.

- *Family Branding:* Under this branding approach new products are placed under the umbrella of an existing brand. The principle advantage of this approach is that it enables the organization to rapidly build market awareness and acceptance since the brand is already established and known to the market. But the potential disadvantage is that the market has already established certain perceptions of the brand. For instance, a company that sells low-end, lower priced products may have a brand that is viewed as an economy brand. This brand image may create customer confusion and hinder the company if they attempt to introduce higher-end, higher priced products using the same brand name. Additionally, with family branding any negative publicity that may occur for one product within a brand could spread to all other products that share the same name.
- *Co-Branding:* This approach takes the idea of individual and family branding a step further. With co-branding a marketer seeks to partner with another firm, which has an established brand, in hopes synergy of two brands on a product is even more powerful than a single brand. The partnership often has both firms sharing costs but also sharing the gains. For instance, major credit card companies, such as Visa and MasterCard, offer co-branding options to companies and organizations. The cards carry the name of a co-branded organization (e.g., University name) along with the name of the issuing bank (e.g., Citibank) and the name of the credit card company. Besides tapping into awareness for multiple brands, the co-branding strategy is also designed to appeal to a larger target market, especially if each brand, when viewed separately, does not have extensive overlapping target markets with the other brand. Thus, co-branding allows both firms to tap into market segments where they did not previously have a strong position.

- *Private or Store Branding:* Some suppliers are in the business of producing products for other companies including placing another company's brand name on the product. This is most often seen in the retail industry where stores or online sellers contract with suppliers to manufacture the retailer's own branded products. In some cases the supplier not only produces product for the retailer's brand but also markets their own brand so that store shelves will contain both brands.
- *No-Name or Generic Branding:* Certain suppliers supply products that are intentionally "brandless." These products are mostly basic commodity-type products that consumer or business customers purchase as low price alternatives to branded products. Basic household products such as paper products, over-the-counter medicines such as ibuprofen, and even dog food are available in a generic form.
- *Brand Licensing:* Under brand licensing a contractual arrangement is created in which a company owning a brand name allows others to produce and supply products carrying the brand name. This is often seen when a brand is not directly connected with a product category. For instance, several famous children's characters, such as Sesame Street's Elmo, have been licensed to toy and food manufacturers who market products using the branded character's name and image.

DEVELOPING NEW PRODUCTS

By its nature marketing requires new ideas. Unlike some organizational functions, where basic processes follow a fairly consistent routine (e.g., accounting), successful marketers are constantly making adjustments to their marketing efforts. New ideas are essential for responding to changing demand by the target market and by pressure exerted by competitors. These changes are manifested in decisions in all marketing areas including the development of new products.

In addition to being responsive to changing customer tastes and competitive forces, there are many other reasons why new product development is vital.

These include:

- Many new products earn higher profits than older products. This is often the case for products considered innovative or unique which, for a period of time, may enjoy success and initially face little or no competition.
- New products can help reposition the company in customer's minds. For instance, a company that traditionally sold low priced products with few features may shift customers' perceptions about the company by introducing products with more features and slightly higher pricing.

- Fierce global competition and technological developments make it much easier for competitors to learn about products and replicate them. To stay ahead of competitors marketers must innovate and often create and introduce new products on a consistent schedule.
- Companies with limited depth in a product line may miss out on more sales unless they can add new products to fill out the line.
- Some firms market seasonal products that garner their highest sales during a certain time of the year or sell cyclical products whose sales fluctuate depending on economic or market factors. Expanding the firm's product mix into new areas may help offset these fluctuations. For manufacturing firms an additional benefit is realized as new products utilize existing production capacity that is under-used when seasonal or cyclical products are not being produced.

CATEGORIES OF NEW PRODUCTS

New products can fall into one of several categories. These categories are defined by the type of market the product is entering (i.e., newly created, existing but not previously targeted, existing and targeted) and the level of product innovation (i.e., radically new, new, upgrade).

- *Creates New Market with Radically New Product or Product Line:* This category is represented by new breakthrough products that are so revolutionary they create an entirely new market. Recent examples include digital music players, such as Apple's iPod, that have spawned new delivery methods (downloadable music) and new media (podcasting). Highly innovative products are rare so very few new products fall into this category.
- *Enters Existing But Not Previously Targeted Market with New-Product or Product Line*: In this category a marketer introduces a new product item or product line to an existing market which they did not previously target. Often these products are similar to competitors' products already available in the market but with some level of difference (e.g., different features, lower price, etc.). Microsoft's entry into the video gaming system market with their Xbox is an example.
- *Stays in Existing and Previously Targeted Market by Enhancing Existing Product or Product Line*: Under this development category the marketer attempts to improve its current position in the market by either improving or upgrading existing products or by extending a product line by adding new products. This type of new product is seen in our earlier example of Procter and Gamble's Tide product line which contains many product variations of the basic Tide product.

HOW NEW PRODUCTS ARE OBTAINED

Marketers have several options for obtaining new products. First, products can be developed within an organization's own research operations.

For some companies, such as service firms, this may simply mean the marketer designs new service options to sell to target markets. For instance, a marketer for a mortgage company may design new mortgage packages that offer borrowers different rates or payment options.

At the other extreme companies may support an extensive research and development effort where engineers, scientists or others are engaged in new product discovery.

A second way to obtain products is to acquire them from external sources. This can occur in several ways including:

- Purchase the Product - With this option a marketer purchases the product outright from another firm that currently owns the product. The advantage is that the product is already developed, which reduces the purchasing company's time and cost of trying to develop it themselves. On the negative side the purchase cost may be high.
- License the Product – Under this option the marketer negotiates with the owner of the product for the rights to market the product. This may be a particularly attractive option for companies who have to fill a product need quickly (e.g., give a product line more depth) or it may be used as a temporary source of products while the marketer's company is developing its own product. On the negative side the arrangement may have a limited time frame at which point the licensor may decide to end the relationship leaving the marketer without a source for the product.
- Purchase Another Firm - Instead of purchasing another company's products marketers may find it easier to just purchase the whole company selling the products. One key advantage to this is that the acquisition often includes the people and resources that developed the product which may be a key consideration if the acquiring company wants to continue to develop the acquired products.

NEW PRODUCT DEVELOPMENT PROCESS

Because introducing new products on a consistent basis is important to the future success of many organizations, marketers in charge of product decisions often follow set procedures for bringing products to market. In the scientific area that may mean the establishment of ongoing laboratory research programs for discovering new products (e.g., medicines) while less scientific companies may pull together resources for product development on a less structured timetable.

In this section we present a 7-step process comprising the key elements of new product development. While some companies may not follow a deliberate step-by-step approach, the steps are useful in showing the information input and decision making that must be done in order to successfully develop new products. The process also shows the importance market research plays in developing products.

We should note that while the 7-step process works for most industries, it is less effective in developing radically new products. The main reason lies in the inability of the target market to provide sufficient feedback on advanced product concepts since they often find it difficult to understand radically different ideas. So while many of these steps are used to research breakthrough ideas, the marketer should exercise caution when interpreting the results.

Idea Generation

The first step of new product development requires gathering ideas to be evaluated as potential product options. For many companies idea generation is an ongoing process with contributions from inside and outside the organization. Many market research techniques are used to encourage ideas including: running focus groups with consumers, channel members, and the company's sales force; encouraging customer comments and suggestions via toll-free telephone numbers and website forms; and gaining insight on competitive product developments through secondary data sources.

One important research technique used to generate ideas is brainstorming where open-minded, creative thinkers from inside and outside the company gather and share ideas. The dynamic nature of group members floating ideas, where one idea often sparks another idea, can yield a wide range of possible products that can be further pursued.

Screening

In Step 2 the ideas generated in Step 1 are critically evaluated by company personnel to isolate the most attractive options. Depending on the number of ideas, screening may be done in rounds with the first round involving company executives judging the feasibility of ideas while successive rounds may utilize more advanced research techniques. As the ideas are whittled down to a few attractive options, rough estimates are made of an idea's potential in terms of sales, production costs, profit potential, and competitors' response if the product is introduced. Acceptable ideas move on to the next step.

Concept Development and Testing

With a few ideas in hand the marketer now attempts to obtain initial feedback from customers, distributors and its own employees. Generally, focus groups are convened where the ideas are presented to a group, often in the form of concept board presentations (i.e., storyboards) and not in actual working form. For instance, customers may be shown a concept board displaying drawings of a product idea or even an advertisement featuring the product. In some cases focus groups are exposed to a mock-up of the ideas, which is a physical but generally non-functional version of product idea. During focus groups with customers the marketer seeks information that may include: likes and dislike of the concept; level of interest in purchasing the product; frequency of purchase (used to help forecast demand); and price points to determine how much customers are willing to spend to acquire the product.

Business Analysis

At this point in the new product development process the marketer has reduced a potentially large number of ideas down to one or two options. Now in Step 4 the process becomes very dependent on market research as efforts are made to analyse the viability of the product ideas. (Note, in many cases the product has not been produced and still remains only an idea.) The key objective at this stage is to obtain useful forecasts of market size (e.g., overall demand), operational costs (e.g., production costs) and financial projections (e.g., sales and profits).

Additionally, the organization must determine if the product will fit within the company's overall mission and strategy. Much effort is directed at both internal research, such as discussions with production and purchasing personnel, and external marketing research, such as customer and distributor surveys, secondary research, and competitor analysis.

Product and Marketing Mix Development

Ideas passing through business analysis are given serious consideration for development. Companies direct their research and development teams to construct an initial design or prototype of the idea. Marketers also begin to construct a marketing plan for the product. Once the prototype is ready the marketer seeks customer input. However, unlike the concept testing stage where customers were only exposed to the idea, in this step the customer gets to experience the real product as well as other aspects of the marketing mix, such as advertising, pricing, and distribution options (e.g., retail store, direct from company, etc.).

Favorable customer reaction helps solidify the marketer's decision to introduce the product and also provides other valuable information such as estimated purchase rates and understanding how the product will be used by the customer. Reaction that is less favorable may suggest the need for adjustments to elements of the marketing mix. Once these are made the marketer may again have the customer test the product. In addition to gaining customer feedback, this step is used to gauge the feasibility of large-scale, cost effective production for manufactured products.

Market Testing

Products surviving to Step 6 are ready to be tested as real products. In some cases the marketer accepts what was learned from concept testing and skips over market testing to launch the idea as a fully marketed product. But other companies may seek more input from a larger group before moving to commercialization.

The most common type of market testing makes the product available to a selective small segment of the target market (e.g., one city), which is exposed to the full marketing effort as they would be to any product they could purchase. In some cases, especially with consumer products sold at retail stores, the marketer must work hard to get the product into the test market by convincing distributors to agree to purchase and place the product on their store shelves. In more controlled test markets distributors may be paid a fee if they agree to place the product on their shelves to allow for testing.

Another form of market testing found with consumer products is even more controlled with customers recruited to a "laboratory" store where they are given shopping instructions. Product interest can then be measured based on customer's shopping response.

Finally, there are several high-tech approaches to market testing including virtual reality and computer simulations. With virtual reality testing customers are exposed to a computer-projected environment, such as a store, and are asked to locate and select products. With computer simulations customers may not be directly involved at all. Instead certain variables are entered into a sophisticated computer programme and estimates of a target market's response are calculated.

Commercialization

If market testing displays promising results the product is ready to be introduced to a wider market. Some firms introduce or roll-out the product in waves with parts of the market receiving the product on different schedules. This allows the company to ramp up production in a more controlled way and to fine tune the marketing mix as the product is distributed to new areas.

MANAGING EXISTING PRODUCTS

Marketing strategies developed for initial product introduction almost certainly need to be revised as the product settles into the market. While commercialization may be the last step in the new product development process it is just the beginning of managing the product.

Adjusting the product's marketing strategy is required for many reasons including:

- Changing customer tastes
- Domestic and foreign competitors
- Economic conditions
- Technological advances

To stay on top of all possible threats the marketer must monitor all aspects of the marketing mix and make changes as needed. Such efforts require the marketer to develop and refine the product's marketing plan on a regular basis. In fact, as we will discuss in a later section of this tutorial, marketing strategies change as a product moves through time leading to the concept called the Product Life Cycle (PLC). We will see that marketers make numerous revisions to their strategy as product move through different stage of the PLC.

PRODUCT DIFFERENTIATION AND COMPETITIVE ADVANTAGE

Having established the *V*alue of product differentiation, we next consider the *R*areness and *I*mitability of product differentiation. The answer to the question of rareness can safely be assumed to be affirmative at this point in the analysis. The assumption is that the focal firm has established a differentiated product, which implies that the product is rare. We therefore turn our attention to the question of imitability. If a product differentiation strategy is costly to imitate, the focal firm can reasonably expect to enjoy a competitive advantage.

Easy to Duplicate

Product Features:

- Are easy for competitors to observe
- Unless there is a patent, competitors face little cost in imitation
- May lead to temporary competitive advantage until competitors are able to imitate
- *Example*: Wrinkle-free, 100% cotton in shirts, blouses, and pants is a product feature that has been rapidly duplicated. This innovation meant that customers could enjoy the feel of 100% cotton without having to iron or professionally launder their clothing. Nordstrom was an early adopter with its SmartCare line. Most other department stores now have their own line of all cotton clothing that is wrinkle-free.

IMPLEMENTING A PRODUCT DIFFERENTIATION STRATEGY

The Organization question of the VRIO Model is perhaps even more important with a product differentiation strategy than with a cost leadership strategy because of the relationship between the focal firm and customers. A successful differentiation strategy depends on creating customer preferences for the products and/or services of the focal firm.

Customer preferences are heavily influenced by customers' experiences in interacting with the focal firm. The focal firm must be able to respond quickly and accurately to customer needs. Customers need to'feel' that the focal firm is catering to their needs. Organizational structure, management control systems, and compensation policies can all be managed to encourage customers to have a preference for the focal firm's products and/or services.

Organizational Structure

At the business level, the U-Form is used to implement product differentiation strategies just as it is to implement cost leadership strategies. However, there are some important differences in the way the structure is used. The U-Form is used in a cost leadership strategy to exploit the efficiencies inherent in the structure due to specialization. With a product differentiation strategy, the specialization of the U-Form structure is exploited through cross-functional teams.

Management Controls

The main idea behind using management controls in the implementation of a product differentiation strategy is that of flexibility. Not only must managers and employees have the freedom to be flexible, they should also be encouraged to be creative and adaptable. Decision making is usually more decentralized in a product differentiation strategy as compared to a cost leadership strategy.

This decentralization means that managers can make decisions and take actions that allow the focal firm to differentiate its products and/or services through a high degree of responsiveness to customers. As a matter of firm policy, decision making guidelines are broader-allowing greater flexibility. Also, managers and employees should explicitly be given the freedom and encouragement to experiment with new ideas. Managers and employees need to know that if experimentation leads to failure they will not be punished for having tried.

Compensation Policies

Compensation policies can be used to help exploit the U-form structure and reinforce the broader management controls. In the simplest of terms, compensation policies should be structured to reward managers and employees for cooperating within cross functional teams and being creative in the process. Compensation policies can be especially effective with regard to experimentation and risk taking. Promised rewards for successful experimentation and the promised absence of punishment for failed experimentation provide strong incentive to be creative.

7

Brand Management

INTRODUCTION

Brand management is the application of marketing techniques to a specific product, product line, or brand. It seeks to increase a product's perceived value to the customer and thereby increase brand franchise and brand equity. Marketers see a brand as an implied promise that the level of quality people have come to expect from a brand will continue with future purchases of the same product.

This may increase sales by making a comparison with competing products more favourable. It may also enable the manufacturer to charge more for the product. The value of the brand is determined by the amount of profit it generates for the manufacturer. This can result from a combination of increased sales and increased price, and/or reduced COGS, and/or reduced or more efficient marketing investment.

All of these enhancements may improve the profitability of a brand, and thus,"Brand Managers" often carry line-management accountability for a brand's P&L profitability, in contrast to marketing staff manager roles to manage and execute. In this regard, Brand Management is often viewed in organizations as a broader and more strategic role than Marketing alone.

The annual list of the world's most valuable brands, published by Interbrand and Business Week, indicates that the market value of companies often consists largely of brand equity. Research by McKinsey and Company, a global consulting firm, in 2000 suggested that strong, well-leveraged brands produce higher returns to shareholders than weaker, narrower brands. Taken together, this means that brands seriously impact shareholder value, which ultimately makes branding a CEO responsibility.

PRINCIPLES OF BRAND MANAGEMENT

A good brand name should:

- Be protected under trademark law.
- Be easy to pronounce.
- Be easy to remember.

- Be easy to recognize.
- Be easy to translate into all languages in the markets where the brand will be used.
- Attract attention.
- Suggest product benefits or suggest usage
- Suggest the company or product image.
- Distinguish the product's positioning relative to the competition.
- Be attractive.
- Stand out among a group of other brands.

BRANDING MANAGEMENT

Branding involves decisions that establish an identity for a product with the goal of distinguishing it from competitors' offerings. In markets where competition is fierce and where customers may select from among many competitive products, creating an identity through branding is essential. It is particularly important in helping position the product in the minds of the product's target market.

While consumer products companies have long recognized the value of branding, it has only been within the last 10-15 years that organizations selling component products in the business-to-business market have begun to focus on brand building strategies. The most well-known company to brand components is Intel with its now famous "Intel Inside" slogan. Intel's success has led many other b-to-b companies and even non-profits to incorporate branding within their overall marketing strategy.

BRAND NAMES AND BRAND MARKS

At a very basic level branding is achieved through the use of unique brand names and brand marks. The brand name, which may be either the individual product name or a name applied to a group or family of products, is important for many reasons including suggesting what the product is or does (e.g., Mop-and-Glow).

The name is also what we utter when we discuss the product (i.e., word-of-mouth marketing). The brand mark is a design element, such as a symbol (e.g., Nike swoosh), logo (e.g., Yahoo! graphic), a character (e.g., Keebler elves) or even a sound (e.g., Intel inside sound), that provides visual or auditory recognition for the product.

ADVANTAGES OF BRANDS

A strong brand offers many advantages for marketers including:

- Brands provide multiple sensory stimuli to enhance customer recognition. For example, a brand can be visually recognizable from its packaging, logo, shape, etc. It can also be recognizable via sound, such as hearing the name on a radio advertisement or talking with someone who mentions the product.

- Customers who are frequent and enthusiastic purchasers of a particular brand are likely to become Brand Loyal. Cultivating brand loyalty among customers is the ultimate reward for successful marketers since these customers are far less likely to be enticed to switch to other brands compared to non-loyal customers.
- Well-developed and promoted brands make product positioning efforts more effective. The result is that upon exposure to a brand (e.g., hearing it, seeing it) customers conjure up mental images or feelings of the benefits they receive from using that brand. The reverse is even better. When customers associate benefits with a particular brand, the brand may have attained a significant competitive advantage. In these situations the customer who recognizes he needs a solution to a problem (e.g., needs to bleach clothes) may automatically think of one brand that offers the solution to the problem (e.g., Clorox). This "benefit = brand" association provides a significant advantage for the brand that the customer associates with the benefit sought.
- Firms that establish a successful brand can extend the brand by adding new products under the same "family" brand. Such branding may allow companies to introduce new products more easily since the brand is already recognized within the market.
- Strong brands can lead to financial advantages through the concept of Brand Equity in which the brand itself becomes valuable. Such gains can be realized through the out-right sale of a brand or through licensing arrangements. For example, Company A may have a well-recognized brand (Brand X) within a market but for some reason they are looking to concentrate their efforts in other markets. Company B is looking to enter the same market as Brand X.

If circumstances are right Company A could sell to Company B the rights to use the Brand X name without selling any other part of the company. That is, Company A simply sells the legal rights to the Brand X name but retains all other parts of Brand X, such as the production facilities and employees. In cases of well developed brands such a transaction may carry a very large price tag.

Thus, through strong branding efforts Company A achieves a large financial gain by simply signing over the rights to the name. But why would Company B seek to purchase a brand for such a high price tag? Because by buying the brand Company B has already achieved an important marketing goal – building awareness within the target market. The fact the market is already be familiar with the brand allows the Company B to concentrate on other marketing decisions.

ONLINE BRAND MANAGEMENT

Companies are embracing brand reputation management as a strategic imperative and are increasingly turning to online monitoring in their efforts to prevent their public image from becoming tarnished. Online brand reputation protection can mean monitoring for the misappropriation of a brand trademark by fraudsters intent on confusing consumers for monetary gain.

It can also mean monitoring for less malicious, although perhaps equally damaging, infractions, such as the unauthorized use of a brand logo or even for negative brand information from online consumers that appears in online communities and other social media platforms. The red flag can be something as benign as a blog rant about a bad hotel experience or an electronic gadget that functions expectations.

CORPORATE BRANDING MANAGEMENT

Corporate branding refers to a company applying its name to a product. The product and the company name become the brand name. The company can advertise several of its products under a single brand name in a practice referred to as *family branding* or *umbrella branding*.

By using corporate branding with a successfully marketed product, a company can familiarize consumers with its products and may create brand loyalty. If the public likes one product from this company, then they may seek out the brand name when buying other products. Corporate branding is usually only successful if the company is well known and sells reputable products with a positive image. One of the disadvantages of corporate branding is that the company can become identified with only one type of product.

To consumers, corporate branding represents a level of quality that they have come to expect from the company. They will expect every product with the same brand name to have the same level of quality that they are familiar with. The company can increase sales by comparing one of their more popular products with a similar product by another company. The value of the brand is determined by the profits the products have made. If profits are high, then the manufacturer is able to charge more for their product.

When applying corporate branding to a product or products, companies need to follow a few guidelines. A corporate brand should be easy to recognize and attract attention. It should also be legally protectable and suggest the company or product image.

Ideally, the brand should be easy to pronounce and easy to remember. A premier brand product typically costs more to purchase than an economy brand. Consumers are paying for the name and the quality of product that name guarantees.

There are a few extensions to corporate branding. One brand name may be used for a number of products in family branding, or all the products may be given different brand names in a practice called *individual branding*. When large retailers buy goods in bulk and then put their own brand name on them, this is called *store branding, label branding,* or *private branding. Co-branding* is when two or more manufactures combine to sell their products. When a company sells the right to use their brand name to another company for use in another location or for non-competitive purposes, this is called *brand licensing.*

Corporate branding has the ability to make a product very successful. If the brand name has a track record of a guarantee of quality, then there are huge amounts of money to be made by using the name. However, just one shoddy product under the brand name may cause bad word of mouth, affecting sales of all the other products under the same name and causing irreversible damage to the company.

FAMILY BRANDING MARKETING MANAGEMENT

Family branding is a type of marketing tactic. It involves using one brand name to market multiple products. For example, a company may use one brand to market soap, lotion, hair shampoo, and nail polish. This differs from branding individual products, which involves giving each product its own name and image. For example, a company may sell lipstick and nail polish, giving each product line a separate marketing identity.

The idea behind family branding is that a company can make a wide range of products both desirable and profitable by giving them all one recognizable name. Then, by building recognition of this brand name, a company can also build customer loyalty. When the company introduces new products or even makes changes to existing products, it can depend on customer loyalty to ensure its market will purchase the new or altered product. Additionally, family branding, makes it possible to use an advertising campaign to successfully market a range of products instead of just one at a time.

Often, companies in the food industry use family branding techniques to market their products. For example, a company may make and sell bread, potato chips, frozen food, and condiments all under one highly recognizable name. This umbrella branding may mean such companies will sell more than they would with individual branding. Some consumers are more likely to choose a product with a familiar name over one that is less well-known, even if the known brand is more expensive.

There is a downside for companies that use family branding, however. In order to keep sales up, they have to maintain consistent levels of quality across their entire product line. If one of the products is perceived as being of lesser quality, this consumer perception could cause sales to drop for the whole family of products. Likewise, a brand that does have consistent quality could suffer if the company that makes it experiences bad publicity.

Interestingly, some companies use both family and individual branding. For example, a company may have a strong brand name, yet choose to market some of its products with individual branding. This may occur, for example, when a product is introduced to a new market. In such a case, individual branding can prevent problems for the family of products if the new product fails. Sometimes an individual brand may be more appropriate because the product is being introduced to another class of consumers; introducing a product designed for budget shoppers under the same brand intended for affluent shoppers may not produce the desired results.

INDIVIDUAL BRANDING MARKETING

Individual branding is the marketing strategy of giving each product in a product portfolio its own unique brand name. This is contrasted with family branding in which the products in a product line are given the same brand name. The advantage of individual branding is that each product has an image and identity that is unique. This facilitates the positioning process.

CONCEPT OF BRAND

A brand is the identity of a specific product, service, or business. A brand can take many forms, including a name, sign, symbol, or slogan. The word brand began simply as a way to tell one person's cattle from another by means of a hot iron stamp. A legally protected brand name is called a trademark. The word brand has continued to evolve to encompass identity - in effect the personality of a product, company or service.

A brand is the personality of a product, service or company and how it relates to key constituencies: Customers, Staff, Partners, Investors etc. Some people distinguish the psychological aspect of a brand from the experiential aspect. The experiential aspect consists of the sum of all points of contact with the brand and is known as the brand experience. The psychological aspect, sometimes referred to as the brand image, is a symbolic construct created within the minds of people and consists of all the information and expectations associated with a product or service.

People engaged in branding seek to develop or align the expectations behind the brand experience, creating the impression that a brand associated with a product or service has certain qualities or characteristics that make it special or unique. A brand is therefore one of the most valuable elements in an advertising theme, as it demonstrates what the brand owner is able to offer in the marketplace. The art of creating and maintaining a brand is called brand management. Orientation of the whole organization towards its brand is called brand orientation.

Careful brand management seeks to make the product or services relevant to the target audience. Brands should be seen as more than the difference between the actual cost of a product and its selling price - they represent the sum of all valuable qualities of a product to the consumer. There are many intangibles involved in business, intangibles left wholly from the income statement and balance sheet which determine how a business is perceived.

The learned skill of a knowledge worker, the type of mental working, the type of stitch: all may be without an 'accounting cost' but for those who truly know the product, for it is these people the company should wish to find and keep, the difference is incomparable. A brand which is widely known in the marketplace acquires brand recognition.

When brand recognition builds up to a point where a brand enjoys a critical mass of positive sentiment in the marketplace, it is said to have achieved brand franchise. One goal in brand recognition is the identification of a brand without the name of the company present. For example, Disney has been successful at branding with their particular script font.

Consumers may look on branding as an important value added aspect of products or services, as it often serves to denote a certain attractive quality or characteristic. From the perspective of brand owners, branded products or services also command higher prices.

Where two products resemble each other, but one of the products has no associated branding, people may often select the more expensive branded product on the basis of the quality of the brand or the reputation of the brand owner.

BENEFITS OF GLOBAL BRANDING

In addition to taking advantage of the outstanding growth opportunities, the following drives the increasing interest in taking brands global:

- Economies of scale
- Lower marketing costs
- Laying the groundwork for future extensions worldwide
- Maintaining consistent brand imagery
- Quicker identification and integration of innovations
- Preempting international competitors from entering domestic markets or locking you out of other geographic markets
- Increasing international media reach is an enabler
- Increases in international business and tourism are also enablers

GLOBAL BRAND VARIABLES

The following elements may differ from country to country:

- Corporate slogan
- Products and services
- Product names
- Product features
- Positionings
- Marketing mixes

These differences will depend upon:

- Language differences
- Fifferent styles of communication
- Other cultural differences
- Differences in category and brand development
- Different consumption patterns

- Different competitive sets and marketplace conditions
- Different legal and regulatory environments
- Different national approaches to marketing

Local Brand

A brand that is sold and marketed in a relatively small and restricted geographical area. A local brand is a brand that can be found in only one country or region. It may be called a regional brand if the area encompasses more than one metropolitan market. It may also be a brand that is developed for a specific national market, however an interesting thing about local brand is that the local branding is mostly done by consumers then by the producers. Examples of Local Brands in Sweden are Stomatol, Mijerierna etc..

Brand Name

The brand name is quite often used interchangeably within "brand", although it is more correctly used to specifically denote written or spoken linguistic elements of any product. In this context a "brand name" constitutes a type of trademark, if the brand name exclusively identifies the brand owner as the commercial source of products or services.

A brand owner may seek to protect proprietary rights in relation to a brand name through trademark registration. Advertising spokespersons have also become part of some brands, for example: Mr. Whipple of Charmin toilet tissue and Tony the Tiger of Kellogg's. Local Branding is usually done by the consumers rather than the producers.

Brand Identity

A product identity, or brand image are typically the attributes one associates with a brand, how the brand owner wants the consumer to perceive the brand - and by extension the branded company, organization, product or service. The brand owner will seek to bridge the gap between the brand image and the brand identity.

Effective brand names build a connection between the brand personality as it is perceived by the target audience and the actual product/service. The brand name should be conceptually on target with the product/service. Furthermore, the brand name should be on target with the brand demographic.

Typically, sustainable brand names are easy to remember, transcend trends and have positive connotations. Brand identity is fundamental to consumer recognition and symbolizes the brand's differentiation from competitors.

Brand identity is what the owner wants to communicate to its potential consumers. However, over time, a product's brand identity may acquire, gaining new attributes from consumer perspective but not necessarily from the marketing communications an owner percolates to targeted consumers.

Therefore, brand associations become handy to check the consumer's perception of the brand. Brand identity needs to focus on authentic qualities - real characteristics of the value and brand promise being provided and sustained by organisational and/or production characteristics.

Visual Brand Identity

The recognition and perception of a brand is highly influenced by its visual presentation. A brand's visual identity is the overall look of its communications. Effective visual brand identity is achieved by the consistent use of particular visual elements to create distinction, such as specific fonts, colours, and graphic elements.

At the core of every brand identity is a brand mark, or logo. In the United States, brand identity and logo design naturally grew out of the Modernist movement in the 1950's and greatly drew on the principals of that movement– simplicity and geometric abstraction. These principles can be observed in the work of the pioneers of the practice of visual brand identity design, such as Paul Rand, Chermayeff and Geismar and Saul Bass.

Brand Parity

Brand parity is the perception of the customers that all brands are equivalent.

BRANDING APPROACHES

Company Name

Often, especially in the industrial sector, it is just the company's name which is promoted. In this case a very strong brand name is made the vehicle for a range of products or even a range of subsidiary brands.

Individual Branding

Each brand has a separate name, which may even compete against other brands from the same company.

Attitude Branding and Lconic Brands

Attitude branding is the choice to represent a larger feeling, which is not necessarily connected with the product or consumption of the product at all. Marketing labeled as attitude branding include that of Nike, Starbucks, The Body Shop, Safeway, and Apple Inc.

"A great brand raises the bar — it adds a greater sense of purpose to the experience, whether it's the challenge to do your best in sports and fitness, or the affirmation that the cup of coffee you're drinking really matters. Iconic brands are defined as having aspects that contribute to consumer's self-expression and personal identity. Brands whose value to consumers comes primarily from having identity value comes are said to be "identity brands".

Some of these brands have such a strong identity that they become more or less "cultural icons" which makes them iconic brands. Examples of iconic brands are: Apple Inc., Nike and Harley Davidson. Many iconic brands include almost ritual-like behaviour when buying and consuming the products.

There are four key elements to creating iconic brands:

1. *"Necessary conditions"*: The performance of the product must at least be ok preferably with a reputation of having good quality.
2. *"Myth-making"*: A meaningful story-telling fabricated by cultural "insiders". These must be seen as legitimate and respected by consumers for stories to be accepted.
3. *"Cultural contradictions"*: Some kind of mismatch between prevailing ideology and emergent undercurrents in society. In other words a difference with the way consumers are and how they some times wish they were.
4. *"The cultural brand management process"*: Actively engaging in the myth-making process making sure the brand maintains its position as an icon.

"No-brand" Branding

Recently a number of companies have successfully pursued "No-Brand" strategies by creating packaging that imitates generic brand simplicity. Examples include the Japanese company Muji, which means "No label" in English and the Florida company No-Ad Sunscreen. Although there is a distinct Muji brand, Muji products are not branded. This no-brand strategy means that little is spent on advertisement or classical marketing and Muji's success is attributed to the word-of-mouth, a simple shopping experience and the anti-brand movement. "No brand" branding may be construed as a type of branding as the product is made conspicuous through the absence of a brand name.

Derived Brands

In this case the supplier of a key component, used by a number of suppliers of the end-product, may wish to guarantee its own position by promoting that component as a brand in its own right. The most frequently quoted example is Intel, which secures its position in the PC market with the slogan "Intel Inside".

Brand Extension

The existing strong brand name can be used as a vehicle for new or modified products; for example, many fashion and designer companies extended brands into fragrances, shoes and accessories, home textile, home decor, luggage, glasses, furniture, hotels, etc. Mars extended its brand to ice cream, Caterpillar to shoes and watches, Michelin to a restaurant guide,

Adidas and Puma to personal hygiene. Dunlop extended its brand from tires to other rubber products such as shoes, golf balls, tennis racquets and adhesives.

There is a difference between brand extension and line extension. A line extension is when a current brand name is used to enter a new market segment in the existing product class, with new varieties or flavours or sizes. When Coca-Cola launched "Diet Coke" and "Cherry Coke" they stayed within the originating product category: non-alcoholic carbonated beverages. Procter and Gamble did likewise extending its strong lines into neighbouring products within the same category, dish washing detergents.

Multi-Brands

Alternatively, in a market that is fragmented amongst a number of brands a supplier can choose deliberately to launch totally new brands in apparent competition with its own existing strong brand; simply to soak up some of the share of the market which will in any case go to minor brands. The rationale is that having 3 out of 12 brands in such a market will give a greater overall share than having 1 out of 10. In its most extreme manifestation, a supplier pioneering a new market which it believes will be particularly attractive may choose immediately to launch a second brand in competition with its first, in order to pre-empt others entering the market.

Individual brand names naturally allow greater flexibility by permitting a variety of different products, of differing quality, to be sold without confusing the consumer's perception of what business the company is in or diluting higher quality products. Once again, Procter and Gamble is a leading exponent of this philosophy, running as many as ten detergent brands in the US market.

This also increases the total number of"facings" it receives on supermarket shelves. Sara Lee, on the other hand, uses it to keep the very different parts of the business separate - from Sara Lee cakes through Kiwi polishes to L'Eggs pantyhose. In the hotel business, Marriott uses the name Fairfield Inns for its budget chain.

Cannibalization is a particular problem of a"multibrand" approach, in which the new brand takes business away from an established one which the organization also owns. This may be acceptable if there is a net gain overall. Alternatively, it may be the price the organization is willing to pay for shifting its position in the market; the new product being one stage in this process.

Private Labels

With the emergence of strong retailers, private label brands, also called own brands, or store brands, also emerged as a major factor in the marketplace. Where the retailer has a particularly strong identity this"own brand" may be able to compete against even the strongest brand leaders, and may outperform those products that are not otherwise strongly branded.

Individual and Organizational Brands

There are kinds of branding that treat individuals and organizations as the"products" to be branded. Personal branding treats persons and their careers as brands. The term is thought to have been first used in a 1997 substance by Tom Peters. Faith branding treats religious figures and organizations as brands. Religious media expert Phil Cooke has written that faith branding handles the question of how to express faith in a media-dominated culture. Nation branding works with the perception and reputation of countries as brands.

8

Modern Marketing Management

INTRODUCTION

From earliest history, man has been dependent upon agriculture and upon some forms, however crude, of handicraft or manufacturing activity. Only in very recent times have people, especially in the United States, lived in an economy dominated by marketing-oriented organizations. The rather youthful character of our marketing system as it exists today may be better understood by giving very brief attention to historical changes from primitive times, through the emergence of a middleman system, down to current marketing conceptions.

EARLY DEVELOPMENTS

The origin of marketing is lost in antiquity. Certainly there is ample evidence of the existence of trade among the ancient Egyptians. Numerous references to trade are to be found in the Old Testament, and the Phoenicians in their heyday were regarded as a nation of wholesalers. Both wholesale and retail trade were well developed during the era of Greek supremacy and in the period of Roman domination.

To be sure, articles traded in the early days of civilization were few. They were restricted largely to luxuries purchased by the rich, due to the costliness and dangers of transportation and the low standards of living. Differentiation of production in the various parts of a country and deficiencies in essentials such as common salt and spices in certain countries also stimulated trade, but in relatively few items. Even as late as the year 1000, villages were characterized by their agrarian, independent nature and by economic self-sufficiency. In every village attempts were made, by methods now considered crude and wasteful, to raise the necessary food supply and to produce other necessaries of existence. With the fall of the Roman Empire, trade seems to have suffered an eclipse for some centuries.

Beginning with the latter part of the Middle Ages the advance from the manorial or village system to the town was rapid. The town became a place of craftsmen and traders. In this handicraft stage, skilled workers set themselves up in their homes as craftsmen, making goods to order. Enterprising craftsmen began to use apprentices and often produced a surplus which was sold at local markets or fairs.

This resulted in the organization of markets and in the holding of fairs at periodic intervals. Craftsmen soon organized into guilds, which controlled both manufacturing and marketing by minute regulations, much to the detriment of progress in both. The domestic system, whereby the products of the craftsmen were sold by businessmen, superseded the handicraft stage. With increased protection by stronger and more stable governments, towns grew rapidly and markets gradually expanded. Toward the close of the fifteenth century a period of discoveries began.

It resulted in marked improvements in maritime transportation, thereby supplying an added impetus to commerce. With the development of national governments, guilds finally outlived their usefulness, and during the early part of the sixteenth century mercantilism became the guiding principle of state policy. In brief, mercantilists argued that a country could become opulent if it sold more merchandise and services to foreigners than it bought from them.

Only in this way could it increase its stock of precious metals that was received in payment required by a "favorable balance of trade" and which, at that time, was considered the ultimate desideratum. Naturally, this movement stimulated commerce to no small degree.

The Industrial Revolution

In the latter part of the eighteenth century the Industrial Revolution began to usher in marked improvements in form utility production. These were continued throughout the early part of the nineteenth century, but were greatly accelerated in the United States in the period following the Civil War. The domestic stage of manufacture was supplanted almost entirely by factories in which large numbers of specialized workers were employed.

Elaborate steam- or motor-driven machinery replaced handicraft methods. Industry became localized, largescale output became the goal of manufacturers, and a minute division of labour began to be considered an essential prerequisite to efficient operation. Specialization reached such a point that whole communi-ties or areas sometimes devoted a major part of their energy to the making of a single commodity.

Thus, Pittsburgh and Gary became known for iron and steel products; Detroit for automobiles; Wisconsin for cheese and other dairy products; California, Florida, and the Rio Grande valley for citrus fruits; and so on. xhe geographical chasm separating farm or factory and consumer widened considerably.

The agricultural producer, the processor, or the manufacturer cannot ordinarily seek out the final consumer or user of his wares. He finds it more economical to devote his major effort to physical production, where he is presumably of maximum service, and for the most part allows a marketing system to dispose of his finished goods and even to assemble his raw materials for him. Similarly, the consumer or business user finds that any attempt on his part to purchase the numerous commodities necessary to satisfy his increasing and varied wants, directly from their makers, is the height of absurdity. He is, therefore, only too glad in the vast majority of cases to be relieved of the necessity of buying direct and to let the marketing system do it for him.

Effect of Industrial Revolution

It thus becomes obvious that the present middleman system is the outgrowth of changed conditions, the outcome of a growing civilization and industrial progress. As long as towns were economically self-sufficient, producer-consumer contact was feasible except for trade between countries. As localized, large-scale physical production developed, and cities grew in importance, maladjustments made their appearance, marketing risks increased, and an elaborate middleman system was called into existence to bridge over the ever-widening gap that separated the consumer or business user from the manufacturer.

To these factors may be added the constant pressure to increase both the scale of industrial output and production for sale instead of own use, both of which are direct results of our factory system.

Need for Middlemen

From this brief historical sketch it is apparent that few, if any, middlemen existed in primitive society—a condition that still obtains in underdeveloped parts of the globe. There is hardly any surplus to exchange in primitive or highly underdeveloped communities. Each family is making practically all that is used in the home. Whenever any surplus of products of the soil, chase, or craftsman's art becomes available, the members of the tribe or village effect exchanges directly among themselves. Even during the early part of the handicraft stage in Europe, consumers either visited the shops of craftsmen or the latter abandoned their loom or bench at frequent intervals in order to find buyers for their wares.

On the other hand, whenever a country advanced in civilization, trade flourished as it did in ancient Sumeria, Babylonia, Phoenicia, and Egypt. In later years the Persians, Greeks, and Romans engaged in trade to a considerable extent, which decreased in importance as these nations declined in power. In modern times the ascendancy of trade resulted

largely from the Industrial Revolution. This presented in its early days what appeared to be insuperable marketing problems. Marketing functions were therefore shifted more and more to middlemen who specialized in their performance, so that in the latter part of the nineteenth century the basis for the present system of marketing was fairly well established.

Even today in the transfer of title to goods, direct contact may be established. Manufacturers sometimes buy raw materials directly from original producers, and they often purchase semimanufactured goods, parts, equipment, and supplies direct.

Similarly, the consuming public buys a limited amount of merchandise direct from farmer or manufacturer. The bulk of farm products and manufactured goods, however, is bought and sold indirectly through one or more middlemen.

Middlemen are, then, individuals, firms, or corporations that stand between prime producers and ultimate consumers, assume title or assist directly in its transfer, and receive a profit for the risks they assume in addition to being paid for the cost of their services or take whatever losses are incident to the assumption of an entrepreneur's functions. Salesmen are excluded from this group, for they are not in business for themselves and, consequently, assume none of the risks of entrepreneurs and receive no profit, nor do they sustain losses from their sales efforts as such.

Classification of Middlemen

Undoubtedly the most useful classification of middlemen is that based on ownership of the goods. From both legal and practical aspects the relationship to the transfer of title is a most significant factor in defining the position of any group of middlemen. On this basis, *all middlemen can be divided into merchant and functional middlemen. Merchant middlemen buy the goods outright and necessarily take title to them.*

Wholesalers and retailers are common examples. *Functional,* or nonmerchant, middlemen ordinarily assist directly in effecting a change in ownership, but they *do not themselves take title to the goods in which they deal. They specialized in the performance of a single marketing function or of a limited number of such functions,* one of which is usually related to the transfer of title. Functional middlemen are best represented by auction companies, brokers, commission houses, manufacturers' agents, and selling agents.

Growing out of the major distinction between merchant and functional middlemen is a difference in degree of risk. All middlemen bear entrepreneurial risks, since they are in business for themselves and they may or may not be successful in securing the necessary volume for profitable operation. Merchant middlemen must, however, bear the additional risk resulting from the uncertain ability to dispose of the goods they own at remunerative prices.

Functional middlemen, on the other hand, act for others in the purchase or sale of goods; hence the risks of a changing price level and of uncertain demand or supply conditions are borne by the principals in whom title to the goods vests. There are, of course, other organizations, institutions, or agencies which facilitate the performance of marketing functions by acting in some specialized capacity.

They are not, however, generally regarded as middlemen or as strictly marketing institutions, chiefly because they render no direct assistance in the transfer of title to goods—a characteristic peculiar to all bona fide middlemen and marketing organizations. Among these are railroads, commercial banks, insurance companies, ordinary warehouses, cold storage plants, marketing research agencies, inspectors, and graders. To the extent that they perform distributive and selling functions in certain lines of merchandise, warehouses may be classed among the functional middlemen, and to that extent they constitute an integral part of the marketing system.

Evolution of the Marketing Concept in Industry

Even though marketing functions have long been performed and a middleman system of marketing was well established in the last century, great changes have taken place in the significance attached to marketing by all kinds of companies. In general, this has been a transition from emphasis on selling what a company had to the producing of goods and services that are wanted by the customers that made up the demand side of the market. In the marketing literature of the late 1950's and early 1960's, the newer emphasis has been described as *the marketing concept, marketing orientation, or marketing management philosophy.*

Example of Transition

The evolution may be illustrated by the experience of a well-known manufacturer, The Pillsbury Company, which, like many other organizations, moved through four eras of emphasis. First, there was the era of *manufacturing dominance.* The company was founded in 1869 by Charles A. Pillsbury on the basis of availability of high-quality wheat and proximity of water power.

Major concern was with manufacturing—not marketing. According to a company executive, company philosophy in the era of manufacturing dominance might be stated as follows: "We are professional flour millers. Blessed with a supply of the finest North American wheat, plenty of water power, and excellent milling machinery, we produce flour of the highest quality. Our *basic function is to mill high-quality flour,* and of course (and almost incidentally).

The second era was one of *sales orientation.* By the 1930's, competition had become more significant and the problems of reaching the market had grown much more complex. Company officials became somewhat aware of consumer wants and needs, and formed a commercial research department to develop facts about markets.

More attention was given to strengthening the distributing organization, consisting of wholesale and retail grocers. Company philosophy in this era is described as follows: "We are a flour milling company, manufacturing a number of products for the consumer market. We must have a first-rate sales organization which *can dispose of all the products we can make* at a favorable price. We must back up this sales force with consumer advertising and market intelligence. We want our salesmen and our dealers to have all the tools they need for *moving the output of our plants to the consumer."*

A third era of *marketing orientation* did not begin until the early 1950's. The company had experienced substantial post-World War II sales growth in new products, principally cake mixes. It realized that it could produce hundreds of new products, and faced the necessity of selecting the best ones. It was considered essential to build into the company organization *a new function* which would coordinate the heretofore separate company responsibilities of selling, advertising, marketing research, and product planning, and provide guidance for other areas.

This function was called "marketing," and marketing developed the criteria for determining which products to market. Emphasis shifted from manufacturing and mere sales considerations to a determination of which products would best fit the needs of the company's customers. Company policy for the 1950's was stated as follows: "We make and sell products *for consumers."*

At the beginning of the 1960's the company was moving into a fourth era of *marketing control,* described by a company official as follows: "Marketing today sets company operating policy short-term. It will come to influence long-range policy more and more.... At Pillsbury, as our fourth era progresses, marketing will become the basic motivating force for the entire corporation. Soon it will be true that every activity of the corporation—from finance to sales to production—is aimed at satisfying the needs and desires of the consumer."

CONCEPT OF MARKETING MANAGEMENT

Marketing Management is a business discipline which is focused on the practical application of marketing techniques and the management of a firm's marketing resources and activities. Rapidly emerging forces of globalization have compelled firms to market beyond the borders of their home country making International marketing highly significant and an integral part of a firm's marketing strategy. Marketing managers are often responsible for influencing the level, timing, and composition of customer demand accepted definition of the term. In part, this is because the role of a marketing manager can vary significantly based on a business' size, corporate culture, and industry context.

For example, in a large consumer products company, the marketing manager may act as the overall general manager of his or her assigned product To create an effective, cost-efficient Marketing management strategy, firms must possess a detailed, objective understanding of their own business and the market in which they operate. In analyzing these issues, the discipline of marketing management often overlaps with the related discipline of strategic planning.

STRUCTURE

Traditionally, marketing analysis was structured into three areas: Customer analysis, Company analysis, and Competitor analysis. More recently, it has become fashionable in some marketing circles to divide these further into certain five "Cs": Customer analysis, Company analysis, Collaborator analysis, Competitor analysis, and analysis of the industry Context. Customer analysis is to develop a schematic diagram for market segmentation, breaking down the market into various constituent groups of customers, which are called customer segments or market segmentation's.

Marketing managers work to develop detailed profiles of each segment, focusing on any number of variables that may differ among the segments: demographic, psycho graphic, geographic, behavioural, needs-benefit, and other factors may all be examined. Marketers also attempt to track these segments' perceptions of the various products in the market using tools such as perceptual mapping. In company analysis, marketers focus on understanding the company's cost structure and cost position relative to competitors, as well as working to identify a firm's core competencies and other competitively distinct company resources. Marketing managers may also work with the accounting department to analyse the profits the firm is generating from various product lines and customer accounts.

The company may also conduct periodic brand audits to assess the strength of its brands and sources of brand equity. The firm's collaborators may also be profiled, which may include various suppliers, distributors and other channel partners, joint venture partners, and others. An analysis of complementary products may also be performed if such products exist. Marketing management employs various tools from economics and competitive strategy to analyse the industry context in which the firm operates. These include Porter's five forces, analysis of strategic groups of competitors, value chain analysis and others.

Depending on the industry, the regulatory context may also be important to examine in detail. In Competitor analysis, marketers build detailed profiles of each competitor in the market, focusing especially on their relative competitive strengths and weaknesses using SWOT analysis. Marketing managers will examine each competitor's cost structure, sources of profits, resources and competencies, competitive positioning and product differentiation, degree of vertical integration, historical responses to industry developments, and other factors. Marketing management often finds it necessary to invest in research to collect the data required to perform accurate marketing analysis. As such, they often conduct market research to obtain this information.

Marketers employ a variety of techniques to conduct market research, but some of the more common include:

- Qualitative marketing research, such as focus groups

- Quantitative marketing research, such as statistical surveys
- Experimental techniques such as test markets
- Observational techniques such as ethnographic observation

Marketing managers may also design and oversee various environmental scanning and competitive intelligence processes to help identify trends and inform the company's marketing analysis.

Marketing Strategy

If the company has obtained an adequate understanding of the customer base and its own competitive position in the industry, marketing managers are able to make their own key strategic decisions and develop a marketing strategy designed to maximize the revenues and profits of the firm. The selected strategy may aim for any of a variety of specific objectives, including optimizing short-term unit margins, revenue growth, market share, long-term profitability, or other goals. To achieve the desired objectives, marketers typically identify one or more target customer segments which they intend to pursue.

Customer segments are often selected as targets because they score highly on two dimensions: The segment is attractive to serve because it is large, growing, makes frequent purchases, is not price sensitive or other factors; and The company has the resources and capabilities to compete for the segment's business, can meet their needs better than the competition, and can do so profitably. In fact, a commonly cited definition of marketing is simply "meeting needs profitably." The implication of selecting target segments is that the business will subsequently allocate more resources to acquire and retain customers in the target segment(s) than it will for other, non-targeted customers.

In some cases, the firm may go so far as to turn away customers who are not in its target segment.The doorman at a swanky nightclub, for example, may deny entry to unfashionably dressed individuals because the business has made a strategic decision to target the "high fashion" segment of nightclub patrons. In conjunction with targeting decisions, marketing managers will identify the desired positioning they want the company, product, or brand to occupy in the target customer's mind.

This positioning is often an encapsulation of a key benefit the company's product or service offers that is differentiated and superior to the benefits offered by competitive products. For example, Volvo has traditionally positioned its products in the automobile market in North America in order to be perceived as the leader in "safety", whereas BMW has traditionally positioned its brand to be perceived as the leader in "performance." Ideally, a firm's positioning can be maintained over a long period of time because the company possesses, or can develop, some form of sustainable competitive advantage. The positioning should also be sufficiently relevant to the target segment such that it will drive the purchasing behaviour of target customers.

Implementation Planning

After the firm's strategic objectives have been identified, the target market selected, and the desired positioning for the company, product or brand has been determined, marketing managers focus on how to best implement the chosen strategy. Traditionally, this has involved implementation planning across the "4Ps" of marketing: Product management, Pricing, Place, and People. Now a new P has been added making it a total of 5P's. The 5th P is Politics which affects marketing in a significant way.

Taken together, the company's implementation choices across the 4(5)Ps are often described as the marketing mix, meaning the mix of elements the business will employ to "go to market" and execute the marketing strategy. The overall goal for the marketing mix is to consistently deliver a compelling value proposition that reinforces the firm's chosen positioning, builds customer loyalty and brand equity among target customers, and achieves the firm's marketing and financial objectives. In many cases, marketing management will develop a marketing plan to specify how the company will execute the chosen strategy and achieve the business' objectives.

The content of marketing plans varies from firm to firm, but commonly includes:

- An executive summary
- Situation analysis to summarize facts and insights gained from market research and marketing analysis
- The company's mission statement or long-term strategic vision
- A statement of the company's key objectives, often subdivided into marketing objectives and financial objectives
- The marketing strategy the business has chosen, specifying the target segments to be pursued and the competitive positioning to be achieved
- Implementation choices for each element of the marketing mix (the 4(5)Ps)

Project, Process, and Vendor Management

Once the key implementation initiatives have been identified, marketing managers work to oversee the execution of the marketing plan. Marketing executives may therefore manage any number of specific projects, such as sales force management initiatives, product development efforts, channel marketing programmes and the execution of public relations and advertising campaigns. Marketers use a variety of project management techniques to ensure projects achieve their objectives while keeping to established schedules and budgets.

More broadly, marketing managers work to design and improve the effectiveness of core marketing processes, such as new product development, brand management, marketing communications, and pricing. Marketers may employ the tools of business process reengineering to ensure these processes are properly designed, and use a variety of process management techniques to keep them operating smoothly. Effective execution may require management of both internal resources and a variety of external vendors and service providers, such as the firm's advertising agency. Marketers may therefore coordinate with the company's Purchasing department on the procurement of these services.

Organizational Management and Leadership

Marketing management may spend a fair amount of time building or maintaining a marketing orientation for the business. Achieving a market orientation, also known as "customer focus" or the "marketing concept", requires building consensus at the senior management level and then driving customer focus down into the organization. Cultural barriers may exist in a given business unit or functional area that the marketing manager must address in order to achieve this goal. Additionally, marketing executives often act as a "brand champion" and work to enforce corporate identity standards across the enterprise.

In larger organizations, especially those with multiple business units, top marketing managers may need to coordinate across several marketing departments and also resources from finance, research and development, engineering, operations, manufacturing, or other functional areas to implement the marketing plan.

In order to effectively manage these resources, marketing executives may need to spend much of their time focused on political issues and inte-departmental negotiations. The effectiveness of a marketing manager may therefore depend on his or her ability to make the internal "sale" of various marketing programmes equally as much as the external customer's reaction to such programmes.

Reporting, Measurement, Feedback and Control Systems

Marketing management employs a variety of metrics to measure progress against objectives. It is the responsibility of marketing managers – in the marketing department or elsewhere – to ensure that the execution of marketing programmes achieves the desired objectives and does so in a cost-efficient manner.

Marketing management therefore often makes use of various organizational control systems, such as sales forecasts, sales force and reseller incentive programmes, sales force management systems, and customer relationship management tools.

Recently, some software vendors have begun using the term "marketing operations management" or "marketing resource management" to describe systems that facilitate an integrated approach for controlling marketing resources. In some cases, these efforts may be linked to various supply chain management systems, such as enterprise resource planning, material requirements planning, efficient consumer response, and inventory management systems. Measuring the return on investment of and marketing effectiveness various marketing initiatives is a significant problem for marketing management.

Various market research, accounting and financial tools are used to help estimate the ROI of marketing investments. Brand valuation, for example, attempts to identify the percentage of a company's market value that is generated by the company's brands, and thereby estimate the financial value of specific investments in brand equity. Another technique, integrated marketing communications is a CRM database-driven approach that attempts to estimate the value of marketing mix executions based on the changes in customer behaviour these executions generate.

E MARKETING

Modern information and communications technologies (ICTs) and web based marketing of agricultural produce hold great promise for the socio-economic development of rural hinterlands in India. However, if they are to serve the 'unserved' and spawn innovation at grass root level their implementation must be carefully localised.

This explores several models of ICT deployment and information design issues which have been tried in various parts of the developing world in the context of agricultural marketing over the web and uses that learning with field experience from a live project.

The flexible systems framework is found appropriate and useful to design the next action agenda. The 'anytime-anywhere' advantage of e marketing leads to efficient price discovery and offers economy of transaction for agricultural trading.

This attracts many rural developmental agencies to deploy websites for marketing agricultural produce. But in spite of a core value proposition and significant investment by the Indian government/NGOs and commercial agencies in developing such portals, many have failed. Internet traffic on these websites is either very limited or none at all.

Yet there is a lack of empirical studies on the modes of their failures. This study using the SAP-LAP methodology examines the experiences of a number of internet portals from India and other countries engaged in rural marketing or disseminating rural development information, with usability measures derived from farmers and traders and those suggested by researchers. The findings are used in developing a conceptual framework for e-marketing info design for agricultural market in rural northern India for the portal (DM).

Situation

Common wisdom has it that the advent of modern information and communication technologies (ICTs) such as telephony or the internet holds unprecedented opportunities for rural development. Researchers, policymakers and entrepreneurs alike frequently claim that ICTs represent one of the most powerful tools in the struggle against poverty. The significance of the Web in disseminating information and communicating this effectively to the targeted user has been sufficiently debated.

Most experts agree to it that the Web will have a great impact on the way rural marketing would be conducted in the future, yet there has been little research towards exploring the effectiveness of the provision of agriculture-related and rural marketing information in the electronic form. This study set out to assess the current performance of agricultural websites in some key areas of information provision through such websites maintained by government departments and agencies, private profit-motivated as well as non-governmental organizations (NGOs), and to identify the barriers to communication.

The results offer significant implications for researchers and practitioners interested in development of portal information structure for Web development, multi-dimensional communication, electronic commerce networks and e-commerce trading platforms for rural marketing. There are a number of ways – some obvious and some not-so-obvious ones – in which ICTs may serve the development process. For instance rural entrepreneurs can benefit because ICTs help to improve access to markets or supply chains and provide a broader base for decision-making, thus making risk more calculable.

Moreover, many local communities have experienced that ICTs have increased bottom-up participation in the governance processes and may expand the reach and accessibility of government services and public infrastructure. In Andhra Pradesh, Internet-based Integrated Citizen Service Centres allow for electronic bill payment, issuing of certificates, permits and licenses; or access to public information. The electronic village project of M.S.Swaminathan Research Foundation (MSSRF) in Pondicherry received the Stockholm award for its promise.

However, there is as yet little systematic empirical evidence of the supposed enormous 'developmental' impacts of ICTs. Moreover, in many – especially rural – areas, the private sector is yet to invest significantly in ICT experiments (except for a few like ITC or Tata Chemicals) because of lack of experience with rural markets or low purchasing power of the local population.

This means that, if ICT access is to be expanded, public money will have to be spent – which in turn means that there is important trade-offs to be considered. In many areas, there are serious questions about how much money policymakers should spare for the build-up of ICTs instead of investing further in potable water supply, roads, electricity or other physical infrastructure projects. Given such trade-offs, there is a need to identify which kinds of ICT access deliver the best value for money, and how the limited resources that can be spent on it can be made to best suit the particular needs of rural India. A number of 'models' have so far been tried. One of the most famous projects of successful ICT application for development is the Grameen Village Phone system, undertaken by Grameen Telecom (a member of the Grameen Group). The project aims at ultimately spreading phone access to the over 100 million inhabitants of Bangladesh who are so far 'unwired', made possible by combining the Grameen Bank's expertise in village-based micro-enterprise and micro-credit with the latest digital wireless technology.

The aim is to have selected member borrowers of Grameen Bank purchase the phones under a lease programme and make the phones available to all users in the village on a fee-paying basis. Another model of ICT provision in rural areas of developing countries, and one which attempts to combine phone access with access to the Internet is that of the so-called Telecentres or Information Kiosks or the recently introduced Infothela of MLAKLH.

An Infothela is a common point of access for multiple users (often an entire community), providing a range of ICT services including Internet, fax, phone, e-mail, word processing, and even specialised information retrieval or applications (*e.g.* distance education or matrimonial matchmaking). Telecentres have been established widely in the developing world, and vary in their service provision and means of funding. In Peru, the establishment of numerous 'Cabañas Públicas' created one of the highest concentrations of public internet access and a significant reduction in prices.

Nevertheless, the experience with telecentres has so far been a mixed one. In numerous cases, usage, particularly of PCs, has been lower than expected or commercial viability was not attained. Of the over 70 Community Telecentres established since 1997 by the South African Universal Services Agency, only 40 per cent remain open today, with only 3 per cent making enough money to cover costs. Buried at the end of the World Bank policy paper on the 'Networking revolution: opportunities and challenges for developing countries' is an account of multipurpose community telecentres (MCTs) in rural Mexico.

It turns out that of twenty-three MCTs built in rural Mexico, only five were working two years later. This is a failure rate of 80 percent. The policy paper comments, "Problems encountered included insufficient maintenance funding, inadequate political interest and will, and cultural constraints which hamper community interest in the projects." The paper gives no hint why "political interest and will" might have been inadequate and why community interest might have been constrained by that hold all excuse for failure, "culture."

The paper concludes that the Mexican case "underscores the importance of participatory design and attention to sustainability issues in the development of such programmemes." Internet and Information Kiosks exist in various kinds, each with their respective merits. First, one might distinguish between the small private sector cyber cafes on the one hand and bigger, donor-funded telecentres like e-Seva in Andhra Pradesh or e-Village in Pondicherry on the other hand. Smaller, privately run cyber cafes are often financially self-sustaining – but are thus usually restricted to areas where they expect to be viable (usually urban centres) and are usually neither within physical nor financial reach of the poor.

They are also unlikely to be able to provide local content. – By contrast, larger, often externally funded telecentres are rarely financially sustainable but can focus more on specific 'development' – aspects, including access specifically targeted at rural communities and the poorest in general, as well as a focus on training. A second distinction is according to the institutional context they are embedded in.

This often has a significant influence on the 'developmental impact' of telecentres. Commercial telecentres and commercial franchises (like e-choupals of ITC) are usually closest to commercial viability but, as mentioned, are unlikely to have an impact on the poor outside the economic circle of the e-Choupals. Telecentres run by or with the involvement of developmental NGOs are more likely to target poor and marginalised communities and focus on much-needed additional services like training, content creation, provision of public goods without which ICT access would be of limited developmental use.

Telecentres in village schools for example as another alternative have the significant advantage that for their establishment an existing physical infrastructure only has to be extended and some of the ICT-relevant training can be cost-effectively integrated into the mainstream curriculum of the educational institution. This partnership has successfully worked in the DM project.

One further idea for the Digital Mandi that evolved was Virtual Telephones or village voice mail systems, as have been set up in Brazil. These can provide individuals with their own telephone number and access to a voice mailbox. In other words, the individual need not possess a telephone but can receive calls to a voice mailbox using his/her personal PIN.

Extending this idea to text e-mail access, a South African company assigns e-mail addresses to every Post Office box address in the country, thereby providing electronic mail indirectly to around eight million South African households through public internet terminals located in post offices which users can access with a personal identification number. The Postal Department in India has now taken up a similar programme..

Thus there are a number of alternatives and apparently mutually exclusive business models for ICT implementation in Rural India. On one hand it appears that kiosks run by local entrepreneurs with localized and targeted applications (like e choupals in Northern India or voicemail service in Brazil or matrimonial matchmaking service in Tamil Nadu) will succeed on the other hand following the success model of the world wide web itself one may suggest that if an infrastructure is created and user friendly appropriate interfaces are continuously accessible then local rural folks will develop their own applications and Information Kiosks or Infothela will survive. The Digital Mandi Project conceived as an electronic trading platform for agro-commodities of Northern India and meant to run as a core application on the mobile Infothela faced additional problems.

Barriers to information access may be physical, economic, intellectual or technological, that impede a user's participation in the activities on a website. The barriers may be actively imposed by the architects and website designers or they may be allowed to continue simply through their lack of action or lack of understanding of the critical user conditions.

Such critical user conditions may arise due to particular demographic, geographic, cultural, social, psychological, economic or other factors. Issues related to usability such as ease of use, usefulness, decision effectiveness, user response, user satisfaction and many other aspect of usability have been studied in great detail by researchers. But interactions with focus groups at various agricultural market places around Lucknow-Kanpur showed the need of a more detailed study on Information communication barriers on a more localised set of priorities.

MARKETING ON THE INTERNET

The Internet is a revolutionary development as a communication tool and marketing medium. It offers huge opportunities, but the Internet is not a silver bullet or magic wand for your business. Successful Internet marketing requires a unique approach. If you try to apply old methods from other mediums you will be disappointed. We have some thoughts about Internet marketing based on our experience and those we have worked with. You might also want to check out some other resources like Doing Business on The Internet.

When we explore web sites, we find a huge gap between what those who use the Internet are looking for and what they will find at most sites. It looks very much as if the rush to get in on the WWW has canceled any attempt to really understand and work with the Internet. To be frank, we think most sites are a waste of Internet resources. Sure, there are plenty of "cool" graphics, animation and sound. There are many very artful sites and those that demonstrate a lot of clever thinking, but content is completely missing.

Early TV ads used simple text and display ads with a voice over, borrowed from newspaper techniques. The medium was visual, like a newspaper, but you could provide sound. So, why not just put up a picture and some text and then have somebody read what it said over the air? Well, you could get away with this for awhile. The medium was so new and interesting, people even found looking at the test patterns to be interesting. Not any more.

If you look at most of the current advertising or marketing on the Web, you find that many have simply copied techniques used elsewhere. Many web pages look very much like newspaper ads. Some particularly bad ones "shout" at you with lots of bold type and blinking "signs". High quality graphics and clever displays and "marquees" abound, but after awhile, it all looks the same. TV became the "boob tube". Perhaps the Web will become or has become a new vast wasteland of cheesy ads. The common denominator among Internet users who browse web pages is the quest for knowledge and information. They may be looking for entertainment. They may want to buy something. They may be interested in locating products and services, but the core motivation is curiosity, the desire for information and knowledge.

If you do not respond to this, it will not matter how cool your site is or how wonderful your products are. Your site will be of passing interest and will eventually be passed by. Check this out for yourself, honestly. Look at your own web browsing patterns. Do you honestly go on a simple "shopping trip", looking for ways to spend money? Not likely. We don't and we don't know anyone who does.

Before you try marketing on the Internet, define what information and knowledge you will offer to those who visit your site. It doesn't matter what your product or service is; if you don't have some useful information to share along with your product, you don't have a reason for being on the Net from the customer's point of view. We have developed an example scenario to clarify our point of view.

Every business must choose between two directions for growth. You can only succeed if you focus on one primary direction at a time. Many businesses never figure this out and it shows. All of your marketing including your Internet marketing, must be guided by your basic marketing direction. Without this compass your marketing and your business will drift hither and thither. Here are some pointers for getting your bearings. The best marketing is driven by a clear sense of direction for the business. Everyone wants to grow, but the best prospects for growth are not the same for all businesses. Choosing a primary direction for growth is the first step in developing a marketing plan that works. Your marketing efforts on the Net can be very different depending on the direction you choose.

Some businesses will do best if they concentrate on generating repeat business from existing customers. They don't ignore the need to expand their marketing area, but they focus on repeat sales first. These businesses have a regular opportunity to develop or obtain new products and services that meet the existing needs of their customers. Keeping customers happy and coming back time and again is the key to success.

Emphasis on repeat business is characteristic of these businesses:

- Fast food restaurants
- Banks and Savings and Loans
- Automobile dealers.

The New Pro.ducts Direction

Do you know anyone who doesn't have an opinion about fast food? Most people have pretty stable opinions; they are willing to eat it at least once in a while or they never touch it. If you we are going to start a fast food restaurant would it make sense to focus your marketing on winning over the people who don't eat fast food now? Probably not. It would make more sense to target those who already eat fast food.

Try to get a piece of the existing market by giving them a new choice, don't chase after customers who will be an ultra hard sell. This defines the new products direction. An established market exists and is open to new offerings, choices, options. Look at the marketing of the existing fast food chains. They are battling it out with new products, enhanced versions of their products, new offers, price wars, etc.. You won't find ads wasted on those who aren't currently in the market. Their strategy is focused, their direction is clear.

As products are added or changed to meet the needs of the existing market, the possibility of new markets increases. Think of the changes that have occurred with fast food chains. Most now offer breakfast, salads, alternatives to burgers and fries. As these changes have occurred, the market has actually expanded to include some of those who previously avoided fast food.

They haven't won everyone over, but the market has expanded. Expanding the overall market for fast food is a result of adding new products and improving products. But the primary direction was always to bring existing customers back. The expansion of the market was secondary.

Implications for Internet Marketing

If you pursue a new products direction, your Internet presence must focus on serving the needs of the existing market. Learn as much as you can about what they want, need and can't get. Make your Web site a resource for your current customers first. Use it to communicate with them and keep them informed about what's new. A visitor to your site should feel "at home". The site should tap their existing interests. It should present choices to them that build on the understanding they already have.

Educate them about what you have that is new, better, more functional. They probably aren't there to have you educate them about what they already know. Extend their knowledge instead. If you want to have a section for people new to your product or service, make it a side section. Don't force current customers to wade through it.

Direction Two - New Markets

Some businesses will do best if they concentrate on expanding the market for their current products and services. They don't reject repeat business, but they constantly look for new markets and new applications of what they currently offer. These businesses are good at finding new ways to apply the skills and assets they have to new situations or to new markets. They may have to modify a product slightly or customise their services, but the main goal is always expansion to broader markets.

Emphasis on new markets is characteristic of these types of businesses:

- Mail order businesses
- Consulting businesses
- Hotels and Resorts.

The New Markets Direction

A gift shop located in a small, rural community has established a unique inventory. There is repeat business as they add new items, but it is difficult to expand the range of inventory enough to keep the existing customers coming back. The total number of customers in the community is also self-limiting. The business must expand its market beyond the local boundaries. The larger market for current products will also improve their overall profitability.

This defines the new markets direction. An established business must identify and appeal to new markets to avoid reaching a point of self-limiting growth in repeat business. Look at the growth in mail order companies moving outside of geographic limitations.

The Internet and World Wide Web represent the most striking example of businesses searching for new growth from a new markets direction. Thousands of small businesses are searching for new customers online that they could never have found by staying local.

As new markets are identified, the need for new or modified products grows. The new customers don't have exactly the same needs as previous or existing customers. Accommodations are necessary. As the needs of the new markets are identified, the range of products and services gradually expands. These additions or modifications can bring back prior customers who find new choices and options that appeal to them as well. The search for new markets requires an ability to adapt along the way.

As adaptations occur, the opportunities to offer new products to existing customers expand, but the driving force is always focused on expansion of the market for your product or service. Your marketing choices should be clearly driven by this primary goal.

Implications for Internet Marketing

If you pursue a new markets direction, your Internet presence must focus on education for those who may be new to your products and services. Your Web site should appeal to their curiosity, invite them to dig deeper. Use it to start a relationship instead of assuming one exists. A visitor to your site should feel "intrigued". The site should present choices that allow them to guide and pace their own education. Let them discover what you have to offer by giving them a self-guided tour. Don't assume they know what you are talking about.

Be clear and detailed. The section for existing customers should be accessed from any easy to locate link, but should not be up front and in your face when you first arrive.

Creating an Informative Site

No matter what your business, your web site must be informative to be successful. It must also be publicized, but publicizing a site that offers no information is not going to work. So the first step is to be informative. Every successful site meets the information goal. In our opinion, the majority of sites do not meet this goal. We expect to see a lot of disappointed businesses leaving the Internet.

A Gift Shop

Gift shops are everywhere on the Web. There are times when it begins to seem like a giant flea market. But a good web site can turn a gift shop into a consumer resource. We know a gift shop that offers some unique crystal pieces. While we browsed through the store (they're not on the Web yet), the owner noted that the crystal has some interesting properties. For example, it is resistant to staining when used in a location like ours with particularly hard water. She explained why and went on to share what she knew about caring for crystal in general and how that had led her to select these pieces for her store. It was clear she had a strong personal interest in fine crystal and that had led her to educate herself about her products.

A "bad" web site would trumpet the crystal, skip its resistance to stains and provide you with an immediate link to an ordering page. A nice graphic of the crystal would be provided, but nothing else to get in the way of your desire to Order Now! By the way, several parts of the text would be blinking or scrolling just to make sure you didn't miss them.

The opportunity to educate and inform visitors would be ignored or lost in the hype. A functional site would place the crystal in a context of knowledge and understanding. The unique value of the crystal would emerge as a logical conclusion, not as a marketing claim. Visitors to the site would carry away something other than hype. The owner would have an opportunity to share her enthusiasm and draw others into a dialogue supported by the communication link of the Internet.

We found a very small, but good example of an informative site at Access Market Square. This site is not big or fancy. There are no super cool graphics or clever animated gifs. The goal is to offer useful information. You can get free information on key points to consider when selecting day care for your child. They offer books for new parents that address the needs of today's families. This site will not win awards for being cool or for being clever. Their purpose is not entertainment.

On the up side, they won't make the list of worst sites on the Web either. They have a clear business purpose, simply executed in a manner consistent with the needs of their visitors. We would like to see the site grow and become even more useful to young parents. However, they may find they need to do no more than they already have to make their Web marketing effective.

MARKETING PLANNING AND STRATEGY

In particular, we focus attention on the importance of marketing planning with special attention given to the role marketing strategy plays in the planning process. For marketers planning is an essential task that must be continually undertaken. As we will see, shifting market conditions, including changing customer needs and competitive threats, almost always insure that what worked in the past will not work in the future, thus requiring revisions in how a product is marketed.

Marketing planning is also important since it is often a prerequisite for obtaining funding whether one is a marketer in a large corporation seeking additional money for his or her department or is part of a small startup company looking for initial funding. To aid in our understanding of planning we introduce a key concept in marketing: the Product Life Cycle. We will see the Product Life Cycle offers valuable insight and guidance for marketing decisions.

In this tutorial we also discuss different types of marketing strategy that can be followed to meet marketing objectives. Additionally, we look at how innovative products are adopted within a market and how this impacts marketing planning.

IMPORTANCE OF MARKETING PLANNING

Marketers consider many factors when making decisions. Of course the main factors are those directly associated with how customers (including distribution partners) respond to an organization's marketing efforts, such as how they may react to changes in a product, new advertisements, special pricing promotions, etc.

But when making decisions marketers face other concerns that are not directly customer related. For instance, we have discussed how marketing decisions (e.g., lowering price) may place pressure on other areas of the organization (e.g., production, shipping). Other examples include:

- As we noted in our definition of marketing, decisions must be made with an understanding of the value these provide not only to customers but to the marketing organization. Consequently, marketers must be well aware of how their decisions fit with the overall objectives of the company. For example, a company whose goal is to be the low-price leader may have concerns if the company's marketing department wants to market a very high-end product, since this would go against the reputation and core strengths of the company.

- We showed that marketers' decisions may affect peripheral stakeholders who are not directly connected to the marketing organization but have the potential to impact the organization if issues arise that draw their attention.
- Marketing decisions also directly affect an organization's financial condition. Marketers' efforts generate the funds (i.e., sales) needed for the company to survive, but do so while using company resources, in particular, expenditure of funds. Controls must be put in place to insure the results of what the organization spends through marketing (i.e., return on investment) meet expectations.

Because marketing decisions have both internal and external impact, marketers are wise to make their decisions only after engaging in a careful, disciplined planning process. Marketers who make hasty, off-the-cuff decisions without regard to the implications are taking risks that may lead to problems.

Instead, marketing decisions should be made with consideration of how these affect others and the resources (e.g., funds) required to carry out the plan.

THE MARKETING PLAN

The central point in planning for marketing decisions is the Marketing Plan. The plan serves several functions including:

- Forcing marketing personnel to look internally in order to fully understand the results of past marketing decisions.
- Forcing marketing personnel to look externally in order to fully understand the market in which they operate.
- Setting future goals and providing direction for future marketing efforts that everyone within the organization should understand and support.
- Serving as a key component in obtaining funding to pursue new initiatives.

The scope of the Marketing Plan depends on the company and industry. A small technology startup company may, for instance, have a less elaborate plan that is highly flexible (e.g., does not identify exactly where advertising money is spent) to meet the needs of a rapidly changing market. A more established marketing organization, such a large consumer products firm, may create a very structured plan that clearly identifies all activities that take place over a 12-month period.

Whether the marketer is creating a short plan intended to cover a narrow timeframe or a full-blown document laying out plans for a year or more, any plan requires undertaking significant market research to better understand the market. With knowledge of the market, the marketer can then begin to build the plan which will include the following key concepts:

- *Organizational Mission*: Represents the guiding force of an organization by identifying the long-run vision for what the organization hopes to achieve. The mission comes from the top leaders of the organization and often remains unchanged for many years.
- *Objectives*: Reflects what the organization expects to achieve with its marketing efforts. As with the mission, objectives also flow from the top of the organization down to the marketing department. Objectives can be in the form of financial goals (i.e., profits) or marketing goals (e.g., achieve certain level of market share).
- *Marketing Strategy:* Achieving objectives requires the marketer engage in marketing decision-making which indicates where resources (e.g., marketing funds) will be directed. However, before spending begins on individual marketing decisions (e.g., where to advertise) the marketer needs to establish a general plan of action that summarizes what will be done to reach the stated objectives.
- *Tactical Programs*: Marketing strategy sets the stage for specific actions that will take place. Marketing tactics are the day-to-day actions that marketers undertake and involve the major marketing decision areas. As would be expected, this is the key area of the Marketing Plan since it explains exactly what will be done to reach the organization's objectives.
- *Marketing Budget*: Carrying out marketing tactics almost always means that money must be spent. The marketing budget lays out the spending requirements needed to carry out marketing tactics. While the marketing department may request a certain level of funding they feel is required, in the end it is upper-management that will have final say on how much financial support will be offered.

SALES PROMOTION/SPONSORSHIPS/EXHIBITIONS

Sales Promotion

Sales promotions are direct inducements that offer extra incentives to enhance or accelerate the product's movement from producer to consumer. Sales promotions may be directed at the consumer or the trade. Consumer promotions such as coupons, sampling, premiums, sweepstakes, price packs, low-cost financing deals, and rebates are purchase incentives in that they induce product trial and encourage repurchase.

Consumer promotions may also include incentives to visit a retail establishment or request additional information. Trade promotions include slotting allowances, allowances for featuring the brand in retail advertising, display and merchandising allowances, buying allowances, bill back allowances, incentives to salespeople, and other tactics to encourage retailers to carry the item and to push the brand. Two perspectives may be found among marketers regarding sales promotion. First, sales promotion is supplemental to advertising in that it binds the role of advertising with personal selling.

This view regards sales promotion as a minor player in the marketing communication programme. A second view regards sales promotion and advertising as distinct functions with objectives and strategies very different from each other. Sales promotion in this sense is equal to or even more important than advertising.

Some companies allocate as much as 75 per cent of their advertising/ promotion dollars to sales promotion and just 25 per cent to advertising. Finding the right balance is often a difficult task. The main purpose of sales promotion is to spur action. Advertising sets up the deal by developing a brand reputation and building market value. Sales promotion helps close the deal by providing incentives that build market volume.

Sales promotions can motivate customers to select a particular brand, especially when brands appear to be equal, and they can produce more immediate and measurable results than advertising. However, too heavy a reliance on sales promotions results in "deal-prone" consumers with little brand loyalty and too much price sensitivity. Sales promotions can also force competitors to offer similar inducements, with sales and profits suffering for everyone.

Sponsorships

Sponsorships, or event marketing, combine advertising and sales promotions with public relations. Sponsorships increase awareness of a company or product, build loyalty with a specific target audience, help differentiate a product from its competitors, provide merchandising opportunities, demonstrate commitment to a community or ethnic group, or impact the bottom line. Like advertising, sponsorships are initiated to build long-term associations. Organizations sometimes compare sponsorships with advertising by using gross impressions or cost-per-thousand measurements.

However, the value of sponsorships can be very difficult to measure. Companies considering sponsorships should consider the short-term public relations value of sponsorships and the long-term goals of the organization. Sports sponsorships make up about two-thirds of all sponsorships.

Exhibits

Exhibits, or trade shows, are hybrid forms of promotion between business-to-business advertising and personal selling. Trade shows provide opportunities for face-to-face contact with prospects, enable new companies to create a viable customer base in a short period of time, and allow small and midsize companies that may not be visited on a regular basis by salespeople to become familiar with suppliers and vendors.

Because many trade shows generate media attention, they have also become popular venues for introducing new products and providing a stage for executives to gain visibility.

PERSONAL SELLING

Personal selling includes all person-to-person contact with customers with the purpose of introducing the product to the customer, convincing him or her of the product's value, and closing the sale. The role of personal selling varies from organization to organization, depending on the nature and size of the company, the industry, and the products or services it is marketing. Many marketing executives realise that both sales and non-sales employees act as salespeople for their organization in one way or another.

One study that perhaps supports this contention found that marketing executives predicted greater emphasis being placed on sales management and personal selling in their organization than on any other promotional mix element. These organizations have launched training sessions that show employees how they act as salespeople for the organization and how they can improve their interpersonal skills with clients, customers, and prospects. Employee reward programmes now reward employees for their efforts in this regard.

Personal selling is the most effective way to make a sale because of the interpersonal communication between the salesperson and the prospect. Messages can be tailored to particular situations, immediate feedback can be processed, and message strategies can be changed to accommodate the feedback. However, personal selling is the most expensive way to make a sale, with the average cost per sales call ranging from $235 to $332 and the average number of sales calls needed to close a deal being between three and six personal calls.

Sales and marketing management classifies salespersons into one of three groups: creative selling, order taking, and missionary sales reps. Creative selling jobs require the most skills and preparation. They are the "point person" for the sales function. They prospect for customers, analyse situations, determine how their company can satisfy wants and needs of prospects, and, most importantly, get an order. Order takers take over after the initial order is received.

They handle repeat purchases and modified rebuys. Missionary sales reps service accounts by introducing new products, promotions, and other programmes. Orders are taken by order takers or by distributors.

INTERNET MARKETING

Just as direct marketing has become a prominent player in the promotional mix, so too has the Internet. Virtually unheard of in the 1980s, the 1990s saw this new medium explode onto the scene, being adopted by families, businesses and other organizations more quickly than any other medium in history. Web sites provide a new way of transmitting information, entertainment, and advertising, and have generated a new dimension in marketing: electronic commerce. E-commerce is the term used to describe the act of selling goods and services over the Internet.

In other words, the Internet has become more that a communication channel; it is a marketing channel itself with companies, CDNow, eBay, and others selling goods via the Internet to individuals around the globe. In less than 10 years advertising expenditures on the Internet will rival those for radio and outdoor.

Public relations practitioners realise the value that web sites offer in establishing and maintaining relationships with important publics. For example, company and product information can be posted on the company's site for news reporters researching stories and for current and potential customers seeking information. Political candidates have web sites that provide information about their background and their political experience.

The interactivity of the Internet is perhaps its greatest asset. By communicating with customers, prospects, and others one-on-one, firms can build databases that help them meet specific needs of individuals, thus building a loyal customer base. Because the cost of entry is negligible, the Internet is cluttered with web sites. However, this clutter does not present the same kind of problem that advertising clutter does.

Advertising and most other forms of promotion assume a passive audience that will be exposed to marketing communication messages via the mass media or mail regardless of their receptivity. Web sites require audiences who are active in the information-seeking process to purposely visit the site. Therefore, the quality and freshness of content is vital for the success of the web site.

THE FUTURE OF MARKETING COMMUNICATION

Marketing communication has become an integral part of the social and economic system in the United States. Consumers rely on the information from marketing communication to make wise purchase decisions. Businesses, ranging from multinational corporations to small retailers, depend on marketing communication to sell their goods and services.

Marketing communication has also become an important player in the life of a business. Marketing communication helps move products, services, and ideas from manufacturers to end users and builds and maintains relationships with customers, prospects, and other important stakeholders in the company.

Advertising and sales promotion will continue to play important roles in marketing communication mix. However, marketing strategies that stress relationship building in addition to producing sales will force marketers to consider all the elements in the marketing communication mix. In the future new information gathering techniques will help marketers target more precisely customers and prospects using direct marketing strategies. New media technologies will provide businesses and consumers new ways to establish and reinforce relationships that are important for the success of the firm and important for consumers as they make purchase decisions. The Internet will become a major force in how organizations communicate with a variety of constituents, customers, clients, and other interested parties.

9

Management in Marketing Promotion

INTRODUCTION

The audience for an organization's marketing communication efforts is not limited to just the marketer's target market. While the bulk of a marketer's promotional budget may be directed at the target market, there are many other groups that could also serve as useful target of a marketing message.

Targets of a marketing message generally fall into one of the following categories:

- *Members of the Organization's Target Market:* This category would include current customers, previous customers and potential customers, and as noted, may receive the most promotional attention.
- *Influencers of the Organization's Target Market:* There exists a large group of people and organizations that can affect how a company's target market is exposed to and perceives a company's products. These influencing groups have their own communication mechanisms that reach the target market and the marketer may be able utilize these influencers to its benefit. Influencers include the news media (e.g., offer company stories), special interest groups, opinion leaders (e.g., doctors directing patients), and industry trade associations.
- *Participants in the Distribution Process:* The distribution channel provides services to help gain access to final customers and are also target markets since they must recognize a product's benefits and agree to handle the product in the same way as final customers who must agree to purchase products. Aiming promotions at distribution partners (e.g., retailers, wholesalers, distributors) and other channel members is extremely important and, in some industries, represents a higher portion of a marketer's promotional budget than promotional spending directed at the final customer.
- *Other Companies:* The most likely scenario in which a company will communicate with another company occurs when the marketer is probing to see if the company would have an interest in a joint venture, such as a co-marketing arrangement where two firms share

marketing costs. Reaching out to other companies, including companies who may be competitors for other products, could help create interest in discussing such a relationship.

- *Other Organizational Stakeholders:* Marketers may also be involved with communication activities directed at other stakeholders. This group consists of those who provide services, support or, in other ways, impact the company. For example, an industry group that sets industry standards can affect company products through the issuance of recommended compliance standards for product development or other marketing activities. Communicating with this group is important to insure the marketer's views of any changes in standards are known.

FACTORS AFFECTING PROMOTIONS CHOICE

With four promotional methods to choose from how does the marketer determine which ones to use? The selection can be complicated by company and marketing decision issues.

Company Issues

- *Promotional Objective:* As we discussed, there are several different objectives a marketer may pursue with their promotional strategy. Each type of promotion offers different advantages in terms of helping the marketer reach their objectives. For instance, if the objective of a software manufacturer is to get customers to try a product, the use of sales promotion, such as offering the software in a free downloadable form, may yield better results than promoting through Internet advertising.
- *Availability of Resources:* The amount of money and other resources that can be directed to promotion affects the marketer's choice of promotional methods. Marketers with large promotional budgets may be able to spread spending among all promotion options while marketers with limited funds must be more selective on the promotion techniques they use.
- *Company Philosophy:* Some companies follow a philosophy that dictates where most promotional spending occurs. For instance, some companies follow the approach that all promotion should be done through salespeople while other companies prefer to focus attention on product development and hope word-of-mouth communication by satisfied customers helps to create interest in their product.

Marketing Decision Issues

- *Target Market:* As one might expect, customer characteristics dictate how promotion is determined. Characteristics such as size, location and type of target markets affect how the marketer communicates with customers. For instance, for a small marketer serving business markets with customers widely dispersed, it may be very expensive to utilize a sales force versus using advertising.

- *Product:* Different products require different promotional approaches. For the consumer market, products falling into the convenience and shopping goods categories are likely to use mass market promotional approaches while higher-end specialty goods are likely to use personalized selling. Thus, products that are complex and take customers extended time to make a purchase decision may require personal selling rather than advertising. This is often the case with products targeted to the business market. As a product moves through these stages the product itself may evolve and also promotional objectives will change. This leads to different promotional mix decisions from one stage to the next.
- *Distribution:* Marketing organizations selling through channel partners can reach the final customer either directly using a pull promotion strategy or indirectly using a push promotional strategy. The pull strategy is so named since it creates demand for a product by promoting directly to the final customer in the hopes that their interest in the product will help "pull" more product through the distribution channel. This approach can be used when channel partners are hesitant about stocking a product unless they are assured of sufficient customer interest. The push strategy uses promotion to encourage channel partners to stock and promote the product to their customers. The idea is that by offering incentives to channel members the marketer is encouraging their partners (e.g., wholesalers, retailers) to "push" the product down the channel and into customer's hands. Most large consumer products companies will use both approaches while smaller firm may find one approach works better.
- *Price:* The higher the price of a product the more likely a marketer will need to engage in personalized promotion compared to lower priced products that can be marketed using mass promotion.

OBJECTIVES OF MARKETING PROMOTIONS

The most obvious objective marketers have for promotional activities is to convince customers to make a decision that benefits the marketer (of course the marketer believes the decision will also benefit the customer). For most for-profit marketers this means getting customers to buy an organization's product and, in most cases, to remain a loyal long-term customer. For other marketers, such as not-for-profits, it means getting customers to increase donations, utilize more services, change attitudes, or change behaviour (e.g., stop smoking campaigns). However, marketers must understand that getting customers to commit to a decision, such as a purchase decision, is only achievable when a customer is ready to make the decision. As we saw in Consumer Buying Behaviour and Business Buying Behaviour, customers often move through several stages before a purchase decision is made. Additionally before turning into a repeat customer, purchasers analyse their initial purchase to see whether they received a good value, and then often repeat the purchase process again before deciding to make the same choice.

The type of customer the marketer is attempting to attract and which stage of the purchase process a customer is in will affect the objectives of a particular marketing communication effort. And since a marketer often has multiple simultaneous promotional campaigns, the objective of each could be different.

TYPES OF PROMOTION OBJECTIVES

The possible objectives for marketing promotions may include the following:

- *Build Awareness:* New products and new companies are often unknown to a market, which means initial promotional efforts must focus on establishing an identity. In this situation the marketer must focus promotion to: 1) effectively reach customers, and 2) tell the market who they are and what they have to offer.
- *Create Interest*: Moving a customer from awareness of a product to making a purchase can present a significant challenge. As we saw with our discussion of consumer and business buying behaviour, customers must first recognize they have a need before they actively start to consider a purchase. The focus on creating messages that convince customers that a need exists has been the hallmark of marketing for a long time with promotional appeals targeted at basic human characteristics such as emotions, fears, sex, and humour.
- *Provide Information:* Some promotion is designed to assist customers in the search stage of the purchasing process. In some cases, such as when a product is so novel it creates a new category of product and has few competitors, the information is simply intended to explain what the product is and may not mention any competitors. In other situations, where the product competes in an existing market, informational promotion may be used to help with a product positioning strategy. Marketers may use promotional means, including direct comparisons with competitor's products, in an effort to get customers to mentally distinguish the marketer's product from those of competitors.
- *Stimulate Demand:* The right promotion can drive customers to make a purchase. In the case of products that a customer has not previously purchased or has not purchased in a long time, the promotional efforts may be directed at getting the customer to try the product. This is often seen on the Internet where software companies allow for free demonstrations or even free downloadable

trials of their products. For products with an established customer-base, promotion can encourage customers to increase their purchasing by providing a reason to purchase products sooner or purchase in greater quantities than they normally do. For example, a pre-holiday newspaper advertisement may remind customers to stock up for the holiday by purchasing more than they typically purchase during non-holiday periods.

- *Reinforce the Brand:* Once a purchase is made, a marketer can use promotion to help build a strong relationship that can lead to the purchaser becoming a loyal customer. For instance, many retail stores now ask for a customer's email address so that follow-up emails containing additional product information or even an incentive to purchase other products from the retailer can be sent in order to strengthen the customer-marketer relationship.

CHARACTERISTICS OF DIFFERENT PROMOTIONS

Before we discuss the different types of promotion options available to a marketer, it is useful to gain an understanding of the features that set different options apart. For our discussion we isolate seven characteristics on which each promotional option can be judged. While these characteristics are widely understood as being important in evaluating the effectiveness of each type of promotion, they are by no means the only criteria used for evaluation. In fact, as new promotional methods emerge the criteria for evaluating promotional methods will likely change.

For our discussion we will look at the following characteristics of a promotional method:

- Intended Audience: Mass vs. Targeted
- Payment Model: Paid vs. Non-Paid
- Interaction Type: Personal vs. Non-Personal
- Message Flow: One-Way vs. Two-Way
- Demand Creation: Quick vs. Lagging
- Message Control
- Message Credibility
- Effective Cost of Promotion

Intended Audience: Mass Promotion vs. Targeted Promotion

Promotions can be categorized based on the intended coverage of a single promotional message. For instance, a single television advertisement for a major sporting event, such as the Super Bowl, World Cup or Olympics, could be seen by millions of viewers at the same time. Such mass promotion, intended to reach as many people as possible, has been a mainstay of marketers' promotional efforts for a long time.

Unfortunately, while mass promotions are delivered to a large number of people, the actual number that fall within the marketer's target market may be small. Because of this, many who use mass promotion techniques find it to be an inefficient way to reach desired customers. Instead, today's marketers are turning to newer techniques designed to focus promotional delivery to only those with a high probability of being in the marketer's target market.

For example, Google, Yahoo and other Internet search engines employ methods for delivering highly targeted ads to customers as they enter search terms. The assumption made by advertisers is that customers who enter search terms are interested in the information they have entered, especially if they are searching by entering detailed search strings (e.g., phrases rather than a single word).

Following this logic, advertisers are much more likely to have their ads displayed to customers within their target market and, thus, receive a higher return on their promotional investment. The movement to highly targeted promotions has gained tremendous traction in recent years and, as new and improved targeting methods are introduced, its importance will continue to grow.

Payment Model: Paid Promotion vs. Non-Paid Promotion

Most efforts to promote products require marketers to make direct payment to the medium that delivers the message. For instance, a company must pay a magazine publisher to advertise in the magazine. However, there are several forms of promotion that do not involve direct payment in order to distribute a promotional message. While not necessarily "free" since there may be indirect costs involved, the ability to have a product promoted without making direct payment to the medium can be a viable alternative to expensive promotion options.

Interaction Type: Personal vs. Non-Personal

Promotions involving real people communicating with other people is considered personal promotion. While salespeople are a common and well understood type of personal promotion, another type of promotion, called controlled word-of-mouth promotion (a.k.a., buzz marketing), is emerging as a form of personal promotion. Unlike salespeople who attempt to obtain an order from customers, controlled word-of-mouth promotion uses real people to help spread information about a product but is not designed to directly elicit orders.

One key advantage personal promotions have is the ability for the message sender to adjust the message as they gain feedback from message receivers (i.e., two-way communication). So if a customer does not understand something in the initial message (e.g., doesn't fully understand how the product works) the person delivering the message can adjust the promotion to address questions or concerns. Many non-personal forms of promotion, such as a radio advertisement, are inflexible, at least in the short-term, and cannot be easily adjusted to address questions that arise by the audience experiencing the ad.

Message Flow: One-Way vs. Two-Way Communication

Promotions can be classified based on whether the message source enables the message receiver to respond with immediate feedback. Such feedback can then be followed with further information exchange between both parties. Most efforts at mass promotion, such as television advertising, offer only a one-way information flow that does not allow for easy response by the message receiver.

However, many targeted promotions, such as using a sales force to promote products, allow message recipients to respond immediately to information from the message sender.

Demand Creation: Quick vs. Lagging

As we discussed earlier, the success of promotional activity may not always be measured by comparing spending to an increase in product sales since marketers may use promotion to achieve other objectives. However, when a marketer is looking to increase demand, certain promotional activities offer advantages in turning exposure to promotion into a quick increase in demand.

In general, these activities are most effective when customers are offered an incentive to make the purchase either in a monetary way (e.g., save money) or in psychological way (e.g., improves customer's perceived group role or status level).

Message Control

Most promotions are controlled by the marketer who encodes the message (or hires specialists such as advertising agencies to create the promotion) and then pays to have the message delivered. However, no marketer can totally control how the news media, customers or others talk about a company or its products.

Reporters for magazines, newspaper and websites, as well as posters to Internet forums may discuss a company's products in ways that can benefit or hinder a company's marketing efforts. This is particularly true with non-paid promotions where a marketer is looking to obtain a free "mention" by an influential message medium (e.g., newspaper article).

Message Credibility

The perceived control of the message can influence the target market's perception of message credibility. For example, many customers viewing a comparative advertisement in which a product is shown to be superior to a competitor's product may be skeptical about the claims since the company with the superior product is paying for the advertisement. Yet, if the same comparison is mentioned in a newspaper article it may be more favorably viewed since readers may perceive the author of the story has possessing an unbiased point-of-view.

Cost Effectiveness

Promotional cost is measured in several different ways though the most useful are measured in terms of cost-per-impression (CPI), cost-per-targeted impression (CPTI), and cost-per-action (CPA). The CPI metric (also measured in terms of cost-per-thousand impressions or CPM) relates to how many people are exposed to a promotion in relation to the cost of the promotion. A national or international television advertisement, while expensive to create and broadcast, actually produces a very low CPI given how many people are exposed to the ad.

Yet, a low CPI can be misleading if a large percentage of the promotion's audience is not within the marketer's target market, in which case the CPTI may be a better metric for gauging promotion effectiveness. The CPTI approach looks at what percentage of an audience is within the marketer's customer group and, thus, legitimate targets for the promotion. Clearly, CPTI is higher than CPI, but it offers a better indication of how much promotion is reaching targeted customers.

An even more effective way to evaluate promotional costs is through the cost-per-action metric. With CPA the marketer evaluates how many people actually respond to a promotion. Response may be measured by examining purchase activity, number of phone inquiries, website traffic, clicks on advertisements, and other means within a short time after the promotional message was delivered.

Unfortunately, measuring CPA is not always easy and tying it directly to a specific promotion can also be difficult. For example, a customer who purchases a snack product may have first learned about the snack product several weeks before from a television advertisement. The fact that it took the customer several weeks to make the purchase does not mean the advertisement was not effective in generating sales, though if the CPA was measured within a day or two after the ad was broadcast this person's action would not have been counted..

With the growing trend to more targeted promotions, especially those delivered through the Internet, combined with the development of sophisticated customer tracking techniques, the ability to compare promotion to actual customer activity is bound to one day be the dominant method for measuring promotional effectiveness.

THE COMMUNICATION PROCESS

The act of communicating has been evaluated extensively for many, many years. One of the classic analyses of communication took place in the 1940s and 1950s when researchers, including Claude Shannon, Warren Weaver, Wilbur Schramm and others, offered models describing how communication takes place. In general, communication is how people exchange meaningful information.

Communication Participants:

For communication to occur there must be at least two participants:

- *Message Source*: The source of communication is the party intending to convey information to another party. The message source can be an individual (e.g., salesperson) or an organization (e.g., through advertising). In order to convey a message, the source must engage in message encoding, which involves mental and physical processes necessary to construct a message in order to reach a desired goal (i.e., convey meaningful information). This undertaking consists of using sensory stimuli, such as visuals (e.g., words, symbols, images), sounds (e.g., spoken word), and scents (e.g., fragrance) to convey a message.
- *Message Receiver:* The receiver of communication is the intended target of a message source's efforts. For a message to be understood the receiver must decode the message by undertaking mental and physical processes necessary to give meaning to the message. Clearly, a message can only be decoded if the receiver is actually exposed to the message.

Communication Delivery:

Communication takes place in the form of a message that is exchanged between a source and receiver. A message can be shaped using one or a combination of sensory stimuli that work together to convey meaning that meets the objectives of the sender. The sender uses a transmission medium to send the message. In marketing the medium may include the use of different media outlets (e.g., Internet, television, radio, print), promotion-only outlets (e.g., postal mail, billboards), and person-to-person contact (e.g., salespeople).

Additionally, communication can be improved if there is a two-way flow of information in the form of a feedback channel. This occurs if the message receiver is able to respond, often quickly, to the message source. In this way, the original message receiver now becomes the message source and the communication process begins again.

OBSTACLES TO EFFECTIVE COMMUNICATION

While a message source may be able to deliver a message through a transmission medium, there are many potential obstacles to the message successfully reaching the receiver the way the sender intends.

The potential obstacles that may affect good communication include:

- *Poor Encoding:* This occurs when the message source fails to create the right sensory stimuli to meet the objectives of the message. For instance, in person-to-person communication, verbally phrasing words poorly so the intended communication is not what is actually meant, is the result of poor encoding. Poor encoding is also seen in advertisements that are difficult for the intended audience to understand, such as words or symbols that lack meaning or, worse, have totally different meaning within a certain cultural groups. This often occurs when marketers use the same advertising message across many different countries. Differences due to translation or cultural understanding can result in the message receiver having a different frame of reference for how to interpret words, symbols, sounds, etc. This may lead the message receiver to decode the meaning of the message in a different way than was intended by the message sender.

- *Poor Decoding:* This refers to a message receiver's error in processing the message so that the meaning given to the received message is not what the source intended. This differs from poor encoding when it is clear, through comparative analysis with other receivers, that a particular receiver perceived a message differently from others and from what the message source intended. Clearly, as we noted above, if the receiver's frame of reference is different (e.g., meaning of words are different) then decoding problems can occur. More likely, when it comes to marketing promotions, decoding errors occur due to personal or psychological factors, such as not paying attention to a full television advertisement, driving too quickly past a billboard, or allowing one's mind to wonder while talking to a salesperson.
- *Medium Failure:* Sometimes communication channels break down and end up sending out weak or faltering signals. Other times the wrong medium is used to communicate the message. For instance, trying to educate doctors about a new treatment for heart disease using television commercials that quickly flash highly detailed information is not going to be as effective as presenting this information in a print ad where doctors can take their time evaluating the information.
- *Communication Noise:* Noise in communication occurs when an outside force in someway affects delivery of the message. The most obvious example is when loud sounds block the receiver's ability to hear a message. Nearly any distraction to the sender or the receiver can lead to communication noise. In advertising, many customers are overwhelmed (i.e., distracted) by the large number of advertisements they encountered each day. Such advertising clutter (i.e., noise) makes it difficult for advertisers to get their message through to desired customers.

SALES PROMOTION

In a time when customers are exposed daily to a nearly infinite amount of promotional messages, many marketers are discovering that advertising alone is not enough to move members of a target market to take action, such as getting them to try a new product. Instead, marketers have learned that to meet their goals they must use additional promotional methods in conjunction with advertising. Other marketers have found that certain characteristics of their target market (e.g., small but geographically dispersed) or characteristics of their product (e.g., highly complex) make advertising a less attractive option.

For these marketers better results may be obtained using other promotional approaches and may lead to directing all their promotional spending to non-advertising promotions. Finally, the high cost of advertising may drive many to seek alternative, lower cost promotional techniques to meet their promotion goals. Sales promotions are used widely in many industries and especially by marketers selling to consumers. We will see that the objectives of sales promotion are quite different than advertising and are specifically designed to encourage customer response.

SALES PROMOTION

Sales promotion describes promotional methods using special short-term techniques to persuade members of a target market to respond or undertake certain activity. As a reward, marketers offer something of value to those responding generally in the form of lower cost of ownership for a purchased product (e.g., lower purchase price, money back) or the inclusion of additional value-added material (e.g., something more for the same price).

Sales promotions are often confused with advertising. For instance, a television advertisement mentioning a contest awarding winners with a free trip to a Caribbean island may give the contest the appearance of advertising. While the delivery of the marketer's message through television media is certainly labeled as advertising, what is contained in the message, namely the contest, is considered a sales promotion.

The factors that distinguish between the two promotional approaches are:

- Whether the promotion involves a short-term value proposition (e.g., the contest is only offered for a limited period of time), and
- The customer must perform some activity in order to be eligible to receive the value proposition (e.g., customer must enter contest).

The inclusion of a timing constraint and an activity requirement are hallmarks of sales promotion. Sales promotions are used by a wide range of organizations in both the consumer and business markets, though the frequency and spending levels are much greater for consumer products marketers. One estimate by the Promotion Marketing Association suggests that in the US alone spending on sales promotion exceeds that of advertising.

OBJECTIVES OF SALES PROMOTION

Sales promotion is a tool used to achieve most of the five major promotional:

- *Building Product Awareness*: Several sales promotion techniques are highly effective in exposing customers to products for the first time and can serve as key promotional components in the early stages of new product introduction. Additionally, as part of the effort to build product awareness, several sales promotion techniques possess the added advantage of capturing customer information at the time of exposure to the promotion. In this way sales promotion can act as an effective customer information gathering tool (i.e., sales lead generation), which can then be used as part of follow-up marketing efforts.

- *Creating Interest:* Marketers find that sales promotions are very effective in creating interest in a product. In fact, creating interest is often considered the most important use of sales promotion. In the retail industry an appealing sales promotions can significantly increase customer traffic to retail outlets. Internet marketers can use similar approaches to bolster the number of website visitors. Another important way to create interest is to move customers to experience a product. Several sales promotion techniques offer the opportunity for customers to try products for free or at low cost.
- *Providing Information:* Generally sales promotion techniques are designed to move customers to some action and are rarely simply informational in nature. However, some sales promotions do offer customers access to product information. For instance, a promotion may allow customers to try a fee-based online service for free for several days. This free access may include receiving product information via email.
- *Stimulating Demand:* Next to building initial product awareness, the most important use of sales promotion is to build demand by convincing customers to make a purchase. Special promotions, especially those that lower the cost of ownership to the customer (e.g., price reduction), can be employed to stimulate sales.
- *Reinforcing the Brand:* Once customers have made a purchase sales promotion can be used to both encourage additional purchasing and also as a reward for purchase loyalty. Many companies, including airlines and retail stores, reward good or "preferred" customers with special promotions, such as email "special deals" and surprise price reductions at the cash register.

TYPES OF SALES PROMOTION

Sales promotion can be classified based on the primary target audience to whom the promotion is directed. These include:

- *Consumer Market Directed:* Possibly the most well-known methods of sales promotion are those intended to appeal to the final consumer. Consumers are exposed to sales promotions nearly everyday, and as discussed later, many buyers are conditioned to look for sales promotions prior to making purchase decisions.

- *Trade Market Directed:* Marketers use sales promotions to target all customers including partners within their channel of distribution. Trade promotions are initially used to entice channel members to carry a marketer's products and, once products are stocked, marketers utilize promotions to strengthen the channel relationship.
- *Business-to-Business Market Directed:* A small, but important, sub-set of sales promotions are targeted to the business-to-business market. While these promotions may not carry the glamour associated with consumer or trade promotions, B-to-B promotions are used in many industries.

CONSUMER SALES PROMOTION

Consumer sales promotions encompass a variety of short-term promotional techniques designed to induce customers to respond in some way. The most popular consumer sales promotions are directly associated with product purchasing.

These promotions are intended to enhance the value of a product purchase by either reducing the overall cost of the product (i.e., get same product but for less money) or by adding more benefit to the regular purchase price (i.e., get more for the money).

While tying a promotion to an immediate purchase is a major use of consumer sales promotion, it is not the only one. As we noted above, promotion techniques can be used to achieve other objectives such as building brand loyalty or creating product awareness. Consequently, a marketer's promotional toolbox contains a large variety of consumer promotions.

The following 11 types of consumer sales promotions:

1. Coupons
2. Rebates
3. Promotional Pricing
4. Trade-In
5. Loyalty Programs
6. Sampling and Free Trials
7. Free Product
8. Premiums
9. Contests and Sweepstakes
10. Demonstrations
11. Personal Appearances

Coupons

Most consumers are quite familiar with this form of sales promotion, which offers purchasers price savings or other incentives when the coupon is redeemed at the time of purchase. Coupons are short-term in nature since most (but not all) carry an expiration date after which the value may not be received. Also, coupons require consumer involvement in order for value to be realized. In most cases involvement consists of the consumer making an effort to obtain the coupon (e.g., clip from newspaper) and then presenting it at the time of purchase.

Coupons are used widely by marketers across many retail industries and reach consumers in a number of different delivery formats including:

- *Free-Standing Inserts (FSI)*: Here coupon placement occurs loosely (i.e., inserted) within media, such as newspapers and direct mail, and may or may not require the customer to cut away from other material in order to use.
- *Cross-Product:* These consist of coupons placed within or on other products. Often a marketer will use this method to promote one product by placing the coupon inside another major selling product. For example, a pharmaceutical company may imprint a coupon for a cough remedy on the box of a pain medication. Also, this delivery approach is used when two marketers have struck a cross promotion arrangement where each agrees to undertake certain marketing activity for the other.
- *Printout:* A delivery method that is common in many food stores is to present coupons to a customer at the conclusion of the purchasing process. These coupons, which are often printed on the spot, are intended to be used for a future purchase and not for the current purchase which triggered the printing.
- *Product Display:* Some coupons are nearly impossible for customers to miss as they are located in close proximity to the product. In some instances coupons may be contained within a coupon dispenser fastened to the shelf holding the product while in other cases coupons may be attached to a special display where customers can remove them (e.g., tear off).
- *Internet:* Several specialized websites, such as HotCoupons.com, and even some manufacturer's sites, allow customers to print out coupons. These coupons are often the same ones appearing in other media, such as newspapers or direct mail. In other cases, coupons may be sent via email, though to be effective the customer's email programme must be able to receive HTML email (and not text only) in order to maintain required design elements (e.g., bar code).
- *Electronic:* The Internet is also seeing the emergence of new non-printable coupons redeemable through website purchases. These electronic coupons are redeemed when the customer enters a designated coupon code during the purchase process.

Rebates

Rebates, like coupons, offer value to purchasers typically by lowering the customer's final cost for acquiring the product. While rebates share some similarities with coupons, they differ in several keys aspects. First, rebates are generally handed or offered (e.g., accessible on the Internet) to customers after a purchase is made and cannot be used to obtain immediate savings in the way coupons are used. (So called "instant rebates", where customers receive price reductions at the time of purchase, have elements of both coupons and rebates, but for our purposes we will classify these as coupons due to the timing of the reward to the customer.)

Second, rebates often request the purchaser to submit personal data in order to obtain the rebate. For instance, customer identification, including name, address and contact information, is generally required to obtain a rebate. Also, the marketer may ask those seeking a rebate to provide additional data such as indicating the reason for making the purchase.

Third, unlike coupons that always offer value when used in a purchase (assuming it is accepted by the retailer), receiving a rebate only guarantees value if the customer takes actions. Marketers know that not all customers will respond to a rebate. Some will misplace or forget to submit the rebate while others may submit after a required deadline.

Marketers factor in the non-redemption rate as they attempt to calculate the cost of the rebate promotion. Finally, rebates tend to be used as a value enhancement in higher priced products compared to coupons. For instance, rebates are a popular promotion for automobiles and computer software where large amounts of money may be returned to the customer.

Promotional Pricing

One of the most powerful sales promotion techniques is the short-term price reduction or, as known in some areas, "on sale" pricing. Lowering a product's selling price can have an immediate impact on demand, though marketers must exercise caution since the frequent use of this technique can lead customers to anticipate the reduction and, consequently, withhold purchase until the price reduction occurs again. Promotional pricing is also considered within the framework of the Price marketing mix component.

Trade-In

Trade-in promotions allow consumers to obtain lower prices by exchanging something the customer possess, such as an older product that the new purchase will replace. While the idea of gaining price breaks for trading in another product is most frequently seen with automobile sales, such promotions are used in other industries, such as computers and golf equipment, where the customer's exchanged product can be resold by the marketer in order to extract value.

Loyalty Programs

Promotions that offer customers a reward, such as price discounts and free products, for frequent purchasing or other activity are called loyalty programs. These promotions have been around for many years but grew rapidly in popularity when introduced in the airline industry as part of frequent-filer programs. Loyalty programs are also found in numerous other industries, including grocery, pizza purchasing and online book purchases, where they may also be known as club card programs since members often must use a verification card as evidence of enrollment in the programme.

Many loyalty programs have become ingrained as part of the value offered by a marketer. That is, a retailer or marketing organization may offer loyalty programs as general business practice. Under this condition loyalty programme does not qualify as a sales promotion since it does not fit the requirement of offering a short-term value (i.e., it is always offered). However, even within a loyalty programme that is part of a general business practice, a sales promotion can be offered such as special short-term offer that lowers the number of points needed to acquire a free product.

Samples and Free Trials

Enticing members of a target market to try a product is often easy when the trial comes at little or no cost to the customer. The use of samples and free trials may be the oldest of all sales promotion techniques dating back to when society advanced from a culture of self-subsistence to a culture of trade. Sampling and free trials give customers the opportunity to experience products, often in small quantities or for a short duration, without purchasing the product. Today, these methods are used in almost all industries and are especially useful for getting customers to try a product for the first time.

Free Product

Some promotional methods offer free products but with the condition that a purchase be made. The free product may be in the form of additional quantities of the same purchased product (e.g., buy one, get one free) or specialty packages (e.g., value pack) that offer more quantity for the same price as regular packaging.

Premiums

Another form of sales promotion involving free merchandise is premium or "give-away" items. Premiums differ from samples and free product in that these often do not consist of the actual product, though there is often some connection. For example, a cellphone manufacturer may offer access to free downloadable ringtones for those purchasing a cellphone.

Contests and Sweepstakes

Consumers are often attracted to promotions where the potential value obtained is very high. In these promotions only a few lucky consumers receive the value offered in the promotion. Two types of promotions that offer high value are contests and sweepstakes. Contests are special promotions awarding value to winners based on skills they demonstrate compared to others. For instance, a baking company may offer free vacations to winners of a baking contest. Contest award winners are often determined by a panel of judges. Sweepstakes or drawings are not skill based but rather based on luck. Winners are determined by random selection.

In some cases the chances of winning may be higher for those who make a purchase if entry into the sweepstake occurs automatically when a purchase is made. But in most cases, anyone is free to enter without the requirement to make a purchase.

A sub-set of both contests and sweepstakes are games, which come in a variety of formats such as scratch-off cards and collection of game pieces. Unlike contests and sweepstakes, which may not require purchase, to participate in a game customers may be required to make a purchase. In the United States and other countries, where eligibility is based on purchase, games may be subjected to rigid legal controls and may actually fall under that category of lotteries, which are tightly controlled.

Demonstrations

Many products benefit from customers being shown how products are used through a demonstration. Whether the demonstration is experienced in-person or via video form, such as over the Internet, this promotional technique can produce highly effective results. Unfortunately, demonstrations are very expensive to produce.

Costs involved in demonstrations include paying for the expense of the demonstrator, which can be high if the demonstrator is well-known (e.g., nationally known chef), and also paying for the space where the demonstration is given.

Personal Appearances

An in-person appearance by someone of interest to the target market, such as an author, sports figure or celebrity, is another form of sales promotion capable of generating customer traffic to a physical location. However, as with demonstrations, personal appearance promotion can be expensive since the marketer normally must pay a fee for the person to appear.

PROMOTION STRATEGY

The manager must develop a promotion strategy, including advertising, nonfunctional package-design features, publicity, promotions, and sales-force activities that are consistent with the product position.

External factors:

- What values does the segment hold that can be used in our communications? Which should be avoided? Cultural values include spending time with family and friends, and consumption-specific values such as convenient shopping and fast service. Cultural values such as sexy/vain should be avoided as it contrasts with their values.

- How can we communicate to our chosen segments in a manner consistent with the emerging gender-role perceptions of each segment? In general, since the segment has similar views as males, their perception of the women doing shopping at Lopez could be accepted. This does not mean that only women shop at Lopez, but at least this is an acceptable way to communicate.
- What is the nonverbal communication system of each segment? Traditional symbols or items that symbolizes heritage and family.
- How, if at all, can we use reference groups in our advertisements? Having images of grandparents, mothers, or any extended family member shopping at Lopez.
- Can our advertisements help make the product part of one or more role-related product clusters? Yes.
- Can we reach and influence opinion leaders? Yes. This segment go for advise to their parents, grandparents, and friends. If an opinion leader is someone they know their parents or friends trust, this segment might get a reinforcement for buying at Lopez.
- If our product is an innovation, are there diffusion inhibitors that can be overcome by promotion? No. Lopez is known by this segment for tradition.
- Who in the household should receive what types of information concerning our product? Those who are the decision makers or influence, and/or make a purchase.

Internal factors:

- Have we structured our promotional campaign such that each segment will be exposed to it, attend to it, and interpret it in the manner we desire? At times Lopez uses the word "tradition" and "family" when it comes to some of their advertisements. Advertising should continue to be done through the "Bargain Book", but should take use of other medias. Radio is one option, but should be done in the mornings when this segment is getting their kids ready for school. Late morning should be available if targeting those who don't work. Advertising through the web should be considered only for those who work or might have a computer. These kinds of ads should be on local TV channel and community web sites.
- Have we made use of the appropriate learning principles so that our meaning will be remembered? Yes and because the reference groups are considered.
- Do our messages relate to the purchase motives held by the segment? Do they help reduce motivational conflict if necessary? By using the word tradition, it covers the family believes that they've learned from.
- Are we considering the emotional implications of the ad and/or the use of our product? No. Currently, they concentrate on the savings, and additional services they offer by having images of the products

or by showing big numbers on the prices that are under three dollars. One thing to keep in mind is that their competitors are following the same strategy. Lopez needs to work the advertising aspect to distinguish themselves from the rest. One way would be by showing images or symbols of family values and traditions in their ads

- Is the lifestyle portrayed in our advertisements consistent with the desired lifestyle of the selected segments? In a way. If part of the segment's lifestyle consists on savings, then yes. Other than that, they don't portray a desired lifestyle.
- If we need to change attitudes via our promotion mix, have we selected and prop-erly used the most appropriate attitude-change techniques? Yes.

Situational influences:

- Does our campaign illustrate the full range of appropriate usage situations for the product? Yes. Using flyers with items on "sale" it makes the consumer feel that they are in for a bargain.

Decision-process influences:

- Will problem recognition occur naturally, or must it be activated by advertising? Should generic or selective problem recognition be generated? For this segment, problem recognition will occur naturally. They know they need to buy the basic needs such as milk and cereal for their kids, and that they need to buy meat in case they having a family reunion.
- Will the segment seek out or attend to information on the product prior to problem recognition, or must we reach them when they are not seeking our information? Can we use low-involvement learning processes effectively? What information sources are used? There is low-involvement when it comes coming to Lopez since, again, they are familiar with it.
- After problem recognition, will the segment seek out information on the product brand, or will we need to intervene in the purchase-decision process? If they do seek information, what sources do they use? By default, they will come to Lopez. If there's for example a new Lopez location, they might use word-of-mouth as a source.
- What types of information are used to make a decision? Family and friends.
- How much and what types of information are acquired at the point of purchase? Very little information and type are acquired at the point of purchase since most of it was gained by learning.
- Is post purchase dissonance likely? Can we reduce it through our promotional campaign? No. They already fear rejection from their family and friends if they buy from other store that is not Lopez.
- Have we given sufficient information to ensure proper product use? Yes. By experience, they already know what to expect from Lopez.

- Are the expectations generated by our promotional campaign consistent with the product's performance? Yes. They already expect the sales that are advertised.
- Are our messages designed to encourage repeat purchases, brand-loyal purchases, or neither? This segment is already familiar with Lopez. Lopez advertise the store usually by catalogs and newspaper. By those advertising mediums, Lopez announces current special offers, and products that are at discount prices. Seasonal products are also advertised using the same mediums. Its marketing strategy focus more on detailing special offers of products and services, rather than the store itself. Promotion of Lopez pursue the goal of position the store as a local one who shares their customs, to make consumers identify themselves with the store, and use this store image in order to attract customers to come to buy their groceries at Lopez, rather than any other supermarket store.

PRODUCT

The marketing manager must be certain that the physical product, service, or idea has the characteristics required to achieve the desired product position in each market segment.

External influences:

- Is the product designed appropriately for all members of the segment under con-sideration, including males, females, and various age groups? Yes. Anyone at any age, gender can shop at Lopez Supermarket. Lopez stores have an Hispanic environment, where people feel like in their homes. Store emphasizes on a familiar setting, where customers are treated with individual attention. The general store atmosphere enhances the Mexican/American culture, and transforms the shopping activity into an enjoyable and exciting one, for those customers that identify with this culture. People feel great from buying at Lopez because they feel as part of the group, because they identify themselves with the store image, and share the values and traditions promoted by the store. A friendship environment is enhanced at the store, and people buying there, feel proud of their culture and resemble to the shopping activities of their ancestors, such as the way the meat is cut and deliver like the traditional "carniceria" use to do it in Mexico.
- If the product is an innovation, does it have the required relative advantage and lack of complexity to diffuse rapidly? It has the advantage that is known for tradition.
- Is the product designed to meet the varying needs of different household members? This store is designed to meet different household members and their needs. Customer can buy both grocery and convenient products.

Internal influences:

- Will the product be perceived in a manner consistent with the desired image? For years, Lopez has a good reputation among Brownsville citizens. It is identified as the local grocery store where our parents and old relatives bought their food supplies. Since its initiation, Lopez has had a great standing in society for its contribution to some charity institutions, and for the awareness they show for Brownsville community. Lopez has gained citizen's good will due to a variety of contributions to education, such as scholarships, and even the local school that includes its name, Lopez School. The following are the Dimensions of the Store Image that will need to be taken under consideration:
  - *Merchandise*: Products sold at Lopez are of average quality, depending on the brand selected. Well-known and high quality brands are sold at the store also. Lopez is famous for its fresh meat, which is cut and packaged at client's desire, as well as for its chicken and turkey, which Mexican people go to the store to buy them exclusively.
  - Lopez is a grocery store which offers a varied selection of products, including food, food-related supplies and other products such as paper tissue, house cleaning products. The price charged by Lopez is a little higher than competitors. Price is not a competitive advantage of the store, but it tries to compensate this difference by adding value to customer in other areas, such as the characterized friendly service offered.
  - *Service*: Besides providing convenience shopping, Lopez Supermarket offers other services such as payment of utility bills. They also accept debit cards, credit cards, W.I.C. Vouchers, and Lone Star Card, as they cash checks and money orders, sell lottery tickets, and have Western Union for money transfer. Lopez has a great friendly service provided by store employees, which is a major attraction of the store. Employees have a general knowledge about products attributes and different brands, and know where all items are located. They are very concerned about consumers satisfaction, and are willing to help them when they need it.
  - *Clientele*: For the most part, Mexican-American culture. Customers of Lopez are generally those living close to the store. In general they are low-income Mexican/Hispanics with limited resources, including the segment studied in this project. They are a Spanish-speaking clientele, and the majority of consumers are women from varied ages, who consider food as a purchasing priority. This people are willing to spend a large portion of their disposable income in groceries. Usually, Lopez customers include

direct immigrants from Mexico, and first and second-generation U.S. citizens, with a mixed of Mexican and American culture. Generally they have strong values, high ties to family and tradition and the majority practice the Catholic religion. In overall, Lopez clientele includes a closed segment that shares important beliefs, activities, lifestyles, attitudes, and consumer behaviour.

- *Physical Facility*: Ten locations in Brownsville. Physical facilities are considered an advantage of the store. Since the store is relatively small, customers may easily find the products they are looking for in a short time period. Shopping at the Lopez is easiest and fastest than in other bigger stores such as HEB. Merchandise is located just as to the type of product, and are easy to reach, since the shelves are not very tall for women, specially old ones. Store is always clean, and it is attractively decorated just as to the season.
- *Convenience*: Located on non-commercial locations, close to neighbourhoods. Location is a primary advantage of the store, since the majority of customers lives close to the store, and do not have any automotive vehicle to travel long distances. Lopez is strategic located in neighbourhoods rather than in commercial places as their competitors, and also, Lopez stores are near to the border between U.S. and Mexico, where many of its customers live.
- *Promotion*: Lopez advertise the store usually by catalogs and newspaper. By those advertising mediums, Lopez announces current special offers, and products that are at discount prices. Seasonal products are also advertised using the same mediums. Its marketing strategy focus more on detailing special offers of products and services, rather than the store itself. Promotion of Lopez pursue the goal of position the store as a local one who shares their customs, to make consumers identify themselves with the store, and use this store image in order to attract customers to come to buy their groceries at Lopez, rather than any other supermarket store. For example, Lopez advertise a top page ad" through the "Bargain Book" a weekly newspaper published every Wednesday. Their emphasis is on items under three dollars. They advertise their others services such as paying utilities bills as "quickly and easily".
- *Store Atmosphere*: Lopez stores have an Hispanic environment, where people feel like in their homes. Store emphasizes on a familiar setting, where customers are treated with individual attention. The general store atmosphere enhances the Mexican/ American culture, and transforms the shopping activity into an enjoyable and exciting one, for those customers that identify with this culture.

- *Institutional*: To this segment, the store is known as high quality, friendly store. Lopez has a good reputation among Brownsville citizens. It is identified as the local grocery store, where our parents and old relatives bought their food supplies. Since its initiation,. Lopez has had a great standing in society for its contribution to some charity institutions, and for the awareness they show for Brownsville community. Lopez has gained citizen's good will due to a variety of contributions to education, such as scholarships, and even the local school that includes its name, Lopez School.
- *Post-Transaction*: When buying at Lopez, customers feel satisfied by the products/services, and many of them return to buy there, showing loyalty to the store. Lopez symbolizes many things to customers. The more relevant issues include that buying at Lopez, a local store, customers are defending their community, their culture, and are supporting the well–being of their society. All these feelings increase the satisfaction of customers, and balance between the benefits obtained and the relatively high price than competitors. People buying at Lopez feel great approval from their reference groups, such as their family, friends, neighbours, and even their employers, which as a result reinforce their activity of shopping there, and will continue to do so.

- Will the product satisfy the key purchase motives of the segment? Yes. Lopez offers the basic needs for the segment.
- Is the product consistent with the segment's attitude towards an ideal product? Yes. Since Lopez is an expectation from their family and friends to shop at what they perceive as the ideal supermarket.

Situational influences:

- Is the product appropriate for the various potential usage situations? Yes. They can buy housing goods, groceries, small party supplies, pay utility bills, and cash checks.

Decision-process influences:

- Does the product/brand perform better than the alternatives on the key set of evaluative criteria used by this segment? They do. Since they see this supermarket as a way they identify themselves, as opposed to other segments who perceive Lopez in a negative way due to poor lighting and smell.
- Will the product perform effectively in the foreseeable uses to which this segment may subject it? Yes. If the segment demands it, Lopez could introduce demanding products or services into Lopez.
- Will the product perform as well or better than expected by this segment? This segment already has an expectation for this outlet. But this segment for sure will accept any improvements.

10

Advertising Management

INTRODUCTION

In the next five sections of the Principles of Marketing Tutorials we begin an in-depth look at each promotional mix item. In this tutorial we present the first of a two-part examination of advertising with a discussion of basic concepts and trends. Our coverage of advertising continues in our next tutorial, Managing the Advertising Campaign, where we look at what decisions are needed to carryout a successful advertising campaign.

In this tutorial we cover several fundamental issues in advertising including examining what advertising is and why it is important to the marketing organization. We also look at managing the advertising effort by comparing in-house management to that offered by advertising professionals, such as advertising agencies. Finally, the tutorial identifies different types of advertising and addresses trends facing the advertising industry.

DEFINE ADVERTISING

Advertising is a non-personal form of promotion that is delivered through selected media outlets that, under most circumstances, require the marketer to pay for message placement. Advertising has long been viewed as a method of mass promotion in that a single message can reach a large number of people. But, this mass promotion approach presents problems since many exposed to an advertising message may not be within the marketer's target market, and thus, may be an inefficient use of promotional funds.

However, this is changing as new advertising technologies and the emergence of new media outlets offer more options for targeted advertising. Advertising also has a history of being considered a one-way form of marketing communication where the message receiver (i.e., target market) is not in position to immediately respond to the message.

This too is changing. For example, in the next few years technologies will be readily available to enable a television viewer to click a button to request more details on a product seen on their favourite TV programme. In fact, it is expected that over the next 10-20 years advertising will move away from a one-way communication model and become one that is highly interactive. Another characteristic that may change as advertising evolves is the view that advertising does not stimulate immediate demand for the product advertised. That is, customers cannot quickly purchase a product they see advertised. But as more media outlets allow customers to interact with the messages being delivered the ability of advertising to quickly stimulate demand will improve.

THE BEGINNINGS OF ADVERTISING

Advertising, then, is nearly as old as civilization. There are records more than three thousand years old of announcements advertising for runaway slaves, written on papyri and exhumed from the ruins of Thebes. The Greek and Roman advertisements of gladiatorial exhibitions are reminiscent of the modern "billing" of circuses. There is linguistic proof of the existence of the town crier in early Hebrew civilization, and of hawkers of retail wares in Roman times. The excavations of Pompeii have revealed various "bills"—tablets attached to pillars—on the walls of that ancient city, and there are records in literature of signs over shops and stalls in Rome advertising crafts and merchandise.

As early as the late seventeenth century, advertising was already a source of profits for the first newspapers. From the first daily published in England in Queen Anne's time until the nineteenth century, newspaper advertising was limited to announcements identifying craftsmen, merchandise and services for sale. Even in the early nineteenth century, the newspaper was a local venture usually religious or political in nature. Few had large circulations. If a company wished to advertise, it dealt 6 directly with the paper. There was no particular skill involved in newspaper advertising in the early stages. A simple announcement served both the advertiser and the public.

After the phase of Great Expansion—industrial, geographical and modern mass production methods—production facilities were greatly in excess of natural demand. This brought about the necessity of the persuasive sales appeal—the need to create new markets and new customers. The businessman began to feel the need to *persuade* prospective customers. The businessman *and* the periodicals felt the need to cover wider geographic areas in a more persuasive manner. The problems and profits inherent in this situation were the foundations of the modern advertising agency.

The Rise of the Agency

The first advertising agent was a middleman or jobber in advertising space. He contracted space from publishers, which in turn he retailed to advertisers at a profit.

In 1820 there were about 360 newspapers published in the United States. In 1830 there were over one thousand. In 1841 there is the first definite record of the advertising agent, who, according to Rowell, was Volney B. Palmer. Palmer set himself up in Philadelphia as an agent for country newspapers, obtaining orders for advertising, forwarding the copy to the paper and collecting payment. Palmer was closely followed by others and before long there were a number of agents in the business. Only a few years passed before the jobbers changed their methods of operation.

They soon began to act as space brokers. They made contracts for space on their own accounts and resold the space to advertisers. The early days of the agency business occupy a unique position in business history in that the affairs were conducted in confused state. The early agents were at once agents for the advertiser and for the publication, and space brokers on their own behalf, while some dealt also in printers' materials; and, finally, a few published their own periodicals, selling advertising in these periodicals to the same newspaper for which they acted as agent and whose space they brokered.

It was indeed a catch-as-catch-can business, with payments sometimes being made in "supplies" and with great "flexibility" of rates, etc. Yet since about Palmer's time, for over a hundred years, the agency has been the nerve-center of the advertising business. But it is only today that the advertising agent has achieved the stature of a professional man. The last lap in the progress of the agency began about 1930.

It was a fork in the road for the agency: Either fold-up or gear-up. Business couldn't depend on old-fashioned methods to help push it out of the red. The agency had to devise new ways to serve. That agency which was able to gear-up to the new demands of the early '30'$ was the agency which was successful. It is that agency which represents what is typical in the new attitude of the agency business which has made a simple sales job into a complex professional service.

The Evolution of Advertising

In the nineteenth century a substantial part of advertising consisted of what would now be termed announcements and of items we now find in the classified advertising section of newspapers. In addition to these, however, the advertising agencies sold a quantity of space to the "patent medicine" business. During the period around 1870, modern medicine was in its infancy. As a result there was a considerable field for the sale of all sorts of remedies. These accounts, which almost any agency would frown on today, were perhaps the backbone of the early agency business.

Those were the days of rugged individualism, not of professional ethics. It was the pioneering period. There was no social legislation and, looking backward, it appears that there was little conscience or application of a moral standard in most business. Thus it was natural that the advertising agency seldom investigated the merits of the product it advertised.

Actually, it can scarcely be said that the agency was responsible for the advertising that it sold and placed. In most cases, the advertiser and not the agency prepared the copy for the advertisement. All the agent did was to sell the space, forward the advertising copy and instructions to the publisher, and collect for the advertisement. In addition to the classified and patent medicine advertising, the early agency placed what we today might consider legitimate advertising, including local notices and the advertising of farm implements and a few other products.

Mail-order houses and manufacturers of farm products, books and machinery were some of the first industries to use advertising as a sales tool. The 1870 advertisement is a far cry from the elaborately designed advertisement for the same store today; while the 1911 advertisement for the Buick Motor Company shows that the trend was beginning to change into what is used in present-day styles of advertising.

The nature of the advertising agency business, as it was first constituted, was bound to cause trouble. Nearly all agencies were committed for large amounts of space in the publications which they represented. Consequently, it was profitable for them to urge their clients to use those particular papers. This, of course, was not economically sound.

In addition, if the advertiser wanted to use space in periodicals that the agency did not have direct representation for, it was necessary for the agent to try some makeshift negotiations for the space. Agencies were in constant competition with each other in an effort to secure the space that an advertiser wanted. At the best, the agencies' basis of operations was not conducive to creating confidence between the advertiser and the agent since it was never clear to whom the agency was responsible.

This confused state of affairs finally stimulated a clarification of the business, and toward the close of the nineteenth century the agencies began to give up the position of space jobber by instituting what was called the open contract.

The Open Contract

Under the open contract plan, the agency became the representative of the advertiser. The open contract provided that the advertiser have free access to all of the information available to the agency. The agency promised to buy the space needed by the advertiser at the lowest possible rates, and in return charge a commission for its services. The agency began to promise the advertiser unbiased recommendations concerning circulation, population, general reputation of the paper, etc.

The open contract clearly was the beginning of the system existing today for remunerating advertising agencies through a commission paid by the publication. In 1891, George Batten opened an agency in New York City. From the very beginning, he adhered to the new principle of buying space for the advertiser at the lowest possible cost. To this cost he added fifteen percent for his services. In contrast to the questionable speculative profit that agencies had received when they jobbed space, this new basis provided a reasonable profit margin. It placed the agency in a more secure position and enabled it to develop services for the advertiser. As agencies throughout the country began to adhere more and more to the open contract system, two important developments occurred:

1. They had made their decision to work for the advertisers' interests exclusively.
2. In addition to buying space for the advertiser at the lowest possible cost, they began to provide additional services and to be known as service organizations.

It is during this period that we first hear of "copywriters." Simultaneously with this development in the advertising agency business, publishers began to stabilize their rates so that those agencies which still acted as space brokers had difficulty in buying space below the market. By about 1890, many newspapers had arranged to pay advertising agencies a commission of fifteen percent on the space placed.

National magazines at that time were paying agencies a commission of ten percent. During the period from 1890 to about 1930 when agencies were making the transition from space brokers to service organizations, there were many agencies and advertisers who still were wedded to the old idea of buying space below the market.

This brought about the vicious practice of price cutting, which the agencies accomplished by rebating a part of their commissions to the advertisers. In 1910, out of twenty-five reasonably large advertising agencies doing business with the Curtis Publishing Company, ten were suspected of rebating commissions. In 1920, six of these ten price-cutting agencies were still in business, but by 1930 only one of them remained.

During the period from 1890 to 1930, publishers began to see that the advertising agency was a valuable tool for legitimately creating advertising business. There was a real incentive for them to protect the agency from price cutting and unsound competition, for the publisher wanted the advertiser to get his money's worth. Since the publishers were not in a position to conceive the advertising campaign, select the media, prepare the copy and visualize the art work, the advertising agency was the perfect answer to their problem.

In 1893, the American Newspaper Publishers' Association adopted a resolution which provided that agencies' commissions be paid only to advertising agencies and that no similar price reduction be allowed to advertisers. The Curtis Publishing Company in 1901 put into effect a new contract arrangement with advertising agencies. This new contract provided for a commission of ten percent to approve advertising agencies. To be approved the agencies agreed to charge advertisers the full card rate, less only the cash discount for prompt payment.

The agreement provided that in the event an agency quoted space in the Curtis publications for less than the published rate, such a quotation would be considered a violation of the contract. The contract provided that upon a second violation, the agent would be dropped from the approved list of advertising agencies. Gradually, all publishers and other media fell in line with the commission system which stabilized advertising rates and the income of the advertising agencies.

Magazine publishers increased the commission basis first from ten to thirteen percent. In 1918, the American Association of Advertising Agencies sought to increase the commission basis of magazines from thirteen to fifteen percent, with an additional two percent cash discount for prompt payment. Today, the fifteen percent agency commission is standard with only inconsequential exceptions.

On various occasions from 1890 to the present time, publishers and advertisers have questioned both the commission system itself and the rate of commission paid; but since 1925, it has been more or less standard practice for the advertising agencies to receive a fifteen percent commission allowed by the publishers and other advertising media.

MANAGING THE ADVERTISING CAMPAIGN

We continue our discussion of advertising by taking a closer look at the decisions involved in creating an advertising campaign. Whether a marketer employs a professional advertising agency to handle its advertising campaign or chooses to undertake all advertising tasks on its own, a successful campaign requires a number of important decisions including:

- Setting the Advertising Objective
- Setting the Advertising Budget
- Creating a Message
- Selecting Media for Message Delivery
- Evaluating Campaign Results

For major consumer products companies that spend large sums to promote their products each of these decisions will be intensely evaluated. On the other hand, smaller companies with limited budgets may be forced to focus what little money they have on only one key decision, such as selecting media, and give less attention to other areas. In either case, knowledge of all advertising campaign decisions is important and should be well understood by all marketers.

SETTING THE ADVERTISING OBJECTIVE

As we noted, marketing promotion, which includes advertising, can be used to address several broad objectives including: building product awareness, creating interest, providing information, stimulating demand and reinforcing the brand. To achieve one or more of these objectives, advertising is used to send a message containing information about some element of the marketer's offerings. For example:

- *Message About Product:* Details about the product play a prominent role in advertising for new and existing products. In fact, a very large percentage of product-oriented advertising includes some mention of features and benefits offered by the marketer's product. Advertising can be used to inform customers of changes that take place in existing products. For instance, if a beverage company has purchased the brands of another company resulting in a brand name change, an advertising message may stress "New Name but Same Great Taste".

- *Message About Price:* Companies that regularly engage in price adjustments, such as running short term sales (i.e., price markdown), can use advertising to let the market know of price reductions. Alternatively, advertising can be used to encourage customers to purchase now before a scheduled price increase takes place.
- *Message About Other Promotions:* Advertising often works hand-in-hand with other promotional mix items. For instance, special sales promotions, such as contests, may be announced within an advertisement. Also, advertising can help salespeople gain access to new accounts if the advertising precedes the salesperson's attempt to gain an appointment with a prospective buyer. This may be especially effective for a company entering a new market where advertising may help reduce the uncertainty a buyer has about a new company.
- Message About Distribution – Within distribution channels, advertising can help expand channel options for a marketer by making distributors aware of the marketer's offerings. Also, advertising can be used to let customers know locations where a product can be purchased.

ADVERTISING CAMPAIGN APPROACH

An advertising campaign is a series of advertisement messages that share a single idea and theme which make up an integrated marketing communication. Advertising campaigns appear in different media across a specific time frame. The critical part of making an advertising campaign is determining a champion theme as it sets the tone for the individual advertisements and other forms of marketing communications that will be used.

The campaign theme is the central message that will be communicated in the promotional activities. The campaign themes are usually developed with the intention of being used for a substantial period but many of them are short lived due to factors such as being ineffective or market conditions and/or competition in the marketplace and marketing mix.

TIPS FOR AN EFFECTIVE ADVERTISING CAMPAIGN

The goal of advertising is to cost-effectively reach a large audience and attract customers. If done correctly, advertising can enhance the success of your business.

Here are 10 advertising tips to pay attention to:

1. *Go after your target audience*: An advertising campaign should be geared to your niche market. It is a common mistake to create generic ads that do not speak the language or grab the attention of your potential customers.
2. *Highlight your competitive advantage*: One of the keys to all advertising is to accentuate the pros of your company, those factors that give you your competitive edge. Too many ads are clever but fail to sell the benefits of the product or service.
3. *Establish an image*: You can recognize the McDonald's arches while whizzing by on the highway. Likewise, there are plenty of products that you recognize by their packaging or logo. Image counts when it comes to advertising and promoting your business. Too many advertisers do not work to build a consistent image. Check out Three Brand Identity Myths That Will Bring Your Business Down for additional issues to avoid.
4. *You have to spend money to make money*: There are ways to save money, but typically advertising is not the place to cut corners. It will affect sales, and that affects the bottom line. Successful advertising may cost some money, but that is because it works. Check out More Bang for Your Advertising Buck for cost-cutting tips that won't cut your goals.
5. *Advertise in the right places*: *Your* favourite magazine, radio station, or even television programme might not be a favourite of your audience. Know what they read, watch, and listen to, and advertise in media that reaches your target market.
6. Don't allow your budget to run your advertising campaign. If you budget $5,000 per month for advertising, you've made it very easy from a bookkeeping perspective. However, if like most businesses you have seasonal highs and lows, you are spending too much money advertising during down times and not enough when you want to attract customers. Too many entrepreneurs do not budget according to their seasonal advertising needs.
7. *Diversify*: It is all too common for business owners to choose the best place to advertise based on price and potential rate of returns and then stop. As is the case with investing, you do not want to put all of your eggs in one basket. Spread your advertising dollars around.
8. *Don't try to be everything to everyone*: No product or service will appeal to everyone. Many business owners, including corporate executives, try to come up with ways to reach every market. Typically, this does not work. It can spell disaster for small businesses, who cannot afford to spread themselves too thin. Therefore, find your market and be everything you can be to that audience.

9. *Test your ads in advance*: If you have the time or money to invest in focus groups, you should test your ads on other people. Do they understand and accept the message that you are trying to convey? For further information, read Focus Groups: How They Can Work for Your Small Business. There are other less-expensive ways to test your ads as well: questionnaires, for example.

CHECKING ADVERTISING

The purchaser of an article wants to be sure he receives it and wants to verify the quantity and quality before he pays for it. Printed advertising is purchased in accordance with definite terms and conditions as to quantity, quality and time of publication. Before the agency makes payment to the publisher, it is desirable to check the advertising to determine whether it meets the specifications in accordance with the contract and order. In most agencies one or more persons are assigned the job of checking the advertising. This is a routine job and usually follows a more or less standard pattern.

News Papers

A copy of each newspaper insertion order is sent to the checking department. Newspaper orders are filed by state and city in which the paper is published. Upon receipt of publications, agencies usually sort them in the same manner in which insertion orders are filed. Then, by referring to the insertion order bearing the same name as the publication, the checker is able to determine what advertising to look for. For example, if the checking department receives a copy of the Chicago *Sun,* the checker then looks in the file under "Illinois, Chicago, *Sun"* A copy of the insertion order covering the advertising should be filed there.

If the title discloses an insertion order for "Illinois, Chicago, *Sun"* covering an insertion in a particular edition on a specified date, the checker then looks at the order further to find the name of the advertiser and the product, after which he runs through the paper to locate the advertisement. When this is located, the checker examines it for quality and correctness. Assuming that the correct advertisement has been published and that the quality of printing is acceptable, the checker then measures the advertisement to determine the amount of space occupied by it.

Newspaper space is usually sold in lines or inches. Daily papers usually sell space by lines; the small papers and weekly papers usually sell it by inches. An inch represents fourteen lines of "agate" type. The insertion order indicates whether the space is purchased by lines or inches. The checker is furnished with a rule calibrated in both. A line of space is the depth measure, a column is the width measure. In other words, if an advertisement occupies three columns in width and ten lines in depth, the space measurement would be thirty lines. The same rule holds true when the unit is inches instead of lines; that is, if an advertisement is three columns wide and three inches deep, the measurement would be nine inches. Some agencies have established the practice of rating the various positions in which advertising appears in newspapers.

The purpose of such a rating system is to determine whether or not a particular newspaper is giving the advertiser reasonably good positions in the paper. Generally, advertising which appears on the first few pages of a newspaper is considered to be more effective than that appearing far back in the paper. Advertising appearing in the upper right-hand corner of a page generally may be considered more effective than advertising appearing on the left bottom corner, etc.

After advertisement positions are rated, position reports are prepared to show the number of advertisements that secured the best position, the number that secured the second best position, etc. With these reports, the space buyer is in a position to determine which papers have been giving the advertiser reasonably good advertising positions and which have not. He can then call the representative of the paper that is not giving the advertiser reasonably good advertising positions and can demand greater consideration in the future.

Where the agency rates the positions of advertising, the key or code for such positions is noted on the insertion order at the time the checker examines and measures the advertisement. The position indication would be as follows: Date of Insertion Ad Number Space Ordered Space Used Position.

Magazines and Trade Papers

Checking magazine and trade-paper space is considerably simpler than checking newspaper space. Space in magazines is usually purchased in units of pages or fractions thereof, although occasionally magazines arid trade papers sell space by columns or inches.

The usual magazine advertisement occupying a page, half-page, quarter-page, etc. is not subject to shrinkage. This is because electrotypes and half-tones are used instead of mats. These are built to occupy the exact amount of space ordered. The checker, then, needs to inspect a magazine advertisement only for quality of print and position.

Some agencies, in addition to checking the appearance of advertising for quality and quantity, wish to determine the position secured in either a paper or a magazine.

There are different methods of rating the comparative position of advertisements, but among the most important factors to be considered are:

1. The page number on which the advertisement appears.
2. The section in which the advertisement appears (such as buyer's guide, society section, financial section, etc.).
3. The position on the page.
4. Whether or not the advertisement appears adjacent to competitive copy.

Where the agency is interested in rating the position of the advertising, the checker usually is furnished with a code for this purpose. The code is entered on an accounting record from which the agency can prepare a report showing the various positions secured from the different publications.

Radio

The checking of radio advertising is, obviously, a different matter from checking printed advertising. Usually the broadcasting station sends the agency an affidavit certifying the fact that each message or programme was actually broadcast. Such affidavits are required by agencies before bills for broadcasting are paid. At times, advertising agencies have attempted to listen to each broadcast to check the message or programme, but this practice was never general.

Most agencies rely on the honesty of the broadcasting stations and on other reports secured from the advertiser or his distributors in each town where a programme is broadcast. These distributors, of course, are acquainted with the facts concerning the advertiser's programme. Since the advertising is important to the distributor, it may be expected that the distributor would report any omissions or other defects in the radio advertising campaign.

In addition, there is a radio checking service available on both the East and West Coasts. Clients are furnished with actual recordings of what is said on the air waves on a particular programme, product or topic, or, occasionally, with programme scripts. There is available, also, a spot-checking service, with listeners or monitors in several hundred cities. Agencies and advertisers are advised whether the spots were actually used at the time they were scheduled; what the adjacencies were; the caliber of the presentation; and other pertinent data bearing on the effectiveness of the spot message.

Other Media

It is not a general practice for agencies to check the appearance of outdoor advertising and car cards. Lithographs or other material are sent to the outdoor advertising plants, which certify the actual placing and appearance of the advertising. It would be extremely difficult for an agency to check the posting date and the quality of the posting of each outdoor sign. The cost of such checking would not be warranted. For this reason, agencies do little or no checking of outdoor advertising space.

The National Outdoor Advertising Bureau does render a valuable service in this regard. In addition to checking the appearance of outdoor advertising, the Bureau furnishes other services.

One agency checked every outdoor location to determine the date on which each billboard was posted and the quality of the posting. In addition, for several years, this agency made intensive studies to determine the comparative value of the locations used. This practice was discontinued by the agency after a few years when it was found that the outdoor plants billed correctly for the space used and that the statistics furnished by the plant owners were reliable. This, they concluded, made independent checking and study of little value. Checking the appearance of advertising in the manner discussed is a service that the agency renders to the advertiser in consideration of the commissions received from the advertising media. No special or extra charge is made for such service.

Advertising Materials, Publicity and Miscellaneous

Certain materials are necessary to produce a printed advertisement. These are called mechanical production or advertising materials. They include art work, photography, typography, engravings, half-tones, electrotypes, mats, stereos, Photostats, etc.

Why Agency Should Specify, Advertising Materials

It is highly desirable and almost essential for the agency to specify and purchase these materials, for only in this way can it control the final result or appearance of the advertising. Production work starts almost as soon as the contact man and the client have agreed on an advertising campaign, at which time it becomes necessary to visualize, at least roughly, the various advertisements as they are to appear.

To do this, the agency prepares rough sketches of each advertisement. Sometimes these sketches merely take the form of rough lay-outs that are quickly penciled up by the agency's art department. In other cases, the visuals become more comprehensive and include an explanation of the final art work and a paste-up of the whole advertisement including the type, etc.

In any event, when the kind of advertisement has finally been approved by the client, the agency sets about procuring the necessary materials for printing it. The agency at the outset prepares a timetable showing on what dates each item of material is required, because it is necessary to secure the art work before plates can be made, etc., and all materials, including the final mats or half-tones, must be complete in time to send them to the publisher for printing the advertisement.

Production Orders

Orders are issued in the production department of an advertising agency for each of the materials as it is required; and, as the materials are received with bills from suppliers, all of the production elements for the advertisement are gathered together until the final piece of material is received.

The engraving, electrotype, mat or stereo is forwarded to the publication and the cost of all of the items is invoiced to the client. In some agencies, the art work required for the production of advertising is segregated from the other materials. In such cases, the securing of the needed art work becomes the function of the art director or art department and the securing of the other materials is delegated to the production manager or production department.

There is no standard of procedure in the operation of production and art departments of advertising agencies but there is some uniformity of operation among agencies in regard to certain parts of the art and production work. Most agencies prepare rough lay-outs and nearly all agencies undertake to secure the final art work required, either by creating the art work in their own department or by purchasing it on the outside.

Nearly all agencies undertake to secure the other materials required, such as type, electros, half-tones and mats. The difference in the operation of production departments among agencies comes in the charges made for performing the functions. This subject will be discussed in the chapter "Basis of the Agency's Compensation."

Some agencies operate production departments in which the entire responsibility for securing all required mechanical elements rests within the department. This includes the scheduling of materials so that they are received when they are required. It also includes the responsibility of getting the final plates or mats to the publisher before a closing date. In other agencies, the production department is charged merely with the responsibility of purchasing the advertising materials required; the scheduling and expediting duties are delegated to a separate traffic department.

Publicity

Publicity, in the sense it is used here, may be defined as the dissemination of information regarding products or industries without the overt purpose of selling. It takes the form of news stories and feature articles in the press, in national magazines, in trade papers and in farm papers. Some publicity is also accomplished through the radio in connection with news and other programs.

There is a growing feeling among agencies that publicity campaigns can be best conducted by publicity or public relations firms which specialize in this work. This feeling is emphasized by the attitude among publishers that advertising agencies, in attempting to secure publicity, are actually endeavoring to divert what should be paid advertising into free publicity.

Nevertheless there are a number of agencies that have completely organized publicity departments. These agencies plan, create, develop and place publicity as an extra service to certain clients. Unless the advertiser's account is very large and highly profitable, the agency cannot afford to provide a publicity service without arranging for a special fee to cover the cost of the work. On the other hand, most agencies do counsel and advise with their clients concerning publicity. They further assist the clients by cooperating with the publicity firms which handle that phase of service for the client.

SETTING THE ADVERTISING BUDGET

Setting an advertising objective is easy, but achieving the objective requires a well-thought out strategy. One key factor affecting the strategy used to achieve advertising objectives is how much money an organization has to spend. The funds designated for advertising make up the advertising budget and it reflects the amount an organization is willing (i.e., approved by high-level management) to commit to achieve its advertising objectives.

Organizations use several methods for determining advertising budgets including:

- *Percentage of Sales:* Under this approach advertising spending is set based on either a percentage of previous sales or a percentage of forecasted sales. For example, an organization may set next year's advertising budget at 10% of this year's sales level. One problem with this approach is that the budget is based on what has already happened and not what is expected to occur. If the overall market grows rapidly in the following year, the 10% level from the previous year may be well below what is necessary for the company to maintain or increase its market share. Alternatively, companies may consider allocating advertising funds based on a percentage of forecasted sales. In this way advertising is viewed as a driver of future sales and spending on advertising is linked directly to meeting future sales forecasts. However, since future sales are not guaranteed, the actual percentage spent may be considerably higher than expected if the sales forecast is greater than what actually occurs.
- *What is Affordable:* Many smaller companies find spending of any kind to be constraining. In this situation, advertising may be just one of several tightly allocated spending areas and, thus, the level spent on advertising may vary over time. For these companies, advertising may only occur when extra funds are available.
- *Best Guess:* Companies entering new markets often lack knowledge of how much advertising is needed to achieve their objectives. In cases where the market is not well understood, marketers may rely on their best judgment (i.e., executive's experience) of what the advertising budget should be.

SELECTING MEDIA OUTLETS

With an objective and a budget in place, the advertising campaign will next need to focus on developing the message. However, before effort is placed in developing a message the marketer must first determine which media outlets will be used to deliver their message since the choice of media outlets guides the type of message that can be created and how frequently the message will be delivered.

An advertising message can be delivered via a large number of media outlets. These range from traditional outlets, such as print publications, radio and television, to newly emerging outlets, such as the Internet and mobile devices. However, each media outlet possess different characteristics and, thus, offer marketers different advantages and disadvantages.

The characteristics by which different media outlets can be assessed include the following seven factors:

- Creative Options
- Creative Cost
- Media Market Reach
- Message Placement Cost
- Length of Exposure
- Advertising Clutter
- Response Tracking

Creative Options

An advertisement has the potential to appeal to four senses – sight, sound, smell and touch. (It should be noted that promotion can also appeal to the sense of taste but generally these efforts generally fall under the category of sales promotion which we will discuss in a later tutorial.) However, not all advertising media have the ability to deliver multi-sensory messages.

Traditional radio, for example, is limited to delivering audio messages while roadside billboards offer only visual appeal. Additionally, some media may place limits on when particular options can be used. For instance, some search engines or websites may only accept graphical-style ads, such as images, if these conform to certain large dimensions and limit small advertising to text-only ads.

Creative Cost

The media type chosen to deliver a marketer's message also impacts the cost of creating the message. For media outlets that deliver a multi-sensory experience (e.g., television and Internet for sight and sound; print publications for sight, touch and smell) creative cost can be significantly higher than for media targeting a single sensory experience. But creative costs are also affected by the expectation of quality for the media that delivers the message.

In fact, media outlets may set minimal production standards for advertisements and reject ads that do not meet these standards. Television networks, for example, may set high production quality levels for advertisements they deliver.

Achieving these standards requires expensive equipment and high cost labour, which may not be feasible for small businesses. Conversely, creating a simple text only Internet advertisement requires very little cost that almost anyone is capable of creating.

Media Market Reach

The number of customers exposed to a single promotional effort within a target market is considered the reach of a promotion. Some forms of advertising, such as television advertising, offer an extensive reach, while a single roadside billboard on a lightly traveled road offers very limited reach.

Market reach can be measured along two dimensions: 1) channels served and, 2) geographic scope of a media outlet".

- Channels Served: This dimension relates to whether a media outlet is effective in reaching the members within the marketer's channel of distribution. Channels can be classified as:
  - *Consumer Channel*: Does the media outlet reach the final consumer market targeted by the marketer?
  - *Trade Channel:* Does the media outlet reach a marketer's channel partners who help distribute their product?
  - *Business-to-Business:* Does the media outlet reach customers in the business market targeted by the marketer?
- *Geographic Scope:* This dimension defines the geographic breadth of the channels served and includes:
  - *International:* Does the media outlet have multi-country distribution?
  - *National*: Does the media outlet cover an entire country?
  - *Regional*: Does the media outlet have distribution across multiple geographic regions such as counties, states, provinces, territories, etc.?
  - *Local*: Does the media outlet primarily serve a limited geographic area?
  - *Individua:* Does the media outlet offer individual customer targeting?

Message Placement Cost

Creative development is one of two major spending considerations for advertising. The other cost is for media placement; the purchase of ad time, space or location with media outlets that deliver the message. Advertising placement costs vary widely from very small amounts for certain online advertisements to exorbitant fees for advertising on major television programs.

For example, in the United States the highest cost for advertising placement occurs with television ads shown during the National Football League's Super Bowl championship game where ad rates for a single 30-second advertisement exceed (US) $2.5 million. By contrast, ads placed through online search engines may cost less than (US) $1 dollar.

Media outlets set placement cost using several factors though the most important are determined by audience size, audience type and an advertisement's production characteristics:

- *Audience Size*: Refers to the number of people who experience the media outlet during a particular time period. For example, for television outlets audience size is measured in terms of number of programme viewers, for print publications audience is measured by number of readers, and for websites audience is measured by number of visitors. In general, the more people experiencing a media outlet, the more the outlet can charge for ads. However, actual measurement of the popularity of media outlets is complicated by many factors to the point where the media outlets are rarely trusted to give accurate figures reflecting their audience. Today nearly all media outlets rely on third-party audit organizations to measure audiences and most marketers rely on these auditors to determine whether the cost of placement is justified given the audited audience size.

- *Audience Type:* As we have discussed many times in the Principles of Marketing tutorial, the key to marketing is aligning marketing decisions to satisfy the needs of a target market. A well-defined target market is critical to successful marketing and vital to a successful advertising campaign. When choosing a media outlet, selection is evaluated based on the outlet's customer profile (i.e., viewers, readers, website visitors) and whether these match the characteristics sought by the marketer's desired target market. The more selectively targeted the audience, the more valuable this audience is to advertisers since with targeted advertising promotional funds are being spent on those with the highest potential to respond to the advertiser's message. The result is that media outlets, whose audience shares very similar characteristics (e.g., age, education level, political views, etc.), are in a position to charge higher advertising rates than media outlets that do not appeal to such a targeted group.
- Characteristics of the Advertisement: Media outlet also charge different rates based on creative characteristics of the message. Characteristics that create ad rate differences include:
  - Run Time (e.g., length of television or radio ads)
  - Size (e.g., print ads size, billboard size)
  - Print Style (e.g., black-and-white vs. colour)
  - Location in Media (e.g., back magazine cover vs. inside pages)

Length of Exposure

Some products require customers be exposed to just a little bit of information in order to build customer interest. For example, the features and benefits of a new snack food can be explained in a short period of time using television or radio commercials. However, complicated products need to present more information for customers to fully understand the product. Consequently, advertisers of these products will seek media formats that allot more time to deliver the message.

Media outlets vary in how much exposure they offer to their audience. Magazines and other publications provide opportunities for longer exposure times since these media types can be retained by the audience (i.e., keep old magazines) while exposure on television and radio are generally limited to the time the ad was broadcast.

Advertising Clutter

In order to increase revenue, media outlets often include a large number of ads within a certain time, space or location. For instance, television programs may contain many ads inserted during the scheduled run-time of a programme.

A large number of advertisements create an environment of advertising clutter, which makes it difficult for those in the targeted market to recognize and remember particular advertisements. To break through the clutter advertisers may be required to increase the frequency of their advertising efforts (i.e., run more ads). Yet greater advertising frequency increases advertising expense. Alternatively, advertisers may seek opportunities that offer less clutter where an ad has a better chance of standing out from others. This can be seen with online downloads (e.g., podcasts) of sports and news programming where a 5-10 minute story will be presented with a single 30-60 second ad.

Response Tracking

Marketers are embracing new technologies that make it easier to track audience response to advertisements. Newer media developed using Internet technology offer effective methods for tracking audience response compared to traditional media. But Internet-media are not alone in providing response tracking. Other advertising outlets, such as advertising by mail and television infomercial programming, also provide useful measures of audience reaction.

IMPORTANCE OF ADVERTISING

Spending on advertising is huge. One often quoted statistic by market research firm ZenithOptimedia estimates that worldwide spending on advertising exceeds (US) $400 billion. This level of spending supports thousands of companies and millions of jobs. In fact, in many countries most media outlets, such as television, radio and newspapers, would not be in business without revenue generated through the sale of advertising.

While worldwide advertising is an important contributor to economic growth, individual marketing organizations differ on the role advertising plays. For some organizations little advertising may be done, instead promotional money is spent on other promotion options such a personal selling through a sales team. For some smaller companies advertising may consist of occasional advertisement and on a very small scale, such as placing small ads in the classified section of a local newspaper.

But most organizations, large and small, that rely on marketing to create customer interest are engaged in consistent use of advertising to help meet marketing objectives. This includes regularly developing advertising campaigns, which involve a series of decisions for planning, creating, delivering and evaluating an advertising effort.

MANAGING ADVERTISING DECISIONS

Delivering an effective marketing message through advertising requires many different decisions as the marketer develops their advertising campaign. For small campaigns, that involve little creative effort, one or a few people may handle the bulk of the work. In fact, the Internet has made do-it-yourself advertising an easy to manage process and has especially empowered small businesses to manage their advertising decisions.

As we will see, not only can small firms handle the creation and placement of advertisements that appear on the Internet, new services have even made it possible for a single person to create advertisements that run on local television. For instance, a company called SpotRunner allows users to select from a list of high-quality television ads that can be customized and then placed within local cable television programming.

For larger campaigns the skills needed to make sound advertising decisions can be quite varied and may not be easily handled by a single person. While larger companies manage some advertising activities within the company, they are more likely to rely on the assistance of advertising professionals, such as those found at advertising agencies, to help bring their advertising campaign to market.

ADVERTISING AGENCY FUNCTIONS

Professionals at advertising agencies and other advertising organizations offer a number of functions including:

- *Account Management:* Within an advertising agency the account manager or account executive is tasked with handling all major decisions related to a specific client. These responsibilities include locating and negotiating to acquire clients. Once the client has agreed to work with the agency, the account manager works closely with the client to develop an advertising strategy. For very large clients, such as large consumer products companies, an advertising agency may assign an account manager to work full-time with only one client and, possibly, with only one of the client's product lines. For smaller accounts an account manager may simultaneously manage several different, though non-competing, accounts.
- *Creative Team:* The principle role of account managers is to manage the overall advertising campaign for a client, which often includes delegating selective tasks to specialists. For large accounts one task account managers routinely delegate involves generating ideas, designing concepts and creating the final advertisement, which generally becomes the responsibility of the agency's creative team. An agency's creative team consists of specialists in graphic design, film and audio production, copywriting, computer programming, and much more.

- *Researchers:* Full-service advertising agencies employ market researchers who assess a client's market situation, including understanding customers and competitors, and also are used to test creative ideas. For instance, in the early stages of an advertising campaign researchers may run focus group sessions with selected members of the client's target market in order to get their reaction to several advertising concepts. Researchers are also used following the completion of an advertising campaign to measure whether the campaign reached its objectives.
- *Media Planners:* Once an advertisement is created, it must be placed through an appropriate advertising media. Each advertising media, of which there are thousands, has its own unique methods for accepting advertisements, such as different advertising cost structures (i.e., what it costs marketers to place an ad), different requirements for accepting ad designs (e.g., size of ad), different ways placements can be purchased (e.g., direct contact with media or through third-party seller), and different time schedules (i.e., when ad will be run). Understanding the nuances of different media is the role of a media planner, who looks for the best media match for a client and also negotiates the best deals.

TYPES OF ADVERTISING

If you ask most people what is meant by "type" of advertising, invariably they will respond by defining it in terms of how it is delivered (e.g., television ad, radio ad, etc.). But in marketing, type of advertising refers to the primary "focus" of the message being sent and falls into one of the following four categories:

Product-Oriented Advertising

Most advertising spending is directed toward the promotion of a specific good, service or idea, what we have collectively labeled as an organization's product. In most cases the goal of product advertising is to clearly promote a specific product to a targeted audience. Marketers can accomplish this in several ways from a low-key approach that simply provides basic information about a product (informative advertising) to blatant appeals that try to convince customers to purchase a product (persuasive advertising) that may include direct comparisons between the marketer's product and its competitor's offerings (comparative advertising).

However, sometimes marketers intentionally produce product advertising where the target audience cannot readily see a connection to a specific product. Marketers of new products may follow this "teaser" approach in advance of a new product introduction to prepare the market for the product. For instance, one week before the launch of a new product a marketer may air a television advertisement proclaiming "After next week the world will never be the same" but do so without any mention of a product or even the company behind the ad. The goal is to create curiosity in the market and interest when the product is launched.

Image Advertising

Image advertising is undertaken primarily to enhance an organization's perceived importance to a target market. Image advertising does not focus on specific products as much as it presents what an organization has to offer. In these types of ads, if products are mentioned it is within the context of "what we do" rather than a message touting the benefits of a specific product. Image advertising is often used in situations where an organization needs to educate the targeted audience on some issue. For instance, image advertising may be used in situations where a merger has occurred between two companies and the newly formed company has taken on a new name, or if a company has received recent negative publicity and the company wants to let the market know that they are about much more than this one issue.

Advocacy Advertising

Organizations also use advertising to send a message intended to influence a targeted audience. In most cases there is an underlying benefit sought by an organization when they engage in advocacy advertising. For instance, an organization may take a stand on a political issue which they feel could negatively impact the organization and will target advertisements to voice their position on the issue.

Public Service Advertising

In some countries, not-for-profit organizations are permitted to run advertisements through certain media outlets free-of-charge if the message contained in the ad concerns an issue viewed as for the "greater good" of society. For instance, ads directed at social causes, such as teen-age smoking, illegal drug use and mental illness, may run on television, radio and other media without cost to organizations sponsoring the advertisement.

BILLING THE ADVERTISING

The advertising agency is semiprofessional, offering a combination of commercial and professional services. The agency attempts only to assist the advertiser by selecting the media to be used, by conceiving the advertising campaign and by developing it into the final advertising message. Today agencies do not compete with one another by offering different payment terms or by claiming that they can buy space below published rates.

AGENCY SHOULD NOT ACT AS A BANKER

The agency should not act as the banker for the advertiser, In fact, the average advertising agency has a smaller capital than most of its clients. The agency serves a useful professional function through the special skills of its employees. It renders inconsequential service to the advertiser in its financial dealings with media vendors. For these reasons it is a cardinal principle of the advertising-agency business that all advertising space and radio time should be billed to the client sufficiently in advance to provide for payment to the agency prior to the date upon which the agency is obligated to pay the media.

Invoices for magazine and trade-paper space are usually prepared and sent to clients fifteen days before the date on which the agency is required to pay the publication. If the advertiser wishes to earn the cash discount, he must pay the agency prior to the date on which the agency must pay the publication. In practice, no well-run agency will continue to serve the advertiser who does not discount his bills. Magazines and trade papers have various payment terms, so no general rule can be established concerning the time of the month in which magazine and trade-paper advertising is billed. The billing time varies according to the terms of the publication.

Liability may be Substantial

It is very important to note that the agency's liability for magazine advertising may be much more substantial than is often realized. Frequently, the advertising agency takes a greater financial risk than any other creditor of the advertiser. This is because magazines often go to press months in advance of publication. After the magazine is once on the press, the agency's liability has been fixed. Thus it will be seen that an agency can be and often is liable to magazines for advertisements for a cumulative period covering two or three months.

Magazines have established "closing dates" and "cancellation dates." The cancellation date is the last day upon which the advertiser can cancel the advertising. The closing date is the date on which the publication goes to press. Unless the advertising agency has convincing proof that the advertiser is fully capable of meeting its obligations, it is desirable to invoice advertising space so as to collect from the advertiser on or before the cancellation date for each magazine. After this date the liability of the agency is fixed regardless of whether the advertiser can pay the agency.

Newspaper advertising space, of course, can appear throughout an entire calendar month. Newspapers usually bill on a monthly basis, although some weeklies bill after each issue. Advertising agencies usually invoice newspaper space on a monthly basis. Since, as has been noted under the subject of checking newspaper advertising, newspaper space ordered is subject to shrinkage, it is impossible to complete accurate billing on a space-used basis until after all the newspaper advertising for the month has been measured.

It is common for advertisers to use newspapers that are published hundreds and thousands of miles distant from the place of business of the advertising agency. For this reason, copies of newspapers frequently reach the agency from five days to a week after the issuance of the paper. This means that checking of a month's newspaper advertising frequently cannot be completed until about the tenth of the subsequent month.

If an agency were to defer billing until newspaper advertising for a calendar month was checked, frequently the bill could not be sent to the advertiser until after the tenth of the subsequent month. The standard payment terms of most newspapers call for payment by the agency to the newspaper on either the tenth, fifteenth, twentieth or twenty-fifth of the month subsequent to the advertising.

From this it is evident that final accurate billing for newspaper space cannot be accomplished early enough to permit the receipt of the funds by the agency before the date on which the agency must pay the newspaper. It is necessary for agencies to find a method by which they can secure payment from the advertiser in advance of the date upon which they must make payment to the newspapers. Two different methods of billing for newspaper space have been developed to accomplish the desired result.

Billing on a Space-ordered Basis

One method is to bill all space ordered during a month on the basis of space ordered. Where this method is used, the agency sends its invoice to the client by the first or second day of each month to cover the advertising space ordered for the previous month. After all the advertising space has been checked, the agency sends the client a credit memo to cover omissions and shrinkage.

This method, which is sometimes called "billing on a space-ordered basis," has the disadvantage of involving double work. First, a detailed invoice on a space-ordered basis must be prepared; second, a credit memo covering omissions and shrinkage is prepared. The method has the same disadvantages for the advertiser in that he must audit both the original bill and the credit memo.

Billing on a Prebill Basis

The more desirable method for billing newspaper space so that the agency secures payment before it must pay the publishers is to "prebill." A prebill is simply a commitment billing. It consists of an invoice, sent on the first of the month following advertising and containing one line only, something like this:

- Newspaper space for the month of June—$92,000

The amount of the monthly prebill can be secured by reference to the media recommendation, which is sometimes later refined and called an "estimate." On the twentieth or twenty-fifth of the month following advertising, the agency prepares a complete detailed invoice on a space-checked basis.

The advertiser's first reaction to the prebill method is, often, that he is paying the agency a large sum of money without any proof of the actual debt.

This is without basis because: First, the advertiser knows what his advertising programme calls for and receives copies of the newspapers containing the advertising almost currently with its appearance; and second, by the time the advertiser pays the agency (the tenth of the month following insertion) the agency has already committed itself in substantial amounts for advertising that will appear prior to the payment of the previous month's invoice.

Many of the largest advertisers in the country are paying their agencies on a prebill basis which has the distinct advantage of avoiding duplicate work, since only one detailed invoice is prepared by the agency and audited by the advertiser.

Radio time is often invoiced on a weekly basis, invoices being issued immediately following each week's broadcasting. It is a simple matter for the agency to prepare an invoice covering radio time. Such bills are mailed to advertisers either on the first day of each week covering the prior week's broadcasting, or on the first or second day of each month covering the broadcasting of the previous month.

Radio talent is usually invoiced on a weekly basis, invoices being prepared by the agency and sent to advertisers on the first day of each week covering the talent costs of the prior week. Sometimes agencies prefer to invoice for radio talent on a monthly basis in which case the agency must meet current weekly payments and collect from the advertiser after the close of each month. Agencies usually add either 15 or 17.65 percent to the cost of radio talent.

When the 15 percent is added, the commission is only 13 percent; whereas when 17.65 percent is added, the commission is the standard 15 percent which agencies also earn on printed space. Outdoor space is billed monthly and invoices cover posting for the current month. All bills are due ten days from the date of issuance.

Billing Advertising Materials

Advertising materials purchased by the agency for the advertiser include such items as art work, typography, engravings, electros, half-tones, mats, stereos, photostats, radio transuip-tions and lithography used for outdoor advertising.

It is more or less standard practice for the agency to group all of the advertising materials purchased for a particular advertisement and to bill them on one invoice. There are two methods: (i) billing monthly for all items purchased during the month, and (2) billing jobs for all materials for one advertisement when they have been secured. There is no standard method for fixing the price of the advertising materials billed by the agency to its clients.

Perhaps the most common current method is for the agency to add 15 or 17.65 percent to the cost of the items purchased. Many agencies add 17.65 percent so that the selling price provides for a 15 percent commission. The subject of the agency's fee in connection with the purchase of advertising materials will be discussed in more detail later. The same rule is not always followed in connection with the creation and preparation of catalogs, house organs, dealer helps and direct-mail advertising.

Agencies usually provide for a special fee in connection with the preparation of these items which require the time and effort of the creative personnel of the advertising agency, since any commission based on a percentage of the cost of these items could not possibly compensate the agency for creative work. This creative work when it is used in connection with regular advertising media is compensated for by the commission received on the space used.

Basis of the Agency's Compensation

The service that an advertising agency performs for a client is always tailored to fit the particular client's requirements. No two agencies deliver exactly the same services, and no one agency delivers exactly the same service to any two of its clients. The answer to the question of what an agency should charge its client for the work performed must of necessity be based on the quantity and quality of the work.

The commission system of compensation is a historical part of the agency business. Although attempts have been made to get away from the commission form of compensation for personal service in this business, such efforts have not been successful. Under the commission system, the agency's compensation (a commission paid by the advertising media to the agency based on a percentage of the advertising space or time purchased) is figured on the volume of advertising space and materials purchased rather than on the amount or quality of work required.

To determine what services can be performed for the commission to be received from the advertising media, the agency must weigh the commission revenue against the estimated cost of performing the service. When this is done, it is found that many extensive services can be performed for one client, where only limited service can be performed for another.

Three Types of Agencies

It is necessary, then, to survey the several types of advertising agencies and the several types of advertising accounts before the elements of service performed and the basis of the agency's compensation for performing them can be discussed.

For convenience, agencies may be classified as follows:

1. General advertising. In this category may be placed agencies whose accounts consist of those in which the client's product is advertised to the general public through the customary advertising media, including newspapers, magazines, trade papers, farm papers, radio, outdoor displays and car cards.

2. Industrial agencies. In this category may be included the advertising agencies that specialize in industrial accounts which advertise machinery, electrical devices, tools, equipment and other articles to the industrial consumer and not to the general public. In exceptional cases, articles that the agency is trying to sell to industrial consumers are actually advertised to the general public in order to secure a public demand for a product. An example of this type of advertising is the advertising of thermostatic controls which eventually become a part of heating systems.
3. Agency specialists. In this group may be placed agencies not included in groups one and two, such as, for instance, those specializing in foreign, retail store, financial, classified, fashion or theatrical advertising.

The differentiating factor in classifying the agencies into the three types has been the type of account handled. Each of the three types can be subdivided further according to the general character of services rendered. The agency whose most powerful selling appeal is created through art work may be typed as the art agency; the agency whose principal selling appeal is the advertising copy may be typed as the copy agency; the agency whose principal strength is in the field of radio advertising may be termed the radio agency, etc.

Effect of Size of Account

Before the basis of the agency's compensation can be intelligently discussed, it is necessary to classify advertising accounts by size of advertising appropriation.

An account whose annual advertising appropriation is $50,000 or less may be considered a small account; one whose annual advertising appropriation is from $50,000 to $150,000 may be considered a medium-sized account; an account whose annual advertising appropriation is from $150,000 to $500,000 represents a large advertiser; an account whose annual advertising expenditure exceeds $500,000 is a very large account.

General advertising agencies in fixing the basis of their compensation on large or very large accounts usually find that they can perform all of the services listed in the chapter "Functions Performed by the Modern Advertising Agency" in consideration for the commissions received from the sale of advertising space and materials. The only exception would be research studies and publicity.

Services Rendered

General advertising agencies in determining the basis of their compensation in connection with handling medium-size accounts as a rule find that they are able to deliver the following services in consideration of the commissions received.

1. Developing the advertising campaign.
2. Writing the copy.
3. Selecting the art work and supervising its preparation.
4. Analyzing and selecting media.
5. Buying the advertising media.
6. Buying the production materials.
7. Checking the advertising.
8. Billing the advertising.

General agencies handling medium-size accounts bill production materials at cost, plus 17.65 or 15 percent. General agencies in fixing the fees for handling small accounts usually find that they cannot afford to perform the services required by the advertiser without securing a fee in addition to the commissions received. The cost of planning the campaign, writing the copy, etc., when added to the contact cost and the general overhead of the agency can, and does in many cases, exceed the commissions that an agency receives from the advertising.

When this condition occurs, the agency must arrange for a service fee or minimum charge per month or year. This fee is fixed by the agency after it determines the cost of the services required by the advertiser. Agencies make special arrangements with each client where service fees are required. The annual appropriations of industrial advertisers, by and large, are much smaller than are those of general advertisers. The cost of space in trade papers is relatively low and consequently the industrial agency's commission income per page of advertising is much less than that of the general agency whose clients advertise in national magazines or in large papers.

In addition, the industrial agency advertises specialized and technical products which require special skills and experiences to handle. Furthermore, the industrial account usually requires many collateral or miscellaneous services in connection with point-of-sale material, salesmen's manuals, descriptive folders, convention or business-show materials, etc. Because of these factors, it follows that the commission income from most industrial advertising accounts is insufficient to pay the cost of doing the needed work. The industrial account usually calls for a service fee or some other basis of compensation that will augment the commission received.

Agencies falling in the third, or specialists, classification differ so widely from one another that no generalization as to basis of compensation can be made. Each case will depend on the particulars. The agency often requires experience with an account before it can fix its compensation properly. All agencies have difficulty in determining the basis of compensation for research studies, but by far the larger number of agencies charges a special fee for conducting any but the most cursory investigation of markets or products. A few very large agencies maintain research departments and they offer certain services free to some larger clients. Because of the historic commission basis of compensation, an advertiser spends two or three million dollars a year in large costly space provides the agency with a large commission income allowing a sufficient margin for many "extras." Such accounts are rare. Research studies which have a direct bearing on advertising should be initiated and supervised by the agency. In most cases, these studies are billed to clients at cost plus a commission to cover the supervisory service.

Consultations with the advertiser concerning advertising, merchandising, selling and development of the advertising campaign are nearly always a part of the service the agency renders to its client for the media commissions and service fees received. It is in this area that the agency performs it's most vital and costly service. In the larger agency, one or more executives are assigned to an account.

They are called contact men. These men are usually graduates from other departments, top men in the agency, and they carry the responsibility for planning and developing the campaign and coordinating the various services performed. In a small agency, the owners take on the responsibility for counseling and for planning and developing the campaign. This service is a free service in nearly every case.

The production activity of the agency, which includes the securing of the art work and advertising materials for the production of advertising, is one of the early functions of advertising agencies. Under the first open-contract arrangement, agencies purchased advertising space and materials for advertisers at cost plus a commission. Later, instead of adding a commission to the cost of the space, the various media allowed a commission to the agency. As long as advertising materials have been purchased by agencies, they have added a commission to compensate them for this service.

Different agencies use different commission rates in fixing the billing price of advertising materials. Many industrial and specialized agencies add 17.65 percent to the cost of advertising materials. Agencies dealing in low-cost space and agencies handling small accounts often add a higher percentage. Some general agencies handling medium-size and even large accounts add 17.65 per cent, but many of the general agencies add 15 percent to the cost of advertising materials.

This practice of adding a fifteen percent commission to the cost of advertising materials nets the agency only thirteen percent. Actual cost studies show that production departments cannot operate on a thirteen percent margin. Perhaps ten or fifteen years ago there was a sufficient margin of profit from space commissions to make up for a loss incurred in handling the advertising materials.

This is not the case today. With the advertiser clamoring for more and more service, and the increasing cost of experienced personnel, the agency is facing the difficult job of making both ends meet. There is considerable current opinion that production departments must meet expenses. This has caused many agencies to add 17.65 percent to the cost of advertising materials purchased.

Agency Terms and Conditions

Many agencies carefully define the services that they offer for the fees that they charge. The functions performed, fees charged and other conditions are often incorporated by agencies into a booklet or other outline carrying a title such as "Standard Terms and Conditions." In the final analysis, what an agency has to sell is the accumulated experience of its personnel.

The fees it receives from clients must be based on the amount and cost of services performed for them. In other professions, the services are first performed and then the fee is fixed based on the amount and cost of such service. In the agency, because of the "commission system," the fee is fixed first, after which the amount and quality of service must be determined. If the cost of the service exceeds the commission income, either the cost of the service must be reduced or an extra fee charged.

In the early days of the agency business, few services were performed and then the profit margin was large. But as each year passed, clients demanded additional services. Now an agency must analyze its business in order to determine the cost of performing the tailor-made service on each account. It must be in a position to tell the client what services can be performed for the commissions received and what must be compensated for by an extra charge.

BILLING THE ADVERTISING

Before the agency can accurately bill its client for newspaper advertising space, each advertisement must be checked and measured to determine that it was properly inserted to meet the specifications set up, and to determine the number of lines or inches used by the advertisement and therefore to be billed. In addition, it is an established practice for agencies to pay the newspaper and bill the client for the lesser of the amount of space computed, whether it be that measured by the agency's checking department or that billed the agency by the paper.

It is not infrequent for the newspaper to measure the advertisement as one line more or less in depth than the measurement computed by the agency. Because the agency wishes to give its client the benefit of the doubt where two people measure differently, it is necessary to compare the linage billed by the newspaper with that measured by the agency.

It is a cardinal principle in agency finance that the advertiser must pay the agency for advertising space prior to the date upon which the agency is required to pay the publisher. Newspaper publishers require payment for advertising space on the tenth, fifteenth, twentieth or twenty-fifth of the months following the advertising. A large portion of the publishers require payment on the tenth or fifteenth of the month following publication.

In any sizable newspaper advertising campaign, advertisements will appear in newspapers that are published hundreds of miles distant from the agency's place of business. Where advertisements appear during the last few days of a month, the tear pages or checking copies of publications, which are frequently sent second- or third-class mail, may not be received for from five to fifteen days after the date of publication.

Newspapers send bills to agencies once a month. They usually submit a separate bill to cover the advertising of each client (although a few papers send one bill to cover all the advertising purchased by the agency). Newspapers usually require a few days after the first of the month in which to complete the invoicing. The reader will see that, because of this procedure agencies cannot receive bills from newspapers before the third fourth or fifth of the month following advertising. In some case invoices are not received until after the tenth of the following month.

Because it is impossible for agencies to send accurate invoice for newspaper advertising in time to secure payment from client before the agency must pay the publication, it is necessary to develop some procedure through the operation of which the agency can collect substantially all the money due for the news paper advertising before it has to pay the papers. Obviously, to accomplish this, it is necessary for the agency) to get an invoice of some kind to the advertiser on or about the first day of the month following the month of advertising.

In other words, on June first an agency should send invoices to it, clients covering all of the newspaper advertising for the month of May. This invoice cannot represent the exact amount due for space used since the space has not yet been checked and audited with bills from newspapers. Several methods are commonly used to secure payment from the advertiser so that the money is received before the agency must pay the publication.

They are:

1. Billing on a space-ordered basis.
2. Billing checked space as checked, and unchecked space as ordered.
3. Prebilling on an estimated basis.

Billing on a Space-ordered Basis

Where this method of billing is used, all of the insertion orders are secured from the checking department, and the total linage ordered is multiplied by the rate in order to compute the billing price, which is noted on the insertion order. An in voice is then typed by reference to the insertion orders. Insertion orders are returned to the checking department, and after they have been completely checked, they are routed to the accounting department for auditing against publishers' bills.

When this procedure is completed, the difference between the linage ordered and the linage to be paid for (the linage measured by the have been completely checked, they are routed to the accounting department for auditing against publishers' bills. When this procedure is completed, the difference between the linage ordered and the linage to be paid for the linage measured by the are issued once a month and usually appear in a form. While this method of billing provides a basis for securing payment from the client in time for the agency to pay the papers, it is a cumbersome procedure causing considerable duplicated work for the advertiser as well as for the agency, because, when the first invoice is prepared, all computations must be made to compute the billing price of the space ordered in each paper.

If the advertiser uses precaution in checking invoices, he will want to check all the computations appearing on the invoice. The credit memo that will be issued later to show the amount of credit due to the advertiser will again require a series of calculations and a complete new typing job. Because of the method used by newspapers to print advertising, the great majority of advertisements will appear in less space than that ordered, and consequently there will be a credit due to the advertiser for almost every paper used in the advertising campaign during the month.

This means that the original invoice on a space-ordered basis will show the details of the advertising ordered in each paper and that the credit memo which is issued later will again show the details of the advertising ordered in each paper, as well as the amount of space that actually was used and the credit to which the advertiser is entitled. For the client to determine the net cost of the advertising in each paper, he must deduct the credit issued from the original billing for the same paper, and this is a cumbersome procedure.

Billing Checked Space as Checked, and Unchecked Space as Ordered

To accomplish this manner of billing, it is necessary for the accounting department to secure all of the previous month's insertion orders on about the first or second day of the month following the advertising. These insertion orders are taken from the checking department where advertisements have been checked with tear sheets as the tear sheets have been received.

Obviously, on the first or second day of the month following the advertising, all of the advertisements ordered for the previous month will not have been checked by the checking department; but where tear sheets have been received, the checkers will have checked the advertisements and measured the space used.

Based on the information contained on the insertion orders, a detailed invoice is now made up by the accounting department by billing the space that has been checked and measured on the basis of the number of lines measured by the checking department. Advertisements that have not yet been checked or measured are billed on the basis of the space ordered. Obviously, this form of hybrid billing is usually unsatisfactory to both the agency and the advertiser because, following such billing, it is necessary to review all of the work in order to issue credits or additional charges to adjust the final billing for the amount of space to be paid for.

To accomplish this final billing, it is necessary to return all of the insertion orders to the checking department where there are one or more items on an order that had not been previously checked. These orders must remain in the checking department until the tear sheets are received and the advertisements measured.

They are then taken from the checking department and reviewed by the billing department to determine the difference between the space billed on the ordered basis and the space actually used (after auditing with publisher's bill).

When such differences are isolated and computed, an additional invoice or credit memo must be prepared to account for the differences. This operation is more complicated than it sounds, for it often occurs that two or more different advertisements are ordered for one client to appear within one month.

At the time of the first billing, some of the advertisements will have been checked and measured, but others will not have been measured. In making up the bill to the client, the agency should indicate which of them have been measured and checked in, and which have not.

Also, after paying the invoice, the client should hold the invoice aside and later verify the adjustment for the items that had not been measured and checked at the time the invoice was prepared. This type of billing—that is, billing some items on the basis of space ordered and others on a checked basis —is highly unsatisfactory. Newspaper billing should be performed on an estimated basis, which is next explained.

Prebilling on an Estimated Basis

The properly operated advertising agency secures an approved or signed estimate covering the newspaper space to be ordered before insertion orders are issued to papers. If, before the advertising appears, changes are made, each such change should be represented by an approved estimate revision.

Unless some form of authorization is received by the agency from its client, the agency may be in an embarrassing position. Since agencies make huge commitments at the special request and for the benefit of clients, it is important for both advertiser and agency that such expenditures are approved in writing.

This point cannot be overemphasized, and such written approvals have served to eliminate many misunderstandings. Approved estimates form the basis for determining the amount of an advertiser's commitments for a period. If, in preparing such estimates, each estimate is limited to one type of advertising medium and one month of advertising, there will be a separate estimate to cover each month's newspaper advertising.

These estimates will show the total commitment of each client. Prebilling is accomplished simply by preparing a one-line invoice which usually reads as follows.

Newspaper advertising for the month of May, 1948, as per estimate #567.............................. $90,000.00

Less 10% tentative allowances for shrinkage and omissions 9,000.00

An invoice similar to this is sent to the client on the first day of each month to cover the advertising of the prior month. The reader will note the arbitrary tentative allowance for shrinkage and omissions. By way of explanation, it should be noted that some shrinkage (about one and one-half percent) between the linage ordered and the linage used is expected. In addition, while it is expected that all the advertising ordered will appear, the agency should not ask the client for payment equal to one hundred percent of the expected advertising, since it is entirely possible that some papers may fail to publish.

Bear in mind that this billing on an estimated basis is merely so that the agency secures payment prior to the time it is necessary for it to pay the publishers. This prebill is not intended as an accurate invoice, but the client is asked to pay the prebill and is told that as soon as possible after the space is checked and the publishers' bills audited, a complete detailed invoice will be sent.

After the preliminary bill is sent to the client, the newspaper tear sheets are checked against insertion orders, and the newspaper bills are audited against the linage checked in by the agency's checking department. As soon as the publishers have been paid, the agency prepares a complete detailed invoice to each client. Each newspaper used in the advertising campaign is listed, and that after the newspaper name there are the details of the space used, including the total linage used during the month in each paper and, finally, there is the billing price of the space.

After this detailed invoice is completed, it is totaled; and from the total of the invoice, the amount of the prebill or commitment invoice is deducted, the balance representing the amount due to the agency. This method of first sending a prebill on an estimated basis, followed by a detailed invoice on the basis of checked and audited space, is by far the simplest method that can be used to accomplish the desired objectives. The client has a copy of the estimates which were previous approved. These estimates show the amount of the client's commitments for newspaper space.

The detailed invoice, which is later prepared and sent to the client by the agency, shows the actual amount of space used in each paper for the month, thus eliminating the necessity of making any calculations to determine just how much space was used in a certain paper for a certain period of time. It is only necessary for the client to audit one document, the final invoice, since this is the only document that contains any detail. By the time the final detailed invoice is received by the advertiser, the advertiser should have received tear sheets covering each advertisement, and these tear sheets may be checked against the agency's invoice in order to prove that the advertiser is paying only for the advertising that he had actually secured.

Payments to Publications

The detail of the procedure to be followed to prepare the check for the publisher is given below on the assumption that first the agency prepares an estimated invoice as explained previously, and that later the detailed invoice is prepared after all of the space has been checked with tear sheets and the linage audited against that billed to the agency by the newspaper.

The steps in the procedure are numbered in the order of their normal sequence:

1. Copies of insertion orders are taken from the checking department as bills are received from newspapers. (It is assumed that advertisements have been measured and linage used noted on the insertion orders.)
2. Bills from newspapers are audited with copies of insertion orders, at which time the following is verified:
   - Rate charged per line or inch
   - Agency commission rate allowed
   - Cash discount rate allowed
   - Number of lines charged for on each insertion date.

   (If the newspaper charges for a lesser number of lines than that measured by the agency, the insertion order is corrected to show the linage charged for by the paper.)

   If the rate per line or inch as charged by the paper is different from that shown on the insertion order, the proper or correct rate is ascertained and is used in making further computations.
3. The total linage used is computed by adding the lines used on each date. This is multiplied by the rate per line to determine the gross billing price. The agency's cost, the cash discount and the net payable are then computed.
4. After the computations (listed in 3 preceding) have been made, all the insertion orders for one paper are gathered together and an adding-machine tape is taken of the net amount payable, to determine the amount of the check to be issued to the newspaper.

   When this has been completed, the adding-machine tape is clipped to the copies of the insertion orders for each paper, and they are sent to a disbursing clerk together with the bills from the paper. Previously it has been stated that newspapers send separate bills for each client's advertising and, further, that they forward two copies of each bill to the agency. Even though these requests are made, occasionally a newspaper will fail to meet the agency's requirements. In such case, it is advisable to prepare separate dummy bills for each client by reference to the one bill sent to the agency by the paper, which bill covers the charges on account of all clients of the agency. In addition, if the paper fails to send bills in duplicate, a duplicate copy of the newspaper's bill should be made to be used in the procedure which is explained in the following.

5. When the disbursing clerk receives the copies of insertion orders with adding-machine tapes attached, representing the totals due to each paper, he receives also copies of bills from publications.
   Here it should be noted that where the agency's payment is going to differ from the publisher's bills, the difference should be noted on both copies of the publisher's bill. Such differences occur frequently because of different linage or different rates, and, as stated before, the differences should be shown on both copies of the publisher's bill, and the total of the publisher's bill should be corrected to agree with the computations as shown on the insertion orders.
6. A check is now typed in triplicate. The original copy is sent to the publisher together with one copy of the publisher's bill. Note that this check is designed for use in window envelopes. Under certain conditions, a different check is desirable.
7. Immediately after the preparation of the check, the paid insertion orders are stamped with a rubber stamp to indicate the date on which each item was paid. One copy of the check is stapled to the copies of the publisher's bills, and the check and publisher's bills are filed alphabetically for future reference. The other copy of the check is filed in numerical sequence and constitutes the cash disbursement record of the agency. The third carbon is filed by medium.
8. Insertion orders that have now been paid are filed, awaiting the preparation of the final detailed client invoice. All insertion orders which have been paid, but which have not yet been billed, are lodged in one file.

Details of Billing Procedure

As soon as the payments for the month have been completed, all paid and unbilled insertion orders are taken from the file for the purpose of preparing the client invoice. Insertion orders are now sorted so as to gather all of the orders pertaining to one client. These stacks of orders are then re-sorted so as to bring the orders into alphabetical sequence by the name of the state, the city and the publication. The information contained on the insertion orders for the client is transcribed by the typist to the client invoice, which, when completed.

It is important to note that the copies of the client's invoice which are retained by the agency are wider than the copies which are sent to the client. These office copies, or carbon copies, of the invoice show the agency cost of each item, as well as the gross billing price. This information is needed for the bookkeeping entries which will be discussed later. Clients usually require two copies of each invoice. A third copy is needed for the agency's own records. Sometimes a copy of each invoice is made and it is filed by the treasurer in a tickler file under the date on which payment should be received by the agency. After the invoices have been typed and totaled, the original copies are mailed to clients in window envelopes and the office copies are filed.

The invoice number is now noted on each insertion order that has been billed, and the insertion orders are filed in a completed file containing paid and billed insertion orders.

These files are usually segregated by clients and further segregated alphabetically by state, city and paper name. At the beginning of the description of these detailed billing and paying procedures, it was explained that the assumption was made that a preliminary or estimated bill had been sent to the client. Based on this assumption, the payments are usually made to the papers before the detailed invoice is prepared. Occasionally, for one reason or another, a paper is not paid prior to the time of preparing the detailed client invoice (approximately the twenty-fifth of the month following the advertising).

In exceptional cases payments to papers could be held up because of missing tear sheets, a dispute in rates, a question as to the quality of the printing or for various other reasons. Sometimes clients wish to have all of their billing for a month completed, so they request the agency to include charges for all advertising which has appeared, even though the agency has not yet finally satisfied itself as to the correctness of the charges. As stated previously, in such cases, the agency would not have paid for the item at the time the detailed invoice was prepared for transmission to the client. When this occurs, the insertion orders would have been taken from the checking department file, but at the time of payment they would have been held up because of the questioned items.

Such insertion orders would then be used in preparing the client invoice even though payment had not been made to papers. These insertion orders, which contain no indication of payment, cannot be placed in a paid-and-billed file after the client invoice has been prepared, but must be filed in a billed-but-unpaid file.

Thus there usually are four files of insertion orders:

1. The unpaid and unbilled orders which are kept in the checking department and then sent to the accounting department to be audited against publishers' bills.
2. The paid but unbilled insertion orders which are filed in the accounting department directly following the payment of publishers' bills.
3. The billed but unpaid insertion orders consisting of those items which have been invoiced to clients, but which have not been paid.
4. The paid and billed orders.

ADVERTISING TRENDS

Like most areas of marketing, advertising is changing rapidly. Some argue that change has affected advertising more than any other marketing function. The more important trends in advertising include:

Digital Convergence

While many different media outlets are available for communicating with customers, the ability to distinguish between outlets is becoming more difficult due to the convergence of different media types. In advertising convergence, and more appropriately digital convergence, refers to a growing trend for using computer technology to deliver media programming and information.

Convergence allows one media outlet to take advantage of features and benefits offered through other media outlets. For instance, in many areas around the world television programming is now delivered digitally via cable, telephone or satellite hookup. This delivery method uses the same principles of information delivery that is used to allow someone to connect the Internet.

The convergence of television and Internet opens many potential opportunities for marketers to target customers in ways not available with traditional television advertising. For example, technology may allow ads delivered to one household to be different than ads delivered to a neighbor's television even though both households are watching the same programme. But convergence is not limited to just television. Many media outlets are experiencing convergence as can be seen with print publications that now have a strong web presence.

The future holds even more convergence opportunities. These include outdoor billboards that alter displays as cars containing geographic positioning systems (GPS) and other recognizable factors (e.g., GPS tied to satellite radio) pass by or direct mail postcards that carry a different message based on data that matches a household's address with television viewing habits.

Focus on Audience Tracking

The movement to digital convergence provides marketers with the basic resources needed to monitor user's activity, namely, digital data. Any media outlet that relies on computer technology to manage the flow of information does so using electronic signals that eventually form computer data. In simple form, electronic data is represented by either an "on" or "off" electronic signal.

In computer language this is further represented by two numbers "0" and "1" and, consequently, is known as digital information. All digital information can be stored and later evaluated. For media outlets delivering information in digital form, the potential exists for greater tracking and matching this with information about the person receiving the digital data. And tracking does not stop with what is delivered; it also works with information being sent from the customer. For instance, as we noted earlier, by clicking on their television screen viewers will soon be able to instantly receive information about products they saw while watching a television show. This activity can be tracked then used in future marketing efforts.

Audience Concern with Tracking

While media convergence offers marketers more options for tracking response to advertisements, such activity also raises ethical and legal concerns. Many consumers are not pleased to learn their activities are being monitored when they engage a media outlet.

Yet consider the following examples of how marketers are tracking users:

- *Television Viewing:* As we noted, the advent of digitally delivered television allows cable, telephone and satellite providers to track user activity through the set-top boxes connected to a subscriber's television. Future innovation will make the user television experience even more interactive and, consequently, open to even more tracking.
- *Television recording:* The days of television videotape recording are quickly coming to an end, replaced by recording using computer technology. A digital video recorder (DVR), such as TiVo, can track users recording habits and, based on a viewer's past activity, make suggestions for programs they may want to record. Additionally, advertising services can programme the DVR to insert special advertisements within a programme targeted to a particular viewer.
- *Internet Spyware:* Downloading entertainment from the Internet, such as games, video and software, may contain a hidden surprise – spyware. Spyware is a special programme that runs in the background of a user's computer and regularly forwards information over the Internet to the spyware's company. In some cases spyware keeps track of websites the user has visited. The information is then used to gain an understanding of the user's interests, which then results in delivery of special ads when a user visits a certain site.

Ad Skipping and Blocking

As noted above, television recording devices offer marketers tremendous insight into viewers' habits and behaviour. Yet from the consumer side, the DVR is changing how people view television programs by allowing them to watch programming at a time that is most convenient for them.

Viewer convenience is not the only advantage of the DVR. The other main reason consumers are attracted to the DVR is their ability to quickly skip over commercials. Of course this presents major issues for advertisers who are paying for advertisements. As more DVR devices with ad skipping or even ad blocking features are adopted by mainstream consumers the advertiser's concern with whether they are getting the best value for the advertising money becomes a bigger issue. Advertisers who feel frustrated with television ad-skipping may opt to invest their promotional funds in other media outlets where consumers are more likely to be exposed to an advertisement.

Changing Media Choices

There is a major cultural shift occurring in how people use media for entertainment, news and information. Many traditional media outlets, such as newspapers and major commercial television networks, are seeing their customer base eroded by the emergence of new media outlets.

The Internet has become the major driver of this change. In particular, a number of important applications tied to the Internet are creating new media outlets and drawing the attention of many, mostly younger, consumers. Examples include:

- *Podcasting Audio:* This involves delivering programming via downloadable online audio that can be listened to on music players, such as Apple's iPod. Many news websites and even other information site, such as blogs, offer free downloadable audio programming.
- *Podcasting Video:* While audio downloading has been available for some time, the downloading of video to small, handheld devices, including cellphones, is in its infancy. Many television networks are now experimenting with making their programming available for download, albeit, for a fee.
- *RSS Feeds*: This is an Internet information distribution technology that allows for news and content to be delivered instantly to anyone who has signed up for delivery. Clearly those registering for RSS feeds represent a highly targeted market since they requested the content.
- *Networked Gaming:* While gaming systems have been around for some time, gaming systems attached to the Internet for group play is relatively new and becoming more practical as more people move to faster Internet connections. This type of setup will soon allow marketers to insert special content, such as advertising, within game play.

For marketers these new technologies should be monitored closely as they become accepted alternatives to traditional media outlets. While these technologies are currently not major outlets for advertising, they may soon offer such opportunity. As these technologies gain momentum and move into mainstream acceptance marketers may need to consider shifting advertising spending.

Marketers should also be aware that new media outlets will continue to emerge as new applications are developed. The bottom line for marketers is they must stay informed of new developments and understand how their customers are using these in ways that may offer advertising opportunities.

TYPE OF MEDIA OUTLETS

While just a few years ago marketers needed to be aware of only a few media outlets, today's marketers must be well-versed in a wide range of media options. The reason for the growing number of media outlets lies with advances in communication technology, in particular, the Internet. The number of media outlets will continue to grow as new technologies emerge.

Next we provide an overview of 10 leading media outlets:

1. Television
2. Radio
3. Print Publications
4. Internet
5. Direct Mail
6. Signage
7. Product Placement
8. Mobile Devices
9. Sponsorships
10. Others

Television Advertising

Television advertising offers the benefit of reaching large numbers in a single exposure. Yet because it is a mass medium capable of being seen by nearly anyone, television lacks the ability to deliver an advertisement to highly targeted customers compared to other media outlets.

Television networks are attempting to improve their targeting efforts. In particular, networks operating in the pay-to-access arena, such as those with channels on cable and satellite television, are introducing more narrowly themed programming (i.e., TV shows geared to specific interest groups) designed to appeal to selective audiences. However, television remains an option that is best for products that targeted to a broad market.

The geographic scope of television advertising ranges from advertising within a localized geographic area using fee-based services, such as cable and fibre optic services, to national coverage using broadcast programming.

Television advertising, once viewed as the pillar of advertising media outlets, is facing numerous challenges from alternative media (e.g., Internet) and the invasion of technology devices, such as digital video recorders, that have empowered customers to be more selective on the advertisements they view. Additionally, television lacks effective response tracking which has led many marketers to investigate other media that offer stronger tracking options.

Radio Advertising

Promotion through radio has been a viable advertising option for over 80 years. Radio advertising is mostly local to the broadcast range of a radio station, however, at least three options exist that offer national and potentially international coverage. First, in many countries there are radio networks that use many geographically distinct stations to broadcast simultaneously. In the United States such networks as Disney (children's programming) and ESPN (sports programming) broadcast nationally either through a group of company-owned stations or through a syndication arrangement (i.e., business agreement) with partner stations.

Second, within the last few years the emergence of radio programming delivered via satellite has become an option for national advertising. Finally, the potential for national and international advertising may become more attractive as radio stations allow their signals to be broadcast over the Internet. In many ways radio suffers the same problems as television, namely, a mass medium that is not highly targeted and offers little opportunity to track responses. But unlike television, radio presents the additional disadvantage of limiting advertisers to audio-only advertising. For some products advertising without visual support is not effective.

Print Publication Advertising

Print publications such as magazines, newspapers and Special Issue publications offer advertising opportunities at all geographic levels. Magazines, especially those that target specific niche or specialized interest areas, are more narrowly targeted compared to broadcast media. Additionally, magazines offer the option of allowing marketers to present their message using high quality imagery (e.g., full colour) and can also offer touch and scent experiences (e.g., perfume). Newspapers have also incorporated colour advertisements, though their main advantage rests with their ability to target local markets. Special Issue publications can offer very selective targeting since these often focus on an extremely narrow topics (e.g., auto buying guide, tour guides, college and university ratings, etc.).

Internet Advertising

The fastest growing media outlet for advertising is the Internet. Compared to spending in other media, the rate of spending for Internet advertising is experiencing tremendous growth and in the U.S. trails only newspaper and television advertising in terms of total spending. Internet advertising's influence continues to expand and each year more major marketers shift a larger portion of their promotional budget to this medium. Two key reasons for this shift rest with the Internet's ability to: 1) narrowly target an advertising message and, 2) track user response to the advertiser's message.

The Internet offers many advertising options with messages delivered through websites or by email:

- *Website Advertising*: Advertising tied to a user's visit to a website accounts for the largest spending on Internet advertising. For marketers, website advertising offers many options in terms of:

- *Creative Types*: Internet advertising allows for a large variety of creative types including text-only, image-only, multimedia (e.g., video) and advanced interactive (e.g., advertisement in the form of online games).
- *Size:* In addition to a large number of creative types, Internet advertisements can be delivered in a number of different sizes (measured in screen pixels) ranging from full screen to small square ads that are only a few pixels in size. The most popular Internet ad sizes include banner ads (468 x 60 pixels), leaderboard (728 x 90 pixels) and skyscraper (160 x 600 pixels).
- *Placement*: The delivery of an Internet advertisement can occur in many ways including fixed placement in a certain website location (e.g., top of page), processed placement where the ad is delivered based on user characteristics (e.g., entry of words in a search box, recognition of user via Internet tracking cookies), or on a separate webpage where the user may not see the ad until they leave a site or close their browser (e.g., pop-under).
- *Delivery:* When it comes to placing advertisements on websites marketers can, in some cases, negotiate with websites directly to place an ad on the site or marketers can place ads via a third-party advertising network, which has agreements to place ads on a large number of partner websites.

- *Email Advertising:* Using email to deliver an advertisement affords marketers the advantage of low distribution cost and potentially high reach. In situations where the marketer possesses a highly targeted list, response rates to email advertisements may be quite high. This is especially true if those on the list have agreed to receive email, a process known as "opt-in" marketing. Email advertisement can take the form of a regular email message or be presented within the context of more detailed content, such as an electronic newsletter. Delivery to a user's email address can be viewed as either plain text or can look more like a website using web coding (i.e., HTML). However, as most people are aware, there is significant downside to email advertising due to highly publicized issues related to abuse (i.e., spam).

Direct Mail

This method of advertising uses postal and other delivery services to ship advertising materials, including postcards, letters, brochures, catalogs and flyers, to a physical address of targeted customers. Direct mail is most effective when it is designed in a way that makes it appear to be special to the customer. For instance, a marketer using direct mail can personalize mailings by including a message recipient's name on the address label or by inserting their name within the content of marketer's message.

Direct mail can be a very cost-effective method of advertising, especially if mailings contain printed material. This is due to cost advantages obtained by printing in high volume since the majority of printing costs are realized when a printing machine is initially setup to run a print job and not the because of the quantity of material printed. Consequently, the total cost of printing 50,000 postcards is only slightly higher than printing 20,000 postcards but when the total cost is divided by the number of cards printed the cost per-card drops dramatically as more pieces are printed. Obviously there are other costs involved in direct mail, primarily postage expense.

While direct mail can be seen as offering the benefit of a low cost-per-contact, the actual cost-per-impression can be quite high as large numbers of customers may discard the mailing before reading. This has led many to refer to direct mail as "junk mail" and due to the name some marketers view the approach as ineffective. However, direct mail, when well-targeted, can be an extremely effective promotional tool.

Signage and Billboards

The use of signs to communicate a marketer's message places advertising in geographically identified areas in order to capture customer attention. The most obvious method of using signs is through billboards, which are generally located in high traffic areas. Outdoor billboards come in many sizes, though the most well-known are large structures located near transportation points intending to attract the interest of people traveling on roads or public transportation. Indoor billboards are often smaller than outdoor billboards and are designed to attract the attention of foot traffic (i.e., those moving past the sign). For example, smaller signage in airports, train terminals and large commercial office space fit this category.

While billboards are the most obvious example of signage advertising, there are many other forms of signage advertising include:

- Sky writing where airplanes use special chemicals to form words
- Plane banners where large signs are pulled behind an airplane
- Mobile billboards where signs are placed on vehicles, such as buses and cars, or even carried by people
- Plastic bags used to protect newspapers delivered to homes
- Advertisements attached to grocery carts

Product Placement Advertising

Product placement is an advertising approach that intentionally inserts products into entertainment programs such as movies, TV programs and video games.

Placement can take several forms including:

- Visual imagery in which the product appears within the entertainment programme

- Actual product use by an actor in the programme
- Words spoken by an actor that include the product name

Product placement is gaining acceptance among a growing number of marketers for two main reasons. First, in most cases the placement is subtle so as not to divert significant attention from the main content of the programme or media outlet. This approach may lead the audience to believe the product was selected for inclusion by programme producers and not by the marketer.

This may heighten the credibility of the product in the minds of the audience since their perception, whether accurate or not, is that product was selected by an unbiased third-party. Entertainment programming, such as television, is converging with other media, particularly the Internet. In the future a viewer of a television programme may be able to easily request information for products that appear in a programme by simply pointing to the product on the screen. With the information they may get the option to purchase the product. As this technology emerges it is expected that product placement opportunities will become a powerful promotional option for many marketers.

Mobile Device Advertising

Handheld devices, such as cellphones, personal digital assistants (PDAs) and other wireless devices, make up the growing mobile device market. Such devices allow customers to stay informed, gather information and communicate with others without being tied to a physical location. While the mobile device market is only beginning to become a viable advertising medium, it may soon offer significant opportunity for marketers to reach customers at anytime and anyplace. Also, with geographic positioning features included in newer mobile devices, the medium has the potential to provide marketers with the ability to target customers based on their geographic location. Currently, the most popular advertising delivery method to mobile devices is through plain text messaging, however, over the next few years multimedia advertisements are expected to become the dominant message format.

Sponsorships

A subtle method of advertising is an approach in which marketers pay, or offer resources and services, for the purpose of being seen as a supporter of an organization's event, programme or product offering (e.g., section of a website). Sponsorships are intended not to be viewed a blatant advertisement and in this way may be appealing for marketers looking to establish credibility with a particular target market. However, many sponsorship options lack the ability to tie spending directly to customer response. Additionally, the visibility of the sponsorship may be limited to relatively small mentions especially if the marketer is sharing sponsorship with many other organizations.

Others

While the nine media outlets discussed above represent the overwhelming majority of advertising methods, there are several more including:

- Advertising using telephone recordings (e.g., political candidate's messages)
- Advertising via fax machine (though there may be certain legal issues with this method)
- Advertising through inserted material in product packaging (e.g., inside credit card bill)
- Advertising imprinted on retail receipts (e.g., grocery store, cash machine)

CREATING A MESSAGE

Effective communication requires the message source to create (encoding) a message that can be interpreted (decoding) by the intended message receiver. In advertising, the act of creating a message is often considered the creative aspect of carrying out an advertising campaign.

And because it is a creative process, the number of different ways a message can be generated is limited only by the imagination of those responsible for developing the message.

When creating an advertising message the marketer must consider such issues as:

- General Message Factors
- Message Structure
- Message Testing

General Message Factors

When developing the message the marketer must take into consideration several factors including:

- *Characteristics of the Target Audience:* The makeup of the target audience (e.g., age, location, attitudes, etc.) impacts what is conveyed in the message.
- *Type of Media Used:* The media outlet (e.g., television, print, Internet, etc.) used to deliver the message impacts the way a message will be created.
- *Product Factors:* Products that are highly complex require a different message than simpler products. Additionally, the target market's familiarity with a product affects what is contained in a message. For instance, a new product attempting to gain awareness in the market will have a message that is much different than a product that is well-known.
- *Overall Advertising Objective:* As mentioned, the objective of the advertising campaign can affect the type of ad that is designed. For

example, an advertisement with the objective of stimulating immediate sales for an existing product will be different than an advertisement that seeks to build initial awareness of a new product.

Message Structure

Most advertising messages share common components within the message including:

- *The Appeal:* This refers to the underlying idea that captures the attention of a message receiver. Appeals can fall into such categories as emotional, fearful, humorous, and sexual.
- *Value Proposition:* The advertising message often contains a reason for customers to be interested in the product which often means the ad will emphasize the benefits obtained from using the product.
- *Slogan:* To help position the product in a customer's mind and distinguish it from competitors' offerings, advertisements will contain a word or phrase that is repeated across several different messages and different media outlets.

Message Testing

Before choosing a specific message marketers running large advertising campaigns will want to have confidence in their message by having potential members of the targeted audience provide feedback. The most popular method of testing advertising for the marketer (or their ad agency) is to conduct focus groups where several advertising messages are presented. On the Internet, advertising delivery technology allows for testing of ads by randomly exposing website visitors to different ads and then measuring their response.

11

Customer Value and Service Management

INTRODUCTION

Understanding the business begins with a clear understanding of customer value. Providing a superior customer value requires an understanding of service orientation. Against this backdrop, the rest proceeds to follow the logic that sound decisions and actions cannot be made and performed without a solid understanding of the customer.

You cannot claim to be customer focused if you don't have the appropriate information on the customer. What kinds of customer data are important and why? How do we collect, interpret, and use this data? Where are the opportunities for gathering customer information? Information on all customer preferences, attitudes, and activities associated with the acquisition and use of the product provides a deeper understanding of the customer. This part develops the various methods and approaches to ensuring that the firm is adequately prepared to make customer-focused decisions.

Customer information should drive the design and delivery of customer value. What is involved in conceiving and designing a customer-focused product offering or service delivery? How would a firm go about tracking whether it is maximizing the returns from its value-creating assets? In this part are about effective and efficient value creation and delivery.

Who are the right customers and how can the firm ensure their loyalty to the firm and its products? This part covers topics such as service quality and guaranteeing quality service. When the product fails the customer, what does the firm need to do to recover from that failure in the context of customer service? What must firms do to proactively manage customer defections? \

How does the firm create and maintain a customer-focused culture—a culture that is so focused on the customer that all decisions and actions of all personnel and systems in place create superior value for the customer at a reasonable profit? This final part provides the framework to analyze and manage the firm's value systems to be customer focused.

The principal concepts can be stated as a truism: Businesses cannot succeed in the long term unless they are focused on its customers so as to provide them with superior service. This is how firms attain and maintain a competitive advantage and therefore provide superior customer value at sustainable profits. Thus, the two fundamental and closely related concepts evident here are "customer focus" and "service orientation." After reading this book, you will be able to engage yourself and the firm in a service-oriented mode of designing and delivering customer-focused value to maintain profitable relationships with the right customers.

You will appreciate what is required to sustain a competitive advantage for sustainable profits by:

- Adopting a customer-focused and service-oriented frame of mind
- Understanding the business by understanding customer value
- Capitalizing on the opportunities and use of customer information
- Designing and delivering profitable customer value
- Focusing on the right customer and managing that relationship
- Establishing a customer-focused and service-oriented culture in the firm

Customer-focused firms are the product of customer-focused employees and processes. Customer-focused employees are the responsibility of the executives of the firm. As an executive, you will find that when you stop and think of the ideas and concepts, you will have begun to engage in the intellectual exercise leading to a customer-focused and service-oriented frame of mind. You will be able to specify what the firm should actually be doing to be customer focused.

CUSTOMER VALUE AND SERVICE ORIENTATION

Customers buy solutions, not products. Every firm needs to understand what it is providing the customer in terms of customer value, not by focusing on the product but by focusing on the customer. In doing so, the firm is able to assess whether it is providing superior customer value and whether it has a sustainable competitive advantage. Competitive advantage cannot be sustained unless it can be protected from competitor matching. Any aspect of the product can be matched by the competition. What is most difficult for the competition to match is how the firm approaches and treats the customer. The firm *serves* the customer by providing product enhancements in the form of service. When other firms can provide the same service, the differentiator is in the service orientation of the firm.

CUSTOMER VALUE

Many firms focus on the product rather than on the customer. When the focus is on the customer, the business is defined in terms of customer value, not in terms of product. The product is viewed as a customer solution and experience. That is, for any firm, the most fundamental definition of its business. Try this one. What business is Amazon in? That you can buy just about anything on Amazon may not be too much of an exaggeration. The company abandoned or at least cut back on its strategy of buying up companies, as it did with Drugstore.com in 1999. It now handles retail for such established brands as Toys 'R' Us, Target, and Circuit City. Amazon shocked everyone in early 2002, when they announced their first operations profit of $59 million and a net profit of $5 million in the previous quarter. What value does Amazon provide its customer?

Customers don't buy products. They buy solutions. If firms are focused on the customer, they ought to see themselves in the role of providing solutions, not products. The information technology sector has popularized the term "solutions providers, " with labels such as application service providers (ASPs, as they are called) or technology solutions providers. These labels may be appropriate at the very general level and allow people to gloss over and take for granted the real meaning of the term *solutions.* The label has no real meaning as a concept unless it can be translated into customer value terms. Customers buy value in the solutions. Thus, customer value defines the primary purpose of any business.

This presents an approach to conducting a critical analysis of this fundamental question of "defining the business of a firm." In doing so, it defines "customer value" and redefines "products" in the customer-focused perspective. Finally, this briefly indicates the fruits of a customer-focused organization providing superior customer value. Management guru Peter Drucker said in his 1954 book, *The Practice of Management,* "to know what a business is we have to start with its purpose." He goes on to say: "There is only one valid definition of business purpose: *to create a customer.*" Drucker reiterates this concept in a number of different ways, always emphasizing that "it is the customer who determines what a business is." It is not important what the business thinks it is producing.

The customer determines the value of what the business produces based on what the customer thinks he or she is buying. Such a perspective places the final result in focus—what the product *does* for the customer. Thus, the purpose of a business is what it creates for the customer. The first and foremost question for any firm to ask is, what business are we in? How many firms diligently confront this question? And, when they do encounter this question, whose perspective do they take?

Taking the customer's perspective to answer this fundamental question forces a number of thought processes that benefit the firm in different ways. In fact, businesses will find that approaching the question of *what business are we in?* in so fundamental a manner not only allows the firm to understand its existing customers, but will also help open up new market potential. It forces the analysis of value-creating assets, including the firm's skills and knowledge sets. The question also opens up the analysis of who the competition is. When firms strive to beat rivals, they typically end up competing within the confines of existing business. Firms sometimes do not realize that they compete with firms in other industries. They are able to see this if they articulate their business from the customer's perspective. When customers consider their options in meeting a need, they don't limit themselves to one industry. Without realizing it as such, their solutions may involve different industries. Firms are forced to redefine their competitive landscape when they take the customer's perspective because they will find themselves competing outside their well-defined spaces. Kim and Mauborgne call it competing in a "market space.

They urge firms to expand their view of their business by looking "across substitute industries, across strategic groups, across buyer groups, across complementary product and service offerings, across the functional-emotional orientation of an industry and even across time." They argue this point with examples of how Home Depot cultivated the do-it-yourself market from homeowners using contractors, how Intuit saw that people managing personal finances using a pencil and paper calculation actually competed with their software, how overnight package delivery firms FedEx and UPS competed with telephones and fax machines, and how Southwest Airlines competed with driving. This argument illustrates the definition of a business from the perspective of the customer. Not only does it underscore the value that the customer places on what the firm delivers, but it also reveals that the customer's perspective redefines the business.

Well-known Harvard scholar Ted Levitt expanded on Drucker's thesis of efining a business from a customer's perspective when he popularized the concept "marketing myopia, " where firms and entire industries (such as buggy-whip makers) could perish when inwardly focused. He used the example of railroads as an industry that suffered from marketing myopia because it did not see itself in the business of transportation, but rather in the railroad business. Contrast this with a firm like the Williams Companies, one of the world's largest pipeline builders. Until a few years ago, it built steel pipes to move oil and natural gas. Today, it also builds fiber-optic pipes for the big cable companies. Clearly, Williams did not see itself as being in the oil and gas business, but as being in the business of serving big companies that needed to move material (or data) through pipes. Would Williams have seen this opportunity if it had been focused on competing within the oil and gas industry?

To expand your opportunities, you need to look beyond the product horizon and into the customer's space. For example, if a family was looking for something to do on a Saturday, consider their options: have some friends over for dinner, go out for dinner, go to a nearby mall, go to the movies, go to a play or a show, go bowling, go to a miniature golf course, go for a drive to the lake or the beach—and many other options. Now, look at these options in terms of all of the different industries that are competing with each other. If you were a firm in any one of these industries, you could be defining your business the same way as any of the other industries, depending on who your typical customer is. The customer's perspective broadens your own view of your product. Taking the customer's perspective helps firms identify what they are about—their mission and their values. They are better able to understand their strengths and sources of competitive advantage. Firms are better positioned and more effective in allocating resources and efforts, both strategically and operationally. They are better situated to understand what would be considered superior customer value.

PRODUCTS AS SOLUTIONS

Where do you even begin when you want to define your business? Let us consider the basics. What *do* businesses sell, at the most general level? In what terms will your response be made? Do you see services and goods as solutions to a customer problem—a need to be met? Customer needs are problems searching for solutions and firms are providers of solutions to customer problems.

When seen this way, firms draw focus away from products and orient themselves to the customer with the sole purpose of delivering solutions to problems. The business is defined in terms of customer solutions. Firms suffering from a product focus define their product by its capabilities in terms of product features and promptly lose sight of the customer. The solutions-to-problems approach emphasizes the customer rather than the product. It emphasizes product benefits rather than product features.

Firms must align processes, people, and their entire culture to serving the customer rather than on making and selling products. In customer-focused firms, processes are designed with customers in mind. The output of the processes, the product, is defined by the customer need it serves. In serving the customer, firms offer a combination of benefits or values. Are all products, therefore, a service to the customer? In a sense, yes! The solution represents the value that the firm is providing customers by serving their needs.

Firms' activities produce solutions as value bundles that we call products. All products involve a mix of value producing components—tangibles and intangibles—in value bundles.

The proportion of tangibles and intangibles in the entity that the customer takes title to prompts the artificial distinction between services and products. This unfortunate dichotomy detracts from the necessary customer focus in the conception of the product. Regardless of whether the total product is predominantly a packaged good or a service, in a business-to-business (B2B) or business-to-consumers (B2C) context, all solutions to customer problems can be seen as bundles of benefits or value bundles designed to deliver value by meeting customer problems or needs.

This book adopts the approach that all products are a mix of physical goods and services in some proportion. Some solutions employ more tangibles (physical goods) than intangibles (services) in meeting customer needs, while others may provide an intangible (service) involving physical objects. The important question is, what is that total solution from the customer's perspective? It is more important to understand what the value bundle *does* for the customer than what the bundle *is*. To identify the value bundle, one needs to identify and understand the customer.

DELIVERING SUPERIOR CUSTOMER VALUE

What characterizes firms that can provide *superior* customer value? To answer this question, we have ample evidence from research on such firms. Every firm in any industry provides some customer value. The firm that provides superior customer value is the one that has a sustainable competitive advantage. Firms compete with each other on differentiable aspects of the total solution. If we can conceptualize that every product has parts that are commodities and parts that differentiate it from others, superior value is in the augmented product, not in the conceptual core.

For example, all airlines provide transportation from point A to point B. But the total solution includes aspects other than the physical transportation of the person itself, such as amenities on the airplane. A firm must seek opportunities to differentiate itself from the competition in ways that are meaningful and relevant to the customer. How do firms find opportunities to differentiate themselves in a way that it is sustainable?

Consider how CDW creates superior customer value. CDW is the leading B2B e-commerce firm selling technology equipment to small and medium-sized firms. Wall Street analysts claim that the firm uses a "clicks and people" strategy. Supposedly, their competitive advantage is superior customer service and lower customer acquisition costs. The firm's Web site is tailored to each specific customer as a "custom extranet." How are they able to sustain this competitive advantage? Their own chief financial officer, Harry Harczak, notes that retaining people is key. In his experience, the productivity difference between an employee who has been at the firm six months versus one there three years is a factor of six. CDW values employee commitment.

What are the generalizable characteristics of firms that create superior customer value? A team of Harvard Business School researchers set out to discover exactly this and concluded that successful firms such as BancOne, Intuit, Southwest Airlines, ServiceMaster, USAA, Taco Bell, and MCI made employees and customers paramount. These researchers modeled the findings from their case studies into a framework they called "the service profit chain." Their cases provided data to establish powerful relationships between profitability, customer loyalty, and employee satisfaction, loyalty, and productivity. Evident in the whole model is the focus on the customer and the service orientation of satisfied employees, and the implications on investors and other stakeholders of the firm.

As firms focus on customer needs and become service oriented to deliver satisfaction, there are favourable ripple effects throughout the firm. Consistent delivery of customer satisfaction persuades customers to be loyal because perceived risk in buying a product from that firm is substantially reduced.

When providers of solutions to customer needs are able to consistently deliver expected value, customers are more likely to be consistently satisfied. By way of their continued patronage, they become more valuable to the firm. When customers are loyal to the provider by choice, it is also in their best interest to support the provider because the prosperity and longevity of the provider is beneficial to the customer. Similarly, with regard to employees, research has shown that when employee satisfaction is high employees are more likely to be loyal to the company. When employee loyalty is high, employees are likely to be more productive and to be providing quality products and service.

Neither employees nor customers are likely to be loyal unless their expectations are met and they are satisfied. Therefore, customer satisfaction and employee satisfaction are inherently tied to each other, in that, when employees are loyal to the firm, they provide superior performances driving customer loyalty. When employees are productive and customer loyalty is high, the firm is successful and can command a premium.

With increased profitability and growth prospects, investors are attracted to the firm, which in turn makes more resources available to the firm. With more resources available to the firm, capital is available to continuously improve value-creating assets (people and processes) and to produce consistently superior customer value in its products and service. This sequence of events, presented as the "loyalty circle", contributes to profitability and growth and requires that people and processes are aligned to deliver superior customer value. Delivering superior value should be a relentless endeavor for the firm.

IDENTIFYING THE CUSTOMER

To understand the customer is to understand your business. To understand the customer's perspective is basic to defining a business. The first obvious question is, who is the customer? If the firm defines the customer too narrowly or without context, any subsequent analysis is flawed. Firms either focus on their end users as packaged-goods firms tend to do, or as in the case of industrial firms, the focus is on the immediate customer. Both cases reflect a narrow view and a lack of understanding of the context. To determine who the customer is, the question to ask is, how does what we produce or provide add value to the client's value creating process?

Most important, what do customers see as the value we are providing to their value creation process? This point is central to what we know as the "value chain" concept. An understanding of customers requires an understanding of the customers' value chain that includes the set of their value consumption activities. If the value created by the immediate customer creates value for a subsequent customer, that customer is also an indirect customer of the firm. We really need to identify the customer as a first step to determine whose perspective we should take and to understand the customer value that we are providing.

Performing the analysis of the customer sometimes forces the redefining of the customer. For Bright Horizons, a workplace child care and early education service company, it made a huge difference in how they went about their business when they viewed employers, and not parents, as their primary customers. The company could now tap into the financial and other resources of corporations and gain access to a much wider pool of parents. The value they were providing to the employer became the focus of the company. Chase Manhattan, for example, figured that its child care centre was yielding 110 percent return on investment through reduced absenteeism. Similarly, Merck found that its employee retention rate among those who were young parents went up dramatically.

The customer-focused perspective blurs the boundaries between entities in the value chain. Take the case of Aramark Corp., a firm that caters special events and runs cafeterias for big corporate clients. Nancy Naatz, resident district manager for business services for Aramark, has an office in the premises of her customer, Sears, in Chicago. Since Ms. Naatz is on location at her client's company, she is able to observe and interact with the local vendors Aramark has contracted to supply and serve Sears. Ms. Naatz is able to understand Sears executives' and employees' nutritional needs and interact with the vendors to ensure that the appropriate choices are made available. In this case, Aramark matches the food vendors' solution with the needs of the Sears employees who are the real customers.

So, who is the customer? The perspective of *which* customer I inspect and analyze, so as to help determine the business of my business, is the question. This question also raises the fundamental marketing decision of what or who our target market should be. It is a logical place to start before making any marketing or operations decision. Of all the potential customers that make up the market, which particular type of customer is most appropriate for our solution? The analysis involves segmentation, and the decision involved is one of targeting.

We are able then to determine which particular type of customer from the universe of all customers for this product would find most value in what our value-creating assets can produce. We thus segment the market and target those segments for whom our value-creating assets can provide differentiation and a cost advantage. To know who the customer is necessitates an understanding of the typical customer in that segment at a general or aggregate level.

Traditionally, customer profiles have come out of the segmentation exercise. Segmentation variables in the B2C context have included demographic, psychographic, and behavioural variables. For customer-focused management we need information on all of the characteristics of the need or problem or use-situation that the customer is involved in, encompassing all of the activities of the customer that the product is a part of. Consequently, the question, who is the customer? You want to know how the customer purchases and uses the product.

Similarly, the profile of the customer in a B2B context involves understanding the business of the organizational customer. For either the B2C or the B2B context, an understanding of the customers requires analysis of their use-situations, and the contexts within which a product helps them in what they do. Of what value are you to them? Now we begin to hint at the notion of what customer value really is. The answers lie in the *consumption* of the product, not in its production.

Customer Value

Customer value is what the customer thinks he or she is getting in return for what the customer has to part with, reflecting an implicit comparison akin to "give and receive." It has been described as the quotient of quality over price. Understanding the customer is about understanding customer value. Customer value is a complex concept and measuring it is complicated. But in the exercise of trying to understand customer value, the manager benefits from a better understanding of the customer and of the opportunities for a superior solution.

Here are some characteristics of customer value that any manager should examine in an analysis of the firm and its activities: Customer value:

- Is what the customer believes that a product or service provides in a certain use situation.
- Is an implicit comparison between what the customer receives from the provider and what the customer provides in time, effort, and money. The frame of reference is not just the price tag on the product, but also the ease and convenience in the acquisition and use of the product and the whole interactive experience the customer has with the firm.
- Is the customer's rather than the provider's perspective. It has to do with customer perceptions of the product and the firm, and not the provider's perspective of what the firm is delivering.
- Is dynamic, in that it can change over time before, during, and after the purchase, use, over repeated use of the product, and during all the various stages in the relationship with the providing firm.
- Can vary over different use situations. Your automobile may provide less or more value in transporting a group of kids to the ballpark compared to taking the spouse to the boss's house for a party.
- Can be shaped by attitudes, opinions, and behaviours of others, such as friends, family, media, the providing firm, and other competitors in the industry as well as in substitute industries.
- Determines customer satisfaction and the likelihood of brand or firm loyalty. This cause-effect relationship could be affected by comparisons with competitors and other substitutes.

- Is hard to measure and keep track of. Customers may find it hard to articulate all the different dimensions of customer value and firms may find it a rather onerous task to keep track of all the manifestations of customer value.

CATEGORY CHARACTERISTICS OF A SPECIFIC SERVICE

In employing the service orientation, every manager needs to understand that there are different types of services in every product, each with its own manifestations of the fundamental characteristics of services. The nature of these manifestations in different services implies different situations for the customer and the manager. While all services are fundamentally intangible, inseparable, perishable, and variable, services differ from each other along dimensions peculiar to their category. These category characteristics provide the manager with an insight into the specific situations that they have to deal with in their particular service category.

Christopher Lovelock demonstrated that this sort of categorizing is necessary and powerful as a means of understanding the managerial situations specific to each type of service. Service managers should look toward other services that share similar characteristics and expect to find similar challenges and transferable solutions to those challenges. Consider for example that hospitals provide executive-style rooms for the businessperson who is a patient. They learned this from hotels that have executive-style suites for the businessperson. Now consider the service characteristics that are shared between hospitals and hotels.

In both cases, the customer comes to the factory and frequently requires an overnight stay. In both situations, the executive is likely to be away from an office with all its business support for an extended period of time. Both services are similar in the type of customer interactions, even though they are in two completely different service sectors. An analysis represents the benefits of learning from the successes of services that share certain specific service characteristics.

Managers of services can understand the specific challenges and opportunities presented by the characteristics of their product and corresponding situations by examining a number of characteristics that profile a service category.

Here are a few characteristics to examine:

- Tangible or intangible act
- Person or thing as recipient of the act
- Type of interaction between provider and customer
- Service delivered by people or equipment
- Extent of customization or standardization

What are the tangible and intangible acts involved in the services that you are providing? Is the service act delivered on a person or a thing? For example, if you are an entertainment electronics repair and service provider, you perform tangible acts on a DVD player and intangible acts with the customer as you obtain information on what problems the customer has experienced with the DVD player. Now, examine the nature of the acts and the impact on the customer. When you are working on the DVD player, the customer needs not be present and the process that you employ need not be visible to the customer. However, you do interact with the customer at a number of points, from the initial customer call to the final interaction at delivery or pickup of the DVD player.

Similarly, you might analyze your service about the nature of interaction of with the customer. Is it face-to-face or arm's length, via telephone or the Internet? Do you visit the customer or does the customer visit your premises? How much technology is involved in the interface with the customer? Sometimes the customer does not even interact with a person. How much standardization is built into the service? Are there options provided to customers who require a customized interaction? What benefits does this analysis provide the manager?

The challenges and opportunities discussed earlier as fundamental are common to all service managers. By understanding the characteristics of their specific category of services, the manager can find ways to take advantage of the opportunities and address the challenges of their specific situation. Additionally, in understanding how the fundamental characteristic of intangibility manifests itself in their particular situation, managers can understand customers' perceived risk and use the tangibles in the customer experience to reduce the risk that customers perceive.

By understanding the nature of the interaction, managers are in a better place to manage the roles of customers and recognize opportunities for customization and standardization to improve the customer experience and, therefore, customer value. What is most interesting is that you may find that service businesses in a different industry sharing certain characteristics may offer you innovative ideas to meet these challenges and capitalize on opportunities to better serve customers in your business.

In order to understand how the required service-oriented frame of mind needs to be handled in the customer-focused firm, the firm analyzes the various services with which it augments the product. Each service is analyzed from a fundamental and category perspective. The fundamental nature of services requires an analysis of the implications of the intangible, inseparable, perishable, and variable nature of services for managerial action. The analysis of category characteristics specific to each type of service should deal with how these consequences of these characteristics manifest themselves in that situation. The customer-focused analysis should cover the nature and the recipient of the act, the nature of the interaction, and the fluctuation of the demand.

REDUCING CUSTOMERS' PERCEIVED RISK

With products that contain a significant proportion of intangibles and where the core product is a service, managers of services need to continuously monitor and understand the risk customers feel when they purchase the service. What is the nature of the risk? How do you lower this risk? Professional services providers such as lawyers and doctors have certifications prominently displayed on their walls. Consulting firms provide lists of clients, mutual funds companies show off their performance charts. What would be most appropriate for you to do to reduce customer perceived risk? To determine this you begin by understanding what those risk levers might be. What is the source of the anxiety that customers feel? To what would you attribute the risk that they feel?

Only when this is clearly understood can you think about the possible ways you might reduce their perceived risk. To understand the risk, you need to break down the service into the features that contribute value toward the total solution. Which service features produce benefits, and how can the risk associated with each feature-benefit connection be reduced? The degree to which the customer feels assured that expectations of these benefits will be met would depend on how you can instill confidence in the customer that you have the ability to deliver on those expectations. Christopher Hart is credited with the concept of service guarantees that works to reduce perceived risk. L.L. Bean's famed "100per cent satisfaction guaranteed" goes back to 1912, when the founder was marketing the Maine hunting shoe. Service providers who understand their customers' perceived risk seek to address it.

Customization versus Standardization

One of the powerful implications of the fundamental characteristics of services is that they are not produced ahead of time. The service is designed, created, and delivered to customer specifications. While customization is possible, some standardized parameters are also necessary to derive economies of scale. There is opportunity to standardize as well as to customize. Where there is low margin from a service component and the volume provides the profits, perhaps ways to standardize the production process would be appropriate. On the other hand, if there is opportunity for high margin, customization and low volume is the way to go.

Consider the difference between automated telephone-based customer service and a fee sometimes charged for customers who want individual attention. Professional or knowledge based services are generally customized and are high-margin, whereas dry cleaning services are low-margin services and require considerable standardization and the required volume. The opportunity is to increase margins by providing customized experiences and the challenge is in standardizing the process to reduce costs and maintain consistent quality.

Quality Consistency

A related issue to the opportunity to customize is the accompanying challenge posed by the variability of the product. Since services are produced in real time, and they have a high degree of variability, the challenge is to ensure a consistent quality in the service. Managers must assess the sources of variation.

Sources of the variability are typically associated with the people delivering the service. Every interaction with the customer provides or facilitates some aspect of the product bundle, and therefore the quality of the product is dependent on each and every interaction between the service provider and the customer. Therefore, selecting, training, and motivating frontline personnel become very critical.

For example, service firms such as Walt Disney amusement parks and the Ritz-Carlton hotels have a specific profile in mind when they hire people for the front line. These firms provide extensive service training for their frontline employees, and they motivate employees to provide customer satisfaction. FedEx rewards employees who take care of customers in service failures. Empowered frontline personnel are more likely to deliver quality service.

Demand and Capacity Management

Since services are perishable, productive factors that are in place may be idle at low demand times and stretched to capacity at high demand times. The demand is fluctuating, and it might be impossible or at best a serious challenge to stretch or contract capacity. Therefore, smoothing demand and managing capacity become a constant endeavor for the managers of services. The key to managing this challenge is to understand the demand patterns and to figure out the flexibilities in your capacity. To the extent that the demand patterns can be predicted with a good understanding of customer behaviour, service providers can manage demand as well as capacity. Pricing is commonly used in smoothing demand.

Early bird specials, matinee prices, lower fares if you stay over Saturdays are all different ways by which service firms use pricing to manage demand. Reservations and appointments are another way for service managers to smooth demand. Different segments and markets are served at different times and prices to fill capacity. Hotels depend to a great extent on the lucrative conferences and meetings market to ensure capacity utilization.

Such capacity-constrained services rely more on managing demand than on managing capacity primarily because it is harder to adjust capacity. Product mix adjustments are another way of managing capacity, whereas the more versatile the value-creating assets are in producing different services with the same productive factors, the better the capacity management opportunities. For example, ski resorts turn into hiking or whitewater rafting facilities in the summer. Staffing and scheduling are typical capacity-side management options that the service firm employs. Creative use of value producing assets is critical for efficient and effective management of a firm's capacity.

Managing the Customer

Since the customer is part of the process and some degree of interaction with the customer is necessary and inevitable, managers of services must find ways to educate customers on their roles. If the customer fails in playing the appropriate coproducer role, it could ruin the process and the outcome quality. A clear understanding of the steps in the process and how, where, and when customers interact with the process is a must. Doctors, nurses, and pharmacists provide directions and instructions for patient roles. Banks and other financial institutions have specific protocols for various financial transactions.

A key question to ask is how the customer should participate in the process and whether you have the appropriate instructions for your customer. Differences in customer willingness and ability to participate in the production of the process force the issue of segmentation on the service delivery process. Thus, restaurants have self-service, take-out, or drive-through options. Automatic teller machines are an early example of self-service in banking services.

Hotels have express check-in and check-out facilities. Airlines have electronic ticketing options. Self-service checkout facilities have become a standard option at grocery stores in the United States and elsewhere.

It is clear as we think about these issues that not all services are alike. While all services face all these challenges to some degree, the challenges manifest themselves differently in different services. In fact, the management solutions presented are more applicable in some and inappropriate or impossible in others. There is a systematic way of addressing these differences among services by examining characteristics that differentiate services from one another. A service that shares characteristics with another service exhibits similar challenges and opportunities.

CREATING AND DELIVERING SUPERIOR CUSTOMER VALUE

Firms create and deliver customer value as a bundle of benefits contained in a core and supplementary product. Since the core of any product is a commodity, the competitive advantage comes from the supplementary product. Designing and delivering superior customer value is all about adding value to the customer's value chain and doing it better than the competition. Paying careful attention to the details in each and every encounter with the customer ensures a customer-focused delivery of the value created by the firm.

Since the customer-focused firm competes on service, it also faces the classic challenge of any service firm—matching demand and supply. In order to maximize the profitability from its value-creating assets, firms have to determine the most profitable mix of segments for its customer portfolio.

Designing and Developing Superior Customer Value

How do you design customer-focused solutions that compete on service? Let customer information drive the decision on how best to leverage the productive assets of the firm. Market-based as well as asset-based assessments are necessary to configure value-creating assets into core and supplementary product benefits that provide a sustainable competitive advantage.

How does a small startup bank beat the big boys of the banking industry in their own backyard? Commerce Bancorp in New Jersey is not your standard bank. You will find their branches open at 8:00 AM and at 8:00 PM, and for most of the day on weekends. Vernon Hill, founding CEO of the bank, who also owns Burger King franchises, has embraced retailing practices in successful firms such as Walmart, Home Depot, and Starbuck's. The core product at Commerce Bancorp is the business of banking, of course. But the total solution includes access and convenience benefits for the customer that most definitely distinguish it from other banks.

There are even bathrooms for patrons in each branch at Commerce Bancorp. The total solution for any product includes a core product with supplementary features that in combination present a resultant value to the customer. Product differentiation and superior customer value is not in its core product, but in that total solution. The total solution for Commerce Bancorp is not just banking delivered by human or automated tellers in physical branches, it is banking at the customer's convenience when, where, and how the customer wants it.

Indeed, the difference in a customer-oriented firm is very evident at any Commerce Bancorp branch. Commerce bank has found powerful ways of differentiating itself by being customer focused and then it has been able to execute its customer-focused value creation and delivery.

Firms create and deliver value from their assets. Firms must determine how they might be able to create customer value that is superior to the alternatives available to the customer. With a customer focus, the firm seeks to design a superior solution that will provide the firm with sustainable profits. This covers issues and decisions involved in conceiving, designing, and delivering the customer-focused product offering. What must happen to ensure that the productive assets of the firm, facilities, processes, and people, are set up to create and deliver customer-focused value?

Translating Customer Needs to Product Concept

The assessment must be done both at the aggregate, segment level and at the individual, customer level, where appropriate. The aggregate, segment-level assessment orients the firm's thinking about overall product strategy. When a firm directly interacts with its customer, the individual, customer-level assessment helps the firm configure the product within that strategy to the individual customer.

In keeping with the view that a product is really a bundle of benefits, the core value in any product for any firm is the primary benefit that the firm provides. The supplementary product includes as parts of the solution additional benefits that augment the core product.

Typically, a large part of the supplementary product is comprised of services. For the most part, the core product is a commodity, as in the example of Commerce Bancorp. All banks offer deposits, withdrawals, and investments and banking products such as checking and savings accounts, and fixed and variable income securities, and today most banks offer mutual funds. These products comprise the core product for banks.

How these products are different from bank to bank is represented in the supplementary components of the total product. Commerce Bancorp offers free checking and money orders and does not compete on its lower interest on its savings accounts and CDs. Thus, Commerce Bancorp differentiates itself on a number of different supplementary benefits to the customer, ranging from the quality of its customer interactions to a number of facilitating services such as bathrooms in its branches. Similarly, most if not all banks have an online presence, but customers at banks like Allfirst Financial can talk with bank personnel via their home personal computer.

The hotel industry is one that grew out of its room-and-board days to a total product offering that today includes a multitude of facilitating services. "Room and board" was the commodity. As all hotels in a certain level, competitors in the same segment, began offering the same set of supplementary services, such as room service, meeting and conference rooms, a swimming pool, a gift shop, personal grooming salon service, business services, cable, or Internet service in each room, these became commodity and part of the core product.

By March 2001, 78 precent of all Ritz-Carlton hotels offered highspeed Internet. While only two hotel chains—Omni and Westin hotels—have laptops available for guests, most hotels in that class offer two phone lines. Thus, over time, as competing firms add supplementary services, these previously differentiating value components become a commodity and lose their differentiating ability.

Consider the recent "advances" in the form of supplementary services in the hotel industry. Electronic kiosks can not only check you in with your room key and print your bill at checkout, but can also be an electronic concierge providing a guest with directions or maps to locations of interest. Human butlers are back in the hotel industry.

A growing number of hotels at the top end will provide a bath butler to prepare your luxury bath, a technology butler to solve your gadget problems, a private butler to pack your clothes or make your plans. If you are traveling with a baby or young child, you can find a hotel that offers a room for a nanny and kiddie perks such as baby-sitting, some one to read a bedtime story with live actors, or toys and activities for the child.

If you are bringing a pet along, some hotels will even offer you special pet services for a fee! Over time, hotels in the premium category will all be offering some or all of these supplementary features. These features become part of the standard offering and reduce themselves into a commodity for that category of hotels. You can expect that the "technology butler" service will be adopted by hotels for the business traveller segment, briefly providing a differentiating feature only very quickly to become standard fare. In designing superior customer value, a firm must translate customer needs to the specifications of a solution in terms of core and supplementary benefits.

All hotels need not have the same core product. That statement might seem confusing. Consider the Station Inn, in Pennsylvania, between Pittsburgh, and Harrisburg. It sits 125 feet from the railroad tracks. Railroading buffs sleep at the hotel just to see the freight trains, about 60 of them in a space of 24 hours. Same industry as hotels—but a somewhat different core product. Precise definition of a product can only emerge from deep inspection of the "What business are we in?" analysis.

The Supplementary Product

If product differentiation is derived from the enhancement that the supplementary product provides the core benefit, what constitutes supplementary product? Starting with the familiar: customer service is a common supplementary product (sometimes mistaken as the only element in the supplementary product). There are elements of the supplementary product, such as billing and payment, that are also common to all firms. They are required to facilitate the core product. These must also be viewed as part of the supplementary product to the extent that they affect customer value.

A firm can add to the customer value when its billing and payment process is customer focused or can detract from customer value if it is unpleasant in the customer's experience. Thus, there are some supplementary features that are found in all products that may not necessarily be recognized as such. Services marketing scholar Christopher Lovelock visualized this concept as a flower with petals. Think of the supplementary product as composed of elements of the total value bundle that facilitate and enhance (or detract from) the primary benefit sought in a product. Visualize these elements in three broad categories: facilitating services, quality of customer experience, and brand image.

Facilitating Services

Facilitating services are all those features of the product and activities of the firm that serve to facilitate the consumption of the core product. All firms have to provide some of these services at some level. Large retailers such as Sears, Walmart, and Lowe's will provide assembly and installation services for a fee and sometimes for no charge. The four broad categories of facilitating services—complementary services, customer education, customer access, and customer service. Customer-focused firms differentiate themselves by excelling in these facilitating services. *Complementary services* are those related to the consumption of the core product. Some are almost necessary, like the waiting area in a physician's clinic or parking facilities at a hotel. Passengers on long international flights enjoy a wide range of inflight entertainment activities such as films, TV channels, and even casino-style gambling or electronic shopping and services such as being able to rent a car or book hotel rooms from the technology at their seats. Some complementary services are product differentiators.

For example, recognizing that some of its customers were coming in to the bank to conduct their business bringing little children with them, some Wells Fargo branches have a play area with television cartoons, Nintendo, and the like—and even sells toys to children. Washington Mutual offers calculators, pens, and piggy banks for a small fee.

To compete for advertising within its *Mutual Funds* magazine for instance, the publisher, Time, Inc. offers its advertising customers anything from primary research and use of its subscriber list to assistance in customizing gifts and promotions to readers or sponsorship featured on special cover-wraps. These are examples of complementary services that help differentiate value created by different providers.

Only with an intimate understanding of the customer's value chain consumption (and creation) activities can firms begin to see what opportunities there might be to facilitate the consumption of the core product. Sometimes complementary products are outsourced and provided directly to the customer by the supplier, as Wells Fargo did when it invited Starbuck's to open locations at some of its branches.

Ultimately, these complementary products ought to be consistent with the positioning strategy for the product. When a complementary feature is offered by all competitors in a particular product category, it becomes a commodity and part of the core product for that category and ceases to be a product differentiator.

Customer education is a form of facilitating service in that it provides information to the customer about the firm or the product in such a way that it facilitates the acquisition and consumption of the product. Instruction manuals and product support via telephone, fax, or the Internet are examples of customer education. Consider what some banks are doing to be more accessible for customers looking for assistance.

Tellers and managers are dressed in khakis and casual shirts to appear approachable and friendly. Bank of America has tested concierges in their lobby to help direct customer questions. Home Depot provides free classes on home improvement projects. Once again, the service feature might be a necessary component of the total product, but how it is designed and delivered may be a source of product differentiation. *Customer access* has to do with everything that the firm does to make its products available to the customer and to facilitate the acquisition and consumption of the product. The hours of operation and location are a simple example of customer access for a service. The various touch points that are available to the customer to access the services of the firm or to reach someone within the firm would be a measure of the customer access. The methods of billing and payment for the product would relate to access to the product and can be a product differentiator. For example, the convenience of payment by credit card was once a source of competitive advantage. Convenience and ease of use is a critical component of customer value for any product. Services such as financing options are also related to this idea of customer access. If these are not customer-focused, they will fail the customer and the firm.

Customer service is a key facilitating service and includes the commonly understood activity of businesses related to product complaints or failures, product returns, refunds, and such. The accommodation of special requests or adapting to unusual or irregular customer situations would be an example of customer service as well. Poor customer service reduces customer value and risks losing the customer.

Quality of Customer Experience

When the total product provided by all firms contains the same set of facilitating services, the product is not necessarily a commodity. The quality of the service offered remains a source of differentiation and therefore a supplementary feature of the product. Perceived quality enhances, and lack thereof reduces, the value of the core product. For example, even when Internet service is offered by all hotels, the quality of the customer experience with the Internet service is still a differentiator.

One hotel may require you to get into a closet, fish out the cables and force you to shape yourself into a yoga pose to hook up those cables to your laptop, while another hotel may offer wireless Internet access from anywhere on the property. All airlines provide seating and, depending on distance and class, also provide meals and entertainment while transporting you from point A to point B. Differentiation in seating can come in legroom and comfort. First-class services can offer six and a half feet of seat length, single seats, pajamas, and privacy partitions between seats. The quality of the entire customer experience is most definitely a source of differentiation.

Brand Image

Brand image is a supplementary feature of the product in that it adds to customer value. Brand image is the sum total of all the perceptions and attitudes about a brand. The image of the firm in the general media as well as for each individual customer provides a measure of the perceived quality of the product. The reputation of a firm is usually a result of the firm's product and actions. Where there is very little tangible evidence of the product, as in the case of Web-based services, an entire industry of so-called "reputation managers" has emerged. These reputation managers are Web sites that rate the reputation of others! A firm's image is an implicit source of differentiation in the market. Brand image is the ultimate differentiator. When all else can be seen as equal, the brand image captures the essence of the difference in customer value among the alternatives available to the customer. Firms have to determine what their total product offering is and what it should be. The value bundle of core and supplementary product needs to be designed based on what the customers expect as standard from all providers of a solution in a product category. The supplementary product might also contain features that are sources of differentiation among solution providers reflecting the positioning strategy of the firm. Firms must constantly watch the various solutions that are being offered. Sometimes the threat of competition comes from newer business models.

For example, online broker ETrade surprised the banking business when it began to open ATMs with new services. A deep and broad analysis of customer needs could reveal value-creating opportunities.

Matching Product to Customer Value Chain

To determine how best to match the total product as the superior solution to fit customer need, the firm must understand the customer's value chain. This is an integral part of the product concept development of the customer-focused firm. A thorough understanding of the customer needs and the customer value chain will help the firm conceive its product from the customer's point of view. Firms that best relate their own value chain to the buyer's value chain, said Michael Porter, will enjoy a sustainable differentiation strategy.

The value chain is essentially a chain of value-creating and value-consuming activities, where the value created as output from one activity becomes the input to another value-creating activity that in turn creates value as input for another activity, and so on. Thus, any activity can be assessed by the value it creates versus the value it consumes. This is why activity-based costing practices make a lot of sense. As, the value creating activities *within a firm* are those that contribute to the creation of either the core product or the supplementary product.

The value created by these activities is derived by the processing of the productive factors of the firm—its people, facilities, and equipment. There may be assets or value components sourced from external suppliers or intermediaries that contribute toward producing either the core or the supplementary product. Some outsourced services may even be delivered directly to the customer.

When any value component of the total product is outsourced, as in the case of a retailer offering customers outsourced financing options for purchases, or airlines outsourcing catering services, there is the obvious issue of quality assurance in the value creation that is outside the control of the firm. Externally (to the firm) when you relate other firms' value-creation activities into a value chain, you see that the value created by one entity contributes to the value created by the next entity in the value chain. The same idea is referred to by economists, in the context of forecasting, as "derived demand." The demand for a product is dependent on the market for another product, such as aluminum and aircraft sales for example. A homeowner who gets a home improvement job done receives (customer) value from the home contractor who in turn is receiving value from the retailer who in turn receives value in the form of products and services from the supplier or manufacturer.

Customer Information Management

Technology has revolutionized customer information management. Information technologies allow firms to gather, store, and interpret demographic and behavioural data so that each subsequent interaction with the customer is customized, based on historical data gathered from each customer interaction. Digitized purchase transactions in commerce have enabled numerous opportunities to track customer interactions. Chip technology has progressed so rapidly that soon there could be a computer chip in just about any product that would enable mindboggling links to improve customer value and the customer-firm relationship.

For example, take the Internet and e-commerce. Most Web sites will ask simple unobtrusive questions of customers when they browse the site. This information identifies the customer and tracks the customer's activities or "clickstreams" on the Web site. Subsequently, software can use this information to personalize the Web site and the experience for the customer.

A number of firms have emerged that provide customer information management software. Such software can customize Web pages for each customer depending on the customer's profile, which is created based on the customer's previous interactions with the firm and the Web site. Vignette's software allows Web sites to dynamically generate pages that are custom-made for each customer. Silknet's virtual sales assistant guides customers through a series of questions about their need situations and then makes product recommendations.

Marriott has an enterprise-wide software that integrates information on customers from different departments so that its sales reps can anticipate and respond more quickly to customer needs. Similarly, H&R Block uses software from Clarify to combine and coordinate customer records from its tax offices, discount brokerages, its customer service centre, and its Web site so that customer interaction personnel in each department have access to all of the information on the customer.

There are a variety of methods for analyzing data. Data mining techniques attempt to discern patterns in the data where one set of characteristics affects another set in a certain way. SAS Enterprise Dataminer software helps detect patterns in databases and construct models to predict customer response to the firm's actions. Software from iMarket looks at customers' most recent or most frequent purchase decisions and the monetary value of these purchases for the firm and helps decision makers select a subset of customers for targeting specific promotions or new product introductions. Epiphany and Digimine are examples of firms that use a set of their own proprietary algorithms to analyze customer data for their clients. Early clients of Epiphany included Charles Schwab and Hewlett Packard, and for Digimine include Nordstrom. Edify has software that will link customer feedback such as survey responses to individual customer profiles for anlaysis.

There is also software such as Nudist available for the analysis of qualitative data. When firms are able to sort through their customer databases and group customers by the relevant characteristics with such datamining software, the power of segmentation and targeting is fully realized with such datamining software.

In general, data is useless for decision making unless it is organized for interpretation. When organized appropriately, data can be contextualized so as to be transformed into information. Displaying and disseminating information is critical to the firm's success. Without proper reporting procedures, decision makers do not benefit from the information that the firm has.

For example, ESRI has a programme called Arcview that allows the user to spatially display numerical data. The user can view the data in his or her preferred format to match individual cognitive styles. As Peter Drucker notes, no two executives organize the same information in the same way. Therefore, software that allows the users to display information in their own preferred formats is valuable in customer information management.

The task of the customer information management system is to generate intelligence on the customer so that firm can be more customer-focused in its serving the customer. Intelligence generation capability has been shown to be positively correlated to superior customer value. In a study that involved hour-long in-depth interviews and surveys of sixty-six of the largest one thousand electronic firms by scholars interested in the characteristics of the market-oriented firm, firms are urged to treat learning about the customer as an investment.

Ultimately, customer information is useless unless it is available to the user. Scholars researching the value of information have called this the "value in use" metric. The more the information is used, the more value it has! Customer information management, therefore, involves determining how the information needs to be made available, to whom, when, and in what form. The focus here is on who needs the information.

In the spirit of customer focus, the information system serves an internal customer—the decision maker. What will the user need the information for? What specific information is needed for the firm's decisions and activities? Is the user of the information able to enhance customer value with the information? At what level of aggregation is the information used: policy level and customer level, segment level, and individual level? Such decisions need to be made so as to prioritize the customer information according to its impact on customer value. In making judgments about committing resources to managing and leveraging customer information, the firm should consider the worth of the information in terms of how it would help the firm provide superior customer value at a reasonable profit.

Customer information must drive any business process and activity. Customer-focused management requires a customer-focused analysis of the information necessary for designing processes and making decisions regarding value creation in the firm. These run the gamut of decisions regarding creating and delivering customer solutions, product improvements, attracting and retaining customers, customer service, recovering from product failures, hiring and motivating employees, and ensuring a customer-oriented climate and culture.

Index